Teaching and Learning in Further and Adult Education

L. Walklin

First published in 1990 by Stanley Thornes (Publishers) Ltd
First revised edition published in 1994
Second revised edition published in 2000

Reprinted in 2002 by:
Nelson Thornes Ltd
Delta Place
27 Bath Road
CHELTENHAM
GL53 7TH
United Kingdom

    04 05 06 / 10 9 8 7 6

A catalogue record for this book is available from the British Library

ISBN 0 7487 0145 1 ≈ 1990 ed   C3146

Page make-up by Tech-Set Ltd

Printed and bound in Spain by Graphy Cems

By the same author:
Instructional Techniques & Practice for Driving Instructors
The Assessment of Performance and Competence
Putting Quality into Practice
Instructional Techniques and Practice
Training and Development NVQS

Note
In 2001 the DfEE was replaced by the Department for Education and Skills
(DfES).

CONTENTS

Foreword   v
Acknowledgements   vi
Preface   vii
Introduction to 1994 Revised Edition   viii

CHAPTER ONE   **The Principles of Learning**   **1**
1.001   Developing a favourable learning attitude in your students   1
1.002   Identifying characteristics of different types of learning   5
1.003   How people learn   16
1.004   Applying principles of learning to individual teaching strategies   21
1.005   Student-centred learning and performance judging   31
1.006   Importance of analysis and synthesis in learning development   38

CHAPTER TWO   **The Principles of Teaching**   **39**
2.001   Recognising differences and similarities between students' learning
        characteristics   39
2.002   Choosing appropriate teaching methods   43
2.003   Identifying and evaluating different teaching methods   52
2.004   Matching teaching skills to method   63
2.005   Combining and integrating methods   67
2.006   Planning, preparing and delivering a teaching programme   69

CHAPTER THREE   **Learning Resources**   **78**
3.001   Identifying availability of learning and teaching resources   78
3.002   Selecting appropriate learning and teaching resources   82
3.003   Using the learning resources centre   84
3.004   Using audio-visual aids when teaching   87
3.005   Using computers and data processing aids when teaching   88
3.006   Resource planning   92

CHAPTER FOUR   **Course Organisation and Curriculum Development**   **99**
4.001   Formulating aims and objectives   99
4.002   Defining terminology appropriate to curriculum development   108
4.003   Formulating and justifying aims and objectives for a specific training
        programme   114
4.004   Identifying factors influencing the design of schemes of work   121
4.005   Integrating schemes of work, outcomes, and assessment procedures   125

CHAPTER FIVE   **Assessment**   **134**
5.001   Translating objectives into performance goals   134
5.002   Designing, using and evaluating tests   135
5.003   Objective testing   142
5.004   Assessment methods compared   143
5.005   Classifying and evaluating assessment methods   151
5.006   Planning and preparing assessment procedures   159

CHAPTER SIX   **Communication**   164
6.001   Identifying socio-cultural influences on language   164
6.002   Communicating in teaching and learning situations   169
6.003   The importance of communication style   173
6.004   Selecting the communication mode   179
6.005   Communicating effectively with students   184
6.006   Enhancing student communications   188

CHAPTER SEVEN   **Role**   198
7.001   Describing further and adult education   198
7.002   Identifying institutions and agencies associated with further and
        adult education   200
7.003   Why students enrol for courses   212
7.004   Appraising social and educational backgrounds of student groups   214
7.005   Relating group appraisals to planning   218
7.006   Creating an environment conducive to learning   222
7.007   Health and safety in the learning environment   225
7.008   Counselling, guidance and classroom management   230
7.009   Involving students in curriculum matters   237
7.010   Promoting students' participation in their professional and
        personal development   240
7.011   Identifying the roles of a teacher   244
7.012   Identifying and evaluating characteristics of personal teaching styles 258

CHAPTER EIGHT   **Features of the FAETC NVQ3**   268
8.001   Introduction   268
8.002   Award structure   269
8.003   Portfolio building   269
8.004   Assessment model   271
8.005   Assessment strategy   277
8.006   Identifying individual learning needs   277
8.007   ITN interviewing and planning   278
8.008   Assessing achievement   288
8.009   Working towards D32   290

Appendix A   Making OHP transparencies   301
Appendix B   Writing objective tests   307
Appendix C   Establishing Learning Needs   316
Appendix D   Assessing prior learning and achievement   323
Appendix E   C&G7306 NVQ Level 3 – Unit/Chapter references   331
Appendix F   Professional relationships with colleagues and customers   333

Bibliography   336

Index   338

FOREWORD

Observations of animal life throw up ample evidence of learning as a 'natural process'. The fledgling sparrow is left to perfect its flying techniques through trial and error and is only assisted by being booted out of house and home once its parents consider that the time is right. Our own children, too, have often acquired a good understanding of the rules of English grammar long before they go to school and are able to apply those rules in the construction of appropriate and rather complex linguistic responses to novel situations. The sparrow and the child have managed to extract important lessons from their own experiences of their environment with little direction from others. They have learned principles of flight and rules of grammar through processes of experimentation and reasoning, without ever having been taught.

The point of all this is to remind us that education is principally about learning and not teaching. Learners are active in the construction and development of new knowledge and skills; they are not simply receptacles into which pre-digested knowledge is deposited. At the end of the day, it is the learner who has to make his/her own sense of what is being learned, and that is something that teaching can support but not replace. Of course, we have all been victims at some time or other of those who would seem to view their own teaching as the primary concern of education – the 'full-frontal bores' who resolutely fill all available 'air time' with their own voices and chalkdust in the belief that the more they 'teach', the more we will learn. From these experiences, we know that teaching may even diminish opportunities to learn.

Teaching, then, is about supporting learning in a manner which is sensitive to the profoundly important part that learners themselves have to play in the learning process. The movement away from Dickens' idealised Victorian pedagogue, Mr. M'Choakumchild, whose main preoccupation was to insert facts into learners' heads rather like coins in a slot machine, has been slow but it has certainly happened on a very broad front. Today's teacher is not merely a knowledge dispenser or a model to be imitated but is someone who recognises that effective learning takes place in many different ways, that different learners may have different preferred learning styles, that individual learners' needs must be taken into account if learning is to be satisfactory, that learners have a great deal to contribute to the process of education and that teaching is more about prompting and supporting such contributions than it is about some slick theatrical performance by somebody holding a piece of chalk. The curriculum, too, is not something to be merely 'handed down' to the next generation of learners like a tablet of stone; rather, the learner can have a very important part to play in determining what the curriculum should be. This, in turn, requires that teachers must possess the skills that equip them to identify learners' needs and to negotiate with them what their personal curriculum might be.

These points certainly apply to further and adult education, where our recent experiences inform us that learners value the opportunities to take a major responsibility for their own learning and to be able to use their own experiences of life as a platform for learning. They enjoy and benefit most from their own active participation in the learning process and from a learner-teacher relationship which is more of a working partnership than the superior-subordinate relationship captured in the folklore of teaching and learning.

Les Walklin's book addresses these issues. It provides information about learning, and stimulates thought about teacher responses to learners' needs. It offers appropriate and helpful support to the person intending to become their own teacher; a teacher who is sensitive to the needs of learners.

MARTIN BLOOMER M.Ed., Ph.D
Course Director, Certificate in Education (FE)
University of Exeter

ACKNOWLEDGEMENTS

The author and publishers are grateful to the following for permission to reproduce copyright material:

Adult Literacy and Basic Skills Unit, Fig. 7.1;
Peter Blunt of Strode College for contributing text relating to: 'Education services in prisons and youth custody centres'.
Bournemouth and Poole College of Further Education for lesson notes by Janet Young, Figs 7.6 and 7.7;
City and Guilds of London Institute, Fig. 5.4 and extracts from *Manual of Objective Testing* in Appendix B;
DfEE and the former Employment Department Group – Training, Enterprise and Education Directorate (TEED), formerly the Training Agency, for numerous references to the contents of its publications.
Engineering Industry Training Board, Fig. 2.10;
Peter Finney, Figs 1.11, 1.12, 1.13;
Further Education Unit (FEU) for numerous references to the contents of its publications.
Gill French, Dorset School of Nursing, Fig. 2.8
Edward Fennell for the roles of consultant listed on p. 245;
John McCafferty, Fig. 2.11 (algorithm) from his article 'Innovation and Education' in *Education and Training*, Vol. 22 No. 9, 1980;
Penguin Books for the poem 'Lies' by Yevgeny Yevtushenko from *Yevtushenko: Selected Poems*, translated by Robin Milner-Gulland and Peter Levi S.J. (Penguin Books, 1962), copyright R. Milner-Gulland and Peter Levi;
South Thames College, for extracts from *The Overhead Projector* in Appendix A;
Roy Whitlow, Figs. 5.5, 5.6, 5.7, from *Notes for Guidance*, 1976.

Every attempt has been made to contact copyright holders, but we apologise if any have been overlooked.

PREFACE

This book provides information about teaching and learning relating to the standards for teaching and supporting learning in further education developed by the Further Education National Training Organisation (FENTO). It explores the ideas and sources of relevant knowledge and experience that underpin the standards, and also the elements of competence and performance criteria that apply to a variety of teacher and trainer qualifications designed to meet the demands of teaching and learning in the 2000s.

Candidates working for awards such as the traditional or competence-based City and Guilds Further and Adult Education Teacher's Certificate and modular Certificates in Education (H/FE) will find this handbook useful, since it also embraces the aims and objectives of the highly regarded City and Guilds 730 FAETC that forms the bedrock upon which so many individual teachers' qualifications have been achieved. Such studies need to result in several critically important outcomes, namely:

– improving their approaches to work as teachers
– improving their ability to design and carry through effective teaching programmes
– improving their ability to understand and respond to the needs of their students
– enlarging their awareness of and willingness to exercise the variety of roles in which they have to work as teachers.

Adult learners value opportunities to accept major responsibility for their learning and to play an active role in the process. Flexible methods of course organisation and study are now becoming the pattern in teacher training and continuing education provision and learners will wish to select the most appropriate mode of learning to suit their needs. Teachers must be competent in meeting these requirements and the book seeks to address key competences and areas of expertise that modern teachers need to own and demonstrate while teaching.

Innovation in education and training stimulated by changes in technology, markets and occupations, the introduction of National Vocational Qualifications (NVQs) and Scottish Vocational Qualifications (SVQs), the phasing-in of General National Vocational Qualifications (GNVQs) or vocational A-levels and the role of work-based training and assessment in learners' accreditation have together created a great need for more support in the area of teaching and training method.

This book will be an invaluable resource for teachers in Further and Adult Education and trainers in industry and commerce who wish to gain a new qualification or update their skills. Self-evaluation and self-assessment of teaching activities and learning by reflection on actual experience can be reinforced by referring to the principles, concepts and ideas set out in this book and by seeking better understanding in discussion with others.

Furthermore, the systematic approach to teaching and training described will be of use to Quality Managers and Staff Developers who are seeking guidance about the need to meet the ISO 9000 Quality System requirement that suppliers shall provide for the training of all personnel performing activities affecting quality.

LES WALKLIN
Charlton Marshall 2000

INTRODUCTION TO REVISED EDITION

This book is laid out following the seven major aims of the City and Guilds 730 Further and Adult Education Teacher's Certificate (FAETC) and is therefore useful for the student following either the more traditional-based developmental 7307 as written by City and Guilds, or the competence-based 7306, which follows National Standards set by the Training and Development Lead Body.

Because of the close relationship between many Certificate in Education (H/FE) providers and those offering FAETC, the book also covers the first year curriculum of many Cert. Ed (H/FE) programmes. Furthermore, people wishing to achieve the Assessor Units (124) D32, Assess candidate performance, and (125) D33, Assess candidate using differing sources of evidence, will find a great deal that will be useful in generating and collecting evidence and building up a portfolio for accreditation.

In order to meet modern teacher and trainer qualification criteria, the student is required not only to provide performance evidence at a satisfactory level, but also to demonstrate sufficient knowledge to support the inference of competent performance. A new chapter has now been added giving useful information about some key features of the 'new' FAETC standards. Details of where relevant underpinning knowledge relating to other C&G 7306 Units may be found in this book is given in Appendix E. However, the text continues to meet all City and Guilds aims and objectives of the 730 FAETC and serves as a valuable source of reference for candidates seeking a variety of teacher and trainer qualifications, including any future Level 4 NVQ in Learning Support and Management.

MALCOLM BUTCHER
Project Manager – Teacher Training
City and Guilds Moderator
Bournemouth

How to use this book

The book may be read from cover to cover or used for spot reference whenever information relating to a particular topic is needed. The text is arranged in numbered chapters and sections, each of which may be read individually. Assignments are included in each section and these can be used for self-study or for group discussion.

The chapters and sections have been numbered in accordance with the objectives set out in the City and Guilds of London Institute syllabus, 'Further and Adult Education Teacher's Certificate'.

Appendix E has been added to help candidates for the competence-based C&G7306 FAETC (Level 3 NVQ format) gather information that will be particularly useful when preparing and presenting supplementary evidence, personal reports and product evidence. The text also provides a source of knowledge that can be used by candidates to support naturally occurring evidence and other evidence presented while the qualified assessor is judging performance evidence against Award criteria.

CHAPTER ONE

The Principles of Learning

Aim: To introduce teachers to relevant principles of learning

1.001 Developing a favourable learning attitude in your students

Motivation: a keystone in learning

Motivation describes the arousal, control and sustaining of behaviour necessary to satisfy a need or to attain a goal. A favourable attitude to learning can be developed in students provided they are motivated to achieve some goal that they have set themselves. A teacher can only help students to attain that goal.

Once physical survival needs such as hunger or thirst have been satisfied, people tend to concentrate on needs relating to self-actualisation, such as self-fulfilment, prestige and esteem. **Intrinsic motivators** like challenge, mastery and curiosity frequently lead a person to great efforts in order to attain a goal. The reward for effort comes in the form of an inner satisfaction and feeling of accomplishment after overcoming a problem, acquiring knowledge and experience or mastering some feat of endurance. No obvious reward in material form results from such effort. On the other hand, **extrinsic motivators** involve the satisfaction of needs such as the desire for recognition, praise or financial reward. Gratification can be observed by others and may in some cases be measured in monetary terms, publicity or degree of fame achieved.

Learning takes place from the cradle to the grave. Most people learn something every day, but academic learning is a special case; such learning can only be accomplished through the concentrated efforts of the learner, backed by the teacher. The learner must want to learn, be exposed to an appropriate learning environment, and be interested in the learning material in order to maintain attention. Motivation, interest and attention are therefore closely interrelated.

Motivated experience results from knowledge gained during encounters relating to the satisfaction of needs. Students may be confronted with a wide variety of learning situations and yet walk away with little or no change in their state of knowledge. If the situation appears to have no bearing on their views of the world, or is considered to be irrelevant to their work or future prospects, then they will

1

attend to other matters that seem to them to be more profitable. On the other hand, the desire to qualify so as to improve job prospects, the pleasure experienced in doing a job well, taking a pride in one's work, intellectual achievement and active participation in group activities are all important motivators which can give rise to feelings of satisfaction if addressed in learning situations.

Motivated experience can be promoted by providing the means by which learners' needs may be satisfied. The teacher needs to arrange things so that the learners' interest, and hence attention, is directed to those factors which will prove to be most rewarding to them. The teacher should therefore outline the purpose of the activity and its importance to the learners.

Once the learning process has started, interest may be maintained by feeding back progress reports in the form of knowledge of results and by giving praise and reward for correct responses. The presentation should include a variety of teaching and learning media, while curiosity may be promoted by using discovery learning techniques where possible. Students like to be kept busy, and sometimes an atmosphere of friendly competition creeps in. High morale will often result from such practices.

How motivation can be encouraged

When it becomes necessary to use a teacher-centred approach, the more interested students become in what the teacher is saying or doing, the more attention they will devote to it and the better they will remember it. If they are to learn what is being taught, material relating to the lesson should be presented in such a way that mental images are easily formed. Once formed, the images may be reproduced at a later date to enhance subsequent extensions to that already learned or to aid recall. The presentation of material should also allow students to use as many senses as possible rather than to rely on passive learning methods. Where appropriate, they should be encouraged to see, hear, feel, taste or smell the objects under discussion, and preferably be asked to describe them in their own words.

The foregoing assumes that the students really want to learn in order to fulfil a need or desire to acquire knowledge of the subject being presented. However, attitudes already held as a result of former exposure to the subject or teacher and other factors such as feelings, expectations, thoughts and possibly resentment, will affect the students' perceptions at a given time. Their mental or emotional state will also influence their interpretation of the learning situation.

Motivation affects and alters perceptual experiences, and the students' perception of any instructional content will be evidenced by their responses and resulting modification of behaviour. The teacher must therefore provide a learning environment designed to attract the students' attention and provide the inputs and resources with which their needs may be fulfilled. The students should be made aware of the links between the immediate learning objectives and the overall aims of the instruction, and also the benefits to be derived in the long run.

Incentives, competition, challenge, ego-involvement and examinations all serve to arouse interest and to stimulate the students to greater efforts; but beware of possible unwanted side-effects — the 'confirmation of underachievement' or even failure — where self-imposed standards set by students are not realised. An important influence on performance may be standards set by the teacher. The standard should not be too easy to achieve, but should be difficult enough for the students to attain — if they try.

The drive reduction concept of motivation

Drive is the motivational force causing behaviour — a person feels hungry, seeks food, finds food, consumes it and no longer feels hungry. **Primary drives** are essential to survive, but there are also **secondary drives** which can be acquired through learning. It is the latter which form the basis for understanding a person's behaviour, at work, in class and in the social world outside working hours.

Some of these 'psychogenic needs' have been listed by H.A. Murray[1]:

- needs associated briefly with inanimate objects
- needs expressing ambition, will-power, desire for accomplishment, and prestige
- needs having to do with human power exerted, resisted, or yielded to
- needs having to do with hurting others or oneself
- needs having to do with affection between people
- additionally socially relevant needs.

Assignment 1.1 - Motivation and drive reduction

Consider a study group known to you, examine and describe its needs; and consider how Murray's list of psychogenic needs may be interpreted and related to aspects of teaching and learning. Examine particularly the students' needs concerning

- achievement and recognition
- exhibition and aggression
- self-respect and esteem
- avoidance of failure, ridicule and blame
- dominance, deference and emulation
- relaxation, entertainment and interaction.

Formulate a strategy that will enable you to take account of these factors when you are preparing and presenting instruction or otherwise facilitating student activity.

Teamwork

Teamwork has been found to benefit business situations where it has been encouraged. When members are working co-operatively, the outcomes are often better than when a number of individuals are working in isolation. This principle is transferable to the teaching and learning arena where fulfilment of the expectations of all group members, the teacher and external agents provides an opportunity for involvement of all concerned in a team approach.

It is likely that the teacher will often act as a facilitator or group leader; mature students often expect this, but there will often be times when students take over the role (and this is to be encouraged). The function of the leader will be to negotiate group objectives, to plan, to brief, to control and support members, to inform and to review progress and to evaluate outcomes.

Action-centred leadership theory suggests three sets of needs that overlap and interact in any teamwork activity:

– needs relating to the task
– individual team member's needs
– team maintenance needs.

The need to accomplish the task set will clearly affect each of the other two sets of needs. Individuals' needs such as those proposed by Herzberg, Maslow and Murray must somehow be satisfied, and in this respect good supportive leadership is essential to success. Team maintenance will be reinforced by making good progress with the task and keeping up team morale. A delicate balance needs to be maintained between the three sets of needs in order to get the task completed without losing group cohesiveness or individual support. A favourable attitude to learning through teamwork can be promoted by

– creating a co-operative attitude among the group
– clarifying the success criteria for individuals and the group as a whole
– allocating responsibilities to the persons best suited
– making sure everyone knows what they are required to do
– utilising individual talents
– collectively setting objectives and regularly reviewing progress
– encouraging effective communication within the group.

In industry, management attitudes and behaviour affect rank-and-file motivation and productivity. The same concept applies in education. The teacher as a manager of learning must be careful not to adversely affect student behaviour, motivation and outcomes. Student apathy and lack of effort are not necessarily a matter of mere laziness. Often, they are healthy reactions by normal people to an unhealthy environment — created all too commonly by unsound teaching practices and policies. When you and your students operate as a team, loyalty, co-operation and morale will improve and the group will undoubtedly function more effectively and with higher attainment than could otherwise be expected. Motivation to learn increases and individual talents are utilised for the benefit of the group. Destructive behaviour and lack of support is replaced by positive and helpful effort leading to a responsible attitude and the will to succeed. Outcomes of teamwork are normally much better than the sum of individual efforts. Personal satisfaction also results from helping one another to master tasks confronting the group.

All this sounds fine, but how does one forge a good team? Some teachers have succeeded by communicating well, showing an understanding and caring attitude, setting a good example and involving and encouraging their students right from the start. Effective managers in industry and commerce also have a high level of 'people skills' that contribute to the success of a company. Modern teachers are managers and facilitators of learning, and they too need to be competent in behavioural aspects of team management as well as resource management.

Assignment 1.2 – **Using teamwork**

Consider your attitude towards teamwork in the classroom.

Think about the conditions under which you feel people work best as a team and record your ideas.

Make notes on how you would set about

- shaping a class of new students into a team
- setting and agreeing targets and standards with the team
- fitting into the team.

Discuss your notes with a colleague and consider whether it would be profitable to change existing routines.

1.002 Identifying characteristics of different types of learning

The significance of different types of learning

Strategies adopted by teachers result mainly from their perception of how teaching should be carried out, from their own personality traits, and from the extent to which a given educational psychologist has influenced their beliefs about learning theory. Thorndike's laws of disuse, effect, exercise, frequency, readiness, recency and repetition, Gestaltist configuration-based theories and flashes of insight described as the 'Aha!' experience, Skinner's work on conditioning and programmed learning and other theorists' work all compete for a place in a teacher's depository of values and pedagogical knowledge. However, in the end, it is the teacher who will need to decide how to manage the learning process, having taken into consideration the needs of the particular group who are on the receiving end.

People learn in many different ways, and teaching strategies must take account of such parameters as ability, interest, motivation, difficulty, group mix, physical and intellectual handicaps and many others. No single learning theory can cope with every aspect of group needs. But a teacher armed with a good basic knowledge and understanding of learning principles will be better placed to make a conscious choice of teaching method than one who does not have such an understanding.

The learning process

As we grow older we learn by experience. We are exposed to a wide variety of events in our social environment and learn something during each encounter. We learn by interacting with people, places and things. Without this interaction we should know little more than on the day we were born.

Some things are learned accidentally. We touch a hot object, get burned, and learn that hot objects should not be touched with bare hands. Later, perhaps in the workshop, we may have to handle hot objects in the course of our work. We remember our earlier unpleasant experience and take precautions. We extend our knowledge to include the wearing of protective equipment when handling hot objects.

The tempo of learning can be accelerated by arranging contrived situations in which the learner is exposed to stimuli which would not necessarily be experienced during the process of maturation. The formal learning process, for example, comprises a teacher, a set of behavioural objectives, elements of instruction and interaction between the teacher and learner, responses and reinforcement, and a means of testing and evaluating the outcome. The teacher is responsible for providing a set of conditions under which learning may occur, while the learner must display a willingness to participate actively in the process.

In his book *'The Conditions of Learning'*[2] Robert Gagné defines eight classes of learning, each calling for a different set of learning conditions and higher level of mental ability than that preceding it. The classes are:

– signal learning
– stimulus-response learning
– chaining
– verbal association
– multiple discrimination
– concept learning
– principle learning
– problem solving.

Gagné suggests that each class of learning should be mastered before tackling higher levels. This entails competence in seven classes before attempting problem solving at the highest level. The classes of learning are defined below.

1 Signal learning

This involves the learner in responding to a **signal**. It is a form of classical conditioning of behaviour. Ivan Pavlov (1849–1936), a Russian physiologist and psychologist, discovered it during investigations of the salivation in dogs.

Examples of signal learning include the reaction of a pedestrian to the sound of a car horn or the appearance of the family dog when it hears the sound of a biscuit-tin lid being removed. Classroom examples include the way teachers gain attention at the start of a lesson either verbally or non-verbally and the signal the class takes to pack up at the end.

Teachers can make use of the related theory of **learned association** during both theoretical and practical teaching and learning.

2 Stimulus-response learning

'Trial and error learning', 'operant learning', 'instrumental learning', 'instrumental conditioning' and 'need reduction' are all names used to describe **stimulus-response learning**. The stimulus-organism-response model of learning attempts to explain how it is that learners come to behave as they do when presented with a stimulus. The general argument is: a stimulus is more likely to elicit a response if similar responses have, in the past, been beneficial to the learner and have been rewarded or reinforced by means such as approval, praise, encouraging words and gestures, and material rewards.

Trial and error learning results from trying out one form of response after another until the correct response is discovered. The correct response is often rewarded in some way. E.L. Thorndike (1874–1949), an American experimental psychologist, believed that human behaviour could be studied and analysed in terms of stimulus (change in environment) and response (behaviour resulting from attempts to adapt to the change). He based this belief on research carried out on animal behaviour. As a result, Thorndike drafted his 'law of effect': it suggests that behaviour which is followed by reinforcement will tend to be repeated, while behaviour which is not reinforced or which results in discomfort will be less likely to occur.

Instrumental conditioning is a form of stimulus-response learning in which an active response in the form of desired behaviour is rewarded. The response is 'instrumental' in producing the reinforcement, hence the name. If the required response does not occur, then there is no reinforcement.

A form of instrumental conditioning, known as 'operant conditioning' was introduced by B.F. Skinner (born 1904), an American psychologist. His experiments with rats illustrated how the subject of an experiment operates on the environment in order to produce a desired effect. To illustrate the principle, Skinner used a box later known as the 'Skinner Box' into which a hungry rat was placed. The box was fitted with a bar and a food tray. By pressing the bar, a pellet of food was delivered to the tray. Pressing the bar was instrumental in providing the reinforcer. Motivation for the rat's behaviour was provided by means of its hunger drive, and reinforcement for its bar-pressing activity was in the form of the pellet.

Skinner later investigated reinforcement schedules relating either to the period of time or number of non-reinforced responses between successive reinforcements. This resulted in Skinner concluding that behaviour could be 'shaped' by reinforcement. He listed four categories of reinforcement:

– fixed time interval (A)
– variable time interval (B)
– fixed ratio (number of unreinforced responses per reinforced response) (C)
– variable ratio (first response after variable number of unreinforced responses is reinforced) (D).

Experimenters have shown that schedules B, C and D tend to produce higher levels of response than A.

The practising teacher can make use of Skinner's results to elicit and reinforce learners' responses, and reinforcement techniques are widely used in programmed learning instruction and teaching machines.

Gestalt or insight learning theory stems from speculation about learning by a number of psychologists, including Koffka, Köhler and Wertheimer. Gestalt psychological theory stresses the importance of pattern, organisation and seeing things as 'wholes' rather than as collections of individual elements. Gestaltists believe that the whole is greater than the sum of its individual parts. For example, the sounds of individual notes are meaningless for some, but when combined produce music which may be recognised and enjoyed. A highly tuned and 'blue-printed' racing engine, when reassembled and tested, has many properties not apparent to the observer when laid out as components before assembly. The whole highly organised structure becomes much more meaningful than does knowledge of its elements.

Wolfgang Köhler (1887–1967),[3] a German-born psychologist, considered that there was much more to learning than purely stimulus-response behaviour. In order to justify his beliefs, he carried out experiments designed to investigate how animals solved problems.

In one experiment Köhler placed a banana outside a cage containing a chimpanzee. Two sticks were available to the chimpanzee, neither of which alone was long enough to reach the banana. The chimpanzee tried unsuccessfully to reach the banana with its hands and feet. It then tried using one of the sticks and was once again unsuccessful. After pausing, presumably to cogitate, the chimpanzee suddenly joined the two sticks together and, using the resulting single long stick, was able to reach the banana. It then proceeded to rake the banana towards the cage.

Köhler concluded that the solution came suddenly when the chimpanzee had surveyed the whole problem after its unsuccessful attempts. In a flash of 'insight', the chimpanzee had 'seen' the connection between the two sticks and the banana after perceiving the relationships essential to the solution.

In another experiment yielding the same sort of conclusions, a banana was dangled from the top of a cage beyond the reach of a chimpanzee. A number of boxes were placed inside the cage. The chimpanzee tried to reach the banana by standing on top of one box after another but was unsuccessful. No single box was high enough. The animal tried in vain to reach the banana. Then, after a while, it stacked one box on top of another. It leapt on top and was able to reach the banana. Again, the solution was attributed to insight.

In problem solving, insight is the name given to the process involving the perception of relationships leading to a solution. The learner surveys each element of a problem and calls up previous knowledge and rules from his memory store. Perceptual organisation takes place as he tries to formulate a pattern of activity which will solve the problem or arrange the links connecting various elements into the correct sequence. All aspects of the problem are surveyed; then, in a flash of insight, the solution suddenly becomes apparent and the requisite responses are made. The problem is solved and the method of solution may be repeated or applied to other problems with similar parameters. The problem has been solved by insight brought about by a complete understanding of all relationships appertaining to it.

Teachers can help students to gain insight by using examples and diagrams which illustrate rules and by using the 'Socratic' method of questioning, where the students' replies help them to identify their errors and discover the correct answer for themselves.

3 Chaining

Response chains and **learning sets** are learning structures in which elemental steps are mastered and linked together to form a procedure. Having once acquired the knowledge, a learner will be able to carry out routine sequences almost automatically.

The procedure normally adopted in a formal instructional situation covering the motor responses involved in, say, inspection operations or setting up machines is as follows: the teacher demonstrates each step in the correct sequence; the learner memorises the sequence, performs individual links and then connects each one to the next. The chain is repeated in the correct order with the teacher cueing and reinforcing as required until an error-free demonstration can be repeated many times.

Having acquired the chain, a learner should be able to apply it to new operations of a similar nature.

Participator	Procedure	Remarks
Teacher	Establishes form and content of chain	Discriminates
Teacher	Demonstrates each link	Explains
Learner	Learns each link of chain separately	Verbal prompts
Learner	Repeats sequence in quick succession	Avoids forgetting
Learner	Repeats chain several times	Reinforces
Learner	Masters chain	Satisfaction
Teacher	Rewards learner for correct chaining	Immediately

Figure 1.1 Stages in learning response chains

4 Verbal association

One example of **verbal association** is **naming.** In order to be able to name an object, such as a cone or cube, the observer must see the object, recognise its shape and know its name. If these three conditions are met, the observer will be able to say, 'this is a cone', or, 'this is a cube'. We can see from this that naming is an elementary form of learning met in everyday life.

When unusual objects are experienced or when new concepts are introduced during a lecture the names sometimes give a clue as to their nature. Take the word 'pyrometer'. The word breaks down into two parts: 'pyro' and 'meter'. 'Pyro' relates to fire or heat and 'meter' to measuring. A pyrometer is a temperature-measuring device. The learner associates 'pyro' with an existing mental image, say, a heat-resistant Pyrex® dish or perhaps a pyre, a pile of wood for burning a dead body! Similarly, 'meter' may be associated with a parking meter or speedometer, both used for measuring. The examples drawn from experience act as coding connections and help to give meaning to the new word.

Definitions are frequently made up of several concepts; a statement such as, 'a vector quantity involves both magnitude and direction', can be translated as 'how

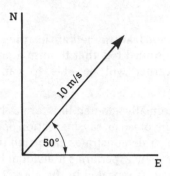

Figure 1.2 Meaning from mental image: a vector diagram

big' and 'course or line'. A mental image of a vector diagram helps to connect the words in a meaningful way (see Figure 1.2).

Poems, quotations, physical laws and procedures for solving mathematical problems are other examples of verbal chaining. The form of a commonly used phrase is often memorised, so that many people will be able to say almost without thinking: 'at this moment in time', 'unaccustomed as I am to public speaking'. 'I regret that I shall be unable to attend the meeting', etc. Many partially formed verbal chains are stored in the brain ready for recall when the opportunity presents itself, so that new chains are more readily learned if the coding cues are strong enough.

5 Multiple discrimination

Discrimination is the act of discerning that which constitutes a difference between two or more objects. It involves making judgements or observing characteristics. In psychological terms it relates to the detection of differences between stimuli in the perceptual field.

Multiple discrimination learning requires the learner to be able to distinguish objects or words from a very wide variety of items, many of which bear similarities and thus lead to problems of interference. The learner must also be able to identify likenesses and differences in objects and to construct chains of words in correct and unambiguous sequences.

In a practical situation the learner must be able to discriminate between physical characteristics of objects or processes. Figure 1.3 below sets out some common applications:

Factor	Concept knowledge
Light/heavy	Relative density
Bright/dim	Luminous intensity
Rough/smooth	Surface finish assessment
Hard/soft	Hardness testing
Wet/dry	Humidity
Hot/cold	Temperature
Colour	Optical spectrum

Figure 1.3 Discrimination based on concept knowledge

6 Concept learning

Groups of objects with common features are known as **classes**, while general ideas about classes are known as **concepts**.

A concept can be defined as the properties, essential qualities or relationships common to a class of objects. Concepts may relate to concrete things in the real world or to abstract ideas such as beauty, fairness, equality, honesty or justice.

If we consider the word 'house', a mental image of several of the following may form: large house, small house, mansion, council house, farmhouse, lodge or villa. The word 'house' probably brings to mind several different types of building, so that when we are thinking about houses we are thinking about a **class** of buildings.

If we are presented with a set of photographs which includes many different types of houses together with a variety of other objects, we shall be able to sort the houses into a class and reject the remaining photographs. This is because the houses incorporate common features such as walls, windows, doors and roofs.

Concepts are formed as a result of experiences within the physical environment as well as through verbal communication related to events. In addition to the physical attributes of a house, such as bricks and mortar, ideas about the functions of a family within the house are also built into the concept. Having once acquired the concept 'house', we are able to discuss houses or read about them using mental images drawn from our imagination and hence learn without actually seeing the real thing.

In the classroom, when a word is written on the chalkboard or spoken by the teacher, a response of some kind will be forthcoming. This is because the words represent real things in the minds of the students. The response may be in the form of physical behaviour at the mention of a word because the word has signal significance. On the other hand, students may recall abstract ideas suggested by the word because the word has semantic significance—going beyond the recognised simple meaning of the word to form a general concept from consideration of particular instances.

In general, when teaching concepts, the teacher should move from the concrete to the abstract, from the known and familiar to the unknown, and should, wherever possible, relate examples or analogies to the students' lives.

7 Principle learning

A **principle** is a fundamental truth on which others may be founded and is made up of a chain of concepts. A chain of concepts such as 'molecules', 'energy' and 'heat' may be combined to form a relationship like: 'molecules gain energy when heated'. In the same way, more complicated principles, such as: 'action and reaction are equal and opposite', 'the force on objects in circular motion is directed towards the centre', and 'pure metals increase in resistance when their temperature is increased', are made up of a number of concepts linked together in a specific sequence. The important point about chaining of concepts is that for the principle to be correctly stated, the appropriate verbal chain must be assembled in the correct sequence.

Principles learned from verbal chaining may or may not be meaningful. If principles are learned by rote, that is, by repeating or performing without regard to meaning, there will be a strong probability that the student will be able to solve only certain examples. Slight changes in the order of wording problems, or problems requiring 'in-depth' knowledge of the application of principles will result in the learner giving in. To be successful in problem solving, the learner will need to be able to recall the verbal chains in correct sequence, to understand individual concepts and to be aware of the relationship between them.

Perhaps a better approach to principle learning is that put forward by Gagné, who suggests that a thorough knowledge of the lower orders of learning should be mastered before attempting principle learning and problem solving.[4] This requires that words denoting general ideas and concepts formed when different objects are seen to possess common features should be forged into well-learned chains making up the principles. Having once acquired a number of principles relevant to a given problem, the learner can combine them in order to solve it.

The teacher can help by relating the teaching of principles to situations which the learner will meet in day-to-day life, and by using appropriate teaching aids. For their part, learners can speed up problem solving by verbalising their repertoire of principles while working on the problem. Such practices tend to produce more accurate solutions, reducing the number of errors made along the way.

8 Problem solving

A problem is a matter in which it is difficult to decide the best course of action. An academic problem usually arises as a question propounded for solution or as a proposition in which some outcome or end-product is required. Such problems involve the application of one or more principles.

Problem solving is the most complicated form of learning behaviour. It leads to the formation of new principles of a higher order. The learner is required to consider the problem and to organise knowledge of several principles at one time in order to reach a successful solution.

If the learners are able to find words to express their thoughts and to talk about fundamental principles bearing on the problem they will be well on the way to solving the problem. This type of activity is met daily at work. A problem arises and two or more people get together to find a solution. We hear conversations like:

'We had this once before. Watercans! Remember Chris? Handles kept breaking away when they were full of water. We used a larger heater element to increase the fluidity of the plastic. Then we were able to reduce the moulding pressure. We can do the same with this job. That will solve it — provided we shorten the cycle time.'
'Yes, but if we do that Ian, will the cavity fill completely? Another thing, will the plastic cool down enough before it's ejected?'
'Mmmm. I've just thought of another problem. Distortion. We had a lot of scrap when we speeded things up.'

The discussion of the problem will probably lead to a decision based upon a mixture of past experiences and principles relating to the moulding process. The example illustrates Gagné's proposition that once a problem has been solved, something has been learned and added to the learner's capabilities.

Trial and error learning can waste a lot of time and the learners run the risk of learning redundant and incorrect responses in their efforts to reach a solution. Problem solving which is guided by a teacher is much more productive. It involves the combination of learned principles to achieve some end, and once this end has been achieved, the principles involved may be transferred to many other situations. Learning achieved by problem solving is long retained and seldom forgotten.

Participator	Procedure	Remarks	
Teacher ↓	Prepares and describes problem ↓		
Learner ↓	Analyses problem and identifies its nature ↓	Exhibits state of readiness ↓	T E A C H E R
Teacher ↓	Outlines possible approaches or lines of thought ↓	Does not reveal solution ↓	
Learner ↓	Keeps all relevant principles in mind and applies them to the problem at one time ↓	Continuity ↓	
Teacher ↓	Cues and directs learners efforts when required ↓	Keeps learner on right track ↓	C E N T R E D
Learner	Discovers solution ↓	Activity is reinforced ↓	
Learner	Forms new higher-order principle from existing principles ↓	Has learned something new ↓	
	Remembers solution and is able to apply principles to other similar but novel problems	Is less likely to forget principles	
Teacher ↓	Provides problem solving opportunity, or encourages learner to select problem to tackle ↓	Makes resources available	L E A R N E R
Learner	Selects and defines problem ↓		
Learner	Analyses problem ↓		
Learner	Devises possible solutions ↓	Learner 'owns' problem-solving skills	
Learner	Reviews implications of each solution ↓		C E N T R E D
Learner	Decides on course of action ↓		
Learner	Implements and monitors problem-solving activity ↓		
Learner	Evaluates outcomes: problem solved or redefined		

Figure 1.4 Stages in problem solving

In formal academic situations the teacher should analyse the problem and ensure that the learner has all essential concepts and principles involved in the problem before being introduced to it. While problem solving is taking place, the teacher should be on hand when needed to guide the learner through the maze towards a solution. Students should be able to see the overall pattern and should make use of any positive transfer of learning available (see Figure 1.4 for the stages involved).

An alternative is to ask the students to identify a problem, and let them sort out what is needed to solve it, while keeping a low teacher profile (see part 2 of Figure 1.4).

Learning skills

Some tasks are performed frequently. They often form basic components of other more complicated tasks, so it is necessary to perform them well, accurately and with as little effort as possible. These basic operations are called **skills** and include walking, manipulating arms and legs, writing, reading and typing. If these skills are not well learned, they consume a great deal of time and energy, and higher order activities of which they form part are less efficiently performed.

Skills demand a lot of practice and eventually their performance becomes more or less automatic. Many skills relate to motor or physical activity only; but there are many parallels in what are almost exclusively mental activities.

Filing metal with a hand file is an example of a **sensorimotor skill** in which muscular movement is prominent but is controlled by sensory stimuli. Filing a block of metal is not purely a mechanical operation but also includes brain activity which may occur without our paying conscious attention to it. This manual skill involves a decision-making process in which a choice of muscular response is made to suit the pattern of incoming sensory signals (see Figure 1.5).

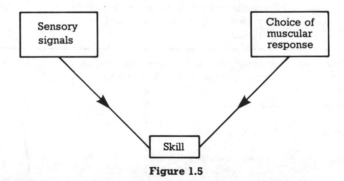

Figure 1.5

A skilled performance involves rather more than carrying out a pattern of skilled movements. The craftsman must discriminate between competing stimuli and select only those appropriate to the task on hand (see Figure 1.6).

When considering the skills involved in a filing operation, the following should be borne in mind: senses such as sight and touch; pressure (kinaesthetic sensitivity); hand and body movements.

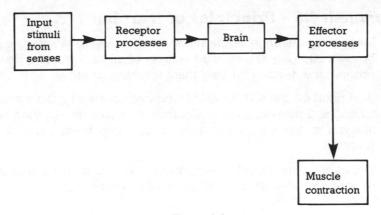

Figure 1.6

In order for a person to pick up the file from the bench, the following must occur:

– the eyes must observe the location of the file
– information is transmitted to the brain
– brain initiates hand movement
– hand grasps file handle and exerts suitable pressure.

This information is represented diagramatically in Figure 1.7.

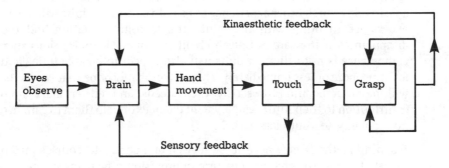

Figure 1.7

Once the filing operation commences, a good many more input signals relating to the filing are received by the brain, and kinaesthetic senses really come into play. A stronger grip is required on the file handle. Downward and forward force is required to actually cut the metal. The file must be stopped momentarily at each end of the cutting stroke to enable a change in direction to take place. The plane of filing must be constantly monitored to ensure squareness and flatness of the surface produced. The cutting force must be adjusted so as to obtain the desired surface texture and to ensure that the component is within specified dimensional tolerances. Inefficient cutting action must be detected and remedial action thought out, and so on.

Assignment 1.3 – **Principles of learning**

Identify and comment on the importance of some relevant principles of learning brought into play during the teaching of all or some significant parts of the programme devised for your main teaching group.

It is important that you are able to demonstrate during the course of preparing, writing and reviewing this assignment that you have carried out a systematic analysis of the interaction between learning theory and its application in practice.

The assignment should be supported by references to and examples of actual experiences shared with the group of learners.

1.003 How people learn

Needs of adult learners

Adult learners come to the learning environment with needs that vary considerably from those of children and young people. Whereas the young will be dependent upon the teacher for guidance and control and are unlikely to be self-directing, the industrial or commercial experience of adults and their experience of living will tend to make them expect to be treated differently, so as to promote self-esteem and self-confidence.

Children's experience will be limited to that gained during interaction with their families and friends and during schooltime and leisure. They will be too young to be able to bring much other experience to bear. In contrast, adults will have a wealth of experience to bring with them into the learning situation and they will be disappointed if they are not given credit for this or if their prior experience and competence is not utilised. Adults will also expect to be able to make use of new learning more or less immediately. They will probably hope that you as their teacher will be in a position to satisfy their needs and either make an important contribution to their future employment chances or help them to gain in other ways from coming to your classes.

Teaching methods may need to be revised and access to courses may need to be adjusted to suit the changing pattern of provision now being encouraged to meet adults' expectations of the service. Potential student groups, especially when comprising the adult unemployed, will contain people with a wide range of ability and attainment. It is dangerously easy to stereotype students on the basis of very little knowledge. Some will have a pretty good idea of where they want to go and how they are going to get there, while others will need a lot of support. This is where a sound knowledge of confidential counselling or sources of referral becomes critical to the success of learning.

As far as the actual learning processes are concerned, there is no doubt that both younger and older adults will respond much better to methods that encourage active involvement in their own learning. However, it is likely that the older students will make more fuss if they do not get what they want. The teacher and adult learner will therefore both need to be committed to a process of consultation and negotiation on content and mode of learning. Study guidance is a priority activity for successfully matching needs to educational provision.

Processing information

Cognitive processes are used to handle mental activities such as perception and thinking by which knowledge may be acquired. Cognitive processing can deal with information being received, regardless of the form in which it is transmitted, whether it be visual, verbal, attitudinal or conceptual. However, many people find it difficult to learn simply by waiting for suitable chunks of information to come their way and relying on their inherent cognitive processing system to do the rest automatically. Efficient learning calls for interaction between the learning task, the teaching and learning methodology, the teacher and the students' cognitive processing systems. This interaction greatly improves the quality and ease of learning.

Not everyone will agree that people learn using the cognitive processing approach, since cognitive processes are unobservable mental activities. B.F. Skinner, for example, suggests that students are able to solve problems because they are able to recall standard methods of solving problems of a certain form from memory. They have learned that certain academic operations produce learning outcomes. Convergent thinkers may well fall into this category since they tend to concentrate on getting the one right answer to a question using standard methods that yield conventionally acceptable answers. On the other hand, divergent thinkers may be less constrained by theory and standard methods of solution, and will often come up with several novel solutions. They tend to perform well when presented with 'open-ended' problems.

Skinner also maintains that the capacity to examine one's thoughts is the outcome of environmental conditioning and is incidental to behaviour rather than the cause of it. Whatever the mechanism may be, many feel that real understanding occurs only when learning is transferred from short-term memory and is stored permanently in the brain.

New knowledge is a result of real and tangible experiences linking in some way with experiences, knowledge, attitudes and concepts that have already been stored in long-term memory. The amount of knowledge and understanding already attained will influence the rate and capability to add subsequent learning.

Barriers to learning

Barriers or blockages to learning may be self-imposed or may result from past involvement with teachers. Some bad experiences in school or earlier college. courses many have coloured adult students' attitudes towards a return to learning. They may feel that they are getting too old to learn and fear that they may be made to appear dense relative to others. They may have physical impairments such as failing eyesight or hearing that would hold them back. They may feel that they have been out of the game for too long and out of touch with modern terminology. There are countless reasons for fears and individual learning differences among adult students but whether a real problem exists or not, the best way to clear the barriers to learning is to ask each student to make a note of their perceived problems and to share their worries with a sympathetic teacher.

The problems which such differences and fears can create in teaching are not insignificant, but they are not insurmountable. However, it has been recommended that when teaching people with learning blocks, the teacher should be aware of the fragile relationship that will initially exist and work hard at dispelling anxieties.

Positive ways of building confidence are to:
- make the student feel at home in class
- explain things carefully, moving from the known to the unknown
- take your time and do not rush things
- avoid getting impatient when students are slow to grasp the point
- encourage questions and reward students who volunteer answers
- present information in small, digestible amounts, giving plenty of practice and reinforcement
- deliver in logical sequence hooking each new piece of information on to the last piece
- avoid jargon and try to avoid being too theoretical
- use frequent checks of learning
- use objective-type tests to evaluate progress rather than lengthy written tests
- turn students' mistakes into valuable learning experiences
- if the concept is particularly difficult to comprehend but essential to the lesson, ask the students to take your word for it. Trying to force understanding could be disastrous for their confidence.
- where appropriate, use computer-based training programs of suitable level and with entry point at appropriate level for the student and help with using the operating system and running the software package
- use mnemonics where applicable as an aid to learning
- give advice on improving study skills and learning out of class
- identify transferable skills and build on students' existing skill ownership
- use a knowledge of Bloom's *Taxonomy*[5] to help break down the learning content into appropriate parts such as recall, comprehension and application depending on the objectives set
- integrate theory and practice and allow time and scope for the latter
- provide plenty of opportunity for learner-centred activities
- allow each student to go at their own pace
- negotiate learning objectives and agendas for action with individuals if possible
- instigate a study guidance and reviewing system
- encourage self-evaluation and quality assurance practices.

How people learn

It has been found helpful to work in small groups when initially considering how people learn. Most people will have in their minds ideas about methods by which they and others learn or they will be able to recall learning experiences of one sort or another.

Methods such as trial and error, watching, reading, stripping things apart (undoing) and finding out how they work, mnemonics, making comparisons, solving practical or theoretical problems, copying, watching demonstrations and listening may spring to mind. The list is endless. By recording and later reviewing all methods of learning suggested by individuals during their group activity the concept of people learning may be understood.

A facilitator starts by asking the groups to write on a flipchart their definitions of 'competence' and 'learning' before going on to list ways in which people learn. This will promote initial discussion and focus attention on the main task of discovering or confirming the three main ways in which people are thought to learn.

After about ten minutes, group leaders are asked to report on their findings and to read out definitions of learning. Well-known definitions can be given and comparison made with those of each group. During the report-back sessions the learning facilitator will be able to introduce the three methods of learning that subsume all that the groups will have written on their flipcharts and label each of their recorded methods with an M, U or D, or a combination of these letters.

It would seem that people learn by **memorising**, **understanding** and **doing** or a combination of these three, hence the letters 'MUD'.[6]

A 'card-sort' is a useful way of reinforcing the MUD idea. A set of 40 cards covering a wide range of concepts is produced. On each card is written one example such as: Ohm's Law, playing snooker, bricklaying, learning a poem, recalling phone numbers, airports, how electric motors work, dates of battles, how plants absorb water, names of Spanish resorts and so on. Each group member is given a set to sort into three piles labelled: 'Memorising', 'Understanding' and 'Doing'.

Having finished the sort, members are paired and asked to compare results. Much discussion usually follows when it is discovered that some of the cards may be correctly placed in more than one pile. This is due to the fact that the concept of 'understanding' is difficult to define and also that it it not often the case that learning falls neatly into only one category such as 'doing'.

Another outcome of the card-sort exercise is that members of the group wish to know more about the different levels of learning behaviour involving 'thinking' and 'doing'. Discussion often focuses on different types of learning activities that can be related to the affective, cognitive and psychomotor domains set out in Bloom's *Taxonomy*.

Briefly, the **affective** domain relates to the feelings, attitudes, emotions and values of the learner. The **cognitive** domain involves knowledge and thinking ranging from simple recall to evaluation at the highest level. The **psychomotor** domain involves motor skills, sensory perception, responding and the development of complex skills in written, verbal and manual forms. These domains will be discussed in more detail in Chapter Four.

Clearly, the level of domain category at which the learning materials and activities are pitched will govern how people will learn, or whether in fact they will learn at all!

Assignment 1.4 – Individual differences in adult learners

Consider a group of adult learners known to you and describe in what ways individual members differ in their approaches to learning. Think about their possible

- level of motivation and expectations
- retention level, long-term and short-term memories
- knowledge, skills, practical abilities and experience
- access to facilities, resources, time and support for study when out of class
- powers of concentration and problem-solving skills
- confidence level and capacity for learning new things.

Record your thoughts and discuss with colleagues what actions you would need to take in anticipation that some or all of your class may need help with aspects of learning listed above.

Decide also how you could make it easier for them to cope with a return to the classroom and what you may need to do to facilitate this.

Assignment 1.5 – Gatekeeping role

'Gatekeeper' is the term used in some colleges to describe the role of a person who is responsible for initially admitting an applicant to a course of study. It could be held that such a person has the power to open the institutional gate to the student or keep it firmly closed.

Giving guidance and advice to applicants seeking admission to a course is a very responsible and demanding duty. It would be easy to turn good prospects away by behaving inconsiderately or thoughtlessly. Mature people may need to be handled sensitively; they may be very demanding in their expectations. Not everyone is suited to the role of gatekeeper in an institution offering education or training.

List some of the ways in which adults may differ from adolescents in their previous experience and entry qualifications.

Prepare a strategy for assessing an applicant's suitability for entry to a course of your choice and consider in particular

- existing levels of skills, knowledge and experience
- level and recency of qualifications or profiles of competence
- relevance, scope and transferability of other training to proposed course.

1.004 Applying principles of learning to individual teaching strategies

More and more further and adult education courses and vocational preparation schemes are concerned with developing basic levels of understanding. They are based on common cores and the need for students to acquire a wide range of basic skills that are transferable over a range of jobs, the aim being that the students will attain levels of competence that will enable them to work in a wide range of occupations and enhance their employability. There is therefore an increasing need for teachers and trainers across the whole education/training spectrum to become aware of and to practise teaching for transfer.

It is the prime responsibility of further education establishments to relate principles, theory and skills to the needs of commerce and industry as well as to provide education in the strictest sense. Reviewing the years from the work of mechanics' institutes and 'night schools' up to the present day FE and adult education institutions will confirm the truth of this, but schools also have an important part to play. They can foster the concept of transfer at a time when pupils are likely to be highly receptive to the philosophy, and as such are accountable to pupils, parents and society in general for the development of a self-reliant and responsible attitude to both the world of work and the world outside work.

One of the most pressing needs is to spread an awareness of the importance of exploiting every skill and every piece of knowledge that teachers teach and learners learn. There are at present far too many teachers who disseminate facts and information without linking their output to real world situations. What is worse, such teachers often refuse to consider the possibility of transfer; fulfilment for them lies instead in the achievement of good examination results and the comfort of knowing that students are able to regurgitate what they have been told during a few hours of formal examination. Reflection, negotiation and the students' experiences over the academic session are largely ignored. Such teachers are too concerned with 'product' and give much lower priority to the 'process' of learning.

Using techniques and strategies to help students develop and become owners of new skills and concepts, to use them in a number of different situations and to recognise their applicability to a range of other contexts, should be of paramount importance to any teacher. This is what teaching for transfer aims to encourage and promote.

Teaching for transfer

The notion of teaching for transfer is outlined in the Further Education Unit (FEU) publication *Basic Skills*[7] and much of the content of the work is reflected in this section. It became the subject of FEU research project 'Teaching for Transfer', one of the aims of which was to explore teaching and learning strategies and principles that might enhance skill transfer in a number of vocational areas.

Given the present uncertain employment situation, teaching and learning for transfer of skills is becoming increasingly important both for young people and for the more mature who may be faced with several job changes during their working lives. Similarly, the types of courses being offered by educational institutions will also have to change across the whole spectrum and sooner or later every department will be affected. We have already seen the introduction of NVQs, New Deal, Traineeships, Modern Apprenticeships, work-based training for adults and young people, open learning, flexistudy and countless other initiatives. More will follow and concepts relating to 'teaching for transfer' will provide an increasingly important foundation for many areas of work-related non-advanced further education and training offered by the Further and Adult Education Services.

In *Basic Skills*, it is suggested that transfer of skills from one situation to another can be aided by

– designing it into the curriculum
– increasing teacher awareness of appropriate teaching and learning strategies
– students appreciating the concept of transferability and the value of 'skill ownership'.

Skills that are learned in one specific occupation, sport or course offer the potential of transfer to other occupations, games or subject areas. A common core checklist of transferable skills includes skills in

– language (reading, writing, speaking and listening)
– number (calculation, measurement, graphs and tables)
– manipulative dexterity
– problem solving
– interpersonal relationships
– computer literacy and learning.

Each of these skills is used in many different situations. What is not so obvious is how teachers might teach for transfer and how to design transfer into everyday lesson plans.

Teaching for transfer is not new. We have all been doing this to some extent since the day we started teaching. What is needed is a fresh look at what we have been doing and an increased awareness of the benefits to be accrued from designing education and training programmes that contain explicit aims and objectives relating to transfer. The next step is to deliberately use teaching strategies associated with promoting transfer.

Before a teacher can generate transfer learning objectives, each of the terms relating to transfer must be understood together with the following three aspects of skill transfer:

– the commonality of skills across occupations or task boundaries
– the ways in which a skill is learned
– the learners' awareness of their own transferable skills and capabilities.

Terminology
In the past the term **skill** has been interpreted by many as the ability to perform some manual occupational tasks; and the word 'skills' as, simply, practised

manipulative abilities. In consequence, when the word 'skill' is mentioned, an image of, say, a farrier producing and fitting a horse shoe, or a cake-maker icing and decorating a cake, or a cabinet-maker repairing antique furniture is formed. However, this concept does not reflect modern thinking on the part of the Department for Education and Employment (DfEE), where it is considered that even apparently simple tasks do in fact require a complex mix of skills from each of the 'domains' given in Bloom's *Taxonomy*.

Observe, for example, a young person operating a point-of-sale terminal in a large departmental store. Notice that the operator does not use manipulative (psychomotor) skills in isolation from the numerical (cognitive) or the inter-personal (affective) skills needed to do the job. As well as recording the cost of items by pressing keys, calculating change (where necessary) and performing stock control duties, the operator has to answer customer queries, ovecome objections, remain pleasant and be able to open and close the encounter efficiently so as to maintain good customer relations. With this in mind it becomes necessary to introduce two new terms to describe the skills involved in the encounter. The terms are: **product skills** and **process skills**.

A **product skill** can be demonstrated by a student and accurately assessed by a teacher using normal techniques for accreditation against objectives specifying behaviour, conditions and standards. An example might be: 'after instruction the student will be able to enter text at a rate of 40 words per minute for a period of five minutes continuous using a standard computer keyboard making not more than four errors.' The performance may be observed and assessed fairly accurately against the objective, but how the typist feels and whether or not he or she will be able to work under pressure in an office remains to be seen, as it is untested. As stated in Basic Skills: 'The acquisition of product skills can be demonstrated by precisely describable behaviour and can be assessed by written and practical tests.'

A **process skill** cannot usually be precisely described in terms of exact behaviours, unlike product skills. Process skills are demonstrated by a person working with others on a task-based activity that involves planning, problem solving and communicating. The kinds of skills involved are the inter-personal skills and problem-solving skills that are encountered at the workplace during day-to-day routines. Process skills cannot be described in terms of exact behaviour but are demonstrated in a person's abilities in tackling problems, working with others on task-based activities and listening, counselling and persuading.

During training and work experience sessions few formal learning methods are employed, often no practical skills testing or written tests are applied and there is no positive measurement of behaviour against carefully written specific learning objectives. Performance can be described rather more subjectively by reference to instances of observed behaviour while undertaking such tasks as group activities relating to painting and decorating a room, setting up a camp-site, or cooking a meal for a large number of people in a catering establishment. Individuals may be assessed if working alone by observing their performance in real life situations. Monitoring the point-of-sale terminal operator's cognitive, affective and psychomotor skill levels while interacting with customers is a good example of this.

When process and product skills are applied in new situations, they are known as **transfer skills** and **transferable skills** respectively. It is important to keep this distinction in mind.

Transfer skills are the process skills (the ability of a person to work with others, to solve problems and to communicate) that enable one to perceive similarities between an old and a new situation so that previous learning can be brought to bear on the new situation. That is, experience gained by past encounters may be transferred to the new situation so that earlier mistakes may be eliminated, and mastery speeded up. There will also be a gain in the learner's confidence to tackle a wider range of problems.

Transferable skills, that is, those product skills demonstrated by precisely describable behaviour that have been assessed against carefully specified objectives, are most generally thought of as skills that have utility in a wide range of settings.

An example of a transferable skill might be the product skills involved in filing a piece of metal flat, square and straight to given dimensions and surface finish tolerances. The learner, having mastered this task, would be able to file a set of contact points for a car ignition system in order to remove pits and defects caused by arcing of electric current, or be able to transfer the skill to filing the edge of a bathroom wall tile to fit a space.

The effect of learning one task on the learning of another and the extent to which past learning can be applied to new situations affects the **transfer of training.** One or more of the following can be identified in most new task situations.

Positive transfer is likely to take place when previous training or experience assists in the acquisition of knowledge or abilities involved in another task. Maximum transfer will occur when the new task is very similar to previously learned tasks.

Neutral transfer applies to a situation where previous learning neither aids nor hinders a learning process and obviously applies to a task that is completely different from anything a learner has experienced before.

Negative transfer occurs when previous learning interferes with and hinders the learning of another task. An example of this might be where the new task is different but bears some similarity to what has been previously learned. In such circumstances stimuli may appear to be the same, but actually require different responses to those at first assumed in order to avoid mistakes.

Lateral transfer is the name given to the transfer of learning when identical elements are present in two or more tasks. For example, if two tasks both involve the use of an office filing system, then the mastery of one system will facilitate the mastery of the other. A pre-requisite for lateral transfer is that component skills that are required in new tasks have been previously learned or experienced as part of one or more earlier tasks.

Plumbing and levelling in the construction trades is another example of lateral transfer. Once the concept of gravitational pull has been grasped and the learner has been given chalk and a plumb-bob on a thin string, it will be possible to produce a vertical chalked line on a wall prior to fixing the first strip of wallpaper. The learner will also be able to check the vertical straightness of walls when bricklaying or install a grandfather clock absolutely upright, either by this method, or by the use of a spirit level.

Keyboard skills may be transferred from typewriters to word-processors, computer terminals, telex machines and even to the operating of post-code machines at main post offices — although a little vertical transfer may be added in some cases.

Vertical transfer relates to the learning of new higher order skills following the prior learning of subordinal skills. Relevant basic skills are first learned so that the learner is fully proficient in the psycho motor and cognitive skills that will be needed in order to perform parts of the new higher order task. The example of a motor mechanic adjusting a set of car engine tappets illustrates vertical transfer.[8] Before the mechanic can successfully adjust the tappets he must first have mastered certain sub ordinal skills such as

- turning over the engine to the correct position before attempting to carry out each adjustment
- using spanners to unlock and correctly re-tighten the locking nuts after making the adjustments
- using feeler gauges to set the correct clearance between valve-stem and rocker arm.

The feeler gauges could be used in the lateral transfer sense to check adjustment of contact points in a distributor, or the points on an electric fuel pump without actually making any adjustments. But the use of feelers in the tappet adjustment task together with other basic skills employed gives rise to vertical transfer – and higher order skills.

Further examples of vertical transfer in this situation, where higher order knowledge and hand skills are needed, include: checking piston ring gaps when fitting pistons into car cylinder blocks and adjusting backlash in crown wheel and pinions in car transmissions.

In a typewriting situation, elementary skills such as inserting paper and carbon, setting margins, tabulating, centring and page layout all go together to give a higher order skill of producing a correctly typed letter or other document.

Transfer in is the term relating to the skills that learners bring with them when they join a learning activity. A learner might possess skills that can make the learning of new skills easier. New learning is more relevant to the learner if it links with or relates to previous knowledge. It is a great boost to the learner's confidence to be made aware or reminded that he or she has already mastered a range of useful skills. An example of transfer in the young person who wants to be a trainee motor cycle fitter and who already owns a motor cycle or car and has a go at servicing the vehicle. The person has probably already acquired a number of skills in motor vehicle servicing and therefore could transfer these into the training course.

Transfer out is the inverse of transfer in. The term relates to those skills that the students take with them when they leave a course of training. These skills are available for transfer into subsequent courses.

Generic skills are skills that are used in and are fundamental to the performance of many tasks carried out in a wide range of occupations.

Occupational area skills are the skills, standards and practices associated with a particular occupation or job.

Skill clusters are groupings of skills, tasks or jobs on the basis of statistical evidence of relationships between them, for example, job clusters could contain jobs requiring similar skills.

Skills across the curriculum refers to curriculum organisation and teacher strategies that aim to use the activity in which the student is involved for wider learning and the acquisition of other basic skills.

Skill ownership is a term that refers to skills acquired through training which emphasise personal knowledge and understanding of principles, rather than just relating skills to a particular job. Young people should be encouraged to think in terms of 'owning' their own 'bundles of skills' which they can apply in a variety of contexts.

Vocational area skills are skills that have been picked up by sampling general areas of training, work experience or other employment.

Transfer-of-training theories

Two general theories apply to the transfer of training: the **identical elements theory** and the **transfer through principles theory**.

The first theory holds that if tasks X and Y contain identical elements, positive transfer from one task to the other will occur and that the rate of learning will increase, giving faster times to 'experienced worker standard' (EWS). (See Figure 1.8).

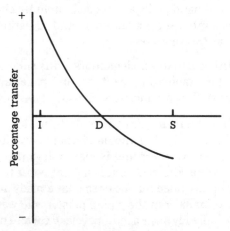

I – Task X identical to task Y

S – Confusing similarity between tasks X and Y

D – Tasks X and Y completely dissimilar

Figure 1.8 Graph showing percentage transfer of training between tasks X and Y

The second theory holds that fundamental principles, once learned, can be applied to a variety of problems based upon general objectives and concepts of certain classes, resulting in positive transfer.

The 'identical elements theory' could apply to the learning of specific skills and the ability to demonstrate 'can-do' competence without necessarily owning knowledge of the underlying principles; whereas the 'transfer through principles theory' requires that the necessary chains of concepts are available to the learner when problem solving, or confronted with novel learning opportunities.

Evaluating transfer of training

A diagram showing the form of an experiment used to evaluate transfer of training is given in Figure 1.9.

The aim of the experiment is to compare the performance of each group in learning task Y. Neither group should have any previous knowledge of task X. The experimental group first learns task X and then learns task Y. The control group does not attempt task X, but attempts task Y. After completing the learning sessions, each groups' performance on task Y is evaluated and compared. If the experimental group performs better than the control group, positive transfer of knowledge from task X to task Y is assumed. If the experimental group performs worse than the control group, negative transfer is assumed. If both groups perform the same, no transfer is assumed.

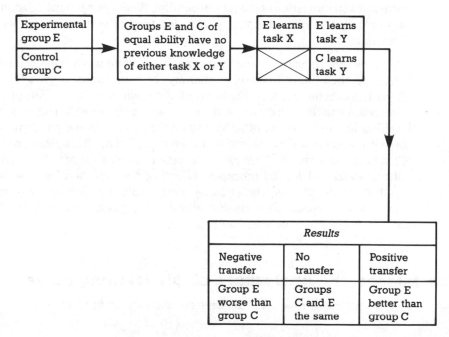

Figure 1.9 Evaluating transfer of training

In industry, when a person is retraining and is faced with performing a new job, previous experience will probably affect performance. As in academic learning there will be elements of both interference and positive transfer and these factors should be allowed for when designing the training programme.

Assignment 1.6 – **Teaching for transfer**

Teaching for transfer involves using techniques and strategies to help students develop and 'own' skills and concepts; to practise them in a number of different situations and to recognise their applicability to a range of other contexts.

With reference to your teaching programme consider how you might

- promote the notion of teaching for transfer as outlined in the FEU publication *Basic Skills*[7]
- explore teaching and learning strategies that might enhance skill transfer
- design transfer of skills into the curriculum
- encourage your students to appreciate the concept of transferability and the value of skill ownership.

Learning curves and plateaux of learning

Learning curves represent in graphical form the rate of progress of a student or trainee who is engaged in learning a task or undergoing skills training. A learning curve may be drawn by plotting performance against a time base. The gradient of the curve gives an indication of the rate of learning. When 'performance', 'acquisition of skill' or 'output' is plotted vertically, then the steeper the curve, the higher the 'rate' of learning.

A learning process usually produces a gain in competence or improvement as time passes but the upward trend will not always be continuous, despite the student's efforts to maintain progress. The time will come when no discernible progress will be recorded and the line drawn on the curve will resemble a plateau — a temporary levelling in the course of otherwise upward progress. Performance remains at a constant level for some time and may even drop. Then, after a while, performance again improves steadily. These plateaux occur in many areas of training and involve both physical and mental processes. Learning proceeds and then, perhaps after tackling a difficult task, comes to an abrupt halt. Reinforcement of previously learned work occurs and information absorbed is processed by the brain. Once this has happened, fresh progress can be made.

Assignment 1.7 – **Analysing a single learning curve**

A learning curve has been drawn from data given in table A.

A

Day	1	2	3	4	5	6	7	8	9	10
Learner performance %	15	27	40	43	47	50	50	65	80	100

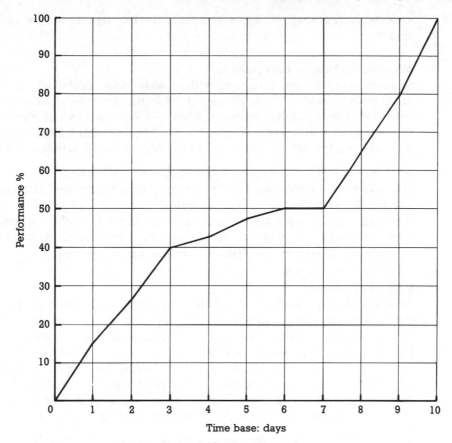

Figure 1.10 A learning curve

Analyse the curve and determine over which period

– the highest rate of increase in performance was achieved
– the lowest rate of increase in performance was obtained.

Describe what was happening to the learner between day 6 and day 7.

Teaching strategies

Some important learning principles have been discussed in this section of the book and there is a need for teachers to understand how these and other underlying principles can be applied to their work.

We started by recognising the importance of developing a favourable attitude towards learning in our students and considering our responsibilities as teachers for providing an atmosphere conducive to learning. We then attempted to identify the characteristics of different types of learning and to appreciate why the need exists for teachers to be able to use a wide variety of teaching strategies. As individual differences in student learning styles, abilities and needs exist we concluded that such differences would inevitably create a need for teachers to apply a range of teaching strategies according to the nature of the class being taught.

Allowing for learner expectations

Learners come to the classroom with a wide range of hidden agendas and expectations of what will happen during the learning sessions. Unfortunately, the outcomes of some teacher-centred and teacher-planned activities may not always be in accord with students' wishes. So there will be a mismatch. Some will vote with their feet and this will be evidenced by the high drop-out rate in some classes.

Teachers may feel constrained by their interpretation of the syllabus and decide that time, examination pressures or other factors prohibit the negotiated approach to learning favoured by some. What is probably true is that where students are encouraged to develop their own powers of learning and to take responsibility for their own learning outcomes as far as they can reasonably be expected to do so, motivation, self-esteem and attitudes towards learning improve.

Skill development

Good relationships based on mutual respect and trust can be promoted by exploring the ways in which your students tend to learn, and by being seen to be sympathetic to their worries and apprehensions. By seeking advice from colleagues who may have had more experience teaching the kind of group that you find yourself teaching, you will be able to concentrate on finding the best way to prepare your delivery. It is also necessary to review the subject matter, to establish the needs of the learners, to find out about their past experiences and consider the general setting of the course in order to determine how learning may best be facilitated.

You will probably need to analyse the course content very carefully and prepare a systematic weekly breakdown bearing in mind the outcomes of the review described above so as to be able to identify and select the most suitable strategy for teaching the group. The best learning environment is one that promotes a continuity of approach to the subject matter, enabling students to build on what has passed before. Planning should include arrangements for helping students with differing abilities and those with special learning difficulties. Learning should proceed at an appropriate rate with flexibility built into the programme. Suitable contexts should be identified whereby appropriate learning objectives may be achieved and where learners may be encouraged to take responsibility for their own learning and collaborate with other students to enhance learning quality. Reviews and discussions should be arranged between course team members, course tutors and external assessors wherever possible in order to compare notes and to learn of teaching and learning strategies that may be in use elsewhere within the college or in other institutions.

All of these suggested areas for skill development relate to those competences that teachers need to own in order to perform their duties effectively with the best interests of the students in mind. In an ideal world perhaps all of the suggestions made would be put into practice, but this is not always the case as for one reason or another teachers are not always in control of their destiny.

The students do need to play an important role in the planning of teaching and learning, particularly as it is they who will need to confirm the quality of the learning process, by demonstrating how effectively they can make use of what has been learned during the course.

1.005 Student-centred learning and performance judging

Learner participation

Active participation of the learner in curriculum design, choice of learning method, selection of learning resources, assessment and evaluation of activities and review of outcomes is now becoming more widespread. The term **student-centred learning** describes learning situations in which learners are expected, within reasonable limits, to take responsibility for identifying and agreeing objectives, planning and implementing their own learning activities and appraising learning outcomes with a tutor.

The curriculum is designed to encourage activity and experience by doing and actively participating rather than passively accepting from the teacher set bodies of knowledge or information. **Heuristic** teaching and learning methods whereby work is planned to enable the learners to discover laws and principles for themselves or with the cooperation of the teacher as facilitator or enabler are thought to encourage more effective and longer-lasting learning.

As long ago as 1920 a teaching plan called the Dalton Plan was developed by Helen Pankhurst at Dalton High School, Massachusetts. The plan required that students be given monthly assignments in each subject that they were studying and that their progress be confirmed and discussed with the teacher and recorded on 'job-cards'. Nowadays, this concept appears in a modified form as a 'negotiated curriculum' or 'learning contract' or 'agenda for action' and 'profiles' are used to record progress and experiences rather than 'job cards'. More recently psychologist Jean Piaget concluded in his studies of children's thought processes that teachers cannot further understanding simply by talking to pupils. He proposed that good pedagogy must involve presenting pupils with situations in which they may experiment and hence learn by actively constructing their own knowledge through interacting with the learning environment.

Student-centred approaches

Learning results from real experience obtained by doing things — by action learning, in other words, by taking an active part in work-related activities, tackling problems or completing assignments.

When this is followed by a review session with someone who has been successful in meeting the objectives set, or with a tutor, learning is more permanent. Recalling strengths and weaknesses of performance during the task and describing how difficulties were overcome by reflecting on and learning from the experience all promote effective learning.

Contrived classroom **action learning** as a substitute for the real thing simulates conditions where learners are encouraged to achieve a greater level of effectiveness than would be likely or possible under more passive learning conditions. Small-group work with four to six participants is favoured for action learning during which the teacher engages in building a good relationship with the students in each group. The more important skills involved include: negotiating learning objectives and goals, introducing learning opportunities and knowledge, summarising progress, facilitating and resourcing, reviewing and reinforcing, offering study guidance when requested and assisting with students' self-assessments or profiling.

The need to actively involve students in the learning process and to encourage independence in the learning situation is of paramount importance. Teachers need to design strategies that will promote each of the three types of learning already described (memorising, understanding and doing — see p. 19) so that each member of the group will be able to achieve at least one level of learning.

Designing activities for student-centred learning is a very demanding task that calls for a planning-led approach to related curriculum development. Facilitating during the activity is even more demanding since the role of expert advisor, supporter, helper and assessor can be far more difficult to undertake than that of a classroom lecturer teaching 'conventionally'.

At this stage there will probably be a division between teachers who are strongly in favour of the negotiated student-centred experiential learning approach and those who strongly support formal academic learning.

In the FEU publication *Curriculum Opportunity*, **experiential learning** is defined as: '. . . the knowledge and skills acquired through life and work experience and study which are not formally attested through any educational or professional certification. It can include instruction-based learning, provided by any institution, which has not been examined in any of the public examination systems. It can include those undervalued elements of formally provided education which are not encompassed by current examinations.'[9] The value of experiential learning to the teacher lies in the fact that it is a way for students to learn outside college hours and also serves to provide a store of knowledge built up over many years. Yet, while teachers will generally agree that students bring to the classroom rich and varied bundles of skills and experiences that can be tapped during the ongoing learning process, many do not trouble to find out about these experiences and how they can be integrated into the current work.

Making an assessment of the substance of past learning helps teachers bridge the gap between learning acquired by adults through life experience and the kind of learning offered by educational institutions.

In further and adult education when using teacher-led participative learning methods, the students are encouraged to make substantial contributions to the learning process so that physical resources, teacher and group are linked in vigorous interaction. Success depends on a co-operative attitude from students, and on the attitude, style, personality, awareness and sensitivity of the teacher, together with knowledge of and skill in using teaching methods which promote student involvement.

Under the general heading **participative learning** the following teaching and learning techniques can be grouped:

– case studies
– role play
– discussions
– simulation exercises
– problem solving
– instrumental team learning.

Instrumental team learning

This is a student-dominated learning method where the teacher acts purely as an administrator. Since this is a method that encourages students to develop their own powers of learning and to judge their own performance, it will be discussed here. The other participative learning methods listed above will be discussed in Section 2.003.

Instrumental team learning comprises three elements:

1 Team effectiveness design
With this technique, students are divided into teams of about five persons. Each individual reads a manuscript and then attempts to answer an associated questionnaire. They then rejoin respective teams. A time limit is set by the teacher and using the completed questionnaires the team discusses answers and formulates a reasoned answer to each question. During the discussion no reference may be made to the original manuscript. When the team has answered all the questions, both individual work and teamwork are scored against a key provided by the teacher. The scores measure both individual and team performances.

If the team interaction has been effective, the team score will normally be higher than any individual score. The key provides the correct answer together with the rationale behind the answer, so that the student is able to reinforce the learning objectives without re-statement by the teacher.

The last stage in team effectiveness design technique is the teamwork critique. A period of time is provided for members to criticise their individual performances within the team and to analyse team effectiveness. The critique may take the form of a guided discussion with the teacher in the chair or the team may wish to undertake the analysis and evaluation themselves. Figure 1.11 on page 34 details an overview of this technique.

2 Team member teaching design
The basis of this instrument is that the student will learn a section of work and then teach other group members. As the teaching is performed by a peer group member nobody will feel out-of-place and discussion of subject matter will occur. The whole

Summary of technique
Stage 1   Individual preparation
Stage 2   Teamwork
Stage 3   Testing and scoring
Stage 4   Teamwork critique

Advantages
Student responsible for learning (motivates)
Immediate feedback of results and achievements
Re-usable subject matter
Direction of learning can be controlled
Teams compete against a standard
Experiences of individual team members are beneficial to group
Teams could influence a disinterested member
Administrator needs to be a subject expert
Students learn to reject inappropriate material
Material can be set up at short notice
Large number of suitable subjects

Disadvantages
Construction of instruments is difficult, time-consuming and requires specialist
    knowledge
No use for acquiring skills, or for subjective material
Students must be literate and capable of participating in group interaction
Failure to complete pre-work reduces group effectiveness
Unco-operative attitude within teams inhibits learning (dominating, 'switching-off')
Material may require frequent updating which could be difficult
Could be used inappropriately because it is easy to administer
Requires accommodation for syndicate work
Needs careful time management

Uses
'Levelling' (testing previous knowledge)
Rules and regulations
Legislation
Product knowledge
Business topics
Facts and comprehension
Codes of practice

(Source: Peter J M Finney)

Figure 1.11 Team effectiveness design

procedure is controlled by students. Group size controls the number of segments that will comprise the subject matter. One subject segment is allocated to each student for individual preparation and at this stage students are told that their understanding of not only the individual material but also that presented by other team members will be tested.

After the team assembles, one student starts by teaching other members his or her segment, without referring to original material. The rest of the team ask questions and take notes to aid learning.

Each student in turn presents a segment and after all segments have been delivered, a test covering the whole subject matter is applied individually, followed by scoring.

At this point four different comparisons are possible:

– total score by each individual
– average individual score for each team
– score each student made in his teaching segment
– a within-team comparison of how well each team member taught his/her segment of information.

The last step is the teamwork critique in which the team gathers to discuss their performance. Within this framework it can be seen that the four different comparisons can be used to great effect in clarifying learning objectives.

Summary of technique
Stage 1   Individual preparation
Stage 2   Teamwork
Stage 3   Testing and scoring
Stage 4   Teamwork critique

Advantages
Promotes in-depth study of one piece of subject-matter
Competitive element motivates team members
Individual effort essential
Requires commitment
Large amount of learning in short time
Easy to administer
Can aid confidence and social skills
Students control learning process (acts as 'subject matter expert')
Re-usable

Disadvantages
Depends on students identifying key points (no control of direction)
Reading/presentation skills of student crucial
Needs close monitoring
Requires concentration and time-consuming preparation
Students concentrate on own subject-matter
Can causes stress/undermine confidence
Subject must be capable of suitable segmentation
Need for full access to all information
Individual ability may not match subject suitability
Absence or poor preparation can jeopardise team results

Uses
Segmented topics of complex nature (extensive application):

– supervisory/management level
– codes of practice
– instructional skills
– technical subjects
– legislation
– products

(Source: Peter J M Finney)

Figure 1.12 Team member teaching design

3 Performance judging design

This instrument allows students to learn the criteria that apply to performing a particular skill. It requires the student to be able to produce a workpiece or report as evidence of his or her skill level. The workpiece can be evaluated using students' own criteria.

A two-page report on a given subject set by the tutor is an example of individual preparation where each student working alone produces some item of work. Teamwork now follows and the object of this is to develop relevant criteria for judging the particular work objective. This may be done in a number of ways. The team may be given 'expert' criteria and asked to discuss them to ensure full understanding, or they may be asked to develop their own set of criteria together with rationale. In order that each team arrives at a similar set of criteria, one member

---

Summary of technique

Stage 1   Individual preparation
Stage 2   Teamwork
Stage 3   Performance judging
Stage 4   Critique
Stage 5   Second assignment
Stage 6   Repeat stages 2–4

Advantages

Responsibility placed on student for learning
Criteria can be set by students
General uplifting of standards
Students learn to exercise critical judgement
Students more receptive to 'in-team' criticism
Reinforces learning by rapid feed-back
Can be used for subjects which can be measured by an original set of standards

---

Disadvantages

Uneven mix of students in team can lead to uneven rate of learning
Possible rejection by colleagues
Criteria that is acceptable to group may not be so to individual
Relies on learning administrator being a subject matter expert
Criteria limited to students' level of knowledge
Could induce negative teaching
No guarantee of correct feedback for students' effort
Disruptive member can have a 'domino' effect on team or group
Complicated to administer
Limited application

Uses

Selected areas such as

– learning a new skill
– to improve and perfect existing skills
– selling techniques
– servicing equipment
– installation of appliances.

(Source: Peter J M Finney)

Figure 1.13 Performance judging design

of each team meets with representatives of other teams to thrash out a common set of criteria.

Judging performance comes next. Individual material is collected by the tutor and coded so that authorship is unknown to others. The material is then passed out to different teams. One group-member reads the report and the other members criticise it against their developed criteria. This procedure is repeated until all reports have been dealt with. A written critique is attached to each report and the reports returned to the tutor who then passes them on to their respective authors. At this stage each author reads his or her report and its critique to the team. This enables the team to offer help, advice and suggestions to individual team members. Each student is then given another assignment which is different, yet similar in nature to the first and is now able to put into practice improved skills and knowledge in the particular subject area. As before, work is coded and distributed for critique. This cycle can be repeated until students reach any pre-determined level of ability.

Assignment 1.8 – Traditional or learner-centred teaching methods?

Consider how you were taught.

- Did your teachers use 'traditional' methods to get their message across?
- If so, how successful were they and how painful was the process?
- Was the point of focus of learning 'the learner' or was it the 'content'?
- Was your Head's educational priority to foster curiosity, initiative and involvement of the pupils or was it directed to academic achievement without much concern for personal development?
- What happened to the 'under-achievers' in your school?
- Presumably you did reasonably well, and if you were taught by traditional methods then they must have been successful?

Recall your own experiences and summarise your thoughts by describing 'what was good' and 'what was not good' about your earlier learning experiences.

Examine some of the learner-centred, experiential and participative teaching and learning methods that have been advocated here and contrast them with the more formal traditional or instructional methods. Write a list of advantages and disadvantages for each method and describe how you would develop teaching methods that encourage learners to take a measure of responsibility for their own learning outcomes and performance judging while making the learning experience enjoyable.

If your preference is for the traditional approach to teaching and learning describe how you would develop a beneficial formal approach that would maximise learning outcomes.

1.006 Importance of analysis and synthesis in learning development

An important motivator for teachers is the desire to be of real value to their learners by promoting learning, acting as a resource for overcoming learning difficulties and fulfilling the learners' need to become competent in their chosen field of study. But the fact remains that whatever learners learn they must learn for themselves. The teacher cannot learn for them but they can however stress the importance of learning by doing, reflecting on experiences, analysing outcomes and using synthesis to find ways of acting to improve matters in learning development and encourage them to do this.

David Kolb described a model of learning, which proposed that learning, change and growth are facilitated by an integrated process. His work on **experiential learning** suggests that all prior learning is brought to bear on new experiences. The Kolb model is represented by a cyclical learning process comprising four stages: concrete experience, reflective observation, abstract conceptualisation and further active experimentation.[10]

With this in mind, and in order to find a way forward, a **cause and effect analysis** could be implemented using the techniques of analysis and synthesis. **Analysis** is effected by probing, dissecting and dividing unsatisfactory outcomes or **effects** into component parts; and then examining principles, theory and detail with a view to discovering the **causes** of poor performance. In doing this a certain amount of learning reinforcement and newly gained knowledge will result, together with a greater understanding of the parts making up the **whole** learning activity.

Then, by progressing from analysis to a synthesis or **rectification mode** the meaning of the results of the analysis and the causes of success or failure can be explained. But how can this be achieved? It can be achieved by comparing and contrasting **effects** noted with past experiences and memories of similar happenings; **causes** of earlier problems and how these were overcome using principles, experimentation or standard solutions; or by drawing on the learner's creativity, imagination and inventiveness so as to frame a proposal for action leading to further beneficial concrete experiences.

Notes and references

1   H.A. Murray, *Explorations in Personality*, John Wiley and Sons, New York 1938. Murray's list helps to explain why people behave as they do, and how secondary drives associated with satisfaction of needs motivates people to do something about fulfilling them.

2   R.M. Gagné, *The Conditions of Learning*, Holt, Rinehart and Winston, New York 1965, p. 58.

3   W. Köhler, *The Mentality of Apes*, Harcourt, Brace and World, New York 1927.

4   R.M. Gagné, *Ibid*, pp 60, 153.

5   B. Bloom (ed.), *Taxonomy of Educational Objectives*, David McKay, New York, 1956.

6   The concept of MUD implicit in any learning activity was introduced in an FEU publication entitled *How do I learn?*, an experimental programme to introduce young people and their teachers to the many ways of learning, December 1982.

7   Further Education Unit, *Basic Skills*, FEU/Longman.

8   As used by researcher Brenig Davies in 'Teaching for Transfer' (FEU research project RP129).

9   *Curriculum Opportunity*, FEU 1983 para 10. See also *Assessing Experimental Learning*, FEU/Longman Group, 1987.

10   See D.A. Kolb, *Experiential Learning: Experience as the Source of Learning and Development*, Prentice-Hall, Englewood Cliffs, New Jersey, 1984; and also Les Walklin, *Training and Development NVQs*, Stanley Thornes, Cheltenham 1996.

CHAPTER TWO

The Principles of Teaching

Aim: To enable teachers to make a conscious choice of teaching methods based on an understanding of learning principles

2.001 Recognising differences and similarities between students' learning characteristics

Group composition

To some extent learning characteristics are related to level of ability, age, social class, previous education and the many other factors that affect learning styles. However, people come to classes for a myriad of reasons and there is no way of classifying students in terms of precise similarities and differences in learning characteristics. What we can do is use our experience to judge as far as possible likely behaviours based on what is known, and be aware of several important factors that may influence student attitudes to learning. For example, an awareness of the effects of self-perception on the one hand, and motivation and learning characteristics on the other hand, can provide an insight to possible differences.

In continuing education the ages of the biggest group range from 18 to about 35 years. There are many more women than men in the system, more lower middle class people than any other class, and more better 'formally' educated people than less well educated people. Senior citizens, many of whom will have left school at the age of 14, are well represented but there are far fewer students in this group than in the biggest group.

Individual self-perception

The importance of self-estimates of ability, self-concepts and self-perceptions in students' approaches to learning cannot be underestimated.

The way people see themselves and the values they place on themselves is referred to as **self-image**. Michael Argyle[1] suggests that each person is constantly being categorised by others and learns to anticipate how he will be categorised, so that he eventually sees himself in these terms. Argyle goes on to say that people are also categorised as being more, or less, rewarding or prestigeful. This too is anticipated, and affects one's self-image.

Teacher expectations

First impressions are important, and the impression formed when meeting someone for the first time will influence behaviour during subsequent meetings.

Teachers tend to stereotype people according to beliefs held about others known to them who have in the past exhibited similar characteristics. Traits are attributed on the basis of whatever information is available at a given time, without real justification. We tend to go beyond the facts and read a situation in terms of past experiences of apparently similar behaviour. On this basis, a student may be labelled as 'thick' — the learning situation provides an arena in which stereotyping can affect progress and performance.

The influence of social expectations has highlighted the fact that people tend to behave as one would expect them to behave in a given social or work situation. Experiments have been conducted in which greatly improved performance has been observed in a classroom when randomly selected children were thought by their teachers to have been specially selected, due to their having 'shown great promise'.

The 'specially selected' children performed better because they believed that greater effort was expected of them. Expectations of high achievement led their teachers to make greater efforts in order to ensure that the group realised these expectations. Categorising, stereotyping and labelling often forms a basis for students adopting the identity expected of them. Teacher expectation and attitude can therefore serve to make or mar the student's approach to learning.

Learner characteristics

Adult students from many sources come to the classroom with widely ranging experience. For some, learning will have derived from what has passed before and learning by experience may have been the main method of learning. Others may have spent many hours in classes learning by formal processes. Whatever the method may have been, the students are now there with a purpose in mind and their motives for being there will affect the choice of teaching method to use.

For teacher-dependent students who have a tendency to become anxious when asked to take responsibility for some of their own learning outcomes, perhaps a didactic method of teaching would be appropriate. Some students are not able to organise themselves and prefer to work to instructions given by the teacher.

With adult classes, using teacher-centred methods may lead to problems, since it is often difficult to establish a norm for the group in terms of tasks and goals, sequence, pace and learning expectations. Highly anxious students may demand that the teacher controls everything whereas others would prefer a move flexible, individualised learning approach.

It can be helpful if teachers are familiar with characteristics that adult learners may exhibit.

Assignment 2.1 – Adult learner characteristics

Ten characteristics that may be associated with teaching adult learners are given below:

- teacher dependence/independence
- field dependence/independence
- hyperactivity/inactivity
- reflectivity and low error rates
- impulsivity and high error rates
- task difficulty and persistence
- anxiety and its effect on performance
- previous learning influences
- variance in rate of learning
- degree of motivation.

Consider the list and add others based on observation of your groups. Discuss how an awareness of these characteristics may influence your teaching style.

The effect of intellectual development on the learning process

Tests now exist for the assessment of verbal comprehension, verbal fluency, numerical ability, perceptual speed and logical reasoning.

IQ tests are used to estimate the mental capacity of a person at a given time, and relate to present performance over a range of intellectual abilities for which the test has been designed. Coaching, rehearsing and practice affects test results as does the attitude towards the test of the person being tested. Test scores are subject to rise and fall with time.

The intelligence quotient (IQ) is given by the ratio:

$$\frac{\text{Mental age} \times 100}{\text{Chronological age}}$$

and for the average person ranges from about 90 to 110, although college graduates may have IQs of 120 plus.

Intelligence has been defined as 'the faculty of understanding.' It implies the capability to solve problems using abstract language, both verbal and symbolic. In order to learn, a person must be able to perceive and to attach meaning to written and spoken words as well as concrete objects.

Some argue that people are born with innate potential for the development of intelligence, and that knowledge results from exposure to contrived learning situations and interaction with the environment. Low academic achievement (whatever this may mean!) is considered by some to be an indicator of defective intelligence, with mental differences between slow learners and rapid learners increasing over a period of time. Exposure to poorly designed or inappropriate curricular activities relative to the learner's ability also reduces the learning rate. Poor performance judged against academic standards often results in students 'opting out' and sometimes giving trouble.

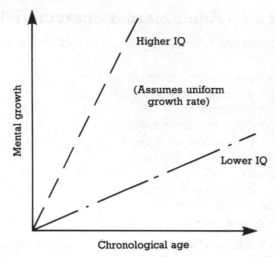

Figure 2.1 Mental growth against chronological age

People develop intellectually at their own rate and should, for prolonged mental growth, be exposed to challenging learning processes for as long a period of life as is possible. Intelligence is maintained by some people throughout life, especially if their IQ is high when younger. In others, with initially lower intelligence, intellectual ability declines progressively from the age of about thirty, while physical loss may also impair intelligence and learning ability. Fortunately, there is a greater maintenance of intelligence with use — if you don't use it, you may lose it!

Assignment 2.2 – **Comparison of learning styles**

Compare the similarities and differences between two of the groups that you teach in relation to their learning styles.

Account for any observations that you have been able to make and describe what action you have taken to adjust the teaching and learning methodology employed with each of the classes to suit the students' needs.

Assignment 2.3 – **Learning characteristics in multicultural classrooms**

There is a need for all persons entering the teaching profession to be aware of the increasingly multicultural nature of British society. Over the past 30 years, immigration has resulted in multi-ethnic mixed communities that wish to maintain cultural identities while at the same time exercising the unquestionable right to equality of opportunity in all aspects of life in Britain today. Ethnic minorities are entitled to a fair deal in the classroom and their needs should be reflected in the design of an international curriculum.

Draw up a list of criteria that you would use when planning a curriculum in multicultural education under the headings:

– cultural similarities and differences
– avoidance of stereotyping and racism
– attitudes and values
– language and communication
– differing needs of new immigrants and those of second-generation, British-born residents
– selection of aims, objectives, content and experiences
– teaching and learning strategies
– mode of delivery
– materials development
– guidance and counselling
– assessment and standards.

Assignment 2.4 – Understanding the needs of students with learning difficulties

There is a need to provide special educational facilities for about 20 per cent of young people during their childhood and early adolescence, due to **learning difficulties** — a concept that describes physical, behavioural and emotional conditions that hinder learning. While the modern approach is to recognise the fact that learning difficulties do exist and to integrate those concerned in ordinary classes, in some cases there will be a requirement for special education.

Describe the procedure that you would adopt if you felt there was a need to support someone in your class that you suspect may have learning difficulties.

Outline the referral procedures operating within your establishment.

Explain what is meant by the terms

– physically handicapped
– developmentally delayed
– visually impaired
– hearing impaired
– communication disordered.

Discuss what should be done if a student with an extreme behavioural problem became so disruptive that you were unable to continue your lesson.

2.002 Choosing appropriate teaching methods

At least three different methods of instruction are used in further and adult education: **didactic**, **socratic**, and **facilitative**.

Didactic materials are instructional materials that assist teaching and learning. The term **didactic** is also used to describe methods of instruction that are designed to allow the passing of information or facts with little intellectual activity on the part of the students.

Teachers may resort to the use of didactic methods simply because they perceive the method as being the best way to 'teach' a curriculum rigidly imposed, say, by an examining board or other external agency. Students are expected to learn precisely what the teacher transmits and later to regurgitate the knowledge without necessarily really understanding what they repeat.

The method can be valuable when the knowledge transmitted to the students is operated on by them. Reviewing, analysing and evaluating the given information and asking the teacher questions instigates student/teacher interaction and higher levels of cognitive domain activity may result.

Socratic questioning, or the 'Socratic method' as it is sometimes known, derives from an early style of teaching practised by a Greek philosopher and refined by Socrates. A series of carefully planned questions are asked with the intention of leading the students towards the statement of a principle or truth, a conclusion, or the solution to a problem; using step-by-step questioning.

Searching questions that encourage insight, contemplation and active and creative participation by all, are more valuable than simple 'yes/no' decisions calling for little effort on the part of students.

Facilitative teaching is student-centred rather than teacher-centred and is designed to encourage a high level of participation, with students accepting considerable responsibilities for their individual learning outcomes.

The teacher acts as a catalyst, supporter and helper who provides resources and opportunities for students to learn by problem solving, discussion and student instigated activities. Help in reviewing, guiding, counselling and evaluating may be given to the students as appropriate.

Differences between groups of students and their learning characteristics affect the choice of teaching and learning method to be employed. The teacher needs to be familiar with each of the methods described above and careful to select the teaching method that will yield the best outcomes for the students.

Judging appropriateness of a chosen teaching method

The teacher is responsible for the management of teaching and learning and for the deployment of resources to the best effect, the aim being to arrange things so that students may learn effectively. In judging the appropriateness of methods, the teacher needs to consider six main elements of the programme: planning, resources, method, activities, feedback and supervision. One way of judging the method is to prepare a checklist of questions relating to each element. A sample checklist is given here.

1 Planning
Does the method take account of

- the analysis of competences and core objectives involved?
- size and nature of group?
- pre-requisite skills needed?
- what is to be learned?
- how the student is to learn?
- degree of motivation to learn?
- different learning styles and abilities?
- relevance to work experience and real world?
- need to transfer generic skills?
- need to incorporate practice for learner in defining problems and formulating solutions?
- ways of presenting material?
- need to agree contracts or learning agendas with learners?
- need to complete a profile or other certification?

2 Resources
Are the following resources available?

- accommodation
- training aids
- training media
- simulations
- illustrated case studies
- assignments
- group/individual projects
- locally based activities
- assessment materials

3 Methods
Is the teacher aware of the following methods?

- job instruction training
- programmed instruction and teaching machines
- lecture
- demonstration and practice
- project work
- algorithms and fault diagnosis
- case studies
- role play
- discussion and simulation exercises
- computer aided learning
- other methods described in Section 2.003

Is the teacher familiar with eight varieties of learning suggested by R M Gagné?

- signal learning
- stimulus response learning
- chaining

– verbal associate learning
– multiple discrimination
– concept learning
– principle learning
– problem solving

Is the training best achieved by

– teacher exposition (teacher talk)?
– self instruction?
– student-centred learning?
– individual learning packages
– work experience opportunities?

4 Activities
Does the method provide learners with opportunities

– to understand the roles they will be called upon to play?
– to reinforce studies at work or at home?
– to participate in and to solve work related problems?
– to practise and transfer skills?
– to try out and apply alternative strategies and reflect upon results?
– to get 'hands-on' experience of several types of apparatus or equipment relating to the task?
– to practise reviewing, interview and discussion skills?

5 Feedback
Does the method provide an opportunity to

– test theory in practical situations and relate practice to theory?
– obtain knowledge of results quickly?
– attend reflection and guidance sessions?
– undertake diagnostic and remedial procedures?
– contrast experiences gained during educational and works projects or media presentations with experiences gained elsewhere?

6 Supervision
Does the method provide opportunities

– to apply alternative strategies?
– to support learner by negotiating and guiding?
– to relate training to previous experiences?
– for the teacher to help learners meet objectives and performance criteria?
– for the teacher to act as enabler rather than disseminator or fountain of knowledge?
– to arrange for assessments?
– to provide early feedback to learners?

Summary
In order to write a relevant teaching and learning programme based on a list of desirable competences identified, the teacher should be able to

– fulfil the need to provide realistic learning experiences
– explain the criteria on which performance standards are set, in order to assess competence
– translate aims describing experiences into training objectives
– judge the relevance of teaching methods and projects that have been designed to enable learners to be effectively occupied in an academic and vocational sense.

After the course programme has been implemented, the teacher should be able to revise methods or content, acting on feedback from learners, employers and other concerned parties.

Guides to training

It is easy to be lulled into a false sense of satisfaction about the way one teaches. Some teachers unquestionably accept the status quo and seem content to plod on as they have always done. Why should they change? They still have students and they are probably well liked by them.

In order to monitor what is actually happening in the classroom and confirm systematically that all is well, it may be helpful for teachers to judge the relevance of their methods using a set of 'Guides to training.'

Assignment 2.5 – Preparing a set of 'Guides to training' for use when judging relevance of teaching methods to a particular group of learners

Teacher's assignment objectives
To be able to construct guides in the form of block diagrams relating to analysis of
– training modes
– instructional systems
– objective-subjective learning
– acquisition of knowledge
– control of learning.

To be able to use the guides as aids to judging the open-endedness and suitability of course design.

Method
1   Identify important factors listed under the six main elements of programme construction: planning, resources, method, activities, feedback and supervision.

2   With these in mind, list groups of factors to be incorporated in the block diagrams to be constructed.

3   Construct the block diagrams.

4   Obtain a sample scheme of work or lesson plan and analyse the content using the block diagrams.

5   Consider whether the existing teaching and learning method is the most appropriate for the group of learners and training objectives involved.

6   Modify the training schedule incorporating more open-endedness where desirable.

Specimen

For each guide

– identify factors relevant to your classes (see below)
– draw up a central column with a box for each factor
– identify diametrically different dimensions relating to each factor
– enter and box-in the dimensions with the highest open-endedness in a column to the right-hand side of the paper and the lowest open-endedness to the left-hand side.

Using the guides produced, the sample schedule or lesson plan may now be analysed.

List of relevant factors:

Training modes	– passive/active
Instructional system	– instructional method
	– learning method
	– rate of presentation
	– standards
Objective-subjective learning	– instructional procedures
	– experiences provided
	– learning methods
	– source of knowledge
Acquisition of knowledge	– procedures
	– outcomes specified
	– experiences
	– thinking abilities
Control of learning	– aims, goals and objectives
	– content
	– method
	– assessment

Guides produced are given in Figures 2.2 to 2.6.

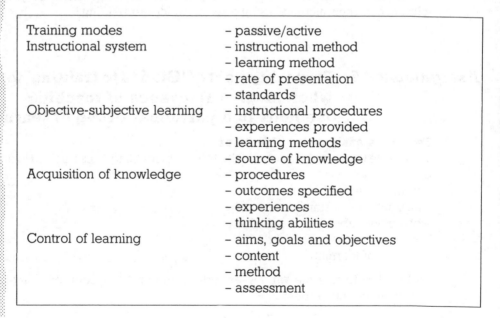
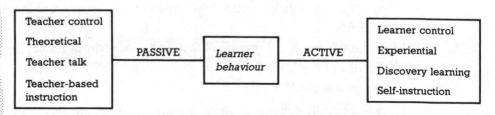

Figure 2.2 Training modes

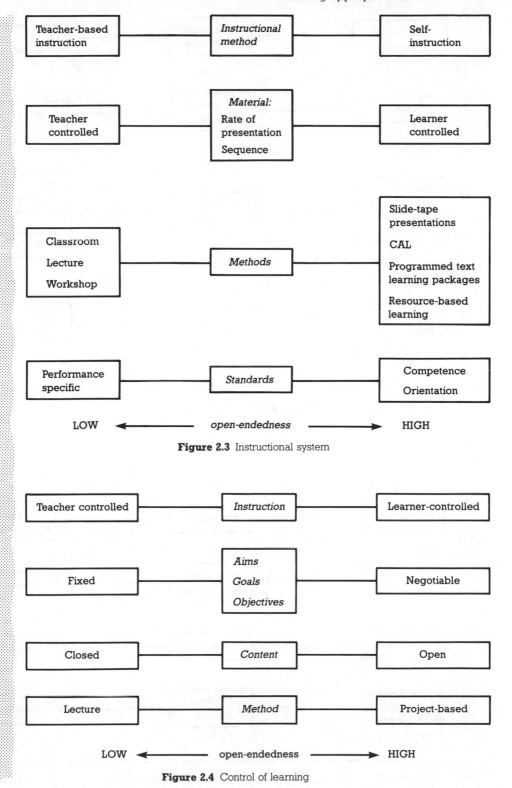

Figure 2.3 Instructional system

Figure 2.4 Control of learning

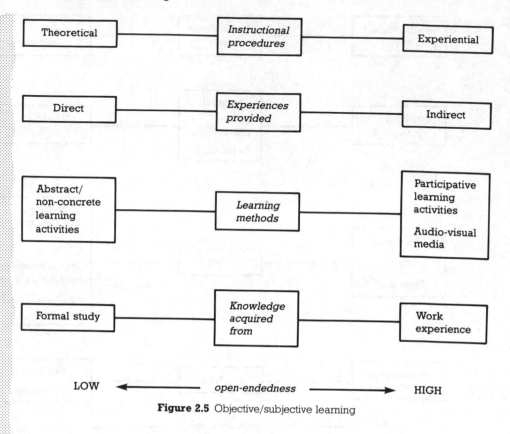

Figure 2.5 Objective/subjective learning

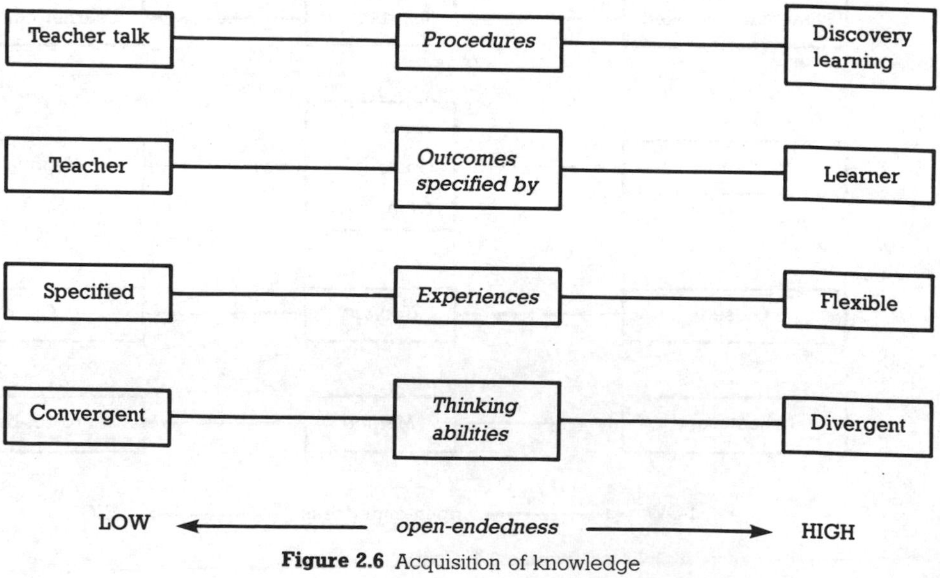

Figure 2.6 Acquisition of knowledge

Assignment 2.6 – **Choosing teaching methods**

For any one of your classes consider the learning characteristics of the student group and review your main strategies when teaching the group.

Make a list of students from the register and against each name note their individual learning characteristics.

Analyse your observations and try to establish a learning style appropriate to the group as a whole.

Do you feel that your present teaching method is appropriate to the underlying learning styles and needs of your students?

Assignment 2.7 – **Classroom seating arrangements**

The physical arrangement of the classroom furniture contributes to success with a class. Sometimes it is not easy to arrange the room allocated to suit the proposed teaching and learning method, but a teacher should be able to demonstrate an awareness of the role of seating in classroom management.

Observe the layout of your classroom and sketch the existing arrangement on squared paper or graph paper. Remember to include the teacher's desk, chalkboard, OHP, students' desks and any other equipment.

Part A

Rearrange the layout to suit your own class and make a drawing of your design. You are expected to be able to position the teacher's desk so that all students can see you and gain access should they wish to consult with you. The way you arrange the students' furniture will depend on the nature of the group and subject.

Part B

Review your design with a colleague and be prepared to justify the arrangements in terms of:

– the need for all students to be able to see the board, computer monitor/TV and OHP screen
– the teacher's view of the class when seated at the desk
– student access to the teacher
– teacher access to the students, board, computer(s) or OHP
– maintenance of effective class control at all times
– your choice of layout relative to the learning process.

Part C

Consider the various layouts used for individual, pair, group and whole class working and for each layout produce diagrams showing the students' seating arrangements and teacher's operating position.

Describe how the layout can affect students' attitudes to learning and their interaction with each other and the teacher. Explain why there may be a need to change the arrangement to suit the activity you have in mind, such as in the case of a change from formal lecturing to discussion group or to pair work.

2.003 Identifying and evaluating different teaching methods

Teaching and learning methods may be grouped under several main headings that include

– teacher-centred methods based on exposition, direction and control of activities, some of which are described below;
– student-centred methods, both in groups and working individually.

Individuals may be using resource-based learning techniques including computer assisted learning, or forms of experiential learning, or distance learning. They may be working on assignments or they may be involved in a personalised system of instruction such as the Keller Plan.

Students working together may be members of brainstorming teams, buzz groups, panels or games sides; or they may be out on field trips, study tours or visits. For some, membership of a seminar or workshop group may provide a successful teamwork approach to learning. In the case of social and community care workers, therapeutic groups or 'T' groups may be a good method of developing human relations skills using a group approach to explore attitudes, traits, interpersonal events and relations.

There are literally hundreds of teaching and learning methods from which to choose when deciding on the method to use for a particular class. Skill is needed in identifying and classifying those methods that could be of use to the individual teacher and students, and in evaluating the outcomes achieved.

Job instruction training: traditional method

With the advent of World War II came a rapid increase in demand for armaments and many other war materials. Factories were drained of manpower in order to swell the armed forces and these men had to be replaced. Large numbers of workers were recruited to cope with the vastly increased demands made of British industry. Female labour was introduced on a large scale and men were directed to factory work from non-essential industries. These workers needed to be trained, and trained quickly. To meet this need, job instruction techniques were developed which are still widely used today.

The traditional method of job instructional training involves the seven main stages set out in Figure 2.7. The whole job is demonstrated and explained by a teacher while the learner observes. The learner then tries to emulate the teacher and endeavours to reach experienced worker standard. During this process learning plateaux are sometimes encountered which hold up progress. After a while the learner overcomes the difficulties and reaches the required standard.

The analytical method

The analytical method is based upon a skills analysis for the job concerned. The job is studied and broken down into skills elements which are demonstrated separately. The learners practise and master each element after which they are required to combine the individual skills into a complete job. Time to reach experienced worker

Analytical method	Traditional method
Analyse job ↓	Demonstrate whole job ↓
Carry out skills analysis ↓	Demonstrate whole job with explanation ↓
Demonstrate and explain whole ↓	Demonstrate whole job slowly ↓
Demonstrate each skill element ↓	Learner practises whole job while teacher supervises and corrects ↓
Learner practises each skill element until proficient ↓	Learner builds up stamina ↓
Move to next skill element ↓	Transfer learner to production situation ↓
Combine skills into whole job ↓	Follow-up
Learner builds up stamina ↓	
Transfer learner to production situation ↓	
Follow-up	

Figure 2.7 Comparison of job instruction methods

standard by this method is usually shorter than by the traditional method. Learning plateaux are reduced or eliminated with consequent savings in training time, while the learners benefit by experiencing less frustration.

Before preparing a job instruction plan, the job itself should be analysed and the following questions asked:
– What is done?
– Why is it done?
– When is it done?
– Where is it done?
– How is it done?
– Who does it?

Having established answers to these questions and agreed the method, a **skills analysis** is carried out. A 'skill' is the ability, either innate or acquired by practice, which enables a person to perform a job expertly. The purpose of the skills analysis is to separate job factors into their component parts, so that a training plan can be devised and used to train people to perform their work effectively. Each factor is analysed under three headings:

– function
– knowledge
– skills involved.

The example shown in Figure 2.8 is the procedure for administering an intramuscular injection. It involves the nurse in carrying out a sequence of well defined actions. In order to do this correctly, the nurse must learn the sequence, and the knowledge and skills needed to perform the task. Careful co-ordination of hand

Function	Knowledge	Skill
1 Clean hands	Effective handwashing Modes of infection	Wash and dry hands
2 Select drug for administration	Interpretation of prescription sheet (a) Indications for use of drug (b) Normal dosages and frequency (c) Side effects and contra-indications of drug (d) Routes of administration (e) Manúfacturers advice for diluting drug Location of drug and dilutent	Read chart correctly Select drug and dilutent
3 Load syringe with drug	Location of equipment (a) Gauge length of needle (b) Size of syringe Recommendations for mixing drug Required dose Consequences of air emboli	Select and assemble needle and syringe Reconstitute drug with dilutent Draw up correct amount of drug Expel excess air from syringe
4 Identify patient	Location of correct patient	Check patient's name band and hospital number against prescription sheet
5 Administer injection	Sites for intramuscular injections Method for giving injection (a) Angle of needle (b) Consequences of needle entering blood vessel (c) Method of injecting large volume of drug	Select site for injection Swab injection site Insert needle Draw plunger back slightly Inject drug steadily Withdraw needle quickly Apply slight pressure to injection site with swab
6 Record drug given on prescription sheet	Recognition of layout of prescription sheet	Enter date, time and dose in appropriate place Sign chart
7 Disposal of equipment	Modes of cross-infection Location of disposal container	Place syringe and needle in Sharpax box
8 Clean hands	Effective handwashing Modes of infection	Wash and dry hands

(Source: Gill French, Dorset School of Nursing)

Figure 2.8 Skills analysis for administering an intramuscular injection

and eye movements ensures that the injection is skilfully administered and that the patient suffers the least possible discomfort.

The advantages of carrying out a skills analysis are that the following are identified:

- sequence of operations
- key elements of task
- hand skills involved
- other sensorimotor skills involved
- necessary co-ordination of movement
- kinaesthetic senses involved
- need for learning aids
- need for special exercises and practice
- estimate of cognitive aspects of task
- estimate of training time.

Computers, programmed instruction and teaching machines

Students may use a computer with CD-ROM drive and Internet connection or a teaching machine. Using linear programmes, the subject matter is presented in discrete steps known as frames, each of which poses a problem or gives one unit of information. Each frame requires a response, usually asking the student to answer a question or complete a statement based upon the information given.

In branching programmes the frame contains much more information than that of the linear programme and is usually followed by a multiple choice type question. The student selects an answer from the options provided and presses a key which signals the choice to the machine. The machine communicates the correctness or otherwise of the choice to the student, and if correct, moves to a new frame which often indicates why the answer is correct and presents new information. If incorrect, the student is directed to that part of the programme which is designed to remedy the error.

Having entered the programme at a level commensurate with existing knowledge of the subject, maximum participation from students is ensured because they work alone at their own pace and receive adequate reward and reinforcement for correct answers. The programme presents a challenge, and the immediate feedback of results helps to maintain motivation so that students are encouraged to give all their attention to the programme.

The advantage of the programmed learning method is that the subject matter is carefully presented in small interrelated steps and is graded in difficulty to reduce levels of student error. The method ensures a high probability of successful learning.

The lecture

The lecture is an economical means of transmitting factual information to a large audience, although there is no guarantee that effective learning will result. The method is autocratic in form and allows little or no room for active audience participation, while at the same time providing little feedback to the speaker as to the effectiveness of presentation.

The method is popular in universities and institutions which aim to provide a framework of ideas and theories which can be developed and considered in detail subsequently, either by private study, or in seminar groups supervised by a tutor. The lecture cannot cope with a wide diversity of ability and in itself provides little opportunity for the audience to clarify misunderstandings although a limited question and answer session usually follows.

A famous educationalist once declared that a university lecture is a means whereby the contents of the speaker's notes are taken down into the students' notes without passing through the minds of either. If the lecture is read from notes by an uninspiring speaker, the audience will soon fall asleep. It is difficult for a person to concentrate for very long, due to lack of active participation and some experiments have suggested that twenty minutes is the best one can hope for.

However, lectures can be very successful if they are well prepared, rehearsed, and supported by audio visual material. Where lecturers exhibit enthusiasm and imagination, they can set the scene for meaningful and intrinsically motivating learning experiences.

In general, lectures do not result in a noticeable change in attitudes held, and retention of information disseminated is also poor. Tests on recall applied immediately after lectures have shown that students may retain less than 40 per cent of content, falling to 20 per cent one week later. Those results show how ineffective the lecture is as a means of teaching, especially in the case of below average students.

Instructing by demonstration

A **demonstration** is a practical display or exhibition of a process and serves to show or point out clearly the fundamental principles or actions involved. Teaching by demonstration is a useful tool available to the teacher and plays an important part in the teaching of skills. The recommended sequence for planning and delivering a demonstration is given in Figure 2.9.

Practice session

A practice session should follow a demonstration immediately in order to reinforce procedures. If the actual equipment is delicate or expensive, a cheaper simulator should be substituted for the real thing.

Learners learn best by doing. There is no substitute for practice in the acquisition of a skill. During the practice session, the teacher should give individual attention and should correct errors and omissions quickly. Bad habits and unsafe working procedures are difficult to unlearn once established.

After confidence has been built up, factors such as accuracy, style, rhythm, speed and quality can be concentrated on; while ensuring that any target set is within each learner's mental and physical capacity.

Sequence	Remarks
Preparation Plan demonstration	Include key factors Logical sequence
Obtain apparatus Rehearse demonstration	Do not leave anything to chance Perfect sequence and delivery
Delivery Lay out apparatus	Each element in correct order
Establish rapport	Create suitable atmosphere for learning
State aims	What you intend the learners to achieve by the end of the session
Show end-product	Establishes in learner's mind the need to participate
Demonstrate silently at normal speed	Repeat several times. Allows learner to focus attention on process and arouses curiosity
Demonstrate at slow speed	Describe hand or body movements and senses involved
Ask learners to explain process	Learners think for themselves and are actively involved
Discuss safety aspects	Forewarns and creates awareness of inherent dangers
Ask for volunteer to attempt demonstration	Encourages competition Other learners asked to spot mistakes
Each learner attempts demonstration	Remainder watch and comment Teacher corrects faults

Figure 2.9 Instructing by demonstration

Watch for signs of boredom. Once learners have mastered a technique there is no further challenge. Move them on to another stage, but do not confuse boredom with fatigue. Reward with praise wherever possible, since this acts as a reinforcer. Aim to stimulate, not to distress. Never blame a student; no one deliberately sets out to make mistakes. Be positive. If there are difficulties, look at your instructional method and try a new way.

Project work

Student behaviour in the learning situation has been grouped by Bloom into three domains or areas: cognitive, affective and psychomotor (see Section 4.001). The use of project work provides a means by which the teacher can develop abilities in each of these fields.

A project may be set either as an individual task or a small group undertaking. The project may be designed as a learning process in which group members are faced with new concepts and unfamiliar activities, or as a device for the integrating of several previously mastered individual skills.

The **cognitive domain** will embrace such thought processes as identifying key factors inherent in the problem, seeking information relevant to mastery of the problem and using the information to solve it. This domain also includes the ability to plan and to implement a scheme of work designed to complete the task and the ability to communicate the contents to other group members.

The **affective domain** provides for the development of latent aptitudes or traits such as perseverance, leadership and creativity; and the ability to provide teamwork spirit or individual effort.

The **psychomotor domain** includes design work and practical skills involved in working on and assembling project components.

If a group project is set, account must be taken of each student's social skills as shown by the way they get along with other group members. As a teacher, once again, you must know your students traits and try to arrange membership so that the group will be cohesive.

Modern research has shown that when appointing a group leader it should be borne in mind that successful leaders are usually more intelligent than the other group members and are often assertive and self-confident extroverts. They tend to have a high rate of participation in group discussion, to integrate group activity and to be task orientated. In the event of a snag or problem, they suggest remedial action and attempt to secure group co-operation and consensus.

Allocation of work to each group member is the responsibility of the group leader, who will have to decide whether each member will be made responsible for a particular stage of the work or whether they will be involved in all aspects of the project. Before decisions can be made, the leader will have to consider whether to allocate a task on the basis that a member is good at a particular type of work or because practice is needed in a given area.

Time available to completion and the probability of achieving objectives set at the right quality level must, of course, be an important factor when making these decisions.

Algorithms

An algorithm is a set of instructions designed for solving problems in a finite number of steps. It should be laid out in such a way that the reader knows exactly what is to be done in order to solve the problem as quickly as possible.

Algorithms usually have only one entrance or starting point although they may have several exits or finishing points corresponding to the possible solutions or outcome of the problem.

Each step of the algorithm should be unambiguously laid out and should be easy to interpret. It should leave the reader in no doubt as to what to do next, so that if instructions are correctly followed, a successful solution is guaranteed.

The algorithm shown in Figure 2.10 illustrates the general principle of 'go, no-go' gauging used in an engineering inspection situation. It forms part of a training element, prepared by the Engineering Industry Training Board, designed to assist teachers and students in the development of satisfactory levels of skill in operator training.

The starting point, in this case, is the box containing the command 'Try the "go" end of the gauge to the workpiece'. Then follows a set of Yes/No decisions when a question is asked either leading to further commands or to a logical conclusion. The algorithm has three possible exits or conclusions, one of which indicates that the gauged component is acceptable, the other two rejecting it as unacceptable.

Algorithms are excellent aids to problem solving and are ideal teaching devices in a practical situation. They can also be used for the solution of mathematical problems. A typical application for an algorithm is in the diagnosing of faults in motor cars and electrical devices reducing the role of the teacher to a minimum while student activity is maximised.

In his article 'Innovation and Education',[2] John McCafferty, introduced the algorithm shown in Figure 2.11 in order to draw the attention of the reader to
– the issue of whether an innovation problem exists in his or her company
– the need to investigate some initial stages of the problem solving process.

In other words, he was not only trying to stimulate the reader's interest, but also using the technique as a method of problem identification, together with some suggestions as to what the initial stages of the analysis should be.

The simplicity of an algorithm can encourage individuals to make the first steps in problem analysis, and in McCafferty's view is useful in tackling problems, for example in pre-negotiation meeting plans where industrial relations issues are being discussed. The design of algorithms has the advantage that it disciplines a person to think in a realistically structured way towards a whole range of problems. Finally, it helps others to focus on appropriate options open to them.

Case studies

Case studies are based on real-life situations or problems which are 'frozen' and presented in one of the following forms:
– written
– spoken (taped)
– film, video, CD-ROM
– role-play.

Case studies create subject awareness and interest and by actively participating, people can learn from others. As peer groups are frequently involved, there are less inhibitions within the group and participation by all members helps to fill out an

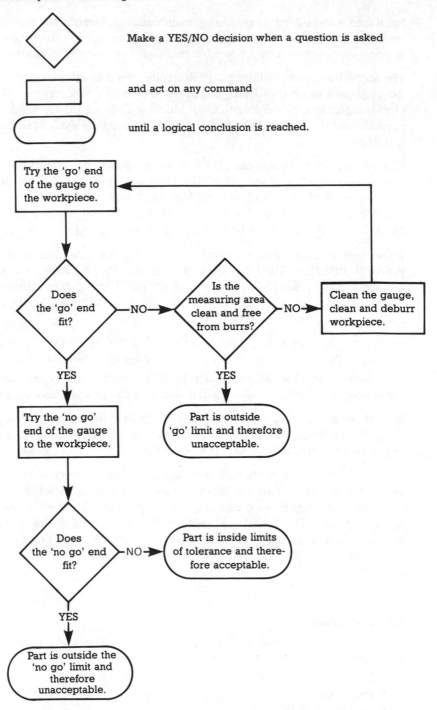

Make a YES/NO decision when a question is asked

and act on any command

until a logical conclusion is reached.

Figure 2.10 Developing the skill of using the gauges through an algorithm

experience giving an understanding of behaviour. The method can also be used to pass on skills, knowledge and attitudes.

In general, complex cases should be avoided in order to eliminate overloading the students' capacities, although suitably difficult cases may be written for use by management students or even degree students.

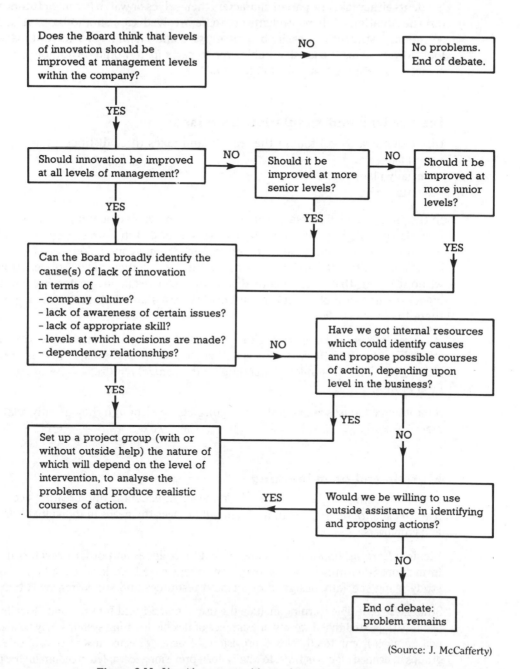

(Source: J. McCafferty)

Figure 2.11 Algorithm as a problem-solving mechanism

Role play

Role play is a dynamic version of the case study and is often based on counselling or human relations problems. Role play itself gives many of the advantages of the case study method but is limited to very simple situations where only one or two learning objectives are involved.

Students either take the part of characters themselves or watch actors or tutors play out the situations. Where students are to be involved, care should be exercised in selection. A student can easily be embarrassed and mentally shattered if made to look silly. Perhaps the most suitable type to participate would be outgoing people sometimes described as 'social extroverts'.

Discussions and simulation exercises

Discussion is a useful tool of the teacher and takes three distinct forms:
– pre-planned
– partially planned
– spontaneous.

In the pre-planned discussion, conclusions are known and opening statements are formulated, together with important factors arranged in correct sequence. With partially planned discussions, opening statements and conclusions may be known but the rest of the discussion must be planned as the theme is developed. It goes without saying that spontaneous discussions can result in greater freedom and bigger rewards in that the tutor can grasp certain statements made and expound them to any level.

However, care must be exercised to ensure that the tutor is fully conversant with the subject matter otherwise chaos will ensue. All three discussion types may be either guided or non-guided, depending on the control required by the situation or by the tutor.

Simulation exercises are very similar to discussion although they usually relate to practical work.

Flexible and open learning

Flexible learning has been defined as 'a means of widening and creating access to learning and training opportunities tailored to meet the needs of individual learners and employers.

Flexible learning opportunities are offered by colleges and other providers in the form of open-learning schemes involving college based, work-based or home-based study using specially designed or adapted resources and supported by tutors.

Strategies for flexible learning include the use of home-based Internet and IT facilities, and it is suggested that a variety of examples of flexible learning systems may be identified, ranging from: 'totally closed provision – teacher directed instruction of selected groups in defined blocks of time; to totally open provision – complete freedom on the part of learners to design their own curricula and pursue them at their own convenience'.

Open learning provides opportunities for people to fill gaps in their education and training, and to attain additional qualifications post school; and also to update their work-based skills and meet identified training needs.

Teacher skills needed to support open-learning include: an awareness of what flexible learning is all about; competence in tutoring and counselling; writing and adapting open-learning materials and working on curriculum development directly relating to open-learning needs; and monitoring and evaluating resources and methods.

The Open College, described by Lord Young as 'the college of the air', is one in a series of initiatives within the field of flexible learning designed to enhance and update the skills of people already in work and those who are not available for work. It is a relatively new national approach to education and training which places emphasis on learning rather than teaching.

The College follows other leaders in the field of open learning such as The Open University and The National Extension College. It is intended to attract people back into education and training and to provide interesting and easy-to-study, high-quality, cost-effective training.

The Open College uses open-learning techniques supported by broadcasting and local centres where guidance and facilities are made available, so as to provide learning where, when and how it is needed. Successful performance in Open College courses provides credits which may lead to NVQs and the award of other qualifications by Awarding Bodies such as City and Guilds, RSA, AEB, BTEC and SCOTVEC.

Assignment 2.8 – Identifying main features of various teaching methods

List all teaching methods that you use and tabulate advantages and disadvantages of each method.

Identify main features of three methods that you most frequently use and explain why you consider these methods to be most applicable to the type of work that you are involved with.

Compare your list with that of a colleague and together evaluate your preferred methods.

Seek your students' opinions as to the validity of your choices.

2.004 Matching teaching skills to method

The use of objectives

Behavioural objectives are specific and contain an indication of observable terminal behaviour expected, important conditions under which it will occur and a standard of acceptable performance. **Non-behavioural objectives** are more abstract and relate to concepts that cannot readily be measured, such as sales staff attitudes towards customers, and the establishment of relationships. In practice, it is not easy to classify objectives as being either behavioural or non-behavioural, because attitudes and feelings become inextricably mixed with specific identifiable behaviour.

Course, unit and lesson planning, and the choice of learning materials and methods to be employed are all based on selected objectives. Behavioural objectives can be instrumental in promoting effective learning outcomes, and all foreseeable activities relating to the accomplishment of goals can stem from carefully written objectives previously negotiated with the learners.

The approach to writing objectives for vocational training differs from that used in traditional educational planning. In the case of established academic courses, objectives may be written using an externally imposed syllabus, past examination papers, examiner's reports or teaching experiences as a starting point. With vocational training, however, the skilled craftsperson, experienced sales assistant, service engineer or other job holder provides the model on which to base the learner's expected final performance and outcomes of training.

Matching teaching method to objective mode

Cognitive domain objectives concern knowing and thinking and may be taught using lecture, case study, problem solving, assignment and project methods. The choice of method may depend on the conditions of learning and taxonomy level at which the students will be required to perform; ranging from recall or memorising to problem solving.

Affective domain objectives may be taught using role play, discussion and work-based activities. When formulating affective domain objectives to meet an aim such as: 'After training the trainee salespersons will be able to control and express their feelings without offending others', it is helpful either to draw on personal experiences of past incidents or to use role-play situations that allow students to compile a set for themselves. (A case study that involves the writing of affective domain objectives is given at the end of this Section in Assignment 2.10.)

Psychomotor domain objectives relate to doing things and carrying out manipulative tasks. Some actions are performed frequently and often form parts of more complicated tasks, so it is necessary to perform them accurately with as little effort as possible. A manual skill involves a decision-making process in which a choice of response is made to suit the pattern of incoming signals from the senses.

The ability to perform a job expertly may be acquired through training and practice. The teaching and learning mode selected should therefore match an appropriate skill development pattern such as

- picking up information about the task through the five senses
- interpreting information received about the task
- planning resulting action
- translating plan into activity, movements or behaviour

– executing all actions needed to complete task
– storing new knowledge for transfer to other tasks.

A craftsman in a practical situation given a problem to solve or task to carry out usually adopts the following procedure:

– read the instructions or job card or listen to the customer's requests
– look over the job and prepare a plan of action
– form a clear picture of how to tackle the work
– select appropriate tools and equipment
– obtain spare parts or materials needed for the job
– use tools skilfully in carrying out the job
– monitor quality and check work.

Sometimes, leadership skills are necessary to ensure that others involved in the task work together smoothly and efficiently and that all equipment and materials are to hand.

Assignment 2.9 – Matching psychomotor domain objectives to teaching and learning method

Details of a practical skills training case are given below.

Discuss the training requirements with colleagues and specify the most appropriate teaching and learning method to meet the objectives.

Alternatively, use the information as a model for designing practical training for one of your own classes.

Job: Trainee service engineer
Problem: Customer returns toaster for repair under guarantee complaining that the elements will not heat up.
General objective: Test against purpose and rectify if necessary.
Specific objectives: After instruction, the trainee service engineer will be able to

– select appropriate equipment needed to test toaster components
– carry out test procedures including:
  testing the fuse located in a 13 A plug
  checking connections and continuity of the mains lead
  testing heating elements
  testing switches
– assemble tools needed to strip and reassemble the toaster
– dismantle heating elements
– identify faulty parts
– specify and select correct replacement parts
– fit replacement parts
– reassemble the toaster using tools skilfully
– test, clean and despatch toaster
– return tools and test equipment to storage
– clean up work areas.

Assignment 2.10 – Matching affective domain objectives to teaching and learning methods

Part A

Read the case study given below.

Disharmony at work

Clare Davis, one of the sales staff allocated to the white-goods section of a large electrical retailer has left and will not be replaced. The white-goods section sells washing machines, tumble driers, refrigerators and other domestic appliances. The audio-visual section of the same retailer, selling television sets, video recorders, hi-fi and radio has a much higher level of sales than the white goods section, so that much more commission is earned. In general, a high percentage of customer enquiries for audio-visual products result in an immediate sale, whereas sales of white-goods need much more effort on the part of the sales staff and purchases are frequently delayed for several weeks. Often, a lot of time is devoted to potential customers without securing a sale. Such customers are regarded by staff as 'time-wasters'. Bernie Hodges is one of your part-time students and he is employed as a junior salesperson at the electrical retailers. He has until now been allocated permanently to the audio-visual section. However, Bernie is now called into the manager's office and given a new brief: 'Due to Clare Davis' sudden departure, the white-goods section will be one short. Under the new arrangements there will be occasions when that section will need a hand to cope with customers. This will be particularly necessary at peak periods on Saturdays and at lunchtimes. I want you to act as a back-up, so that if customers are waiting for attention there, you will have to leave the audio-visual section and attend to them promptly.'

Bernie is unhappy about the new arrangement. He feels that some of the older staff on his section are less effective than himself and that one of them should be given the 'stand-in' job. He realises that his commission will be reduced, due to the time he will be spending on the white-goods section and that he will be paving the way for future sales that another permanent 'white-goods' salesperson will benefit from.

He also feels that advantage has been taken of his youthfulness and junior position. He objects to being used as a dogsbody and is building up hostile feelings.

Bernie's normally good attitude in class changes. You realise something is upsetting him and he tells you what happened at work.

Part B

Put yourself in Bernie's position. Imagine how you might feel and try to predict his likely attitudes and feelings towards the situation.

Suggest ways of counselling Bernie so that his feelings do not cause him to lose self-control and create a poor relationship with other staff.

Part C

Write a set of affective domain objectives that would be helpful in the preparation of students for coping with human relations problems. Your list might include the following training objectives: 'After training the trainee salesperson will be able to

- control the emotional component of attitudes formed
- avoid defensive or retaliatory behaviour based on emotional or irrational feelings
- exclude behaviour that could offend or distress other staff
- act in a mature way and co-operate with others
- maintain a positive and helpful attitude towards customers.'

Add to the list other objectives that would be suitable for preparing Bernie and other trainee salespersons for situations similar to that described in the case study.

Consider how the case study would be edited so as to provide a role-play resource and decide how you might use it.

Assignment 2.11 – **Planning to teach, or facilitating by interaction?**

'Students do better when the teacher uses traditional and systematic formal teaching methods based on carefully devised schemes of work and lesson plans with well-researched and carefully structured aims and objectives.'

'Students do better when a facilitator uses an open education or learner-centred approach that encourages students to take responsibility for their own learning within a negotiated curriculum wherein objectives reflect their invididual needs.'

'It is probably true to say that open education is more effective in areas traditionally regarded as "non-achievement outcomes" such as curiosity, creativity, co-operativeness and independence. Other types of outcome are open to debate.'

Consider the statements given above and decide which one you would advocate. Justify your decision.

Draw up a list of factors to be considered when choosing a method of delivery and specify the mode of delivery you consider to be best suited to the class composition, subject environment, attitudes and expectations. Obviously the mode selected will depend upon individual teaching programmes and employing institutions.

2.005 Combining and integrating methods

Managing change

Dr Ray Bailey, for many years the principal of a large college, said in the foreword to a book concerning teaching and learning:

Until relatively recently educational syllabuses were prescribed in descriptive terms by examining bodies, and teaching staff directly responsible for education and training in classroom and workshop tended to accept the descriptive subject lists provided from those central bodies as being sufficient to outline both the extent of the educational intentions and, by implication, the teaching strategies to be used.[3]

Dr Bailey goes on to say that such attitudes changed, indeed had to change abruptly with the new-found curricular freedoms heralded by Industrial Training Boards, BTEC and at senior levels, the Council for National Academic Awards.

The freedom to be personally involved in detailed construction of curricula and to define their purposes more fully led in turn to a more intense and continuing interest in both the conceptual and practical aspects of the student-teacher relationship and to a concern for the identification of 'aims', 'objectives' and 'goals' specifying educational intent and the expected outcomes of the communication processes. Today, much work is being developed on learning-to-learn and teacher styles, and such work views the learner as the key person in control of the learning process.

Some earlier work on teacher and instructor training tended to view the learner as 'reactive' and placed power and control in the hands of the teacher. However, it is now thought that learning will be more effective if learners take greater responsibility for their own learning outcomes and for the means of acquiring knowledge. If such power is vested in the learners, adjustments will be needed in teaching styles and in the design of the learning process so as to provide a more student-centred approach.

Combining methods in teaching and learning contexts

When devising schemes of work it is important to set aims and objectives in context and to match teaching method to content and students' needs. Although examples given in the text may not exactly fit the different types of learner or subject specialisms of all teachers, it is worth spending time analysing the underlying principles and considering whether any of the ideas are transferable from vocational preparation students to further and adult education students.

Integrating classroom work with off-college activities is now regarded as being an essential part of course design. This is equally desirable for the sponsored trainee, leisure activity student or other type of continuing education student. As expressed by City and Guilds, the modern practitioner will need to be able to: 'show in given teaching contexts how different methods may be combined, and how the elements of combination affect one another.'

There is a requirement for vocational preparation tutors to be able to design on-the-job learning opportunities and work-based projects appropriate to the job. This is not entirely new to teachers since they have always attempted to relate theory to practice and encourage transfer between the two.

Assignment 2.12 – **Effect of combining teaching methods**

For a subject that you teach, describe how different teaching and learning methods may be combined to suit the content and context.

Describe how the elements of such a combination could possibly affect one another.

2.006 Planning, preparing and delivering a teaching programme

A systematic approach to teaching and learning

Before attempting to teach, the teacher must know what it is that he or she intends to teach and what the students are expected to learn as an outcome of the joint effort.

The teacher must have a clear idea of the objectives around which the teaching plan has been developed. What the students are already able to do must be known or anticipated and relative instruction pitched at the right level. The outcome of the teaching and learning process is that terminal behaviour will reflect what the students are able to do as a result of their participation in the learning experience. Learning will be identified as 'a relatively permanent change in behaviour' brought about by this experience.

The diagram given in Figure 2.12 shows teaching as a system. The input is a lesson which depends for its success upon effective communication between teacher and students. During the lesson, teacher activity combined with student activity aims to produce a satisfactory learning experience for all concerned.

Management of learning

A teacher is responsible for the management of learning and for the optimum deployment of resources. The aim should always be to arrange things so that students may learn efficiently and effectively.

Every teacher encounters problems on some occasions. For an inexperienced teacher a lesson can go wrong. Students may become hostile in their attitude, destructive or unhelpful with relatively catastrophic results for the teacher and for those students who are trying to learn despite the disruption. Good practices relating to the management of learning can go a long way towards avoiding pitfalls.

Within industry and commerce a training specification is prepared after a job has been studied, its work content listed and skills needed to carry out the work identified. The job is broken down into separate tasks and a sequence of operations listed. Key break points and areas of difficulty are noted, together with details of standards, resources utilised, safety factors, inspection and quality assurance requirements. A skills analysis, which may be as detailed as necessary, is then produced. It itemises the knowledge and practical 'doing' skills involved in doing

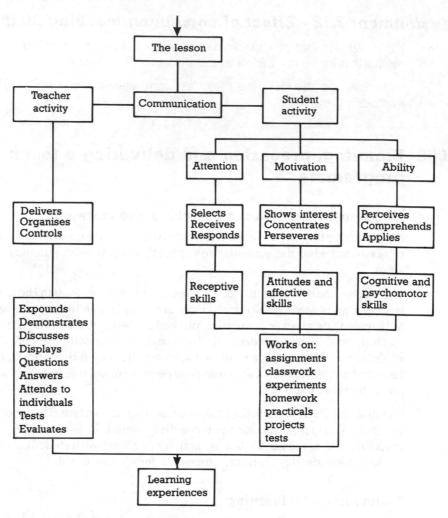

Figure 2.12 Class teaching system

the job effectively and at the right standard. From the data recorded, a training specification is written and an efficient learning programme then designed.

With academic learning, a person often experiences greater difficulty with perceptive and cognitive learning associated with new concepts, than with psychomotor activities. The teacher needs to put a great deal of thought and energy into preparing a suitable lesson plan that will allow students to learn efficiently, confidently and enjoyably.

Integrating study skills and related activities is now, more than ever before, becoming an essential part of lesson planning and course team curriculum development work. A purposeful and organised approach needs to be adopted when setting about the task of promoting and developing an integrated curriculum.

Such an approach is critical in achieving integration through the modular

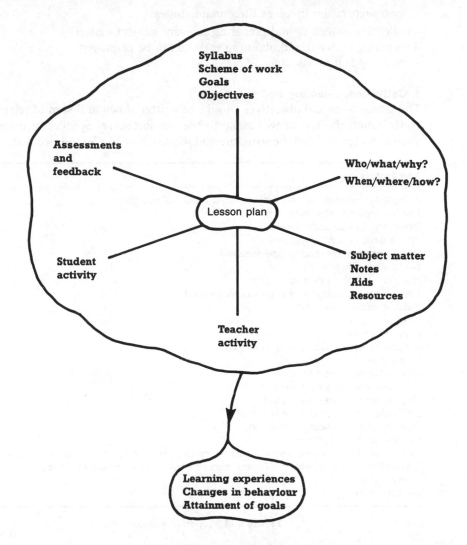

Figure 2.13 Lesson-planning system

approach to curriculum design and delivery that is now becoming increasingly widespread.

The lesson-planning system shown in Figure 2.13 contains the basic elements involved in the production of a lesson plan, while Figure 2.14 sets out some aspects for the teacher to consider when producing a plan.

Designing a lesson plan

Before starting work on your lesson plan, due consideration should be given to the category of students needing to learn, their needs, course requirements, lesson content, resources and methods to be employed.

Lesson preparation involves three main stages:
- collecting, selecting and preparing relevant subject matter
- preparing material and planning methods to be employed
- checking and rehearsing.

1 Collecting, selecting and preparing

The lesson aims and objectives should be written down and should relate to the contribution the lesson will make to the whole course. Sources of information should be explored and the structure and sequence of the lesson decided.

Key factors

Analyse task in terms of concepts, principles and skills involved
Identify important elements
Determine special skills involved
State relevant learning objectives
Decide pre-requisite knowledge required
Set goals for the lesson
Make the lesson content interesting
Relate new knowledge to that previously learned
Build on existing knowledge
Provide continuity
Structure lesson in logical sequence
Integrate learning with real-life situations
Encourage participation
Design lesson around students
Plan for maximum student activity
Employ appropriate learning aids
Include question-and-answer sessions
Provide for assessments of learning
Provide knowledge of results
Incorporate: note-making; frequent summaries and reviews; recapitulation of important information; final summary of lesson content; introduction of next topic together with book references
Set homework

Figure 2.14 Preparing a lesson plan

2 Preparing and planning

The extent of the material to be used and methods appropriate to the content to be taught should be determined. Aids and equipment needed should be recorded and subject-matter notes prepared. The lesson notes should be arranged in logical sequence and should contain: notes to assist teaching, notes and diagrams for the chalkboard or overhead projector, notes for students to write and classwork exercises for class practice. Worksheets or incomplete handouts should be prepared and aids organised.

The lesson plan can then be written and should be used as a basis for controlling the timing and content of the lesson. It should be written in a logical sequence and should provide a framework for development of the subject, being laid out so as to make the most effective use of available time. A variety of activities should be included, together with checks of learning. The plan should also contain details of methods and aids to be employed during the lesson.

3 Checking and rehearsing

Plays are rehearsed before the first night in order to ensure a flawless performance and to check lights and props. In the same way, a lesson should be rehearsed in order to try out aids and chalkboard layout.

Classwork examples should be worked out in advance to verify that no information is missing and that examples set are capable of solution. Teaching 'off-the-cuff' can go wrong! Demonstrations and experiments should be tried out to make certain

---

Date: 20 January   Time: 1500–1600   Group: NEBSM   Room: F4

Students:	14 mature supervisors
Subject:	Communications
Duration:	60 minutes
Aim:	To illustrate methods of presenting statistical data
Behavioural objectives:	The students will be able to construct a:
	pie chart
	bar chart
	ideogram
Equipment:	Chalkboard and chalk (CB)
	Overhead projector (OHP)
	Transparencies (prepared) (T)
	Newspapers (8 of same issue) (NP)
	Homework handout (HO)
	Computer and large-screen monitor (CM)

Time	Stage	Method	Activity	Aids
1500	*Introduction:* the use of charts to convey information	VE[4]		OHP T, CM
1505	*Development:* students check newspapers for charts		Small groups checking	NP
1510	Discuss newspaper charts	Q and A		NP CB
1515	Graphical methods of presenting information explained	VE Q and A		OHP T, CM
1525	Students produce: pie chart, bar chart and ideogram for given example	Individual attention	Drawing charts	
1550	Check students' work against master solutions	VE	Checking	OHP T, CM
1555	*Conclusion:* recap and summary Set homework: ideogram Next week: frequency polygon and cumulative frequency curve	VE Q and A		OHP HO CM

Figure 2.15 Lesson plan A

that equipment is complete and in good working order. Timing should be checked and a decision taken as to what could be omitted if time runs short and what supplementary material could be included if spare time becomes available. A selection of lesson plans is shown in Figures 2.15, 2.16 and 2.17.

Date: 20 May   Time: 1040–1145   Group: BTEC/1   Room: F102

Students:	First-year mechanical technicians
Subject:	Mathematics
Aim:	Solution of simple equations, known on LHS only
Objectives:	To recall the forms of simple equations
	To use the four basic arithmetical operations in their solution
	To complete an exercise
Equipment:	20 worksheets

Time	Stage	Method	Activity	Aids
1040	*Introduction:*			
	if 5 apples cost 24p, how much each?	Q and A		
1045	*Development:* transform to algebraic form	VE		CB
	Define unknown and simple equation meaning of 'solve'	VE		CB
1050	Compare with balance		Note 1	CB
	Ex. 1-division	VE		
1100	Distribute worksheet		Note 2	
	¼ m of cable costs 7.2 p, cost 1 m?	Q and A	Exercise	
	Ex. 2-multiplication	VE		CB
1110	5 cigars, pay 50 p, 21 p change,		Note 3	
	cost of the cigar?	Q and A	Exercise	
	Ex. 3-subtraction	VE		CB
1120	Ex. 4-addition	VE	Note 4	CB
			Exercise	
1130	Class solve remaining examples on worksheet		Note 5	
			Classwork	
			and	
			individual	
			attention	
1140	Conclusion: recapitulation	VE		
	Next week: $5x + 19 = 7 - 4x$ type			
	Set homework			

Comment: Objective NOT formulation of equation. Problem approach used to associate equations with familiar situations.

Figure 2.16 Lesson plan B

Date: 15 October   Time: 1015–1115   Group: Sec 1   Room: G86

Students:	First-year secretarial 16+. No previous knowledge of typewriting
Subject:	Typewriting
Aim:	To achieve correct posture, staccato key action and practice typing on 'home keys'
Behavioural objective:	To touch-type simple words based on the 'home keys' without error
Duration of lesson:	60 minutes
Equipment and preparation:	Typing paper, backing sheets, chart showing facsimile keyboard (pivot presentation), metre ruler, demonstration stand and machine. Paper and backing sheet placed correctly in machines.

Time	Stage	Method	Activity	Aids
1015	*Introduction:* Brief demonstration of touch typing at expert level			Dem. stand
	Discussion of posture (body, fingers, arms)	VE	Adopt	and
	Explanation of staccato action and demonstration	VE and	position	mach-
	Always same finger for same key	DEM	Strike	ine
	Introduction to 'home keys', correct placing of fingers	VE and DEM	keys	
1025	*Development:* Keys asdf practised in order then rearranged, keeping eyes on chart/CB	DEM	Strike keys	Dem. mach- ine
1040	Spacebar and uses	VE and DEM	Practise	Dem. mach- ine
1045	Carriage return lever	VE and DEM	Practise	Dem. mach- ine
1050	Type simple words—add, fad, as lass, flask, keeping eyes on CB throughout	VE	Touch- typing	CB
1100	Type longer words—alas, dad, salads, flasks, falls. Eyes on CB	VE	Touch- typing	CB
1105	Type simple sentences—ask a lad; a lass has a flask	VE	Touch- typing	CB
1110	Paper release lever. Routine for putting work in folders, covering machines	VE and DEM.	Take work from machines	Dem. mach- ines
	Summary	VE	Cover machines	

Figure 2.17 Lesson plan C

Assessing the lesson

Teachers cannot hope to produce a perfect lesson plan for every lesson. In many cases the plan will have to be modified in the light of experience gained during the first presentation of the lesson. As the lesson progresses (and if you remember and are not too pressurised to do so) actual timings should be recorded and a brief note made of any shortcomings in preparation, presentation, aids or methods.

The revised plan based upon consideration of the notes made will give a more realistic outline for use when the lesson is repeated.

A lesson plan assessment sheet is shown in Figure 2.18. The lesson may be rated on the elements shown either by a team member or by another student teacher.

Rating scale:		Score:	
Excellent	5		
Very good	4		
Good	3		
Fair	2		
Poor	1		
Element	**Rating**	**Remarks**
Stating of learning objectives		
Logical development in suitable steps		
Variety of methods and activities		
Use of resources		
Adequacy of student involvement		
Checks of learning		

Figure 2.18 Lesson plan self-assessment sheet

Self-assessment and supportive consultative assessment with peers are two excellent ways of analysing and improving preparation and presentation of lessons. Reflection and review are of prime importance in any modern learning programme and this technique should be practised by teachers during training. Whenever possible micro-teaching sessions should be videotaped and reviewed with other students or discussed with one of the tutorial team.

Aspects of the teaching input to be discussed during evaluation of this type of delivery include

- adequacy of preparation
- objectives to be fulfilled
- context and relevance of the lesson to stated objectives
- logical development of the lesson
- class management and relationships
- body language, mannerisms and maintenance of attention

- delivery style, language, accent and diction
- construction of objectives and objective test items
- evaluation of outcomes: interest, test results, efficiency and effectiveness of delivery in terms of learning.

Assignment 2.13 – **Planning and preparing to deliver a short lesson**

Part A
Karen Hickman is a young woman who is training to become a teacher and hoping to get her first teaching job working part-time for an adult education establishment. She has never planned a lesson nor written a lesson plan before and has been asked to prepare and deliver a sample lesson.

Karen is very concerned to get her preparation right and decides to seek your advice.

What advice on lesson planning would you offer Karen?

Part B
Write a lesson plan and other supportive materials for a lesson that you will need to deliver in the near future.

Part C
Pass your work to a colleague for criticism and comment.

Notes and references
1   M. Argyle, *Social Interaction*, Methuen, Atherton 1969, Chapter 9.
2   J. McCafferty, 'Innovation and Education', in *Education and Training*, Vol 22, No 9, October 1980.
3   L. Walklin, *Instructional Techniques and Practice*, Stanley Thornes (Publishers) Ltd, Cheltenham 1982, p xi.
4   In the lesson plans (Figures 2.15–2.17) the method known as 'verbal exposition' has been shown as 'VE'.

CHAPTER THREE

Learning Resources

Aim: To enable teachers to evaluate and use effectively the resources available to themselves and students

3.001 Identifying availability of learning and teaching resources

The purpose and use of aids

Try this activity first. Stand in front of a group holding a picture of something that they have never seen nor heard of. Try to describe the picture in words without displaying it. Ask the group to name the 'something'. There is a high probability that you will receive a wide variety of suggestions.

As you probably discovered, it is difficult to convey new ideas and unfamiliar information by words alone. We hear words but often have little or no understanding of the ideas and concepts behind them. For words to have meaning they must be related either to personal experiences or to known 'concrete' objects.

We meet with aids in everyday life. While travelling on an Underground train we look up at diagrams showing lines and stations. In the car we observe road signs giving warnings and directions. At railway stations or in airport lounges we observe visual displays showing departures or we listen to announcements.

These types of aids form one-way communications and like a good many educational aids such as films, television and radio they give observers little chance of stopping the presentation to ask questions or to clarify difficulties they may be experiencing. Two-way communication is effectively excluded with any form of mass media.

To be successful in the classroom, aids must supplement the teacher's work and should be flexible in their applications. The learning resource centre may well be jammed full of the latest multi-media teaching aids, but they will be of little use to a teacher who lacks the know-how or time needed to set up and use them.

Before using any aids, teachers must be fully conversant with their operation and application. They must also rehearse the presentation before confronting the class in order to avoid the risk of embarrassment when things fail to work. Transparencies can get mixed up and many mini-tragedies can happen in class if things are left unchecked. Aids serve to open up many more channels for the communication of information and create a variety of sensory impressions. When using aids, teachers do not have to rely solely upon their talking and students listening for the transmission of knowledge to (hopefully) take place. Aids enhance the process of perception and retention and consequently improve the efficiency of learning.

Boredom is an enemy that the teacher is constantly fighting. It is extremely difficult to maintain attention for periods longer than about fifteen minutes without involving the students in active participation. Aids serve to brighten up a presentation and help to maintain attention, while in many cases they substitute for the real thing, which may be unavailable or too large to bring into the classroom.

While the experiences of handling the real thing, participating in a processs or working in a shop, hospital or factory involve the use of all senses and provide the best aid to learning, well-thought-out aids can act as effective substitutes. But remember always that resources can never be a substitute for a proficient teacher.

Pictorial aids and photographs

Visual aids should be large enough to be seen by everyone present and should display the minimum amount of information to be effective. Avoid presenting too much information in one go.

The main value of using **photographs** lies in the fact that they are a true record of something and will be accepted as such by the viewers. The photographs should be presented one-at-a-time for perusal to avoid the tendency for viewers to divert attention to others in a series. There should be enough copies for each class member to view the subject simultaneously.

Many photographs carry too many details which tend to mask essential features. In such cases complementary diagrams should be provided to ensure that the key features are outlined clearly.

Photographs of 'before' and 'after' situations and those taken at frequent intervals during the stages of a project or experiment are valuable aids to recall.

Pictures can be reproduced on handouts and summary sheets. The photocopier can be used to make overhead projector (OHP) transparencies from pictures and significant parts are then highlighted with colour before projection. Important details can be enlarged and 'exploded views' reproduced inside 'balloons' or elsewhere on a transparency. Descriptive pictures contain facts and information and are intended to give meaning to unfamiliar concepts. Action pictures capture images of people doing things or machines working and are used to encourage thought and enquiry. Emotive pictures relate to the 'affective domain' and are used where people are required to discuss their feelings about the subject of the picture.

Diagrams come in the form of tables, wallcharts, graphs, and cartoons. Line diagrams illustrate essential principles without clouding the presentation with excessive detail. Block diagrams may be used to represent mechanisms or processes schematically (see Chapter Six).

Chalkboards are now in relatively limited use as the trend shifts towards using **whiteboards** and **portable flipcharts**. Competence in using boards is high on the list of desirable skills for practising teachers; sketching can be quite a problem for some. If a board must be used rather than an OHP, the outline of complex sketches should be faintly outlined in pencil or chalk before the lesson starts. Untidy boardwork can be confusing to students so keep the board clear of unwanted material and try to maintain a summary in one corner of the board ready for the review. Whiteboards are much cleaner to work with and can be used as projection screens.

Flipcharts may be prepared at home before lessons or seminars begin. Sheets are ordered in lesson sequence and flipped over one at a time in class. A second chart and stand can be very helpful when recording feedback responses from the group. Summary sheets can be displayed on walls.

Magnetic boards are made of steel. The boards attract magnets stuck to the back of cardboard cutouts representing real items. The cutouts can then be moved around on the board, be added to or removed at will.

Projected aids

An **overhead projector** may be used with solid samples, perspex mobiles, diagrams or written work produced on acetate sheets. These are placed on the glass plate. The projector uses a bright lamp and lens to project the image onto a screen set up by the teacher. Some projectors are fitted with rolls of acetate sheet which may be written on using special pens. After use, the acetate is wound across the plate onto a take-up roll exposing a new surface. Moving the OHP while it is switched on will probably cause the lamp to fail. Switch off and allow to cool down before moving.

To view 35 mm **slides**, either a remote control 'carousel' or a 'back projector' may be used. Programmes with synchronised slide change and taped commentary can be made. Slides stimulate interest and can be used to provide subject background or introduce case studies or projects.

Filmstrips and **loops** are still available but many are getting dated now as video and liquid crystal display projection is adopted.[1]

Audio aids

Record players, **hi-fi** and **cassette players** are often used by keep-fit, music, drama, dance and language teachers. Breakdowns, poor quality sound and problems may result from careless handling, finger marks, dust and scratches. Styluses and tape heads should be checked regularly.

Audio-visual aids

Films should be previewed by the teacher and key points noted. Questionnaires act as a reinforcer after showing. Some advocate a short 'viewer briefing' giving hints on what to look out for before switching on.

Closed-circuit television uses a CCTV camera and recorder together with one or more monitors to record a demonstration while a large audience may view in several places. The technique is of great value in the field of training and communication.

There is little doubt that **interactive video** is a highly effective training instrument. It is now becoming more widely used in education and in industrial and commercial organisations, although it is still relatively expensive to purchase or hire professionally-made programmes.

The main advantage of interactive video lies in the fact that the medium enables information to be provided, questions to be asked of the student and assessment and evaluation of the student's comprehension using the power of advanced computer technology coupled with images from laser disk.

An additional advantage is that the method allows students to learn at their own rate in learning resource centres (often open outside standard college hours). Alternatively, interactive equipment and training programmes may be hired.

The method is said to speed up the learning process while at the same time ensuring greater understanding of course content and enhancing the retention of information. Some systems record and identify students' performances in terms of strengths and weaknesses, and highlight areas needing remedial or additional study. Printouts of identified weaknesses are provided. Before students are able to make the most of interactive video it is necessary for them to run through a programme that introduces them to the system and gives information about the function keys, action sequences and computer keyboard.

Assignment 3.1 – **Reproducing pictures and sketches**

Nowadays, pictures and data can be downloaded from the web or desktop publishers can be used to generate high-quality handouts and transparencies, but teachers need to be able to operate when computing facilities may not be available.

Pictures, line diagrams, photocopies of sketches and text can be 'pasted-up' and made into originals for printing handouts or for producing overhead projector transparencies.

Using this technique, produce an original and a transparency for use in one of your classes. For this assignment you will need to cut out the pieces to be used. Once the layout has been planned each piece should be stuck to a plain white sheet of paper or card using glue. When you have finished, the paste-up will serve as an original for copies or transparencies.

Assignment 3.2 – **Identifying a range of learning and teaching resources**

It has been found helpful in some instances to involve students in specifying, designing and making aids for use in the teaching and learning programme for their course.

Some students enrol expecting the teacher to prepare, deliver and control every aspect of the course and will have fixed ideas about a 'conventional teaching role', believing that a passive role for themselves is the right one to adopt. Others will have been involved in adult retraining schemes and the like where a more student-centred negotiated approach to learning has been experienced.

There is little doubt that when students are involved in decision-making, their commitment and attitude to learning improves. If practical experiences of the group are utilised when planning and presenting course material and aids, lessons will be seen to be more relevant to the students.

Negotiate with your students their agreement to work with you to identify and list those teaching and learning resources that would enhance the delivery of course content, make the course more enjoyable and improve learning outcomes.

Present the group suggestions in a matrix with core competences, key objectives or other important features of the course tabulated vertically, and a series of resources horizontally. Correlate by ticking appropriate boxes.

3.002 Selecting appropriate learning and teaching resources

The function of aids

A good aid helps to overcome the limitations of word-only communication. It should appeal to as many senses as possible at one time (see Figure 3.1). Advantages and disadvantages of using aids are compared in Figure 3.2.

Aid	Senses used		
	Eyes	Ears	All
Chalkboard	*		
Blanket board	*		
Books	*		
CCTV	*	*	
Drops and charts	*		
Epidiascope	*		
Films	*	*	
Computers	*	*	
Magnetic board	*		
Models			*
Overhead projector	*		
Radio broadcasts		*	
Slide/tape programmes	*	*	
Tape recordings		*	
TV broadcasts/videos	*	*	

Figure 3.1 Summary of senses used relative to aid employed

Advantages	Disadvantages
Larger groups may be involved	Initial cost may be high
Cost per person is relatively low for large groups	Some programmes prohibit interaction between student and teacher
Demonstration time is reduced	Speed of introduction of facts may be too fast for easy assimilation
Chalkboard work is reduced	Too much detail confuses the student
Form and content of lesson is varied	May be used to entertain rather than purely as an instructional aid
Information is more readily disseminated	
Replay can be immediate	
Management of resource material is straight-forward	
Facilitate perception, transfer of training, reinforcement and retention	
Aids are cheaper than field trips	
Eliminate safety hazards relating to actual equipment	
Avoid need for actual equipment	
Enable teacher to preview and rehearse lesson in advance	
Are better prepared and presented than much classroom teaching	

Figure 3.2 Advantages and disadvantages of audio-visual aids

The overall function of an aid is to supplement the teacher's exposition and to help overcome the limits of verbal communication. The aid should provide a shared experience which cannot be conveyed vividly and realistically purely by word of mouth. Generally, the use of aids goes some way to providing a stimulating classroom environment, promoting a desire to learn and enlivening teaching and learning.

To make the most of resources: use the right aid, at the right time, in the right place, and in the right manner.

The purpose of aids is to provoke some kind of response, in line with agreed learning objectives. As already discussed in Chapter Two, the action plan will have been drawn up and aids prepared well before the presentation. This will allow learning resources and sequences to be arranged to give the best available framework for effective learning.

Aids selected should be chosen for their function and suitability. Slow-motion film may be used, for example, to demonstrate surgical operations or keep-fit routines. Slides or transparencies are effective for almost anything. X-ray films of welded joints may be projected to show defect sites. Music or languages may be played back on tape. Engine construction and operation can be shown by cutaway models, while mobiles can be manufactured from card and projected while moving. Computers can be used to demonstrate or simulate virtually anything.

Any or all of the aids may be used to attract and maintain attention, to illustrate relationships, to help explain the meaning of concepts, or to consolidate what the teacher has said.

Assignment 3.3 – **Presenting and evaluating aids**

The most effective way of checking the suitability of an aid is to present it to a group and invite members to comment. This is best done as part of a micro-training exercise relating to the use of aids in a practical teaching context.

Each group member should write down the assumed objective of the aid as they see it.

The group as a whole should then discuss the impact of the visual message, the design quality and its relevance to the presenter's stated objective.

3.003 Using the learning resources centre

A **learning resource centre** has been defined as 'typically, a collection of all forms of learning resources together with some equipment for their manufacture and use by students and teachers.' A **library resource centre** will contain book collections and will also operate information storage and retrieval systems. Some libraries may also include other resources as described above.

One of the important roles of learning resources centres (LRCs) is that of providing information and materials that will help staff keep up-to-date with developments in their subject specialisms and with their curriculum development work. Similarly, students and the public at large can use the service to help them pursue their studies or to occupy leisure time. By increasing control of their own learning through flexible, open access to learning resources available in such centres, new patterns of learning become possible.

Purpose and aims of LRCs

LRCs exist primarily to serve their clients, whether these are part-time or full-time teachers, or students. They are defined to implement the policy of using resources efficiently to support learning. In assisting with this type of innovation in learning and teaching methods, a learning and teaching resources service

– encourages the effective use of all appropriate media and materials in the support of the curriculum
– makes materials and equipment readily available to enable staff to develop and capitalise on their teaching skills and expertise
– creates the environment, facilities and materials for learning through which individual student differences of abilities, learning skills and speeds may be catered for.

Finding information in the LRC

The first step in finding material is to consult the catalogue located in every centre. Items may be traced by subject number, author and title, and systems such as the Dewey decimal classification may be used to classify stock.

Computer databases and microfiche catalogues give details of books, slides, records and laser discs, cassettes, videos, microcomputer programs and other resources held by the LRC, whose staff will be willing to help in case of difficulty.

There is normally a reference section that holds encyclopedias, dictionaries, subject bibliographies, abstracts, indexes, expensive reference works, trade catalogues, industrial directories and very comprehensive sources of information of all kinds. British Standards, study and information packs and archive materials including old newspapers are normally held.

For up-to-date information relating to industry, commerce and other interests, magazines are a good source and subject indexes are maintained for these. A selection of newspapers is displayed and constantly updated computerised data is available from electronic information services such as Prestel, Ceefax, Oracle, Reuters and on-line searching.

Should clients be unable to find what they are looking for, there are professional librarians available who will be able to help with the search. Where materials are not available locally, there are procedures whereby information on almost any topic can be obtained from other libraries reasonably quickly via the nation-wide inter-library loan service.

Books and other resources may be borrowed for reasonable periods, although popular books will normally be kept in a 'restricted loan' collection so that everyone has reasonable access to them.

Working in an LRC

Quiet study areas are provided in many libraries. Some LRCs have learning laboratories equipped for problem-solving and assignment work, and other rooms available to small groups for discussion purposes or projects. Equipment is installed so that users may watch videos, use slide/tape programmes or listen to audio-cassettes. Microcomputers and software are now readily available and personal computers and word-processors can be used for the preparation of assignment work. Coin- or token-operated photocopiers are installed to enable copies for private study to be taken in accordance with current copyright law.

When preparing for examinations, seeking places in other educational establishments or carrying out job searches, students may use old examination papers, careers literature or college, university and polytechnic prospectuses that are held in resource centres.

Videotex in the LRC

Videotex is a generic term referring to any electronic system that makes computer-based information available via visual display units or properly adapted television sets.

There are two main categories of videotex: **broadcast** and **interactive**. Teletext in the form of Ceefax and Oracle are examples of broadcast videotex, where the information is carried from the computer to the receiver by radio waves. Viewdata (Prestel) is an example of interactive videotex where the information is carried from the computer to the receiver by cable. Telephone lines are usually used for the transmission of signals.

The type of information provided on Prestel includes statistical information, essay type information, response frames such as 'Mailbox', consumer information such as prices of commodities, demonstration pages, pages containing horoscopes, recipes and other topics.

Internet connections, data capture and e-mail facilities are now available in most LRCs, where assistance concerning equipment associated with videotex is normally provided by expert staff employed in the LRC.

Assignment 3.4 – Using learning resources centre catalogues

The listing of all books and audio-visual materials kept in an LRC is often called a 'catalogue' and it is normally stored on microfiche.

Check how to operate the microfiche reader.

Find the three parts of a typical microfiche catalogue:

– author/title catalogue
– classified catalogue
– subject index.

Using the author/title catalogue, find the author entry in the microfiche catalogue for a book of your choice.

Using the subject index and classified catalogue

– find the subject number for a topic that you teach
– now look under this number in the classified microfiche catalogue to find of books about this subject.

Using classified catalogues, find examples of the following resources that would be suitable for your subject:

– an audio-visual aid
– a videotape
– a study pack.

Check the procedure for requesting an inter-library loan and complete a sample requisition.

Assignment 3.5 – Checking out journals and periodicals

Make a list of journals and periodicals relating to your subject specialism that are currently on display in the nearest LRC or library.

Check on the arrangements for obtaining back copies kept by the LRC.

Using the 'British Humanities Index' and the 'Clover Index', select an article from each that concerns your subject and identify

– author of article
– title of article
– name of periodical
– date of periodical
– page numbers of article.

Check whether the actual articles are available in the LRC.

Assignment 3.6 – **Using museums as learning resources**

In her novel *Jacob's Room*, Virginia Woolf wrote: 'There is in the British Museum an enormous mind. Consider that Plato is there cheek by jowl with Aristotle; and Shakespeare with Marlowe. This great mind is hoarded beyond the power of any single mind to possess it.'

Discuss how the physical resources held in museums and the knowledge stored in the 'enormous mind' described by Virginia Woolf might be utilised for teaching and learning purposes today.

List ways and means of getting the best out of student visits to museums.

Assignment 3.7 – **Using other information resources**

Teachers need to be able to demonstrate the ability to identify and effectively use public resources such as art galleries, theatres, concerts, government and local records archives, the Public Records Office, clubs and societies, stately homes and gardens, botanical gardens, industrial and commercial visits, the Stock Exchange and law courts.

Discuss the advantages and disadvantages of this type of activity and the learning value that may derive from using such resources.

Identify ways and means of accessing these sources and consider how administrative and organisational problems in arranging visits can be overcome.

3.004 **Using audio-visual aids when teaching**

Today, a great deal of effort is being devoted to curriculum development and to devising ways and means of improving the presentation of information. The role of audio-visual aids and computers as supplements to chalkboard, textbook and teacher's talk is growing in importance, and ready-made aids are freely available.

There is a tendency for some to adopt the role of innovator or to use aids simply because they are on the shelf. Before using an aid, the following question should be asked: 'Does the learning objective call for a visual aid, and if so, does the available aid meet the objective?' In any event, use of the aid should be validated and its impact evaluated. As with any information to be communicated, planning is essential to success. Planning should include both design and reasons for using the transparency, for example. Overlays, animations and colour contrasts should be planned before making the aid; and when displaying them they should be easy to manipulate. Fumbling can ruin a presentation.

It is a good idea to evaluate transparencies as you use them. Try to judge their effect on learning outcomes and look as them critically to see if you need to modify them before using them again.

Planning, producing and using aids is discussed further in Section 3.006.

Assignment 3.8 – **Reviewing learning experiences and materials**

In order to test the applicability of learning materials in relation to the stated learning objectives, it is necessary to carry out a review and evaluation of lesson outcomes.

The materials to be evaluated may be in the form of completed assignments, in which case the student profile recording system and review sessions carried out with students and colleagues would provide feedback for analysis.

In the case of audio-visual aids that have been used in the teaching process, students should be asked to judge the effectiveness and value of the contribution the aids have made to the learning outcome.

Confirm that you have demonstrated an effective knowledge of the use of audio-visual aids in the teaching process by obtaining evidence that the resources employed in the teaching of your classes have resulted in improved learning experiences.

3.005 Using computers and data processing aids when teaching

In Britain today, there are those teachers who are computer literate and those who are not, but the time will come when it will be necessary for virtually all teachers to come to terms with the fact that the computer is here to stay and somehow or other all will need to be able to use them. (Seek out the nearest college information technology (IT) specialist should you need help in this).

The role of the teacher is to some extent changing to that of a facilitator and manager of learning and the increased use of computers in learning will accelerate that change in role. Computers have already had a dramatic effect on teaching and learning methodology, and their application seems limitless. In college classrooms, workshops, language centres, science and technology laboratories and learning resource centres we see students interacting with the computer. They tap away on keyboards, with gaze fixed on visual display units, apparently oblivious to all other activity; we listen to their computer-generated music; we watch the computer-aided design group's pen recorders whizzing across paper with pens being changed at lightning speeds and coloured lines appearing on drawings as if by magic; we input data to a parts programmer, it feeds instructions to a machine tool and within minutes the machine produces a perfect component. Desk-top publishing and graphics are producing high quality material. There is no doubt that computers can and do influence the efficiency of learning and do allow more time for students to devote to learning new principles freed from the time constraints that were previously imposed by laborious calculation, graph drawing, typing corrections and reworking.

Computer-assisted instruction and related learning methods makes possible the provision of flexible learning opportunities, with the computer replacing the teacher for some of the time. Without the computer, many flexistudy and open learning programmes would be unsustainable; and the special needs of under-achievers would not be as well catered for as they are with computer-aided teaching programmes. Administrative duties, record keeping, timetabling, statistical returns and much of the work concerned with managing colleges efficiently, resource management, strategic and operational planning and many other non-teaching tasks that may now form part of the teacher's role, also encourage the use of computers in education.

When using computers to aid the teaching and learning process, it is important to obtain the commitment of the students concerned and not to impose on them without negotiation the need to use a computer. It is even more important to ensure that the materials in the form of software have been carefully checked out and found to be appropriate for the user group; and that the hardware is set up ready for operation and is reliable.

As far as the use of computers is concerned, personal zeal should be curbed, since students may not enthuse when first introduced to computer applications and may not feel committed to the activity unless they are convinced that it is the best way to learn. Far from enhancing rapport and motivation it is possible that the computer/teacher combination as a delivery mode may be perceived as a barrier to teacher/student interaction unless learner-centred activities are encouraged by provision of one terminal or microcomputer for each student or small group.

It is likely that computers may best be used to help teachers and learners achieve educational outcomes of a higher quality and wider scope than might otherwise be achieved, by utilising the computer's ability to

– store information
– make decisions about data with which it is fed
– carry out tasks at high speed
– communicate a mass of information in an easily understood format.

Teachers need to be aware of some of the uses of computers and of the four main elements of a computer system: input devices, output devices, processors, and storage devices.

Input devices may be peripherals that enable operators to communicate with the computer and teachers may be involved with the application of:

– bar code readers
– card readers

- digitising tablets
- keyboards
- kimball tag readers
- light pens or wands
- magnetic disk or tape
- magnetic ink character readers
- optical character readers
- optical mark readers
- mouse devices
- touch-sensitive screens
- voice input microphones.

Output devices convert information from the computer in the form of binary digits to a form that can be instantly understood by people needing to make sense of messages from the information processing system.

Some devices in common usage include:

- computer output on microfilm or microfiche
- impact and non-impact printers
- laser printers
- plotters
- tapes (punched and magnetic)
- visual display unit
- voice output.

The **central processing unit** comprises all that is necessary to enable the computer to function including a:

- control unit
- arithmetic logic unit
- memory unit.

Backing **storage media** include:

- cassette tape
- data cartridge
- DLT tape
- DVD–RAM
- floppy disk
- hard disk
- laser disk
- rewritable compact disk
- tape cartridge
- ZIP disk

Computer-based training

Computer-based training (CBT) is a highly participative learner-centred method of learning with the teacher, who is able to monitor the learner's performance, acting as a resource. Each student has a computer terminal and software relative to the topic being learnt. The software acts as a presentational medium allowing the student to interact at certain points – often to make a 'Yes' or 'No' response or other decisions in answer to prompts designed into the programme. The student can, at any time, go back to previous sections of the programme, or go forward, thereby progressing at a pace that suits them.

Teacher competences

Teachers need to be able to demonstrate awareness of the uses of computers and other data processing aids in the teaching of their subjects. Computer literacy is an area that has regularly been designated by the DfEE as a 'national priority area' for staff development training; and the text given here is intended to focus attention on the growing importance of information technology and micro-electronics in modern teaching and learning practice.

Outcomes of typical training programmes for teachers include: competence in setting up and using microcomputers and associated hardware units; selecting and using programme packages; maintaining storage and retrieval systems; and ensuring that environmental conditions are non-hazardous.

The teacher as systems analyst

Before introducing computers into the teaching of a subject it is necessary to review the existing teaching and learning system and carry out a feasibility study in order to decide whether it would be in the best interests of the students to change things. It may well be that the students will be better off if things are left as they are, but if the intention is to introduce computers, the feasibility study should include a survey of available resources and the additional cost involved in making the change.

Health and safety aspects

It is possible that working with visual display units may under certain conditions cause or contribute to health problems relating to posture and eyesight. Operators have complained of eyestrain, headaches, migraine, nausea, backache and muscular fatigue, eye irritations and visual fatigue, rashes and other symptoms associated with their employment. The data processing teacher must be aware of these and other hazards that may exist when working with computers or in electronic offices and in particular where VDUs are in constant use.

Students will expect their teacher to be fully conversant with ergonomic considerations (see page 92) and all aspects of the Health and Safety at Work Act relating to that part of the syllabus and the equipment to be used during the learning activity.

Assignment 3.9 – Checking systems and facilities

Carry out a review of your existing teaching and learning strategies and conduct a feasibility study designed to check where and how the use of computers and other data processing aids could enhance the quality and efficiency of learning in your classes.

Find out what computer facilities are currently available and how you can gain access to them.

Check the booking procedures and support services available. Check on the security arrangements. Discover who holds the keys and where you can get help in the evening.

Produce a contingency plan to cope with such things as non-arrival of resources, blown fuses, wires detaching themselves from the plug, running out of computer paper, ribbon cassettes breaking or expiring and the intriguing task of locating the technician.

Find out whether additional facilities are planned and when, how and where they will be allocated.

Consider how the other teachers will react to your proposed changes (if any) in teaching methodology. Will they be hostile? Will they be supportive? Will they feel threatened? What will be their attitude towards you and your innovation?

Determine how your students will react to the proposed change and whether new methods will best meet their needs. Think about how you can gain their support and participation in making the changes.

Discuss your review with others and produce an action plan for implementation of the change.

Assignment 3.10 – **Identifying potential health hazards of using computers and other data processing aids**

Ergonomics is described in the *International Dictionary of Education* as the study of the relationship between man and his occupation, equipment and environment, and particularly the application of anatomical, physiological and psychological knowledge to the problems arising therefrom. (Sometimes known vernacularly as 'fitting the job to the worker'.) Ergonomics is known in the US as **human engineering**, and in education would concern itself with the working and learning environment of the teacher and pupil.

In any working environment there will be health and safety hazards. There may also be health problems specific to automated office systems and other data processing situations.

Examine this topic and identify potential problems that you need to consider when using computers and other data processing aids in the teaching of your subjects.

Publications that may be helpful include:
A Management Guide to Hazard Spotting (British Safety Council)
Recommendations for Safety in Workshops, in Schools and Colleges of Education – BS 4163 (British Standards Institute)
Safety in Further Education (DES Safety Series)

3.006 Resource planning

Compiling a resource file

Resource materials comprise anything that may be used by teachers in planning and carrying out their teaching and by students when working on assignments, projects and investigations. Well-prepared teachers keep files containing aids and consumable materials that will be needed during lessons. They consult their scheme of work from time to time and plan ahead to ensure that they are never caught without necessary resources. For, in the words of Bob Clist, an experienced FAETC course tutor: 'Failing to plan is planning to fail.'

Assignment 3.11 – **Compiling a resource file of teaching aids**

Consider the need for a resource file relating to your subject and compile a folder containing the aids appropriate to and available for the teaching of your chosen subject.

In the case of word-processing[2], for example, a teacher might need to assemble in the folder consumables such as:

- cut sheets
- continuous stationery (rolled or fanfold)
- mounted sheets
- labels
- daisy wheel cleaner (fluid, pad or cotton buds)
- printer ribbons (fabric, nylon cloth or plastic film)
- cartridge ribbons, cassettes or spools
- diskettes and floppy disks
- floppy disk drive cleaning kit
- anti-static spray
- screen cleaning kit
- spare print elements.

Other essential aids would include:

- personal computer or word-processor user instructions and handbook
- spelling dictionary
- software
- assignments
- past examination papers
- model answers
- word processing rules

and what else?

Producing software

Computer programs

Modern developments in software project management requires that anyone who intends to produce software should have an adequate knowledge of the theory and practice in the discipline of software engineering. The increasing complexity of software production demands expertise in the specification, design and systematic development process of validation, testing and quality assurance.

Ownership of such expertise is probably not widespread among further and adult education teachers although there are, of course, some who are very proficient in all aspects of programming and computer technology.

It is likely that competence in software production may for many teachers be limited to the writing of fairly elementary programs or even to the copying of existing disks.

Where programs are written they are likely to be **applications software** that handles user tasks such as payroll, traffic control or medical diagnosis rather than **operating system software** that manages the machine's resources.

Commercially produced software used for computer-aided learning has not always proved to be reliable and free of problems. A much higher quality will be needed in future in the form of programs constructed from certified software components.

Perhaps a more valuable competence for teachers would be the ability to review and assess the suitability of some of the many programs that are available to the educational market. Whether or not a teacher decides to produce software or to purchase programmes off-the-shelf is to some extent a less important issue than the need to appreciate that by the turn of the century the interactive use of computers will pervade virtually all learning environments. There is not much point in believing otherwise.

Software in educational technology

Educational technology embraces all that is involved in the design and implementation of systems of teaching and learning and all that is involved in supporting these systems. Resources in the form of hardware and software are important elements of educational technology, and given that the management of educational institutions provides the human resource and hardware necessary to support the curriculum, software production will normally be devolved to individual teachers or to groups of teachers.

Educational software includes materials such as audio and visual aids in the form of CD-ROM, PowerPoint, tapes, films, overhead projector transparencies, photographs and slides, assignments, worksheets and handouts.

High quality lesson preparation depends to a large degree on the availability of good quality support materials and the production of software is a demanding aspect of a teacher's role.

Assignment 3.12 – **Producing software**

Design and produce an item of software (either as a program or other educational resource) for use as an aid when teaching some aspect of your subject.

Construct a questionnaire designed to objectively evaluate how well the software meets the purpose, aims and objectives that you specify for its use.

Demonstrate your software to the group giving aims and objectives that specify what you hope to achieve with it.

Explain why you chose to use it rather than something else as an aid to teaching the subject.

Immediately after your demonstration get your colleagues or students to complete the questionnaire which you should analyse and respond to.

Making aids appropriate to the subject

Some teachers seem to be gifted. They have a charismatic hold over their students who listen spellbound and hang on to every word that is spoken, regardless of the subject matter. Such teachers never appear to rush, they behave more like storytellers, gradually revealing elements of their story while their audience's attention is riveted on what they are saying. Such performances sometimes produce outstanding results in respect of the quality of recall and learning demonstrated by students during checks of learning or evaluation towards the end of such lessons.

Regrettably, for many teachers this experience does not happen very often. The subject does not always lend itself to a storyteller approach. Teachers may wish to make all their lessons student-centred yet there is a need to press on all the time to cover a very full syllabus. Opportunities to explore new ground or to capitalise on student experiences are therefore sometimes missed – the result: loss of attention and poor motivation. In the end, often nothing more than a ritual has taken place and not much learning.

In order to improve the probability of maintaining interest, holding attention and increasing the rate of learning audio-visual and other aids can be introduced into a lesson. Such aids need to relate to one or more of the learning objectives to fulful their role effectively. It is pointless to go over the top with aids and give a performance akin to that of a conjuror or showman. It has been said that viewers of some very expensive training films spend more time watching the star performer's antics than attending to what is being said, so that learning outcomes are minimal!

Aids must be clearly visible, words must be readable, sounds must be pleasantly audible and samples hygienic, free of noxious odours and not unpleasant to touch.

Obviously, there is no substitute for the real thing but good transparencies, videos, interactive computer programmes, PowerPoint, slide/tape shows and magnetic aids help to bring life to a subject that might otherwise be somewhat boring. But even so, aids alone cannot be effective, they can only complement the teacher.

Transparency-making is described in detail in Appendix A while the methods of making slide tape programmes and magnetic aids are outlined below.

1 Preparing a slide/tape programme

With the aid of a slide projector such as the Elf Ringmaster it is certainly not difficult to produce a punchy and convincing programme yourself. The Ringmaster sound–slide projector combines two projectors in one unit. The picture is transferred from the built-in screen to forward projection on an external screen merely by raising a flap at the back. To position the picture precisely, there is an adjustable foot.

All you need is a projector, a camera, some colour film and a blank cassette. Most slide magazines take up to 80 slides in 5 cm × 5 cm mounts.

First, draw up a draft script and decide on the pictures that will best illustrate the points you wish to make. Then take appropriate photographs which may include cartoons, diagrams, charts, captions and maps as well as objects, people and scenes. Special slides and pictures of buildings or subjects that are inaccessible to the public may often be obtained from libraries. Ready-made sets on such subjects as engineering, science and art can be obtained from the Victoria and Albert Museum or the Science Museum in London, art galleries and other museums.

An ordinary compact cassette is all you need for your recording which can be up to 45 minutes long. The cassette pushes into the slot in the projector. For non-stop repetition of a programme, you use a continuous play cassette with its tape in an endless loop.

Now finalise your script. The best way to lay out a script is to put the commentary/sound on the right-hand side of the paper and brief descriptions of the slides on the left hand side.

Then make your recording using the microphone supplied with the projector, subsequently using the remote-control pulsing switch to add the cues that will change the pictures automatically in step with your words. You can change a slide every second — or hold it on the screen as long as you need. Rewind the tape and you are ready to show your programme.

The projector can also be used for quizzes and for question-and-answer sessions provided that it is equipped with a 'cue stop'. A cue stop enables pre-set pauses to be built into the programme. It is particularly useful for training and for carrying out checks of learning. A pause can be inserted after a question. When the question has been answered, the programme can be restarted at the touch of a button.

2 Preparing magnetic aids

Magnetic aids are very useful when illustrating processes ranging from cake making to producing chemicals using flowline or mass production techniques. They are invaluable when showing how machines are built up and how they work, and before entering a laboratory or workshop, various experiments and tests can be demonstrated using cardboard cutouts and a magnetic board.

This saves a great deal of the teacher's time in the laboratory. The teacher can address the whole group in the safety of a classroom and explain what has to be done using the magnetic aids to simulate the actual equipment to be used in the practical. On arrival in the laboratory, students are able to get on with the actual experiments rather than hanging about in small groups waiting for instructions or explanations before commencing work.

Many good textbooks and manufacturer's manuals provide sketches illustrating machine construction and principles of operation. These may be used as models from which aids may be developed for classroom instruction. Permission to reproduce illustrations should first be obtained from the copyright owners in order to avoid infringing copyright.

The supermarkets provide another valuable source of material from which cardboard cutouts can be made. The packaging and promotional materials are colourful and may, for example, help to illustrate the ingredients to be used in cookery classes and demonstrations. All the ingredients of a particular recipe can be represented by pictures cut from packaging and once the magnets have been glued on the back can be manipulated on the steel board to show the process of preparation. In the case of machinery or construction processes, having selected the diagram from which the aid will be developed, identify the number of cutouts needed and the shape of each piece.

The aid must be large enough to be seen by every member of the group; therefore the diagram will need to be magnified. Decide on the magnification factor. Scale each component from the diagram and multiply each dimension by the magnification factor.

Using white paper, draw each component to the magnified dimensions. Cut out each shape and stick to coloured card.

Cut out each cardboard component and glue magnets or strips of magnetic tape to the back of each. Then assemble them on the magnetic board in the correct sequence.

Practise manipulating the cutouts several times and if necessary mark each card with a number indicating the correct sequence of application. Students have found these aids very useful in that their visual impact is so much more effective than lengthy explanation.

Assignment 3.13 – Design, make, use and evaluate an aid

Design, make and use a teaching and learning aid or a set of aids appropriate to your subject that will be of value to you and the students.

With the help of your students evaluate the aids and determine whether they were effective in making learning easier.

Consider whether redesign or replacements will be needed to improve their impact or to otherwise enhance presentation of teaching and learning material.

Assignment 3.14 – Selecting and using appropriate aids

When selecting audio-visual aids for use in a lesson it is necessary to consider how their use could benefit the students. Having chosen the aid best suited to the particular learning objective, it is necessary to look at the environment in which the aid will be presented and to consider the desirability and feasibility of using the aid in that location.

For your individual subject specialism produce a schedule of aids that specifies

– syllabus
– course week number
– objectives facilitated by use of aid specified
– title and description of aid specified
–alternative to aid specified
– how the aid will be used.

In a small group, produce a matrix giving the subjects taught by each member on one axis, and beneath each subject, a list of commonly used aids appropriate to the teaching of that subject. Discuss the finished work with other groups.

Notes and references
1   Large screen computer presentations are being replaced by LCD (liquid crystal display) projection devices that operate directly from PCs and other computers. The device is placed on the OHP and the projected image is focussed onto the screen or whiteboard. Data such as spreadsheets may be instantly presented to the whole group and output from CAD and CAM programmes easily reproduced for all to see.
2   See M.R. King and A.R. Bone, *Information and Word Processing – An Introduction,* Stanley Thornes (Publishers) Ltd, Cheltenham, 1987

CHAPTER FOUR

Course Organisation and Curriculum Development

Aim: To enable teachers to design appropriate programmes, courses and schemes of work with the active participation of the learning group

4.001 Formulating aims and objectives

Before asking someone to carry out a task, we sort out in our minds exactly what it is that has to be done. Then we establish standards, conditions and time for completion of the task. Only when this has been carried out do we allow work to commence. We monitor progress, support those involved in the task and later follow it up by reviewing and evaluating outcomes. Or do we?

Unfortunately, not everyone thinks along these lines. Time is at a premium, everyone in the institution is making demands on us or so it seems. Instructions given are vague and often ambiguous. We are too busy to check up, and things go wrong. Opportunities to monitor, review and reinforce the good learning experiences are missed; the not-so-good outcomes are ignored, and neither the teacher nor students gain much satisfaction from the activity.

If we happen to be involved in teaching or training we simply cannot afford to be slapdash. Teachers working in educational establishments are now becoming more and more accountable for the efficient management of learning and the effective use of expensive resources. What is more, students — the clients — are coming to expect better value from some areas of the service and now have greater choice of provider.

It is recommended that a planning-led approach be employed when developing a learning opportunity; starting with a set of aims and objectives that will enable the purpose and outcomes of a particular training programme to be clearly specified.

The importance of writing aims and objectives

The importance of classifying, writing and evaluating educational objectives in the field of curriculum development has been recognised for many years. During those years Barnes, Bloom, Coltham and Fines, Ebel, Gagné, Gerlach and Sullivan, Mager, Tyler and others have written important works suggesting methods of stating aims and behavioural objectives with a view to increasing the efficiency of teaching and learning. Their work provides insight into the concept of the curriculum process and is a valuable resource for use in teachers' courses.

Tyler[1] proposed that objectives should be stated in the form that makes them most helpful in selecting learning experiences and in guiding learning. From this, it follows that statements of specific objectives should be written in terms of what the student should be able to do at the end of a course, rather than in terms of what the teacher intends to lecture on. Curricula should therefore require that the student is able to demonstrate competence.

In order to create the necessary framework in which effective learning may take place, teachers must be aware of exactly what they are going to do. To meet this requirement Krathwohl[2] has suggested that objectives be defined at three levels: broad statements of course aims; specific behavioural objectives; and lesson plans specifying precisely how the objectives will be attained. Armed with these statements, teaching materials and sequences may be developed and criterion tests produced.

The *Taxonomy of Educational Objectives*[3] was written to provide a framework for curriculum development. It describes and classifies all kinds of educational objectives and is divided into three domains: **cognitive**, **affective** and **psychomotor**.

The Taxonomy, or classification, is used as a reference against which educational objectives may be compared and analysed when developing the curriculum. Its use facilitates the classification of goals, increases the reliability of communication of intent and provides a system for describing test items and course evaluation.

Another book, entitled: *Preparing Educational Objectives*, by R.F. Mager[4] was written in order to provide specific instruction in the writing of statements of objectives. The preface contains a fable, the moral of which is that if you are not sure of where you are going at the outset, then you are liable to end up elsewhere and not even be aware of it.

Mager insists that before you prepare instruction, before you choose material, machine or method, it is important to state clearly what your goals are. The book sets out to demonstrate the form of usefully stated objectives. Its purpose is to help readers to specify and communicate educational intent; for as Mager says, 'until you describe what the learner will be doing when demonstrating that he "understands" or "appreciates" you have described very little at all'. Throughout the book, Mager offers very sound practical advice on the writing of objectives, and the book is highly recommended to anyone interested in transmitting skills and knowledge to others.

An **aim** is a broad statement of intent and it is written in the early stages of programme design. It is a non-specific guideline and relates to an overall policy or strategy rather than to detailed specifications.

Writing about aims and objectives, Frith and Macintosh[5] say, 'An aim should be the product of considerable thought and discussion. It should be stated simply and concisely and should sum up what is the intended outcome in terms of benefit to the pupil, and should lead to the selection of relevant objectives.'

The negotiated curriculum methodology now in place would seem to confirm the need for early and comprehensive discussion with students when jointly establishing aims and objectives for a particular training programme. Aims should undoubtedly reflect the identified students' needs and should be valid in terms of desired outcomes of the learning programme for which they are written.

An **objective** describes precisely what the learner is expected to be able to do, in order to demonstrate learning. Behavioural objectives contain up to three component parts:

– an indication of the terminal behaviour that will be accepted as evidence that the learner has attained the objective
– a statement describing the important conditions (if any) under which the behaviour is expected to occur
– the acceptable performance level specifying how well or to what standard the student must perform to be considered acceptable.

The advantages of stating objectives in behavioural or activity terms are that they

– help in planning delivery, methodology and resources
– emphasise the students' activities
– provide a means of evaluating learning.

In expressing terminal behaviour when writing objectives, words that do not define behaviour clearly, or are open to wide interpretation, should be avoided. Each of the objectives written should specify exactly what the student is required to do in order to satisfy the aim. Words that do not define behaviour clearly should be avoided. Such phrases as: 'to know', 'to understand', 'to appreciate' and 'to believe' fall into this category — they cannot be used accurately to measure behavioural outcomes. Concrete verbs should be used. Examples of suitable terms are: 'to describe', 'to explain', 'to select', 'to compare', 'to calculate', 'to construct', 'to solve', or 'to list'. These are recommended because terminal behaviour can be measured in terms of what the learner is able to do on completion of the instruction. Behaviour will be observable and will validate learners' claims to skill ownership.

From the learners' point of view, the main advantages of strict behavioural objectives is that they know exactly what is expected of them and they can evaluate their own progress against the specified objectives. The main point about writing objectives is that others can get a clear picture of what the outcome of learning is to be. Unnecessary detail should be excluded from the objective. Only those elements that are required to describe all intended outcomes should be written into the statement.

Examples of correctly stated objectives
The following examples contain some or all of the three component parts that may comprise the objective:

– 'From a metal blank supplied and using a Colchester Lathe, the student will be able to produce, within 45 minutes, a Stepped Shaft Part Number 4920 correct to drawing specification and tolerances.'

– 'After instruction the student will be able to prepare, cook and present for service a two-egg plain omelette.'

– 'The student shall, without reference to any books or notes, write in legible handwriting with not more than four spelling mistakes, a 500 word essay on the role of a receptionist employed in a large beauty therapy salon.'

– 'The student will be able to give an oral translation, in English, of selected Spanish menus.'

– 'The student will be able to carry out the correct safety procedure to be followed in the event of the fire alarm sounding.'

– 'The trainee will be able to tolerate and respond professionally to irrational and unreasonable behaviour from customers at the checkout.'

– 'The student will be able to fit correctly a 13 amp plug to an electric fire.'

– 'The student will be able to list six ancient sites that are located in Dorset.'

Assignment 4.1 – **Writing behavioural objectives**

Discuss the importance and value of the use of specific objectives when developing

– learning aids
– subject matter
– teaching and learning strategies.

Write a list of 20 action verbs that could be used when writing behavioural objectives. Ensure that your list contains verbs that accurately specify what the students should be doing when demonstrating competence and eliminate the possibility of any misinterpretation.

Write three objectives containing details of 'behaviour', 'conditions' and 'standards' that relate to the subject you teach.

Decide whether or not behavioural goals are appropriate to all subjects.

Review your assignment outcomes with colleagues.

Recognising the type of skills involved in a list of objectives

When learning objectives are provided for a given course it is necessary for the teacher to analyse the objectives and break them down into two main categories: those of knowledge and intellectual abilities; and psychomotor or practical 'doing' skills.

In the case of practical work it is necessary for the student to be able to perform a chain of responses, to co-ordinate hand and eye movements and to organise chains into complex response patterns. The teacher therefore needs to understand what is involved in the skilled performance of work.

Given that the student has already acquired the theoretical knowledge needed to carry out the task, it remains for the skills elements to be mastered. By identifying the skills involved in the task the teacher can arrange for each element to be demonstrated and practised by the learner.

Ideally, the students should themselves – with teacher support – sort out the sequence and identify which skills they already own and those that they will need to acquire. Where this is not possible, the teacher will need to produce an operation sheet listing the sequence of operations.

Each operation should then be examined and the skills content listed. This requires a good practical knowledge on the part of the teacher and such knowledge is generally acquired only after considerable shop floor or commercial experience. No amount of book-learning can take the place of knowledge hard won by actually performing the task.

As mentioned earlier, educational or instructional objectives have been classified by Bloom and others into three domains or provinces:

1 The affective domain

The 'affective domain' relates to feelings, attitudes, emotions and values of the student. According to Krathwohl the organising principle is that of **internalisation**. He suggests that the process of internalisation appears to describe the accomplishment of learning and growth in the affective field.

Internalisation is a characteristic quality pertaining to the inner nature or feelings; and describes the act of incorporating within oneself, values, attitudes and interests. Internalisation occurs in stages similar to Piaget's stages of moral development and in some ways resembles the process of socialisation.

Inner growth of affective characteristics commences as the student becomes aware of some stimulus and directs attention to it. This is followed by responses brought about by conforming to the instructions of some external authority such as the teacher. Finally, the student's inner control causes responses to occur in the absence of the teacher or other person in a position of power. The student becomes capable of making value judgements according to codes of conduct and principles which have been internalised over a period of time.

Krathwohl[6] produced five main categories in the taxonomy structure:

- **Receiving (attending)**
  Awareness
  Willingness to receive
  Controlled or selected attention
- **Responding**
  Acquiescence in responding
  Willingness to respond
  Satisfaction in response
- **Valuing**
  Acceptance of a value
  Preference for a value
  Commitment

– **Organisation**
Conceptualisation of a value
Organisation of a value system
– **Characterisation by a value or value complex**
Generalised set
Characterisation

Behaviour within the five categories listed ranges from – at the lowest level – receiving or attending, where the student's role is passive and limited to taking in information rather like a sponge, with little personal concern, up to – at the highest level – the integration of concepts and subject-matter into one's own life-world.

2 The cognitive domain
In the writing of objectives, stress is placed on one or more of the following, each involving a different degree of complexity of thinking:

– **Simple recall of knowledge**
Emphasis placed upon remembering facts or terminology without the need to understand that which is recalled.
– **Comprehension**
Elementary level of understanding. The students should be able to explain what they are doing when using recalled information such as a formula.
– **Application**
Having comprehended the meaning of a given concept, the students are able to relate the knowledge to other different situations. They should be able to generalise, using basic principles and to apply knowledge.
– **Analysis**
The breaking down of a statement or operation into its basic components and the relating of each component to the remainder.
– **Synthesis**
The assembling of a variety of concepts or elements so as to form a new arrangement.
– **Evaluation**
Making value judgements about arrangements, arguments or methods. Highlighting strengths and weaknesses in arguments and assessing the points for and against.

Behavioural objectives relating to the cognitive domain are concerned with information and knowledge. **Cognition** is the name given to mental processes such as sensation, perception and thinking by which knowledge may be apprehended.

Thinking is a complex behaviour involving mental activity such as reasoning, where thought is characterised by a symbol reference. Thinking involves the internal representation of events and may be applied to arithmetical activities and problem solving.

Language is an important source of symbols which acquire meaning and convey information. L.S. Vygotsky, a Russian psychologist, studied the importance of language in the formation of concepts. He exposed learners to situations in which they could acquire concepts and simultaneously learn related verbal symbols. By the process of word association (see **Verbal association**, Chapter One) a physical object can be linked with a word. When the word is heard later, an image of the object or concept can be visualised in the mind. Symbolic representation of the object may be recalled by the process of thinking.

When given a problem, learners will begin to think about it. They will turn the problem over in their minds using symbols which represent real objects. When verbalising the problem, words — another form of symbol — will represent the objects involved.

At an elementary level, practical problems may be solved using images alone, while facts and terminology may be recalled and used to solve academic problems. Higher levels in the cognitive domain require a greater complexity of thinking, and the linking of concepts or principles by means of appropriate language.

Bloom's top three levels of mental performance i.e. analysis, synthesis and evaluation, are grouped together into one known as **invention**. Learners demonstrate inventiveness by breaking down information into parts, identifying the parts, determining relationships, recognising principles and detecting fallacies. They then proceed to synthesise, that is, to combine the elements or parts into a whole. The outcome is an arrangement that did not exist before. Planning or proposing methods and procedures, collating information from several sources and developing abstract relationships, also fall within the process of synthesis. The remaining category, that of evaluation, involves making judgements as to the value or worth of material for a given purpose. Such judgements may take the form of appraisals, comparisons, or contrasts, and the learning outcomes of this category tend to contain elements of all others, combined with the need to make value judgements.

3 The psychomotor domain
This area is concerned with the learning of muscular and motor skills and is by its very nature concerned with the acquisition of such abilities as hand skills in the workshop, typing, manipulation of equipment and the assembling of apparatus. At the lower level of performance, behaviour will be characterised by slow, clumsy and hesitant movements, probably with frequent errors. After following a well-designed training programme and with practice, the learners' skills should improve until, at the highest level of performance, they will be able to demonstrate complete mastery without assistance. This skilled performance will be characterised by a smoothly flowing, error-free and polished demonstration.

Appropriate categories would include: knowledge of operations necessary for performance of a skill; application of a variety of skills to more complex manipulations; and mastery of the skills involved in novel situations which involve one or more of the basic skills learned.

Sensorimotor skills are discussed more fully in Chapter One under the heading **Learning skills** (p 14).

Assignment 4.2 – Identifying a range of competences and formulating objectives

The objectives for this assignment are:

– to identify a range of competences relating to a particular job
– to carry out a task analysis prior to the preparation of a training schedule
– to write aims and objectives for a training schedule for an identifiable group of leaders.

Method:

– specify the job on which the assignment will be based
– state the work to be performed
– write a single broad aim
– list competences to be attained by the learners
– write general objectives based on the list of competences
– carry out a task analysis or prepare and distribute a questionnaire that will elicit information about the task
– produce a draft analysis of competences adding notes of any special factors relating to the competences
– arrange with the learner group a general discussion on how they would set about performing the service using the list of competences as a discussion plan
– appoint learners as discussion leader and secretary and ask them to record comments about the tasks involved in the job and the criteria on which performance standards should be set
– compare the secretary's notes with your own analysis.

The specimen given below may be helpful in getting started on the assignment, or when developing learning materials.

Specimen

Job: Electrical salesperson
Product: Radio
Aim: To sell a radio
List of competences:

Relating customer needs to products by

– identifying customer needs
– answering customer questions on product performance
– knowing characteristics of products
– demonstrating uses
– comparing with other products.

Influencing customer to buy by

– handling objections
– negotiating
– closing sale.

Convert the competences to general objectives by adding the words 'After instruction the trainee salesperson will be able to . . .'
Example: 'After instruction the trainee salesperson will be able to identify customer needs.'

Break down the job into competences using own knowledge and experience gained by working in the job

or

Carry out an analysis of job competences by researching job descriptions, job specifications, advertisements or other sources

or

Carry out an analysis of job competences by questionnaire.

A job description could be recorded using a format such as that in Figure 4.1. Questionnaires may take the form shown in Figure 4.2. They should include a rating on all the competences involved in the job selected for this assignment.

Job description duties and responsibilities	Tasks	Competence areas	
		Knowledge	Skills

Figure 4.1 Job description: format for analysis

Category	Required proficiency level (tick)
Numerical skills:	LOW ⟵⟶ HIGH
Add and subtract money	___ ___ ___ ___ ✓
Work with percentages etc.	___ ___ ✓ ___ ___
Communication skills:	LOW ⟵⟶ HIGH
Converse and give information	___ ___ ___ ___ ✓
Follow written instructions etc.	___ ___ ✓ ___ ___

Figure 4.2 Typical competence questionnaire

From an analysis such as the one given in Figure 4.3, specific objectives can subsequently be written for a scheme of work or lesson plan. Draw up a similar analysis for the competences involved in the job you have selected for this assignment.

Reception of customer	Adopt pleasant manner	Be courteous	
		Be calm	
	Avoid over-eagerness	Observe behaviour	
	Allow customer to look over display		
Identify customer's needs	Establish type of goods required	Establish price range	Mains only
			Mains/battery
			Battery only
Offer choice of radios	Display range	Know characteristics of models	Not too technical
			Neatly stored
		Demonstrate	Encourage customer to handle
		Compare with other radios	Specify advantages
Guide towards decision	Handle objections	Use superior product knowledge	Outline quality, design, construction, durability, running costs and reliability
	Answer questions		
	Control sale	Narrow field	Reinforce good points
		Remove rejected radios	Start with mid-range price
		Observe reactions to price	Move up or down
		Observe gaze	
	Negotiate	Describe 'trade-ins', credit terms, delivery, maintenance, guarantees, after-sales service	
Close sale	Maintain courteous manner	Confirm wisdom of customer's choice	

Figure 4.3 Analysis of competences (electrical salesperson)

4.002 Defining terminology appropriate to curriculum development

The **curriculum** may be defined as:

– 'The planned experiences offered to the learner under the guidance of the school.'[7]

- 'All the learning which is planned and guided by the school, whether it is carried out in groups or individually, inside or outside the school.'[8]
- 'An attempt to communicate the essential principles and features of an educational proposal in such a form that it is open to critical scrutiny and capable of effective translation into practice.'[9]

A curriculum provides a vehicle for planning a course, and the diagram given in Figure 4.4 shows how very complex the curriculum development process is.

Components of curriculum development

Curriculum development comprises eight main components:

- identifying and analysing need
- writing curriculum aims and objectives
- selecting course content
- designing teaching and learning strategies
- structuring the curriculum: teaching and learning programme
- assessment
- resource planning
- monitoring and evaluating responsiveness, quality, efficiency and effectiveness of outcomes.

Each component is interrelated with the others, so the process of curriculum development should be ongoing, with continuous adjustments being made as a result of feedback from monitoring and evaluation.

1 Training needs analysis

A needs analysis is client-centred and may include training needs relating to an individual, group, industrial or commercial enterprise, institution or other external agency. Such needs are often classified as being **demand-led**.

Needs may also be anticipated by a supplier of training or education by referring to a syllabus, new legislation, market trends or otherwise predicting the likely demand for a particular learning service. Such provision is described as **supply-led**.

In either case the design and implementation of the curriculum must, if it is humanly possible to do so, satisfy expectations of the clients, that is, fulfil their needs.

2 Curriculum design and objectives

The design and content of the curriculum is decided and its success measured by the degree to which knowledge of the psychology of learning has been applied to the planning of learning experiences.

Tyler's description of the purpose of formulating objectives during the process of curriculum development explains the relevance of writing objectives to student behaviour and the arena in which it operates:

> The most useful form for stating objectives is to express them in terms which identify both the kind of behaviour to be developed in the student and the content or area in life in which this behaviour is to operate. If you consider a

number of statements of objectives that seem to be clear and to provide guidance in the development of instructional programmes, you will note that each of these statements really includes both the behaviour and the content aspects of the objectives.[10]

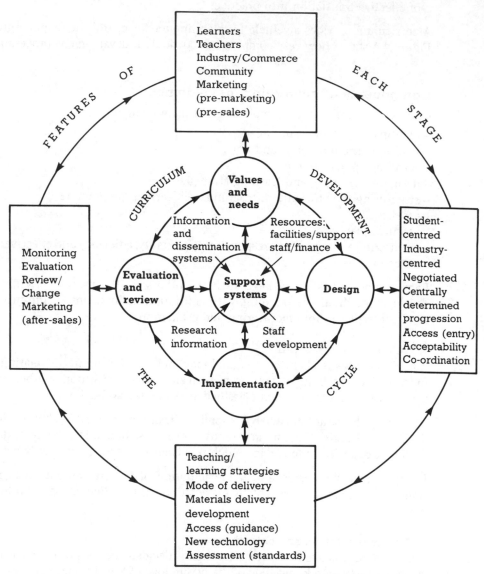

(Source: *Strategy and Processes* FEU, London 1986)

Figure 4.4 Process of curriculum development

3 Course content

The substance of course material may be influenced by the course team or teacher in the role of curriculum developers or by powerful external influences or by the student group itself. When selecting course content the key concept to bear in mind is that the learning experience should be designed to assist the students in their efforts to attain the course objectives set. Content should therefore be arranged in appropriate sequential order, pitched at the right level and delivered at the optimum rate.

4 Strategies

When designing teaching and learning strategies, the teacher is required to structure and organise learning so that account is taken of student-related factors such as need, ability, interest, previous experience, linkages between various subjects and learning style. Provision should be made to involve students actively in decisions about their learning and to recognise the value of two-way negotiation.

Modes of study are changing and computer-based study, distance learning, open learning and work-based learning now feature as important strategies for new programmes. The possibility of providing a flexible learning environment and adequate support for students in the form of counselling and guidance facilities also needs to be considered as does the need to co-ordinate sequences of experiences in an integrated way.

Learning is an active process and the effectiveness of learning will depend on: the learners' understanding of the process in which they are involved; transfer of training; role of perception; reinforcement available; motivation; and group processes operating.

5 Structuring the curriculum

When structuring the teaching and learning programme, early communication of the purpose and value of the course and its activities should be planned. Curiosity should be promoted and a variety of different types of activity scheduled. Commitment to the attainment of valued knowledge or skills that are available to participants should be sought and the relevance of the learning to real world activities assured.

The need to provide continuity and an integrated course that embraces other subjects being studied as well as vocational experience (where appropriate) should be recognised. Linkages between syllabus references, themes, concepts, and topics should be planned and a balanced structure giving a properly weighted allocation of resources made.

From the wide range of learning methods available, techniques should be matched to the method of learning to be applied, whether this be memorising, understanding or doing. Recent curriculum developments require that a good level of skill be demonstrated in the writing of schemes of work and lesson plans, and in the preparing of assignments and other learning materials.

6 Assessment

The purposes of assessment as far as curriculum development is concerned are diverse and many, but some of the commonly used assessment processes involve

- an exercise in communication relating to coursework
- assessment of outcomes

– diagnosis of strengths and weaknesses
– evaluation of effectiveness and efficiency of teaching and learning
– grading or norm-referencing
– guidance in decision making
– placement of students in appropriate courses
– prediction of student performance.

Assessment procedures are an important consideration in curriculum development work and will be discussed in more detail in Chapter Five. In-depth coverage of assessment is provided in *A Teacher's Guide to Assessment*[11] while the subject of profiling is covered in *Profiling: a user's manual.*[12]

7 Resource planning
Resources utilised in delivering the curriculum are either in the form of

– staffing (teaching or non-teaching)
– physical (buildings, accommodation, space, capital equipment or consumables)
– finances
– time.

Now more than ever, we are faced with the need to consider the effectiveness and efficiency of further and adult education in terms of resourcing implications. There is a need to try to establish the efficiency of operation by measuring output against input in much the same way that the efficiency of the burning of fuel is calculated. The message for curriculum developers is therefore: use your resources wisely, effectively and efficiently.

8 Monitoring and evaluation
The final stage in curriculum development is the monitoring, reviewing and evaluation of the responsiveness of the course to the needs identified, and the quality, efficiency and effectiveness of outcomes. Another check that is normally made is that of relating student's actual performances to original objectives. The review and evaluation process identifies the strengths and weaknesses of the course and gives rise to modifications for future planning consideration. The evaluators need to make all of the course team aware of modifications needed and feed back information to all concerned in the course operation.

An element of evaluation that is often over looked is 'client satisfaction', that is, whether the students were happy and contented with the learning experience, and whether or not they thought the course met their needs and expectations.

Monitoring, review and evaluation of the quality of teaching and learning will need to become second nature to all teachers employed in the 1990s.

Other terms appropriate to the curriculum process
A **syllabus** may be defined as an outline or brief description of the main points of a course of study.

A **course** may be described as a series of lessons that are to be delivered over a period of time and at intervals specified by the course provider. In further and adult education many courses are offered that require attendance for one or more sessions weekly over a whole academic year. Courses may or may not be examined or lead to qualifications.

Short courses, fully-costed courses and courses negotiated with students or other clients are examples of courses that are also offered by educational institutions.

A **modular course** is a self-contained unit in a longer course of study. A person studying a car mechanics course may need to take modules in 'engines', 'transmissions', 'brakes', 'steering and suspension' and other aspects; or may wish to take only one module. A modular course structure can be ideal when operating a 'roll-on'/'roll-off' system of enrolment or flexible starting dates; or when taking account of students' previous experience.

A **programme** is a plan of intended proceedings that may be in the form of a descriptive list of schedule of activities. A teaching and learning programme may comprise a series of courses in a particular field of study or in another instance simply a particular instructional sequence. In industrial contexts the word 'programme' may be used rather than the word 'course' to describe staff development training activities.

A **core curriculum** comprises those common elements in a curriculum that are studied by all students taking the relevant programme. Key skills in number, communication and IT are rapidly becoming an integral part of post-16 learning programmes.

A **scheme of work** is a planning document that gives information about the student group; course aims and objectives; organisational factors; methodology and evaluation. Factors that influence the design of schemes of work are discussed in Section 4.004.

Content is all that should be included in the curriculum. Content may be determined by carrying out a 'task analysis' or 'topic analysis', the results of which are then organised into a logical sequence and targeted at a level appropriate to the learners.

Mager[13] suggests that when considering how best to translate content to a set of performance objectives, three questions need to be asked:

'Where are the students going?'
'How will they get there?'
'How will they know when they have arrived?'

The content analysis yields a set of desirable outcomes to be achieved by the learners, perhaps in the form of competences to be demonstrated or in terms of changes in knowledge, skills or attitudes. The analysis shows where the learners are going. **Enabling objectives** signpost how they will get there, since they describe what the students will need to be able to do on their way to attaining the **performance objectives**. These objectives will be written with course content in mind. Assessment of performance against objectives will confirm whether or not the students have 'arrived'.

A **lesson plan** is based on specific learning objectives that describe how the course aims will be satisfied. It amplifies the information given in the scheme of work and it should be carefully structured in logical sequence. Plans are a prerequisite to good lessons and some examples are given in Chapter Two.

Assignment 4.3 – Listing terms appropriate to the curriculum process

Produce a checklist of terms that are appropriate to the curriculum process.

Compare your list with those of colleagues and write definitions or explanations of each term.

Consider how a knowledge of concepts relating to the curriculum development process can help you improve the learning experiences available in a course of study that you are responsible for.

4.003 Formulating and justifying aims and objectives for a specific training programme

In *Practical Curriculum Study* Douglas Barnes says, 'General aims in their nature leave the teacher with the practical decisions still to be made, that is, the decisions about what to teach and how to teach it. . . . Different kinds of subject-matter and of teaching methods require different techniques for planning.'[14]

Barnes suggests five categories that may be helpful when planning. They are: content, concept, skills, problem and interest. Each involves different teaching and learning strategies. Some will require extensive negotiation with students. Student-centred problem solving is a prime example, so also is the situation when learners are free to suggest areas that are of particular interest to them, rather than strictly following a rigidly imposed syllabus.

When planning a teaching and learning activity it is, as Barnes suggests, up to the teacher to make practical decisions as to what will be covered during the learning experience — at least until negotiations with the students begin. It is of little use waiting until the class assembles or until an opportunity presents itself to seek students' views. The teacher needs to plan in advance, regardless of the category of learning that is involved.

The case studies that follow are designed to help in developing skills involved in systematically planning a lesson, although the principle can be applied to planning all the lessons that comprise a course.

Self-assessment and supportive consultative assessment with peers are two excellent ways of analysing and improving preparation of lessons. Reflection and review are also of prime importance in any modern learning programme and this technique should be practised by teachers during training. Whenever possible work should be reviewed with other students or discussed with one of the tutorial team.

Aspects of the teaching preparation to be discussed during the evaluation include

– adequacy of preparation
– logical development of the lesson elements
– objectives to be fulfilled
– context and relevance to the lesson of stated objectives
– construction of objectives
– objective test items and evaluation of outcomes.

It is important to present learners with achievable objectives and to specify suitable contexts through which these may be achieved, together with relevant content. This implies that among other things there will be a need to

– identify learners with special learning difficulties
– provide equal opportunities for all
– pay due regard to gender.

Rather than trying to set out sets of rules for dealing with every conceivable subject or class, perhaps the basic principles underlying the following case studies may be transferable to the reader's own specialism. (Due to limitations of space, lesson plans and the main body of lessons given in the case study have been omitted.)

Planning instruction elements, aims and objectives: case study 1

Karen Hickman is an expert in macrobiotics but like many who are relatively new to teaching, she is not too sure of how to go about planning a presentation.

Karen feels sure that her subject knowledge is more than adequate for the level at which she will be operating. However, getting things in the correct sequence is critically important and Karen fears that she will muddle the order due to the effects of 'stage fright', when delivering the lesson. Friends have tries to reassure that 'It'll be all right on the night'. But, things will not be 'all right' unless she plans carefully.

Karen is friendly with David Hand who likewise is new to teaching. He is training to teach on a community care programme. Fortunately for Karen and David, they have the opportunity to raise their concern with an experienced teacher who favours a planning-led approach to teaching. She suggests they follow the routine:

– consider the planning categories proposed by Douglas Barnes
– think carefully about what it is that the students need to learn about the subject
– write a list of elements comprising the learning content
– write an appropriate aim
– write a detailed set of learning objectives
– design a comprehensive lesson plan
– draft an introduction, main body and conclusion
– write an objective test that will assess learning outcomes
– evaluate the teaching and learning experience.

They go home and after a great deal of effort come up with the following selected drafts.

Karen's draft

An Introduction to Macrobiotics for Catering Students

1 Elements forming the instruction:
a) definition of macrobiotics
b) origins of the macrobiotic diet and first recorded use
c) basic principles of *yin* and *yang* in food
d) brown rice and use of other grains
e) vegetables and fruits in macrobiotics
f) appropriate meats
g) organic growth
h) availability of macrobiotic products
i) introductory effects of macrobiotics on the body
j) positive effects of a macrobiotic lifestyle.

2 Aim:

To suggest the use of macrobiotics as a means of improving life and preventing illness.

3 List of objectives:

The expected learning outcome is that students will be able to

a) define the word 'macrobiotic' from its Greek origins
   specify the correct definition of the macrobiotic diet
b) name the physician who first recorded the use of macrobiotics as a diet
   describe the diet's beneficial effect on the Ancient Ethiopians
   identify the first people to live a macrobiotic lifestyle
c) explain that the principle of *yin* and *yang* is one of balance
   recognise and list the properties of *yin* taste to include feminine, cold and sweet;
   and those of *yang* tastes to include masculine, hot and salty
d) list proportions of *yin* and *yang* in brown rice
   state that millet and rye are good English alternatives to brown rice as they are
   indigenous
e) specify the beneficial balance of fruit and vegetables
   state that the correct use of fruit and vegetables is raw or slightly cooked
f) recognise the detrimental *yin/yang* balance in red meats
g) define the word 'organic'
h) recall that natural products are available from good supermarkets and whole-
   food shops
i) specify the introductory effects of the diet on the body
j) describe the positive outcome of the diet on bodily functions and emotional
   attitudes.

Note how Karen has linked the learning objectives to the elements a)–j).

4 Draft introduction:

Americans today eat 150 lbs of sugar each, per year — that is 10 times more than the maximum safe dose. 17 billion dollars are spent each year on painkillers in the United States and Britain is now in much the same predicament. Since the 1960s when we first became aware of this situation, many elaborate diets have been introduced to promote healthier eating habits and lifestyle. Some of these are useful and some detrimental. But I am going to tell you about macrobiotics — a way of eating simple and natural foods which has been providing people with long and illness-free lives for as long as man has been on the earth, doing away with 'calorie controlling' and reliance on painkillers to survive the day.

5 Draft conclusion:

If you want more proof that a macrobiotic lifestyle is the one to adopt for a long and full life, then think about this: Before Westernisation came to China this century and while the Chinese were still living by macrobiotics, cancer was almost non-existent. A sharp contrast to the frightening medical review made in 1982 by the American body — the National Academy of Science — which revealed that bad diet is responsible for 35 per cent of cancer in men and a staggering 60 per cent in women. Food for thought?

Planning instruction elements, aims and objectives: case study 2

David's draft:

An Outline of Depression for Nursing, Social Work and Community Care Students

1 Elements forming the instruction:

a) definition of depression
b) common causes of depression
c) depression as an indicator of change
d) affective symptoms of depression
e) physical symptoms of depression
f) classifications of depression
g) treatment of depression
h) the positive aspects of depression

2 Aim:

To explain depression, its causes, symptoms, classifications and treatments.

3 List of objectives:

The expected learning outcome is that the students will be able to

– define depression, relate it to personal experience and identify its neurological use
– list some common causes of depression and recognise personal and environmental factors
– recognise the biological use of depression
– list biological causes of depression
– recall its relation to hereditary factors and mental illness
– identify the signs and symptoms of depression
– differentiate between affective and physical symptoms of depression
– explain why depression is not a mental illness
– define its relationship to mental illness as an indicator
– specify four classifications of depression, describe their differences and compare their symptoms
– state four treatments for depression
– specify the types of drugs used in cases of depression
– describe electro-convulsive-therapy (ECT)

– recall what percentage of the population receives treatment for depression
– select communication as a positive means of dealing with depression.

4 Draft opening and introduction:
During this lesson we are going to examine the subject of depression: its causes, symptoms, classifications and treatments.

Depression is something we have all experienced, to a greater or lesser degree — 'My dog has died'; 'I'm never going to pay off my overdraft'; 'I'm just not getting anywhere with my life'; 'How many more tests can I possibly fail?'; 'My wife is very ill.' These are perfectly good reasons for being depressed, yet many of us feel guilty and selfish in admitting to feeling depressed. Many more of us feel depression is unnatural and implies inadequacy.

5 Draft conclusion:
In conclusion, may I once again reinforce the fact that, on the whole, depression occurs to help us in the same way as an alarm system. The most positive way to help yourself is only a friend away. Communicate your feelings, your thoughts and your problems — no matter how petty or stupid you think they are. Do not restrain your feeling of depression — your mind and body are trying to tell you something — ignore them at your peril!

6 Draft objective test to assess retention and learning outcomes:
(please tick correct answer)
  1 A suitable definition of depression is
     a an unnatural chemical response to stress.
     b an unnatural dietary response to a stressful environment.
     c a natural neurological response to ECT.
     d a natural neurological response to stress or trauma.
  2 The neurological use of depression is
     a to indicate fear.
     b as part of a neurological alarm system.
     c to help ease pain.
     d as part of a neurological exercise.
  3 Depression can be caused by environmental stress and an example of environmental stress is
     a bereavement.
     b guilt.
     c stress at work.
     d stress due to illness.
  4 Depression can indicate bodily changes and illness. Which of the following statements is incorrect?
     a Depression indicates changes in puberty.
     b Depression indicates changes during menstruation.
     c Depression indicates mental illness.
     d Depression indicates anorexia.
  5 Which of the following pairs describes two of the physical symptoms of depression?
     a agitation and constipation
     b agitation and despair

  c fatigue and blood loss
  d fatigue and despair
6 Which one of the following statements is true of depression?
  a Depression is a mental illness.
  b Depression always indicates hereditary personality defects.
  c Depression always indicates mental illness.
  d Depression can indicate and be related to mental illness.
7 Which of the following is not a classification of depression?
  a endogenous   c involutional
  b involuntary   d reactive
8 Which one of the following statements is accurate?
  a There is no understandable cause for reactive depression.
  b Simple depression is a mental illness.
  c Endogenous depression is related to environmental stress.
  d Involutional depression occurs in middle age.
9 Which of the following pairs of drugs are recommended by doctors for the treatment of depression?
  a tranquillisers and laxatives
  b antidepressants and hormones
  c antidepressants and mild tranquillisers
  d mild tranquillisers and analgaesics
10 Out of the population, the number of people who will be treated for depression at some time in their life is
  a 1 in 5.   c 1 in 50.
  b 1 in 10.   d 1 in 100.

Assignment 4.4 – Formulating instruction elements, aims and objectives for a specific teaching programme

Comment on the two case studies above with regard to

– logical development of the lesson elements
– relationship between elements of instruction and objectives.

What other, relevant elements might you introduce to ensure student participation and motivation?

Prepare a lesson in your own subject area using the basic principles illustrated by the case studies.

Work-based and fully costed training

Many educational and training providers now offer programmes such as New Deal and work-based training for adults tailored to meet individual needs. Fully costed courses for commercial clients designed to meet the needs of business for professional and industrial updating and retraining are also offered.

Many teachers now need to acquire skills in tailoring courses to meet the needs of their commercial clients; competence in formulating aims and objectives for specific teaching programmes is vitally important in successful marketing of educational services.

Case study: a commercial client calls
Josephine Bain, the Division Leader in the Communications Section is also the College Services to Business Marketing Officer. She receives a phone call from a local company that employs over 200 staff and needs help. The effectiveness of communications within the company is below par.

Josephine explains that under normal circumstances it would be preferable to first carry out a training audit at the factory so that the nature of the problem can be established and a training needs analysis carried out, the object being to find out who needs training and what kind of training should be devised and delivered. However, in this instance the general manager is in no mood to wait, he is very annoyed at having lost valuable contracts through failures of communication within the company and with suppliers. The group he has identified for updating training consists of senior supervisors.

Josephine needs a framework for discussion when she visits the general manager and she requires a drafted set of aims and objectives for a course aimed at rapidly improving matters. The objective is to satisfy the company needs while at the same time generating income for the college by selling fully costed training.

A draft training programme is available for adaptation. It was produced for a NEBS Management Programme course some time ago:

Title: Training programme for senior supervisors
Subject: Communication at work
Aims: To improve the effectiveness of communication within ... by improving the senior supervisors' ability to speak, write, listen, record and observe
Objectives: Each of the objectives listed should be preceded by the words: 'The expected learning outcome is that after instruction and practice the supervisor will be able to ...'

- present information graphically
- record data in tabular form
- construct a 'break-even' chart
- design a safety poster
- draft a bulletin board notice
- draft written orders and instructions
- write an order for spare parts
- complete a stores requisition
- reply to a letter of complaint
- reply to a letter of enquiry
- draft a letter of enquiry
- prepare a technical report
- write a comprehensive memorandum
- précis articles
- recall principles of interviewing
- prepare the structure for an interiew
- conduct an interview

- prepare a short talk
- prepare and deliver a job instruction
- prepare visual aids
- chair a discussion, an informal meeting and a formal meeting
- take comprehensive notes at a meeting
- give verbal orders unambiguously
- achieve a faster reading rate with adequate recall of information
- use a dictionary effectively
- demonstrate clear thinking
- reason logically
- interpret the meaning of non-verbal signals.

Assignment 4.5 – **Improving communication**

Go through the training programme in the case study above, and modify it as necessary to meet your own perception of what the company may be expecting when Josephine goes to negotiate with the general manager.

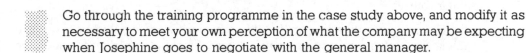 Identifying factors influencing the design of schemes of work

A **scheme of work** is a planning document that gives information about:

- the student group: previous experience, prerequisites and age range
- the course aims and objectives: broad aims giving direction and purpose backed up with more detailed objectives
- organisational factors: location, meeting times, duration, course information, course content, sequence, availability of resources, aids and equipment, lecturers and students involved
- methodology
- evaluation.

A sample scheme of work is shown in Figure 4.9.

Factors influencing the design of a scheme of work

When planning a teaching and learning programme, the scheme of work, together with sets of more detailed lesson plans, is the key to a well organised course; competence is required in each of the important areas outlined above.

1 The student group

The scheme of work should give details of student numbers and age range but more importantly it should reflect the learners' needs and take account of learners with special learning difficulties, gender, class, religion and race.

2 Course aims and objectives

The aims and objectives should be written with a clear idea of the intended outcomes of training in the planner's mind. Where possible, a course team approach should be used with each member contributing to planning and preparation.

Liaison with other course providers, teachers' centres or curriculum bases is very helpful when confronted with curriculum development work for the first time or when there appears to be no one to help you.

When writing a scheme of work, the aims and objectives should be relevant and in the correct context. The objectives should be compatible with the stated course aims and should be appropriate to the needs of the learners rather than the teacher.

3 Organisational factors

Information concerning the venue, timetabling, staffing and other administrative detail is often included in a scheme of work. Planning course content also involves a need to design appropriate learning experiences, learning materials and strategies, preferably in consultation with students or with the aid of feedback from similar courses.

Where a core curriculum is operating, the scheme of work should be constructed against the background of the identified core. Learning experiences should be integrated with vocational activities and work-based assignments set where applicable.

Resource planning is another important factor in the design of schemes of work. The selection of resources is discussed in Section 3.002.

4 Methodology

The teaching and learning strategy specified in the scheme of work will depend on the subject matter, student group and course context. There is no one right strategy for every lesson, course or student group.

The teacher concerned will need to be able to plan, prepare and carry out a teaching programme using different methods and techniques based on a knowledge of the principles of teaching and an understanding of learning principles.

Involving the students in the selection of learning method is recommended, as this is likely to promote a positive and helpful attitude towards learning. When learners are invited to take some responsibility for their own learning and outcomes through experiential learning opportunities, self-reliance is promoted and a greater work output may be possible than where a more passive mode is adopted.

Negotiation may involve regular reviewing and the agreement of learning agendas or contracts with individual learners, especially when individuals are working at their own speed. Learner-centred, participative and experiential methods are worth a try, as is the opportunity to practise skill transfer in a number of different situations.

5 Evaluation

The scheme of work should indicate how checks of learning are to be carried out and how feedback in the form of knowledge of results will be provided. Formative assessments, study guidance and support strategies will need to be worked out and adequate arrangements made for consultation with students in the form of reviews and self-assessment opportunities.

Equal gender opportunities in the curriculum

An important consideration when working on curriculum development projects is that of gender.

In the Coombe Lodge Report *Women in Further and Higher Education Management*,[15] Steve Crabbe gives a 'Checklist for Equal Opportunities (Gender)' 'in order to focus attention on the steps needed to be taken to ensure that educational establishments are providing equal opportunities with respect to issues of gender and sex discrimination.'

The checklist contains a section relating to the curriculum in which the questions reproduced below are posed:[16]

– Have measures been taken to ensure that teaching materials (books, handouts, film, video etc.) do not contain sexist stereotyping?
– Have positive action strategies been developed regarding curriculum development which will encourage both sexes to attempt non-traditional subject areas?
– If a college, are courses for adult women 'returners' provided which:
  a) give advice or information for women returning to work after a career break?
  b) retrain women in non-traditional areas e.g. information technology, engineering, management?

Assignment 4.6 – **Equal opportunities: attitudes and resources**

Examine your attitude towards equal opportunities and check your own curriculum resources and those provided for you by your employer.

Consider the questions asked above. Are you able to answer in the affirmative? If not, what do you intend to do about it?

Assignment 4.7 – **Identifying and countering bias and discrimination**

It is important for teachers to be able to identify and counter bias and discrimination in relation to access to learning opportunities and curriculum entitlement.

– Examine your own attitude towards gender, class, religion and race and consider how discrimination many affect your performance.
– Consider how bias and discrimination may operate during selection and enrolment and with respect to curriculum entitlement.
– Analyse your teaching and learning resources in order to verify that they are free of bias.

Assignment 4.8 – Work experience in the curriculum

Work experience is an increasingly important element of the learning experience. Teachers therefore need to be able to design a curriculum that meets the demand for an integrated approach to work-based and college-based teaching and learning. Work-based learning demands that the curricula must change to meet the needs of widely varying client groups and of rapidly changing industrial, commercial and public service operations.

Consider how you may become more involved in work-experience related curriculum development and what your involvement may be in

– analysing needs and satisfying those needs
– designing new elements and changing the existing curriculum
– implementing changes in curriculum design
– monitoring, reviewing and evaluating the new curriculum.

Discuss with colleagues how developments in work-experience provision have already influenced their profile of activity and how they plan to cope with more change.

Assignment 4.9 – Developing provision for students with special needs

In many educational establishments there is a lack of adequate provision for students with special needs. In some cases, resources, facilities, specifically provided courses and integration with other student groups may need co-ordination or development.

Consider your own classes. Do you feel that your resources and provision adequately meets the needs of students with special needs? If not, outline the changes in curriculum that will need to be made and discuss how you could help to develop a strategy for implementing the changes.

How would the need to accommodate students with special needs affect the design of your scheme of work?

Assignment 4.10 – Developing open learning systems

Open learning provision is becoming more widespread and in order to provide greater freedom of access to learning for adults, it is likely that educational institutions need to devote more resources to this type of learning opportunity. Conventionally taught subjects need to be presented in a form that is compatible with the open learning mode. This requires that teachers concerned are competent in planning, designing, preparing and delivering the appropriate curriculum.

Consider what teachers would need to do in order to meet the challenge presented when designing and implementing open learning systems.

How will open learning affect your teaching programme and scheme of work?

Assignment 4.11 – **Developing resource-based learning**

Some examination boards, HMIs and teachers are promoting a curriculum that has been described as 'resource-led, activity-based learning'. The learning is largely student-centred and facilitated by the provision of, for example, computer-based learning programmes together with a range of other learning resources supported by teachers or tutor-librarians.

Does 'resource-led activity-based learning' take place in your classes?

Does it take place elsewhere in the establishment where you are employed?

What is your attitude towards it? Do you need to do anything about it?

If you decided to implement it, what curriculum development work would be involved?

How would resource-based learning influence the design of your scheme of work?

Assignment 4.12 – **Developing the curriculum: achieving student competence**

The writing of competence objectives, the validation and certification of occupational, intellectual and developmental competences, and provision for recognising and crediting prior learning in education and training are all essential parts of the non-advanced further education curriculum. The demands of such provision are considerable:

> Competence-based standards which place greater emphasis on the 'performance' requirements of employment require programmes of learning that provide opportunities for trainees to develop and practise their competence in a workplace environment or through activities that realistically simulate the requirements of work. In most cases it will be difficult to achieve this through classroom-based learning alone and it becomes progressively more difficult to simulate, the higher the level.[17]

Refer to relevant publications and discuss the implications of providing education and training curricula that will allow prior and ongoing student competence to be recognised and accredited.

How would the recognition of previous experiences and variation in degree of competence be reflected in a properly designed scheme of work?

4.005 Integrating schemes of work, outcomes, and assessment procedures

When planning a unified curriculum experience for students it may be necessary to collaborate with others in order to achieve a proper degree of integration, especially when working with students engaged in cross-college courses. In such cases it is necessary to create a learning environment that demonstrates continuity of approach.

The opportunity to optimise the contributions of colleagues and students should be seized if it presents itself. A team approach can be very productive as can a ready response to colleagues' and external assessors' criticisms and advice.

Effective team planning

The FEU Project Report: 'Staff Development for Open Learning Tutors' suggests that some of the techniques and skills required in the early stages of teamwork involved in curriculum development projects include

- reviewing the curriculum
- planning together with colleagues and students a teaching and learning strategy
- recognising the team leaders' responsibilities in relation to specifically designed resource learning materials and with regard to group decision making and planning processes
- specifying the differences that exist between students in relation to their expected learning characteristics
- developing systems for delivery of the curriculum
- outlining the purpose and importance of the need to coordinate group members inputs so as to improve efficiency and quality of curriculum development project outcomes
- keeping a diary of team meetings, giving a record of work completed during the meetings and of individual work carried out to meet tasks allocated
- maintaining informal contact with the Head, team leader, students and other inter-group members in addition to scheduled formal meetings of the group.

Integrating course components

When integrating the two important course components — activities and resources — the aim should be to arrange learning experiences that encourage demonstrable outcomes. Teaching and learning approaches should be compatible with course aims and with the student group concerned, and a review of learning experiences and course materials in relation to the aims should be conducted regularly. Feedback from the reviews will most probably result in the need to modify and update materials and strategies. A continuous process of self-appraisal, course review and evaluation is advocated.

Material that encourages transfer of training and which applies to situations in a variety of contexts is of great value to learners who may wish to redeploy skills that they already own but may not be able to use at the present time. Being able to adapt materials to the needs of different groups of learners and to integrate learning materials into the overall training programme is an important skill for teachers. Assessment procedures also need to be established with learners and a system of recording set up, either by logbook, profile, review sheets, case studies, diaries or as agreed with standard setting agencies.

All of the above elements need to be considered when devising the scheme of work.

The relative importance attached to each topic and the need to integrate theory and practice should be reflected in the overall plan.

Designing a teaching and learning programme

Before a scheme of work can be produced it is advisable to consider the strategy that will be adopted for the course as a whole and this is where a well thought-out design programme can be of great use.

Figure 4.5 gives a layout that could be used as a basis for programme design. The starting point for any kind of vocational work is the occupation from which a list of competences and job objectives can be derived. It is the ability to demonstrate such competences that determines the outcomes of the teaching and learning process. This is true whether the occupation is that of nursing, horticulture or construction. In the case of academic learning, a syllabus may be the starting point.

Whatever the course may be connected with, it is likely that there will be a need to work towards the achievement of specified teaching and learning aims and objectives.

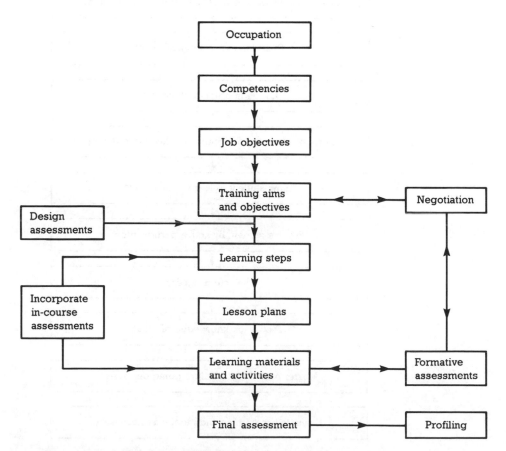

Figure 4.5 Designing the training programme

Once these have been decided, the teaching and learning steps can be planned (see Section 2.005) and lesson plans, assessments, student support, profiling or other certification developed.

Training programme format

An alternative training programme format is given in Figure 4.6. Each step follows a logical sequence. The starting point is the writing of objectives stating in behavioural terms what the student is expected to be able to do as an outcome of the training.[18] Then a programme should be laid out following the form of one or other of the examples shown in Figure 4.7 and 4.8. Detailed lesson plans may then be produced. The remaining steps follow conventional teaching and learning practice.

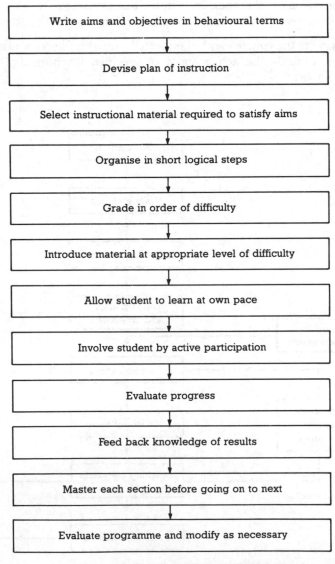

Write aims and objectives in behavioural terms

Devise plan of instruction

Select instructional material required to satisfy aims

Organise in short logical steps

Grade in order of difficulty

Introduce material at appropriate level of difficulty

Allow student to learn at own pace

Involve student by active participation

Evaluate progress

Feed back knowledge of results

Master each section before going on to next

Evaluate programme and modify as necessary

Figure 4.6 Training programme format

Session	Lecture topic	Group activities	Student preparation
1	Introduction to course Components of a lesson Specifying learning objectives	Discussion—further examples of stating objectives Tutor talk on verbal exposition Set assignment	Short talk
2	Lesson-planning and preparation	Discussion on lesson-planning Short talks by students	Lesson plan
3	Interrelationships in the classroom	Presentation of lesson plans by students	
4	Informal methods including questions and answers and discussion	Discussion on use of original methods Presentation of lesson plans by students	Discussion
5	Displaying, demonstrating and the learning of concepts	Examples by tutor of skills analysis and concept-teaching Discussions led by students	Demonstra-tion
6	Classwork, practical and project activities	Presentation of demonstrations by students Brief by tutor on micro-teaching	Micro-teaching
7	Evaluation of work	Micro-teaching	
8	Final review of course	Question-and-answer session Students' comment on course design and presentation	

Figure 4.7 Plan of instruction: practical teaching course

Assignment 4.13 – Designing, applying and modifying a scheme of work

Design a scheme of work that outlines in a logical sequence the way in which you and your students in partnership may best cover the topics in a syllabus. While you are drawing up the outline remember the nature of the learning group; syllabus content; course aims and objectives; timing and duration of main study areas; and reviewing, guidance and assessment procedures. Opportunities to integrate your topic areas with those of other teachers and the need to consider routes for progression to other courses or levels should also be borne in mind.

Review the scheme of work with colleagues or course team members and if necessary modify the scheme taking account of any observations or suggestions.

Use the scheme of work, monitoring its suitability and effectiveness week by week, and subsequently evaluate its effectiveness.

Revise and modify the scheme incorporating ideas for improvement that you collected during the monitoring and evaluation stages; and most importantly, take good account of your students' criticisms and suggestions.

Programme

The lecture programme will consist of a survey of teaching aids and will concentrate on giving the teacher a knowledge of the existing range of media. It is hoped that the students will acquire the practical skills of using these aids and preparing material. There is a range of handout material available, dealing with technical data, methods of preparation and use of those items of equipment covered in this survey.

Period

1   **Introduction** Introduction to the course: aims; programme; resources available for teachers' use; an approach to the use of teaching aids.

2   **Display** A survey of non-projected aids for classroom use: the chalk-board, newsprint pad, felt and magnetic boards; charts, diagrams, classroom displays.

3   **Reprographics** Methods of producing class handouts: spirit and ink stencil duplication; small offset; copying techniques—heat, transfer, dyeline, xerox; economic considerations.

4   **The overhead projector** The projector: its uses; siting; methods of use; as a writing surface; as a projector; masking and overlay techniques; simple movement; experiments.

5   **Still photography** Applications of photography to classroom use; equipment; economics; strip and slide projectors, screens; back projection.

6   **Cine photography** Film projectors: standard and super 8 mm, 16 mm; sound equipment; economics; loop-film projectors.

7   **Recorded sound** The use of sound recordings in the classroom; equipment; record and tape techniques; methods of recording from broadcast and live performances; use of tape/slide synchronisation technique.

8   **Educational radio, TV and ICT** Video recorders; interactive television; information and communications technology (ICT) as classroom aids.

Figure 4.8 Educational technology: an introductory course for teachers

Notes and references

1   Ralph W. Tyler, *Basic Principles of Curriculum and Instruction*, University of Chicago Press, Chicago 1949.

2   D.R. Krathwohl, et al, *Taxonomy of Educational Objectives: Handbook 2 Affective Domain*, Longman, London 1964.

3   B.S. Bloom (ed.), *Taxonomy of Educational Objectives: Handbook 1 Cognitive Domain*, David McKay, New York 1956.

4   R.F. Mager, *Preparing Educational Objectives*, Fearon Publishers, Belmont, California 1962.

5   D.S. Frith and H.G. Macintosh, *A Teacher's Guide to Assessment*, Stanley Thornes (Publishers) Ltd, Cheltenham 1984.

6   D.R. Krathwohl et al, *Taxonomy of Educational Objectives: Handbook 2 Affective Domain*, Longman, London 1964, Chapter 3.

SCHEME OF WORK

Establishment: CHARLTON MARSHALL COLLEGE   **Lecturer:** JACK ANKWILL

Course: FAETC C&G 730	Subject: TEACHING METHODS	One academic year	Additional course information:
Room: 27	Meeting times: Tuesday 6:00 - 9:30 Friday 2:00 - 5:30	Tuesday - Mature 8M 12F (20) Friday - " 4M 16F (20)	Tuesday and Friday classes are run parallel. Students may interchange

Course aims: To enable students to make a conscious choice of teaching method based on the principles of learning and to evaluate and use effectively a systematic approach to teaching and learning.

Notes: Objectives marked * should be preceded by "Students will be able to." Unless otherwise stated all handouts and viewfoils are filed in filing cabinet (room 27)

Figure 4.9 Opening sheets of a completed scheme of work (contd. overleaf)

SCHEME OF WORK:

SHEET NO 1 /

Date	Topic	Objectives / Content	Method	Resources	Notes
① 23 Sept 26 "	INTRODUCTION to Course	* Carry out the procedure to be followed in the event of fire or accident. Describe the basic organisation of the FAETC. Give an individual account of their background and reasons for coming on the course.	Exposition Q & A. Student participation	Health + Safety leaflet Course Calendar	R.F.C. & MB to be in attendance.
② 30 Sept 3 Oct	Course Design Basic Curriculum Development Model	* Describe the basic curriculum development model. Recognise the basic principles of a systems approach. Discuss the teachers activities necessary in the preparation of a course.	Exposition using Q & A, chalkboard and handouts	Chalkboard Handouts 2-1	Assessment Blue Sheet CWA 6 T/o
③ 7 Oct 10 "	Aims + Objectives Theory	* Differentiate between aims, gen. objectives and specific objectives. Recognise "performance, standards" and "conditions" in stated objectives. Identify examples of objectives from the three domains of learning. Write down an objective for a lesson in their own subjects.	Introduction OHP- Video Development: Exposition and Q+A using handouts.	OHP Viewfoils V3-1/4 Video Tape TT 3 PL Book - Objectives	Video tape booklet Library 26.9.87 Students to read PL book as homework and complete examples PL Books in filing cabinet under lesson 3.
④ 4 Oct 17 "	Aims & Objectives Practical	Students will divide into four pre-determined groups and discuss the assignments completed at home. Selected objectives will be written on viewfoils for discussion by the group leaders by the class as a whole	Group discussion Report back Class discussion	OHP Viewfoils - blank " - 4.1 4.2	Assessment Blue Sheet CWA 3 (Ob)

7   D.K. Wheeler, *Curriculum Process*, University of London Press Ltd, 1967, p 11.

8   J. Kerr, *Changing the curriculum*, University of London Press Ltd, 1968.

9   L. Stenhouse, *An introduction to curriculum research and development*, Heinemann Educational Books Ltd, London 1975, p 4.

10   Ralph W. Tyler, *Ibid*, pp 46–7.

11   D.S. Frith and H.G. Macintosh, *A Teacher's Guide to Assessment*, Stanley Thornes (Publishers) Ltd, Cheltenham 1984.

12   D. Garforth, H.G. Macintosh, *Profiling: a user's manual*, Stanley Thornes (Publishers) Ltd, Cheltenham 1986.

13   R.F. Mager, *Preparing Educational Objectives*, Fearon Publishers, Belmont, California 1962.

14   D. Barnes, *Practical Curriculum Study*, Routledge and Kegan Paul, London 1982, p 5.

15   A. Spencer, N. Finlayson and S. Crabbe, *Coombe Lodge Report, Volume 20, Number 3*, 'Women in Further and Higher Education Management', The Further Education Staff College, Coombe Lodge, Blagdon, Bristol 1987, pp 173 and 174.

16   Reproduced here with the permission of Avon County Council.

17   *A TUC Guide to National Vocational Qualifications*, September 1988.

18   National Vocational Qualification (NVQ) awards show what it is that the owner actually can do and to what standard. The NVQ assessment model allows for the assessment of performance-related evidence as well as essential underpinning knowledge. Evidence of occupational competence will therefore comprise a mix of the two.

Performance criteria are used to describe what the candidate will be required to do in order to demonstrate competence in achieving specified outcomes. The criteria provide standards against which candidates will be assessed and their performance judged using the range of evidence available to infer competence.

CHAPTER FIVE

Assessment

Aim: To enable teachers to relate principles of assessment effectively to the aims and objectives of the courses they are teaching

5.001 Translating objectives into performance goals

If we are involved in teaching or training, we need to first negotiate and carefully define the outcomes to be achieved by the learner at or before the end of the course. The means of achieving the desired outcomes and the method of evaluating performance should whenever possible be agreed with the learner.

Learning programmes may, where possible, be designed around a set of aims and behavioural objectives with test criteria built in to measure the effectiveness of teaching and learning. Some teachers consider that this approach is too prescriptive and that it stifles creativity and the freedom to explore diverse avenues of thought and activity.

Testing monitors the student's progress and can also be used to measure the terminal or summative effects of the learning process. The effect of a course of study or training programme can only be truly assessed if the student takes a criterion test both before and after training. If we wait until the coursework is finished before applying the criterion test, no account will have been taken of how much the student already knew about the subject before commencing the course and a false evaluation of our teaching performance may be obtained. What is more, we may have caused a great deal of boredom and loss of motivation on the way.

A **criterion test** is a form of performance test that is based on the desired outcomes of a training programme. Students are tested before the course commences and results are recorded. During the programme further tests are undertaken, providing formative feedback to the students. Finally, at the end of the programme, a test covering the criteria relating to the negotiated performance goals is taken. The difference between performance levels before and after training is a measure of the effectiveness of the teaching and learning.

A **training analysis** or **assessment specification** defines the performance standards to which students need to be trained or educated. Behavioural objectives specifying what the learner is expected to be able to do after training provide the performance goals. For example, a trainee may be required to be able to: 'weigh-up to an accuracy of plus or minus five grammes and pack four 200 gramme sachets of ground coffee in one minute'. The performance goal is precisely stated and competence can readily be established.

Performance testing is a procedure for assessing what a person can do. This can only be properly assessed if the verbs describing the learner's behaviour and related conditions and standards comprising the outcomes of learning can be translated into performance goals.

During 1984 the Oxford Group prepared for the Manpower Services Commission a 'Supervisor's Guide to Standard Tasks' to be piloted in connection with the Youth Training Scheme. The intention was to use **standard tasks** to assess trainees' performance in a job and thus provide credits for the skills displayed. The principle is transferable to many other applications where assessment of practical skill is desirable.

Standard tasks contain all those elements to be assessed and give an accurate indication of the activity that will be carried out while performing the task. Competence is confirmed by completing all the **criteria for success** on a 'can do' basis, thereby eliminating to some extent subjectivity and variation in assessors' opinions.

Criteria for success are specified by re-writing task elements or course objectives relating to the task so that successful completion may be observed. The criteria provide a description of conditions and standards against which performance may be judged.

Assignment 5.1 – Translating objectives into performance goals

Take a list of objectives for one of your courses and write one or more performance goals for each objective. These goals should contain **criteria for success**.

Use the performance specification for course assessment and evaluate the advantages and disadvantages of this method of competence testing.

5.002 Designing, using and evaluating tests

There are many arguments both for and against using formal examinations to assess educational achievement. There is doubt as to whether or not their use should continue. The debate is likely to continue for some time yet, and for many practising teachers there is no alternative but to comply with current regulations.

Some of the factors for and against the use of examinations, and a few suggested advantages for and against the continued usage of examinations for both teacher and student are given in Figure 5.1.

When constructing tests, a teacher should consider what to assess and, in particular, decide what is critical, important, or relevant.

– **Critical material** is that which the learner 'must know' in order to achieve programme objectives.
– **Important material** is that which 'should be known' but is not essential to the successful attainment of specific objectives.
– **Relevant material** is concerned with the matter in hand and 'could be known'. It is pertinent to the subject, but not so important for attaining the immediate objectives.

Case for examinations	Case against examinations
Examinations:	Examinations:
– provide an overall aim for the teacher	– bind teacher strictly to syllabus
– provide a goal for and motivate students	– limit exploration
– measure progress and attainment of objectives	– control curricula
– test ability to discriminate, reason and work at speed	– stress recall and memory
– reveal weaknesses in teaching and learning	– emphasise speed
– provide feedback to employers	– promote rote learning, preparation of model answers and concentration on banked questions

To the learner ⟵ Advantages ⟶	To the teacher
Examinations provide:	Examinations provide:
– a goal	– assessment of student knowledge
– motivation	– evaluation and validation of course content
– competition	– feedback
– reinforcement	Measure effectiveness of teaching
– a sense of advancement	Reveal weaknesses in instructional techniques
	Enable teaching methods to be compared

Figure 5.1 Factors relating to use of examinations

The test should contain questions based on the critical material and be structured so as to satisfy the criteria laid down in the programme in the form of **performance objectives** or as is now the case in so many areas, **competence objectives**. A proportion of questions set on important and relevant material could also be included, but these should be weighted accordingly.

Tests: defining validity and reliability

When designing tests, we must ensure that the test is **valid**, that is, that it covers what we actually intend to test. It is easy to construct a test which unintentionally includes items other than those written into course objectives. Such additional items would be **invalid** in terms of course content, learning experiences and evaluation.

Another feature of any satisfactory test is its **reliability** as a consistent measure of what is to be tested. Subjective marking and assessment unavoidably involves value judgements, opinion and bias on the part of the examiner, especially when the candidates are known personally by the marker. Depending on the nature of the test, one examiner might award a fail grade while another would come down in favour of a pass or even a merit. Similar performance by several students should yield the same grade in any reliable test, and similar results should be obtained by groups of comparable students using the same test on other occasions, even when marked by a different examiner. General factors which may affect reliability include the objectivity of the test and classroom environment, while intelligence testing may be influenced by the effects of coaching and practice. Tutor-related factors such as motivation, language used for instructions, cultural bias, seating arrangements, and method of supervision may also affect test reliability; together with student related factors such as mental, emotional, or physical state, motivation and relationship with the tutor or invigilator.

Validity is inextricably linked with course objectives, so that three important criteria must be fulfilled in order that the complete learning package may be validated. These are

– course content
– learning experiences
– testing.

Assignment 5.2 – **Checking validity**

Select a number of tests that you use and check the validity of the questions, assessment method and accreditation of competence against the course aims and objectives.

Assignment 5.3 – **Checking reliability**

The extent to which a test is dependable and consistent when administered to different groups or at different times is a measure of the reliability of the assessment device. Students operate a 'grapevine' through which intelligence relating to tests, test results, teacher marking styles and other matters of relevance circulates. Whether the intelligence is itself reliable is another matter, but it is nevertheless important for teachers to produce tests that are as free of sources of variability as is humanly possible.

Examine the test results obtained from parallel groups or otherwise check on variations that could be attributed to any of the following:

– student performance factors such as anxiety, out-of-college circumstances, in-college practices and arrangements, or your own assessment style
– the test specification itself and range and suitability of assessment instruments
– differences in content and methodology employed by different teachers involved in the course
– accreditor's judgements of script marker's standards and attitudes
– assessor's workload and ability to manage time and stress.

What can be done to reduce the degree of variation discovered during this assignment?

Evaluating and grading test results

In the following passage, Christine Ward compares the merits and uses of **criterion-referencing** and **norm-referencing**:

> If the marking system used is impression marking, rating scale or checklist, the method of result determination may be classed as **criterion-referencing**; the student passes if he or she fulfils certain predetermined criteria. This is an apparently logical method of determining results, but is only reliable if the criteria are well defined, so that the standard of the assessment remains the same from year to year. For some practical skills it is relatively easy to define the criteria reliably (e.g. 'the student should machine a specified material, to specified dimensions, to a given tolerance') and hence to maintain the standard from year to year. If, however, the criteria are mainly in the minds of the markers, it becomes very much more difficult to ensure that they are applying the same standards as one another and as they did in previous examinations; this is particularly true of essay questions and of oral assessment.
>
> For written examinations and tests, criterion-referencing cannot usually be applied, the paper tests only a sample of the objectives of the course, and in any one year may test an easier or more difficult selection; application questions testing the same objectives may be made more or less difficult.
>
> Unless the questions are all pre-tested and banked, and the marking is of guaranteed reliability, it is impossible to be sure that the paper is of the same standard as that of a previous year. One solution to this problem is to determine results by **norm-referencing**, which assumes that the students are of the same standard from year to year and that therefore any differences in the level of marks awarded are due to the paper or its marking. The same percentage of students is passed each year. This approach can be valid in large national examinations, but its use is questionable in a college or small-entry examination (i.e. where the entry is less than a few hundred), unless there are special reasons for believing the standard to be constant. It is potentially unjust, since the same percentage of students will pass, whether their overall standard is high or low.
>
> Result determination for a written paper therefore takes account of a number of factors, including the mean, standard deviation and range of marks awarded.[1]

The normal curve of distribution

A normal distribution curve is a bell-shaped curve which is often obtained when a large number of test marks are plotted. A typical curve is given in Figure 5.2, which shows that the normal curve is symmetrical about its centre line (average or mean height).

The area under the curve represents all the results. Clearly, the area to the right of the centre line represents the 50 per cent of the population whose mark exceeded the mean mark; and the area to the left of the centre line the 50 per cent who scored less than the mean.

The curve is such that the base line may be divided into six equal divisions known as standard deviations, three either side of the mean. The area under the curve

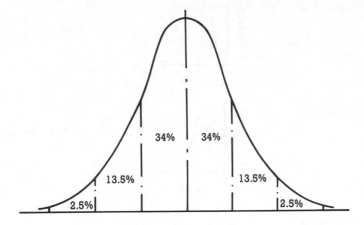

Figure 5.2 Normal curve of distribution

between the mean and plus or minus three standard deviations represents about 99.7 per cent of the population.

The approximate percentage of the population located in each section of the curve is shown in Figure 5.2. The area under the curve between mean and plus or minus one standard deviation is 68 per cent; between the mean and plus or minus two standard deviations is about 95 per cent of the total area.

Whenever any data are obtained by measuring large numbers of components or sizes, a curve which is approximately normal is obtained, unless abnormal factors distort the process being measured.

Interpreting graphs of test results

Figure 5.3 shows graphs of test results.

Graph A is negatively skewed; that is, a high proportion of candidates scored high marks. The graph indicates that the test was too easy.

Graph B is positively skewed; that is, a high proportion of candidates scored low marks. The graph indicates that the test was too difficult.

Graph C shows the results clustered closely about a certain mark. The spread of marks is small. The central value may be located anywhere along the base line (mark axis). The graph indicates a badly designed test.

Graph D shows an approximately normal curve of distribution with a wide spread of marks. The graph indicates a well-designed test.

Graph A

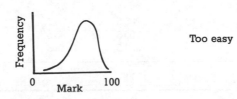

Too easy

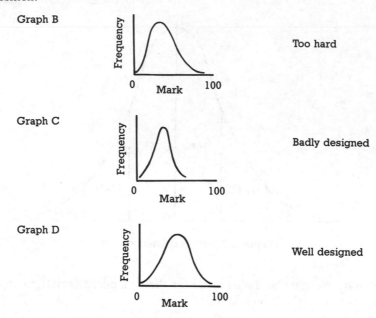

Figure 5.3 Graphs showing examples of test result (not applicable to criterion post-tests)

Calculating the mean and standard deviation of examination results
The table below indicates the results of 200 candidates who sat a single examination. The example which follows shows how the **mean mark** and **standard deviation** are calculated.

Mark	1–10	11–20	21–30	31–40	41–50	51–60	61–70	71–80	81–90	91–100
Mid point (x)	5.5	15.5	25.5	35.5	45.5	55.5	65.5	75.5	85.5	95.5
Frequency (f)	4	10	20	27	40	41	29	16	9	4

Let standard deviation $= s$ Arithmetic mean $= \bar{x}$

Then:

x	f	fx	$(x - \bar{x})$	$(x - \bar{x})^2$	$f(x - \bar{x})^2$
5.5	4	22	−44.5	1980.25	7921
15.5	10	155	−34.5	1190.25	11902.5
25.5	20	510	−24.5	600.25	12005
35.5	27	958.5	−14.5	210.25	5676.75
45.5	40	1820	− 4.5	20.25	810
55.5	41	2275.5	5.5	30.25	1240.25
65.5	29	1899.5	15.5	240.25	6967.25
75.5	16	1208 5	25.5	650.25	10404
85.5	9	769.5	35.5	1260.25	11342.25
95.5	4	382 5	45.5	2070.25	8281
	200	10000			76550

$$\bar{x} = \frac{10\,000}{200} = 50$$

The mean mark $= 50$

$$s = \pm \sqrt{\frac{76\,550}{200}} = \pm \sqrt{382.75} = \pm 19.564$$

The standard deviation $= \pm 19.564$ marks

Calculating the range of examination results
The **range** is the difference between the lowest and the highest mark recorded. If the results are normally distributed, a rough value for the standard deviation may be obtained by finding the range of the data and dividing it by six.

The marks awarded to candidates were as follows:

%	25	30	40	42	51	53	55	57	62	70	81

Range = highest mark minus lowest mark
= 81 − 25 marks
= 56 marks

Evaluating test scores
National education test and examination scores tend to be normally distributed as do pre-tests applied before training commences. On the other hand, local criterion tests tend to be biased towards the high end of the marking scale. This is because criterion tests are designed to measure specific performance and are formulated directly from a limited number of objectives.

A properly designed training programme based upon specific objectives should result in the normally distributed pre-test scores being replaced at the end of training by a 90/90 criterion; that is, 90 per cent of the students should achieve a mark of 90 per cent or over in the terminal test.

There is a wide range of test statistics which can be used in the evaluation of learning. The statistical analysis of test results is a specialised subject area and the selection of test statistics to be employed in analysing the data requires expert knowledge. Interested readers are therefore recommended to consult references such as *Designing a Scheme of Assessment*, by C.M. Ward for in-depth treatment of the subject.

Assignment 5.4 – Calculating mean and standard deviation

One hundred students sat an examination. The results are given in the table. Draw a frequency polygon to represent the results. Calculate

- the mean mark (x)
- the standard deviation (s).

What do you consider would be the minimum acceptable pass mark? Give reasons for your decision.

Mark	Frequency
1–10	1
11–20	1
21–30	2
31–40	3
41–50	36
51–60	37
61–70	12
71–80	4
81–90	2
91–100	2

5.003 Objective testing

An **objective test** may be defined as a series of items, each of which has a predetermined correct answer so that subjective judgement in the marking of each item is eliminated.

The City and Guilds of London Institute (CGLI) and other major examining boards use objective tests as a component of their examinations, and by now many thousands of candidates will have experienced this type of testing.

CGLI is often asked why it uses objective tests. It gives the following reasons:

- an objective paper gives better syllabus coverage
- choice of questions is eliminated
- marking is completely objective giving reliable results
- the preparation of objective question papers is systematic
- there can be more accurate comparison of results from year to year than with a traditional paper
- there is reduced emphasis on penmanship
- results can be issued more quickly
- there is scope for increased teacher participation.

The writing of objective-type questions, usually known as 'items', is very time-consuming. Deciding what to include in the tests and what to exclude is another task that requires a great deal of thought. The tests are difficult to prepare but simple to mark, since each item has only one correct answer.

Examination boards require candidates to indicate their answers on special answer sheets provided. The papers are often marked rapidly by machine. Human error and subjectivity is therefore eliminated. The marking is accurate and consistent, there being only one predetermined acceptable answer.

The items included in a test assess not only the candidates' understanding of the subject, but also their ability to recall facts and to apply knowledge to specific problems. Using objective-type questions, the whole syllabus may be examined in greater detail than by essay method, by asking a large number of questions. The normal response required of the candidate is selection of the correct solution and pencilling in part of a box according to instructions.

As every question used has been pre-tested before incorporation in a given examination paper, the examiners can be sure that no ambiguity exists and that sufficient information has been provided to allow a correct response to be made. Therefore the test paper is fair and adequately examines the candidate's knowledge and understanding of subject-matter.

An extract from the CGLI publication *Manual on Objective Testing* is given in Appendix B. It shows various types of objective items, together with hints on writing items; and notes on the use of computer assisted assessment. A test showing how items have been written in order to check retention after a short teaching input is given in Chapter Four.

Assignment 5.5 – Writing objective items

For one of your subjects write a multiple choice test covering a topic that you wish to assess.
Use the checklist[2] given below to help you to produce a valid and reliable test.

- Is the central question or problem clearly stated in stem?
- Are all distractors feasible?
- Are there no ambiguities in stem or options?
- Are all possible responses about the same length?
- Are responses grammatically correct?
- Do distractors give no clue to key?
- Are the options neither synonymous nor opposite in meaning?
- Does the stem correctly assess level of knowledge specified in objective?
- Is the stem written at appropriate language level for students?

Apply the test and evaluate the results.

List advantages and disadvantages of multiple choice testing.

5.004 Assessment methods compared

Two important areas of testing may be identified: **employment testing** and **educational testing**. The aim of this section is to outline some common types of test.

Employment testing

Employment tests take the form of a set of questions or exercises or other means by which a person's fitness for a particular job may be measured. They are also used to assess a person's suitability for a particular occupation or employment within a particular area or organisation.

1 Aptitude testing

An aptitude is the inherent natural ability to acquire a skill or particular type of knowledge. An **aptitude test** is a test of a person's ability to learn a task or of potential ability to perform a task. This type of test is sometimes called a **proficiency test**: it measures how well a person can perform a given task.

2 Performance testing

This is a procedure for measuring what a person can do. Such tests may be applied during the selection of staff for both skilled and unskilled vacancies, and often take the form of trade tests or tests of hand/eye co-ordination. For unskilled workers, tests are designed to indicate manual dexterity and accident proneness. The ability to co-ordinate hand and eye movements well goes a long way towards accident prevention. This is also very important in college laboratories and workshops where accident risk is likely to be higher.

3 Phase testing

This form of trade testing has been used extensively by vocational training providers. A series of phase tests based on modules of theoretical and practical training has been developed covering various types of training for craftspersons.

At the end of the instructional period, phase tests are administered. The purpose of the tests is to measure the progress of trainees who have undertaken the module. Elements of the assessment include dimensional accuracy, quality and time taken, although many different parameters are used to suit the specific trade concerned. Similar tests would be used as part of the selection process for skilled craftspersons applying for vacancies.

4 Personality testing

Personality testing is a procedure for measuring aspects of a person's psychological, intellectual or emotional characteristics. It is used to help in predicting their ability to fit in with others, or to indicate likely behaviour in times of stress or boredom, or where the ability to make decisions is important. This type of test is also used to discover whether a person has the special attributes required in order to perform a particular job. It is helpful when selecting staff to fill vacancies within a team or existing group, reducing the risk of incorrect placements thereby eliminating 'misfits'.

Educational testing

Testing and assessing is an essential part of the educational process. Tests are used to assess the overall efficacy of teaching and learning and to measure the attainment of objectives. Tests are most commonly used to evaluate knowledge of particular objectives following appropriate instruction and later to assess knowledge of the whole syllabus, or in the case of some courses, the whole unit.

A number of other types of test are used. **Selection tests** or **pre-requisite tests**, for example, may be used to assess a person's suitability for admission to a particular course, while **diagnostic tests** are used to detect weaknesses and to highlight difficulties experienced in specific subject areas.

Attainment tests are applied to large numbers of students with similar backgrounds in a single subject area, so that average performance or a **standardised norm** may be obtained. This may then be reliably used as a norm for smaller classes following the same type of course.

Pre-tests may be used to find out existing knowledge of course objectives before instruction commences, while **post-tests** may be applied at intervals following instruction.

Assessments may be made using internal, external, continuous assessment, periodic assessment or terminal tests. Continuous assessments often amount to 70 per cent of the marks allocated, followed by a 30 per cent terminal or end test, although test specifications for units vary.

Providing systematic formative and summative assessments

Modern techniques such as student-centred learning accommodate assessment in the form of negotiating the training outcomes during counselling and guidance sessions, debriefings and reviews. Democratically agreed outcomes of learning are then recorded on **profiles** or **competence checklists**.

Continuous assessment

As its name implies, this is an ongoing assessment of students throughout the entire course, in contrast to terminal assessment which takes place only at the conclusion.

The purpose of continuous assessment outlined in the IMS Guide[3] are

- to encourage student involvement and motivation
- to monitor and provide feedback on progress
- to help in shaping the student's future learning on the scheme.

The aim of the vocational teacher is to provide the student with a profile of assessment that ranges over the whole set of training objectives and may also include information about unintended learning. This gives a better picture of overall performance. It indicates what the student 'can do' or 'has done' rather than what the student 'knows how to do'.

Profiling

Profiling is a means of recording achievement and competence and it plays an important role in many vocational training courses that are now on offer. The profile or record of achievement produced contains details of the **formative assessments** made during training and a **summative statement of achievement** recorded on completion of the course or training.

According to Garforth and Macintosh[4] the contents of profiles should contain the following three basic elements:

- A list of items forming the basis of the assessment. These may be called 'criteria' and may be in the form of a list of skills or qualities or may be embodied within a course description.
- A means of indicating the level and/or nature of performance reached for each item in this list. Almost any means can be used including marks, grades, percentages, histograms, bar graphs, statements and descriptive assessments.

City and Guilds of London Institute   **Progress**

Main Activities:

	ABILITIES	EXAMPLES OF ABILITIES
COMMUNICATION	TALKING AND LISTENING	
	READING	
	WRITING	
PRACTICAL & NUMERICAL	USING EQUIPMENT	
	NUMERACY (I)	
SOCIAL	WORKING IN A GROUP	
	ACCEPTING RESPONSIBILITY	
DECISION-MAKING	PLANNING	
	COPING	
	OBTAINING INFORMATION	

ADDITIONAL	WORKING WITH CLIENTS	
	USING SIGNS AND DIAGRAMS	
	NUMERACY (II)	
	SAFETY	
	COMPUTER APPRECIATION	

CGL ET3.03069.© 1984 City and Guilds of London Institute

Figure 5.4 Progress profile report of the City and Guilds of London Institute (CGLI)

Profile

Profile No..........

Name of Centre and Course ....
Period covered by this Review　　　　　　　　From ....　To ....
Signed ....　　Signed ....
(Trainee/Student)　　　　　　　　　　　　　(Supervisor/Tutor)

PROGRESS IN ABILITIES

Can make sensible replies when spoken to	Can hold conversations and can take messages	Can follow and give simple descriptions and explanations	Can communicate effectively with a range of people in a variety of situations	Can present a logical and effective argument. Can analyse others' arguments
Can read words and short phrases	Can read straightforward messages	Can follow straightforward written instructions and explanations	Can understand a variety of forms of written materials	Can select and judge written materials to support an argument
Can write words and short phrases	Can write straightforward messages	Can write straightforward instructions and explanations	Can write reports describing work done	Can write a critical analysis using a variety of sources
Can use equipment safely to perform simple tasks under guidance	Can use equipment safely to perform a sequence of tasks after demonstration	Can select and use suitable equipment and materials for the job, without help	Can set up and use equipment to produce work to standard	Can identify and remedy common faults in equipment
Can count and match objects, can recognise numbers	Can add and subtract whole numbers to solve problems	Can use × and ÷ to solve whole number problems	Can add, subtract and convert decimals and simple fractions	Can multiply and divide decimals and simple fractions
Can cooperate with others when asked	Can work with other members of the group to acheive common aims	Can understand own position and results of own actions within a group	Can be an active and decisive member of a group	Can adopt a variety of roles in a group
Can follow instructions for simple tasks and carry them out under guidance	Can follow instructions for simple tasks and carry them out independently	Can follow a series of instructions and carry them out independently	Can perform a variety of tasks effectively given minimal guidance	Can assume responsibility for delegated tasks and take initiative
Can identify the sequence of steps in everyday tasks, with prompting	Can describe the sequence of steps in a routine task, after demonstration	Can choose from given alternatives the best way of tackling a task	Can modify/extend given plans/routines to meet changed circumstances	Can create new plans/ routines from scratch
Can cope with everyday activities	Can cope with everyday problems. Seeks help if needed	Can cope with changes in familiar routines	Can cope with unexpected or unusual situations	Can help others to solve problems
Can ask for needed information	Can find needed information with guidance	Can use standard sources of information	Can extract and assemble information from several given sources	Can show initiative in seeking and gathering information from a wide variety of sources
Can help someone to carry out clients' requests	Can carry out clients' requests under supervision	Can carry out clients' requests without supervision	Can anticipate and fulfil clients' needs from existing resources	Can suggest realistic improvements to services for clients
Can recognise everyday signs and symbols	Can make use of simple drawings, maps, timetables	Can make use of basic graphs, charts, codes technical drawings, with help	Can interpret and use basic graphs, charts and technical drawings unaided	Can construct graphs and extract information to support conclusions
Can estimate answers to tasks involving whole numbers decimals and simple fractions	Can calculate percentages and averages	Can solve problems involving simple ratios and proportions	Can express a problem in terms of a simple formula and solve it	
Can remember safety instructions	Can explain the need for safety rules	Can spot safety hazards	Can apply safe working practices independently	
Can recognise everyday uses of computers	Can use keyboard to gain access to data	Can enter data into the system using existing programs	Can identify potential applications for computers	

– An indication of the evidence used to arrive at the description provided. This element is unfortunately often ignored but it is vital to indicate the context in which a particular skill is assessed if the nature of its performance is to be fully understood.

These three elements can be seen in the progress profile report of the City and Guilds of London Institute (CGLI) shown in Figure 5.4. The level of performance for each item is identified by indicating the most appropriate statement in the five boxes on the right hand side of the report. The tutor then uses the blank section on the left to describe in what context the skill was displayed and to indicate the kind of evidence on which the performance assessment is based.

There are a number of different style profiles in use and it may be necessary for readers to familiarise themselves with some of these or to design their own to suit needs of clients.

Formative and summative assessments

Formal assessment is the formal impersonal testing or measuring of student learning which often leads to the award of a certificate. It is not necessarily a terminal test or examination, since it may occur within a course in the form of continuous assessment. **Informal assessment** is the informal feedback required by students in order that they may be able to assess their own performance. This will include knowledge about their strengths and weaknesses and what they will need to do next in order to master the skills, knowledge and attitudes that are important to them and required in a particular area of study.

Formative assessment or **evaluation** is a process designed to improve the teaching system by feeding back information from tests or negotiations that can be used to justify training methods used or to identify learning difficulties. The process is ongoing so that if regular assessments of progress are made, the system can be modified to overcome problems identified. (It is no good waiting until the end of the course to put matters right!) **Summative assessment** is made at the end of the programme in order to determine the overall effectiveness of training and learning outcomes. This type of assessment can also be made at the conclusion of, or at any break point in course activity to evaluate its effectiveness. It can also be used for certification purposes.

In order to provide systematic formative and summative assessments, teachers must be able to evaluate individual and group performance against learning objectives and provide feedback on achievement during negotiated assessment sessions that are spread over a period of time. They must also:
– explain the purpose of initial assessment in a programme of negotiation and be clear as to his or her own role in the process
– explain the criteria on which performance standards are set
– identify an appropriate range of assessment methods

- use appropriate assessments to measure students' performance or assist students to carry out self-appraisal against each learning objective
- operate a recording and reviewing system founded on the use of initial and ongoing formative assessment.

Purpose of initial assessment

'Initial assessment is intended to influence decisions concerning students' placement and progress.'[5]

It is no use trying to fit a square peg into a round hole. While in many cases school-leavers have not had the opportunity to develop all of their potential aptitudes there will always be some occupations for which they would probably be unsuited. Some form of selection is therefore necessary, and initial assessment is part of this process.

Trainability testing can form part of an initial assessment. It is used to get an idea of a student's suitability for training in given competences. Trainability tests are applied to students before or during induction. The tests are practical and involve the young person in performing a specific job-related task for which they have been given prior instruction. The number of errors made is noted and a performance rating is allocated. The tests measure job aptitude and training potential.

After the test, individual performance is discussed with the students and a mutual decision is made as to whether the applicant is likely to benefit from training in the skills needed to perform the job. This could well be the first negotiating experience for the students, so great care should be exercised to make it a pleasant one.

In *People and Work*[6] the following advantages of trainability testing are given:
- save wasting expensive training on unsuitable applicants
- reduce average training time
- involve instructors in selection
- check claims of previous experience
- channel applicants into work appropriate to their skills
- highlight potential weak spots
- indicate probable length of training required and likely overall level of competence.

Trainability test results can help the students to assess their own potential. The tests enable them to
- demonstrate practical skills
- build up confidence
- get a taste of the job
- meet the teachers
- avoid unnecessary stress caused by failing to meet performance targets during training.

The teacher's role in the initial assessment procedure is to make the students feel at home, to conduct the assessment fairly and efficiently and to encourage them to reflect on their experiences. Negotiation then follows, during which the students' competences and strengths are identified and recorded.

Subsequent assessment

Throughout the training programme, formal assessments can be made by setting criterion tests. Informal assessments may also be made and these involve negotiating with students or carrying out **trainee-centred reviewing.**

Criterion-referenced testing (in which a student is assessed relative to certain pre-determined standards, such as course objectives,) may be used in preference to norm-referenced testing that compares the student's performance relative to other students or to an average for a group of students. With criterion-referenced tests the student will pass if performance against standards is successful. This system of assessment depends to some extent on the teacher adopting a modular approach to training where successful completion of one learning step leads on to the next.

Norm-referenced testing is often applied to nationally-set examinations for a large number of candidates. With this type of testing, individual scores are compared with the scores of all other candidates. Results are collated and then plotted. A normal distribution curve usually results.

Pre-tests applied before training commences tend to yield scores that are normally distributed, whereas **local criterion tests** tend to be biased towards the high end of the marking scale. This is because criterion tests are designed to measure specific performance and are formulated directly from a limited number of objectives.

Norm-referencing is not ideal for vocational training assessment. If results are taken on face value, it would appear that those who score high marks have learned more than lower scorers. This is not always true because unless all training objectives are included in the terminal tests, the scores will bear little relationship with total course content. The effects of coaching and practice on IQ tests and 'question-spotting' in examinations that allow a choice of questions to be answered are well known.

Appropriate range of assessment methods

A selection of the types of test that may be used for assessment purposes is listed here:

- multiple choice
- short answer
- practical work
- workshop projects
- tasks in the field
- model making
- community and social activities
- physical education activities
- project reports
- reports of visits or industrial training
- verbal reports of interviews
- group activity assessments
- tutor observation of students at work
- work experience tasks.

Assignment 5.6 – **Assessing competence within NVQs**

Inconsistency in assessor and verifier practices has been identified by QCA as a serious problem affecting the efficient operation of NVQs. Being aware of this and in order to maintain the quality of assessment for their qualifications, City and Guilds prescribes certain roles and responsibilities for assessors appointed to their Approved Centres. It is the responsibility of the assessor to ensure that:

– agreement is reached on the evidence presented of prior achievement
– an assessment plan is agreed with the candidate
– the candidate is fully briefed on the assessment process
– he/she follows the assessment guidance given by City and Guilds and the centre
– he/she records all questions and responses which are used for the purposes of meeting the evidence requirements and range in the standard
– he/she gives the candidate prompt, accurate and constructive feedback
– he/she confirms that the candidate has demonstrated competence and completes the documentation required by City and Guilds and the centre
– he/she gives constructive feedback on the candidate's competence and agrees a new assessment plan with the candidate if further evidence is required.[7]

To what extent do your current S/NVQ roles, responsibilities and assessment practices conform to those listed above or those recommended by your awarding body?

Assignment 5.7 – **Designing a profile**

For one of your groups, design a student-centred profile that will enable the learners to participate in a form of self-assessment or alternatively complete the profiling jointly with the teacher or peers.

Before designing the profile, examine those already in use in your employing institution or carry out a literature search that may provide insight into the task.

When designing your profile consider some of the key criteria proposed by Garforth and Macintosh:[8]

– What are the main purposes of the profile?
– Who is to be profiled?
– What is to be assessed?
– How is the assessment to be undertaken?
– Who is to be involved in the assessment process?
– How are the results of the assessment to be recorded?

5.005 Classifying and evaluating assessment methods

Tests are set for a variety of reasons and can take many forms. There are also many different types of item format available to test constructors. In his informative *Notes for Guidance*, Roy Whitlow of Bristol Polytechnic has produced a number of tables giving details of test purposes and likely outcomes. Types of test items and their applications are also shown. The tables given in Figures 5.5, 5.6 and 5.7 are an excellent guide to test contructors, in that for each category of test, a note is given of what the test will indicate and of any requirements for pre-testing, sampling and the like. Examples of the various test items are also clearly laid out.

Purpose	Measures/indicates	Requirements
1 Evaluation of instruction	Effectiveness of an instructional sequence or procedure when applied to a particular group.	Pre-test/post-test systems to consider group achievements in terms of overall objectives and skill enhancement.
2 Comparison of instruction	Comparative effectiveness of instructional sequences or procedures, or instructors.	Pre-test/post-test systems in terms of group achievements either cross-sequence or cross-group based.
3 Assessment of individuals (a) for awards	Level of graduation to be accorded, or suggested pass/fail decision.	Sampling of all the individual's work considered relevant, using mainly content-standard test scores.
(b) to determine transfer to higher grade	Suitability, or otherwise, of individual for transfer to the next (higher) part of a course.	Sampling of all work at present grade using mainly content-standard tests.
(c) to measure progress	Degree of mastery of specified objectives and skills	Specific objective-related tests (criterion-referenced) of a progressive nature.
(d) to predict future achievement levels and success expectancy	A prognosis relating the level of achievement that may be anticipated to that required for success, i.e. pass/fail, graduation.	Criterion-referenced tests that can be interpreted in probabilistic terms.
(e) diagnosis of weaknesses and difficulties	Areas of weakness or misunderstanding in specific subjects; individual ability problems, e.g. language, reading difficulty.	Structured and graded criterion-referenced tests in limited areas of study as part of feedback-correction procedures.
(f) self criticism reward by individual.	To the individual, some of the aspects of 3(c), 3(d), 3(e). Provides a measure of reward either in terms of the score or in progress to the next item.	Structured criterion-referenced tests with in-built success pattern, e.g. programmed-learning text.
4 Consolidation of learning	Usually very little except that those completing the test have made the effort and have therefore added to what had been previously taught.	Exercises which extend individuals beyond the levels already achieved; usually with subjective assessment (e.g. essays) or short-scale content-standard tests.

(Source: *Notes for Guidance* R. Whitlow, Bristol Polytechnic)

Figure 5.5 Tests: purposes, indications and requirements

Type/Description	Examples

Multiple-choice   Type M
Test items requiring less
than 3 minutes for
answering or completion
	1 Multi-choice recall
	2 Associative recall
	3 Completion, e.g. of sentence, diagram
	4 Matching and association
	5 Analogies, sets, lists, etc.
	6 Alternative response e.g. true/false, yes/no
	7 Rank-ordering, arrangements
	8 Reaction and association including physical stimulus/
	    cognitive reasoning e.g. picture association, verbal reaction,
	    tactile reaction, etc.

Short answer Type S Test items requiring from 3 to 40 minutes for answering or completion	1 Short essay (associative or critical) 2 Short essay (descriptive) 3 Comparative listings, tabulations, classifications 4 Annotated sketches and diagrams, illustrated definitions, descriptions, etc. 5 Creative short essays and/or sketching 6 Computations, problem solving and analytical exercises
Long answer Type L Test items requiring more than 40 minutes for answering or completion	1 Long essays (descriptive or imitative) 2 Long essays (creative) 3 Problem solving or long analytical exercises 4 Long computation exercises

Practical work   Type P
Items essentially designed
to test psychomotor
skills
	1 Laboratory work including language laboratory, audio/
	    visual exercises, radio/TV exercises and other creative/
	    discovery exercises
	2 Workshop exercises
	3 Exercises in the field, e.g. surveying, site investigation
	4 Technical and/or geometrical drawing
	5 Model making
	6 Fine art exercises
	7 Community and social activities
	8 Physical education activities

Coursework Type C Test items integrated into coursework and the learning process	1 Reports of laboratory and other practical work 2 Reports of projects 3 Reports of visits, industrial training, etc. 4 Commentaries on events 5 Verbal reports, interviews, etc. 6 Group activity assessments, e.g. discussions, seminars 7 Tutor observations of specific objective attainment

(Source: *Notes for Guidance* R. Whitlow, Bristol Polytechnic)

Figure 5.6 Types of test items

Testing individual student attainment

Individual students may be assessed for a number of reasons:

– to provide evidence for profiling recording
– for awards
– to measure progress

– to determine suitability for progression
– to predict future performance levels and outcomes
– to diagnose learning difficulties
– to encourage motivation derived from knowledge of results
– to confirm and consolidate learning.

The type of assessment instrument that could be used to determine individual attainment is given in Figure 5.5.

Type/description	Application
Multiple-choice Consisting entirely of Type M items.	Mainly skill areas ICAF* (in order of decreasing suitability). Intermittent and short stage test, basic abilities grading tests, pre-/post-testing, formative testing, tests associated with programmed and/or packaged learning.
Short answer Consisting entirely of Type S items.	All skill areas generally. Stage tests, terminal tests, both formative and summative, in-class testing, private-study testing. More useful than M for expressive and creative work.
Long answer Consisting of one or more Type L items.	All skill areas generally. More useful than M or S for expressive and creative work, of limited use in terminal testing, well suited to private-study testing.
Practical test Consisting essentially of Type P items.	Specifically to test psychomotor skills, with or without associated intellectual skills.
Coursework Consisting of items integrated within coursework.	That portion of coursework functioning as a test, whether formative or summative, that is to be incorporated in the overall assessment.
Oral test Test question and response given orally.	May include written, visual, aural or tactile stimuli, but strictly oral question and response. Particularly useful for testing level and type of response.
Terminal test Test given at the end of the learning process related to a unit or part.	Usually a timed, unseen examination demanding written and/or graphic response, with or without study aids (e.g. course notes, texts, information sheets, etc.).

*Note: Skills Area   I = Invention
                      C = Comprehension
                      A = Application
                      F = Factual recall

(Source: *Notes for Guidance* R. Whitlow, Bristol Polytechnic)

Figure 5.7 Applications of test items

Testing progress of learning group as a whole

Group assessment profiles provide an excellent means of representing test information. Frith and Macintosh[9] describe the visual presentation of profiles and give three examples of the assessment profiles devised by Overson (1980). The profiles are reproduced in Figures 5.8, 5.9 and 5.10.

The diagrams take the form of a series of concentric circles that represent results of assessments given as percentages, with lines radiating from the centre that

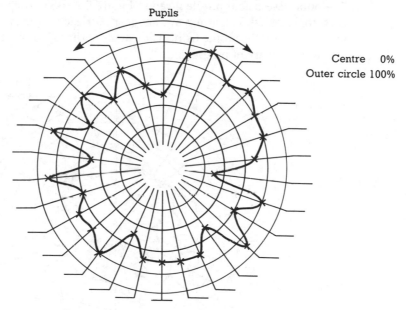

Figure 5.8 Group assessment profile: top set physics group (Test 1)

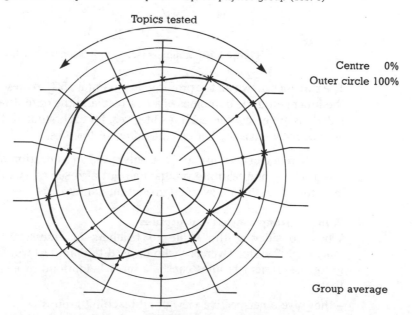

Figure 5.9 Pupil assessment profile: top set physics pupil

represent individual students and in one case topics tested. Although the examples given relate to a physics group the principle can be applied to the assessment of any subject. In the case of Figure 5.8, all individual student results are plotted on a group assessment profile that can be used when evaluating teaching and learning experiences. Subsequent results can be superimposed on the original profile thereby providing intelligence about progress and outcomes that can be utilised during reviewing and monitoring sessions.

The pupil assessment profile given in Figure 5.9 shows the individual's results for each topic tested. The group average mark for each topic is calculated and this is also marked on the profile using a dot, star or other symbol. The profile provides an accurate measure of progress.

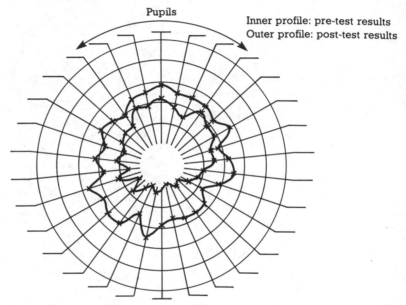

Pupils

Inner profile: pre-test results
Outer profile: post-test results

Figure 5.10 Group assessment profile: mixed ability group

The two lines drawn on the profile given in Figure 5.10 represent two sets of results: the inner being the outcomes of a 'pre-test' and the outer that of a 'post-test'. The radial distance between each result gives, for each student, the **gain score** that is derived by comparing 'before' and 'after' test scores.

The difference between scores not only gives an indication of the effectiveness of the teaching and learning programme but also serves as a diagnostic tool when monitoring methodology and curriculum content.

Value of group assessment profiles

When considering the value to teachers of assessment profiles Frith and Macintosh[10] write: 'Overson [who devised the profiles] would argue strongly that group assessment profiles can be a most helpful aid to modern management in that:

– they give a perspective view of all teaching groups
– the spread of ability within each group is immediately apparent

– the effect of curriculum modification can be monitored
– the effect of a change in teaching methods can be monitored
– they can be used for diagnostic purposes.'

Discovering student learning problems

In industrial terms, the **feedback** concept applies to linking a system's outputs to its inputs, thereby keeping the system under control. In education, feedback provided by various methods of assessment supplies information about the progress of teaching and learning to the 'education and training system'.

Feedback may also be obtained during performance reviews and reflection-and-review sessions when learners are able to appreciate just how well they have done by a process of comparison and verification of performance against standards. Where there is a need to do better, they are able to negotiate further learning opportunities relating to the objectives under discussion.

In some cases feedback is immediately available as a direct outcome of an unsuccessful attempt to achieve something, as in the case of a weightlifter who fails to lift a certain mass. However, the reasons for the failure may be reviewed with a trainer, who having observed the attempt, would be able to give feedback on the process that led to the failure to lift.

In a social and life skills training context, feedback is given by an observer during 'report-back' sessions, the object being to provide information about group and individual behaviour in the hope that behavioural problems may be overcome.

While feedback is unlikely to alter broad course aims, it does bear heavily on the specific behavioural outcomes that are written into the course objectives. It may

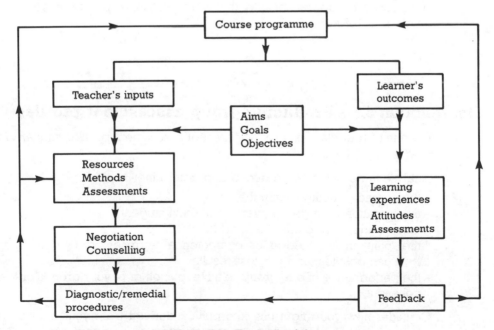

Figure 5.11 The feedback loop

well be that expected behaviour, conditions or standards of performance are revised as a direct result of comments fed back by learners and of performance indicators derived from assessments.

Learners will expect the teacher to act on feedback if motivation and co-operation are to be maintained and performance improved. Analysing feedback may be the best way of discovering a student's learning problems. Using feedback resulting from learning experiences or assessments, necessary changes in both teacher's and learner's contributions may be planned. Feedback can also be used to direct a learner to suitable diagnostic and remedial procedures.

The way that the feedback dimension fits into the course programme is shown in Figure 5.11.

Assignment 5.8 – **Evaluation of assessment procedures in use**

Using Whitlow's 'List of tests, purposes, indications and requirements'; 'Types of test items' and 'Application of test items' (Figures 5.5–5.7) as checklists, carry out an appraisal of those assessment systems that you personally use and consider whether the methods fulfil their intended purpose.

What use is made of the results of the assessments?

Is any part of your assessment process duplicated by others in the institution?

Upon reflection, do you consider that your assessment provision is too little, too much or just right?

Assignment 5.9 – **Producing group assessment profiles**

For one of your classes, produce a set of assessment profiles similar to those devised by Overson.

Analyse the profiles so produced and determine:
- the spread of ability within the group
- the deviation from group average of each student
- those students who may need additional help
- the 'gain' in knowledge or competence represented by the difference between post-test and pre-test results
- the performance of one group relative to another of your groups or that of a colleague.

Consider how you might use information derived from your analysis of the profiles to improve your performance and that of your students.

5.006 Planning and preparing assessment procedures

Test purposes

Before writing a test it is necessary to consider its purpose and to decide what use can be made of the results. It is no use testing for testing's sake.

One of the main outcomes of evaluation by means of a criterion test is that it measures changes in students' behaviour against performance objectives. It measures competence against objectives set. However, other valuable information can be extracted from a set of test results.

Marks are often listed and students ranked in order of 'success' in attaining course objectives. The listing is in itself of some use in identifying regularly high achievers who might in consequence progress to more difficult or demanding work, or to specialised activities. Similarly, low achievers could be singled out and helpful remedial action taken, either to improve their performance in the areas of study with their learning group, or by referring them to a specialist or qualified counsellor for help.

From a teacher's viewpoint, test results show up strengths and weaknesses in the course design and teaching and learning methodology. Where objectives have not been met, the curriculum needs to be modified to overcome weaknesses and if necessary, additional resources employed to remedy shortcomings in performance.

Terminal or **end-test results** are helpful in evaluating the outcomes of learning. Unfortunately, unlike monitoring, the evaluation generally takes place after the course has finished when it is too late to do much for the current year's students. The main point of evaluating end-of-year results is that the course team members will be able to review the curriculum and incorporate improvements when the course is next offered. Performance tests yield valuable data for manpower planners in that they will know exactly what the students should be capable of doing in an industrial or commercial context.

Pre-requisite tests are set in order to assess the suitability of an applicant to undertake a course or training programme. This type of test is not specifically related to theory or detailed knowledge of a given process. It is designed to test the suitability of an applicant to undergo a course of study or training within a given area. Abilities tested may include manual dexterity, spatial ability, literacy or numeracy, while much attention is paid to problem-solving skills and the cognitive, affective and motor skills concepts.

Pre-tests are designed to find out what, if anything, the candidates know about the content of a proposed course of study. If admitted to the course selected, the student will be able to start at an appropriate point in the programme.

Post-tests are given as soon as possible after instruction and practice ends, whether this be at the end of a lesson or at the end of the course. **Retention tests** are given later — some time after the course has finished. They are designed to reveal just how much of the subject matter previously learned can be recalled or demonstrated. If the subject matter or behaviour learned is not reinforced by subsequent repetition, there will in general be a marked difference between post-test and retention test results.

Assessment planning

The first step in the preparation of an assessment plan is to consider the test purposes described in Section 5.005; and then to relate the proposed assessment to the needs of students, and to the requirements of qualification-awarding bodies, employers, higher education, the National Training Organisation (NTO) and the course provider.

Assessment procedures should be introduced in co-operation with the candidates who will be assessed. Where possible, they should incorporate written, practical and oral techniques that enable an adequate and fair profile of competence to be established. They should be planned so that validity, reliability of content and attainment criteria may be ensured, and outcomes should be validated using standardised procedures and forms of certification.

Assessment specifications: example 1

The information reproduced in Figure 5.12 gives the unit breakdown, by topic and types of learning, as a key to the assessment specification for 'Instructional Techniques and Practice'. Each 'Unit topic area' (denoted by a capital letter) subsumes the general objectives, teaching goals, and the specific objectives for student attainment. The specification gives a breakdown of the motor skills and intellectual skills as percentages of each topic assessment. The intellectual skills are sub-divided into categories similar to those given in Bloom's *Taxonomy* (see page 19), each with varying weightings appropriate to the topic. In this case Bloom's top three cognitive categories — analysis, synthesis and evaluation — have been grouped together to form 'Invention'.

Without some form of assessment specification, it is not possible to prepare a reliable and balanced set of test papers or other assessments.

Unit topic area	Topic as % of assessment	% of total assessment				
		Motor skills	Information	Comprehension	Application	Invention
A	45		3	14	14	14
B	11		1	10		
C	8		1	5		2
D	6	2	1	1		2
E	30	5			15	10
% of assessment for entire unit		7	6	30	29	28

Figure 5.12 Assessment specification

Assessment specifications: example 2

Bus and Coach Training Limited circulated nationally agreed standards for Passenger Carrying Driving Instructors that set out general objectives, standards and assessment methods. The assessment scheme covered the following:

– demonstration of driving skills
– knowledge of *The Highway Code*
                    Passenger Carrying Vehicle Legislation
                    Road Transport Regulations
                    basic mechanical principles
                    instructional techniques
                    factors affecting learning
– demonstration of instructional skills.

Candidates needed to have a thorough knowledge of *The Highway Code* and be familiar with the Driving Standards Agency publication *The Official Bus and Coach Driving Manual*. They needed to give a commentary while undertaking a demonstration drive to standards laid down for the PCV driving licence, observed by an assessor.

Questions would be asked concerning all the aspects of knowledge listed above, and candidates would be required to undertake demonstrations of instructional ability in driving and static situations. Assessment was mainly work-based.

Element	Duration (mins)	Method of assessment	Pass mark or standard
Demonstration of driving skills	75	Practical with commentary	Driving Standards Agency PCV driving licence standard
Road Transport Regulations Basic mechanical principles Instructional techniques *The Highway Code*	90	Multiple-choice questions	70% 70% 70% 80%
Demonstration of instructional ability	25 55 30	'In cab' static 'In cab' mobile Lecture	Competence in planning and 'can do'

Figure 5.13 Assessment specification (PCV instructors)

Assessment specifications: example 3

'Experiential learning' is defined as 'learning through experience rather than through study or formal instruction'.[11]

The assessment stages as specified by Norman Evans[12] are:

– identify 'life experience learning' by allowing learner to reflect on experience and review outcomes with accreditor
– relate elements of such learning to course objectives
– verify behaviour using 'can do' evidence of learning

– measure degree of learning
– evaluation against competence objective or other standard
– accredit and record previous learning.

The draft specification given in Figure 5.14 is intended only as an aid to discussion and identification of relevant experience during the reflection-and-review session.

What to assess	How learned	Evidence of learning	How assessed	Accredited by

Figure 5.14 Recognising 'life experience' credits

Assignment 5.10 – Planning and preparing assessment procedures

For one of your courses, design an assessment plan and prepare assessment procedures and instruments.

Relate the plan and assessments to course aims and objectives. Administer and evaluate the outcomes during teaching practice.

Assignment 5.11 – Preparing a marking scheme

Having designed an assessment that is both valid and reliable, it is now necessary to produce a marking scheme that will enable the marker to evaluate the responses as fairly and accurately as possible.

The need to prepare a comprehensive marking scheme becomes even more desirable when the setting is done by one teacher and the marking by others.

Frith and Macintosh[13] recommend the use of the following checklist that may be helpful when preparing mark schemes:

– Are suggested answers appropriate to the questions?
– Are suggested answers technically and/or numerically correct?
– Does the scheme embrace every point required by the question and allocate marks for each point?
– Does model answer include only those points required by the question?
– Are the marks allocated strictly according to the knowledge and abilities which the question requires the candidate to demonstrate?
– Is there adequate provision for acceptable alternative answers?
– Are marks commensurate with degree of difficulty of question and time needed to answer it?
– Is time allowance appropriate for work required?

- Is scheme sufficiently broken down to allow marking to be as objective as possible?
- Is the totalling of marks correct?
- Does scheme reflect undue bias towards one viewpoint at expense of others?

Mark half the students' test papers yourself and ask a colleague to mark the remaining papers, using your marking scheme.

When you have both finished, exchange papers and check for consistency of marking standards against the marking scheme.

Discuss any discrepancies and adjust the marking scheme in the light of suggestions.

Assignment 5.12 – Assessing experiential learning

Conduct a reflection and review session with a student using the draft specification given in Figure 5.14 as an aid to discussion and identification of relevant experience. Use the assessment stages given in the text above or that suggested in the FEU Report by Norman Evans below[14] as a guide to procedure:

- introduction to general idea of the assessment of experiental learning and to the requirements laid upon students
- identification of previous learning experience
- sorting and clarifying those learning experiences
- describing previous learning
- documenting previous learning
- demonstrating previous learning
- evaluating previous learning
- recording and interpreting previous learning.[15]

Notes and references

1 C. Ward, *Designing a scheme of assessment*, Stanley Thornes (Publishers) Ltd, Cheltenham 1980, pp 104–5.
2 D.S. Frith and H.G. Macintosh, *A Teacher's Guide to Assessment*, Stanley Thornes (Publishers) Ltd, Cheltenham 1984, p 61.
3 *Training for Skill Ownership in the Youth Training Scheme*, IMS, Brighton 1983, p 51.
4 D. Garforth and H. Macintosh, *Profiling: a User's Manual*, Stanley Thornes (Publishers) Ltd, Cheltenham 1986, pp 2–4. This is a valuable source of reference for those wishing to familiarise themselves with a variety of performance profiles.
5 *Training for Skill Ownership in the Youth Training Scheme*, IMS, Brighton 1983, p 51.
6 *People and Work*, MSC Training Services Division, London 1979, pp 2–6.
7 *NVQ in Training and Development Level 4 7281/05 Candidate Pack*, City and Guilds, London 1995, p 8.
8 D. Garforth and H. Macintosh, *Ibid.*, pp 21–30.
9 D.S. Frith and H.G. Macintosh, *Ibid*, pp 172–3.
10 D.S. Frith and H.G. Macintosh, *Ibid*, p 173.
11 *Review of Vocational Qualifications in England and Wales*, MSC/DES, London, April 1986.
12 N. Evans, *Assessing Experiential Learning*, FEU/Longman, London 1987.
13 D.S. Frith and H.G. Macintosh, *Ibid*, p 93.
14 N. Evans, *Curriculum Opportunity*, FEU, London 1983, pp 85–6.
15 Evidence gathered could be used by candidates working towards Unit D36 *Advise and Support Candidates to Identify Prior Achievement*.

CHAPTER SIX

Communication

Aim: To develop the abilities of teachers to communicate, thereby enhancing their effectiveness as educators, and to enable them to assist students to develop their own communication skills

6.001 Identifying socio-cultural influences on language

Communication is the art of successfully sharing meaningful information with people by means of an interchange of experience. The important word is 'successfully', which implies that a desired behaviour change results when the receiver takes in the message.

In a teaching situation the teacher could transmit information for the whole period, but there is no guarantee that the information will have been received by the students. The teacher needs to be able to assess problems of understanding, embarrassment and confusion in students. Instruction should be pitched at a level commensurate with their previous knowledge, especially when introducing abstract concepts and technical terms. Simple words carrying the meaning should be used whenever possible.

Socio-economic status

Many teachers are of the opinion that differences in educational opportunity are manifested by the ability or lack of ability of students to form concepts, ideas and attitudes, and to use the vocabularies — mental and verbal — that they possess.

For many people, differences in socio-economic status will inevitably affect life chances and also influence the quality of written and oral communications when in an educational environment. Social class remains a key factor in the degree of benefit that can be derived from educational opportunity. The terms 'socially disadvantaged' and 'socially handicapped' are used to describe people whose family background, accommodation or lifestyle and other social conditions put them at a disadvantage when contrasted with others who have a higher standard of living together with an expectation of a pattern of education that will ensure a decent lifestyle later in life.

Educational disadvantage is often linked with social disadvantage, and the opportunity to be derived from available education provision may well be greatly reduced as a result. There is no suggestion that the principle of equality in education is denied the socio-economically disadvantaged. However although equality of educational opportunity is administratively available, the expectations, attitudes and situations of society's lower status people (in terms of social class), may make them unwilling or unable to seize the opportunities on offer.

Problems in written and oral communications

Written and oral communications may be affected by socio-economic and cultural influences, so teachers need to be aware of the likelihood of differences in performance by students from different backgrounds. Language deficiencies resulting in impaired progress and development are influenced by many factors including: level of intelligence; socio-economic cultural background and degree of verbal stimulation at home; and social dialects resulting from origin and social environment of those concerned.

Underachievement is a term used to describe academic achievement that is below par when compared with expectations raised by results of IQ tests. Performance that does not match expectations may be associated with factors linking with socio-economic conditions, so that problems at home, lack of drive and poor motivation may be inducing problems in class that could be mistaken for lack of ability.

Literacy and the influence of language on learning have been the subject of a great deal of study, and eminent researchers such as Bernstein, Chomsky, Douglas, Floud, Halsey, Labov and Skinner have written volumes on the way people acquire language; the effects of social class on linguistic development; the effects of home life and schooling on language and learning; theories of acquisition by imitation or by innate ability to learn; language competence potential and the relationships between social and cultural constraints on performance. The quantity and variety of this type of research is considerable, and beyond the scope of this book. Only a very brief introduction to the work of Basil Bernstein is included in this chapter.

People with special needs

Special schools and day centres are available for young people with special educational needs caused by physical, emotional or behavioural conditions. Some students with special needs have already been accommodated in mainstream colleges, although there is still a long way to go in providing adequate facilities for them. Efforts are being made by the Government and others to integrate those with special educational needs into mainstream education and training. Schemes such as Lifelong Learning, Basic and Key Skills, and Modern Apprenticeships are paving the way for post-16 education and training provision, but staff development training will need to be available to those teachers wishing to work effectively in this field.

Language codes

Language is the characteristic feature of communication and is the means by which thought processes are manifested. Languages are sets of rules, and the application of these rules makes possible the formation and understanding of sentences. If the rules are known and the appropriate vocabulary available to listeners, then they will be able to interpret sentences that they have never heard before. Similarly, they will be able to assemble words in a form that will be readily understood by others with access to the same language.

Basil Bernstein[1] refers to two main language codes: the **elaborate code** and the **restricted code**. The elaborate code is the language code of the middle classes and is described as 'universalistic' or 'non-specific', while the restricted code is used by the working classes and is 'particularistic' or 'context bound'. Bernstein emphasises the fact that while restricted-code speakers may use the elaborate code from time to time, such instances will be infrequent during socialisation within a family. He goes on to say that speech patterns are influenced by one's position in the social structure. As cultural values and life expectancies are linked to social class, manual workers inevitably find themselves at the lower end of the social scale.

The socialisation of children within a family affects their linguistic styles. In consequence, there are significant differences between the elaborate code of the higher socio-economic groups and the restricted code of the lower classes. The restricted code is characterised by the usage of short, simple and unplanned sentences. This limits the scope of expression. On the other hand the elaborate code enables middle-class speakers to make clear their intended meanings. The possession of a large number of alternative words makes easy the elaborating of statements.

The difference in language codes greatly affects what is learned and the ability to understand the spoken word. This is particularly evident in schools or other academic arenas where teachers almost invariably use an elaborate code. The teacher's language, while readily understood by those already familiar with this code, is not clearly understood by those who use a restricted language code. The danger here is that much of what is said simply washes over the heads of listeners. Consequently, if the language is not understood then the intended concept will not be internalised and many levels of abstraction will be beyond their capacity.

Simple, direct speech has its advantages. Many trade unionists and others with a working-class background have achieved important positions in society due to their ability to put forward an argument in a clear, unambiguous manner. Such clarity need not be lost in the classroom, so long as the teacher's language is kept as simple as the particular concept allows.

Multicultural education

Teacher training relating to staff development in a multicultural society is now a national priority. In the DES circular 9/87 issued in September, 1987, a new category was added to the list of national priorities, namely, 'Training in teaching and planning of the further education (FE) curriculum in a multicultural society'. The circular proposed that all staff training courses should deal with the existence in society of different ethnic groups, cultures and beliefs and should address race, community relations and discrimination.

It is obvious that all teachers undergoing training need to develop competence in working with and teaching people from multi-ethnic groups, whatever the ethnic make-up of the catchment area they serve. This is not to say that some kind of special strategy exclusive to multicultural teaching is either possible or desirable; but it is important to realise that the influence of cultural background, language and experience of racism has a considerable effect on the learning process.

A number of reports, studies and publications recognise that FE in Britain has not in the past served the black communities as effectively as it has the white majority. Equally important is the suggestion that FE has not always used the curriculum opportunities available to challenge racial discrimination, racist assumptions and cultural bias. Changes therefore need to be made at institutional and course level, backed by teachers and students at individual levels.

Managerial staff need to mount awareness-raising projects to inform teachers and students of the need to avoid unacceptable practices or to take corrective action if they are already operating. Staff and students also need to be alerted to the national situation as well as that within their own institution.

To this end a national programme coordinated by Harminder Aujla was instigated and a staff development package was developed in collaboration with and edited by the Further Education Unit (FEU). The package included modules entitled: 'Curriculum Change'; 'Institutional Change'; 'Teaching and Learning Strategies'; and 'Strategies in Mainly White Areas'.[2] Today, many teachers, careers advisers and support workers are striving to meet the educational needs of refugees and asylum seekers and to recognise the special requirements of speakers of languages other than English.

Communicating and consulting with students and trainees

A responsible teacher needs to consult with learners, regardless of their ethnic background; the object being to adopt a sensitive attitude to their views. Some suggest that current practice allows only limited opportunity for black students to voice their views about learning experiences by way of course reviews and evaluations.

Counselling should be available from staff with whom students from ethnic minority groups can relate, and it is a teacher's duty to provide a secure atmosphere in which consultation may take place. In order to demonstrate equal opportunities it is essential that teachers or tutors plan and facilitate counselling and guidance sessions. During these sessions, student perceptions of what they have been experiencing during the learning process can be discussed and comments later fed back to course teams. By this means, co-operation may be promoted and, where necessary, remedial action taken to rectify shortcomings in the curriculum.

Where necessary, appropriate links allowing consultation with ethnic minority groups and their community leaders in the locality should be established. It is also important to ensure that black employers are consulted concerning the nature, form and content of educational provision and its delivery.

All students could be involved in drawing up an ethnic profile of the catchment community that would assist with curriculum planning. This processs would also promote better understanding of realities rather than often held negative attitudes based on stereotyping or prejudice. Better integration within the classroom would also be encouraged through this interaction.

Teaching and learning strategies

Teachers need to be able to assist in developing and introducing new methodology where necessary; and skills in delivering, monitoring progress and quality, appraising outcomes and evaluating the effect of the teaching and learning within the multi-ethnic classroom or workshop need to be acquired.

The role of language in learning, especially where unfamiliar subject-related technical terminology is used, plays a crucial part in the value of the classroom experience and this is particularly true where English is the student's second language. The creative use of the mother tongue in the classroom should be encouraged as this is likely to reinforce learning — student talk is in many cases the most important talk we are likely to hear in the classroom. What the students say to the teacher and to one another is probably one of the better sources of learning experience; for it is language that carries the meaning derived from learning.

Issues of racism within FE and adult education establishments have to be faced and eliminated and the attitude reflected by the teacher will considerably affect the ease with which the issue is resolved; the same goes for work placement situations. Subject matter should be directed towards the history, technology, commerce, commodities or feats of architecture that represent high achievements by other cultures, rather than areas of under-achievement. Incompetent, ignorant peoples did not create the Seven Wonders of the World or massive structures such as the domes seen in temples in the Indian sub-continent.

It has been reported in FEU publications that in terms of culture there is considerable evidence of insensitivity and misconception relating to the background experience and aspirations of the different ethnic minority groups. The modern teacher must be aware of this possibility and lay plans to enlighten people with negative attitudes to minority groups, and be prepared to tackle racism in the classroom and work placements. It is likely that vigorous curriculum change will go a long way towards solving the problem.

Assignment 6.1 – **Identifying the effects of socio-economic and cultural influences on language**

Identify within your student groups any possible effects of socio-economic and cultural influences on language and the problems in written and oral communication that may result. Apply knowledge acquired during this assignment to suggest ways of improving matters.

Student sensitivity to language and terminology

The joint FEU/NUS publication, *FE can really change your life* is based on a seminar held by the National Union of Students, funded by FEU and hosted by the Commission for Racial Equality. The aim of the seminar was 'to give black students an opportunity to talk about their experience of FE, in order to suggest ways in which colleges can respond effectively to their needs and aspirations.'[3] One of the main issues which emerged during the discussions was: 'the sensitivity of the students to issues of language and terminology.'

Under the heading, 'Teaching and curricula' a number of general complaints made by the participants about the way in which they were taught are recorded. Some of these are listed below:

- 'Some teachers use posh words that nobody can understand. They use jargon. They have to bring the language down sometimes'.
- 'Our lecturers come in, give the lecture, do not care if you take notes or not, and move out. That is it.'
- 'To begin with I thought he was a fantastic lecturer. All the essays I handed in I was getting As and Bs. He said, "Don't worry, you're going to pass the lot with flying colours." So I done the exam and got F.'
- 'I think some teachers are saying, "Yes, we know about all these policies" but they are still teaching as if the class is still white dominated . . .'

Assignment 6.2 – **Responding to students' language needs**

Are you responding effectively to your students' needs and aspirations as far as socio-economic and cultural influences on language is concerned?

Having read through the above list of complaints made by students, do you consider that any of the items describes your behaviour or attitude in class?

Discuss the nature of problems in written and oral communication that could result from teaching without due regard for your students' level of ability in language.

What advice would you offer a colleague who approached you for help with a language-related problem?

6.002 Communicating in teaching and learning situations

Gaining and retaining attention

Students need to be motivated before they pay attention to what is going on in a learning environment. Motivation comes in many forms. In the classroom, students need to be aware of the importance of learning to *them,* or they must have some other social or psychological need to learn, if they are to learn anything.

Teaching and learning involves two-way communication, contrary to the belief commonly held by novices that teaching is a one-way process that is achieved simply by the passing of information from teacher to student. Although the teacher may be responsible for preparing and presenting audio and visual stimuli, **communication** forms the link along which information, concepts, opinions and attitudes flow. This requires active participation on the part of both teacher and students.

Poor communication leads to mistakes, misunderstandings and time-wasting. It can have a drastic effect on individual relationships, leading to general feelings of dissatisfaction which spread throughout the group and can result in poor co-operation. Constant effort is required from all concerned to ensure that the flow of communication is maintained.

The ability to establish rapport goes a long way towards providing an atmosphere compatible with effective communication and learning, thereby enhancing group relationships. Both verbal and non-verbal signals play important parts in the communication process, while facial expressions, gestures and body-language substitute for and reinforce other forms of communication.

The importance of non-verbal signals

At first, it may appear that face-to-face communication consists of taking it in turns to speak. While the teacher is speaking the student is expected to listen and wait patiently until the teacher finishes before making any attempt to jump in. However, on closer examination, it can be seen that people resort to a variety of verbal and non-verbal behaviour in order to maintain a smooth flow of communication. Such behaviour includes head-nods, smiles, frowns, bodily contact, eye movements, laughter, body posture, language and many other actions.

Non-verbal cues play an important part in regulating and maintaining conversations. During a meeting, speech is backed up by an intricate network of gestures which affect the meaning of what is said. In a learning situation all will at some time be moving their head, body and hands. These movements are co-ordinated with speech to make up the total communication.

Some movements repeated frequently are known as **mannerisms**. They are unplanned and are carried out quite unconsciously. Mannerisms can provide a source of amusement for observers and if a teacher is involved someone will probably mimic them, leading to disruption or embarrassment.

The facial expression of students provides feedback to the teacher. Glazed or down-turned eyes indicate boredom or disinterest, as does fidgeting. Fully raised eyebrows signal disbelief and half-raised indicate puzzlement. Body posture adopted by group members provides a means by which their attitude to the teacher may be judged and acts as a pointer to their mood during the lesson.

Control of the group demands that a teacher should be sensitive to the signals being transmitted by students. Their faces usually give a good indication of how they feel, and a working knowledge of the meaning of non-verbal signals will prove invaluable to the teacher.

One modern theory suggests that the words and phrases used indicate whether a person thinks in terms of visual, auditory or kinaesthetic terms so that a perceptive teacher will be able to identify the mode of thinking relating to a particular student. Phrases such as: 'I see what you mean' or 'That looks all right', when used regularly suggests a visual mode; 'Sounds good to me' or 'Listen to this suggestion' or 'I asked myself', suggests an auditory mode; while 'It feels OK to me' or 'Let's climb out of this' or 'I can't seem to get to grips with this' suggests a kinaesthetic mode. Another theory suggests that thought patterns, behaviour and attitudes are interrelated so that if one of the three changes then the others will in some way change. Eye-accessing movements are also said to be capable of being read by a trained individual who has studied the requisite theory. It would appear that eye movements to the left or right either upwards, downwards or horizontally reveal how a person thinks, that is, whether in visual, auditory or kinaesthetic forms.

For effective communication perhaps some knowledge of recent developments in the theory of neuro-linguistic programming,[4] the influence of 'matching behaviour' or 'dancing together' on establishing rapport, or of 'forming, storming, norming and performing' on groupwork will become an essential element of teacher training.

Students and teachers talking

During the twelve hours between nine in the morning and nine in the evening there is an awful lot of talking going on in educational establishments. Teachers talking to teachers, teachers to students, students to teachers, students to students and a general free-for-all where everyone present seems to be talking at the same time. The outcome of all this talking and listening should be desirable changes in behaviour brought about by exchange of knowledge, feelings and activities that promote learning.

Language and learning

Language and learning are mutually dependent. Without adequate knowledge of the language related to a given subject, little or no learning can occur. Teacher talk should be pitched at a level to suit the class and should not, in general, take up too much of the available class contact time. As we have seen, analyses of classroom interaction have revealed that all too often, teacher talk dominates the lesson. Some teachers tend to like the sound of their own voices and this does not necessarily result in effective learning by the passive listeners. Even if the students remain attentive to a degree, they will be unable to absorb as much information as is the case when highly participative student-centred learning techniques are used for delivery.

Language used by teachers

As mentioned earlier, it is helpful to be always mindful of the language one is using in class, and avoid language barriers. For example, technical terms produce barriers and hinder learning if used thoughtlessly and without adequate explanation. Students will imitate the teacher and learn to use technical terms without really knowing their meaning. Teachers should therefore ensure, as far as possible, that the meaning is being handed over as well as the words.

Some practising teachers need a far more sophisticated insight into the implications of the language they use. They need to recognise the linguistic and conceptual difficulties experienced by some students. A **register of language** should be built up to suit the teaching and learning environment and teacher talk pitched at the right level to suit the students. Other means of communication should not be overlooked, either. A picture is said to be worth a thousand words. It is better that a concept be understood from a sketch, aid or preferably the real thing, backed up by and reinforced with words, than to rely on words alone.

Trying to make sense of the effects of language on relationships in classrooms and on the processes of teaching and learning has occupied much time. Many researchers have studied the mental processes involved in the acquisition of language and its application in the social context and specifically to its role in education. Two approaches to studying educational language: 'logical-empirical' and 'interpretive', are described by Young, Arnold and Watson in a paper entitled: 'Linguistic Models'.[5]

> To some extent these two traditions have been associated with two different styles of research. The first of these (the logical-empirical) drew its methods from the behavioural sciences and attempted to apply objective categories to counting instances of behaviour ... The interpretive method applied a more intuitive approach aimed at understanding the meaning of language.

They later specify some researchers who have been involved in work associated with the study of language in an educational context:

> The first tradition may be exemplified by the work of Romiett Stevens (1912) and later work by Flanders (1970), Bellack (1966), Smith and Meux (1962) in the United States, and Sinclair and Coulthard (1975)[6] in the United Kingdom. The second tradition may be exemplified by the early work of Barnes et al (1969) in the United Kingdom and more recently by the more systematic work of Hugh Mehan and his colleagues in the United States.

Obviously, the material presented here is somewhat limited, but its purpose is to heighten awareness of the importance of teachers' presentations and of the relatively short time students may spend talking. It will be of value to interested readers to examine the research of those mentioned in this Section and also of pioneers such as Rosen and Gumperz, Labov, and Hymes.

Assignment 6.3 - Analysing periods of oral work

'Despite all that we hear about learner-centred education teachers love the sounds of their own voices.'

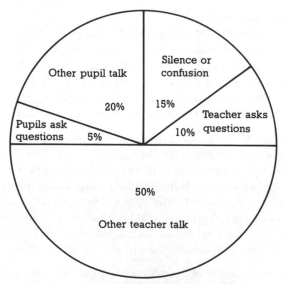

Figure 6.1 Typical analysis of classroom discourse

The table shows that in a class of forty, on average, each student talks for about one per cent of the time available while the teacher may be talking for 60 per cent of the lesson.

– For each of your own groups, estimate the time occupied by each category given in the table.
– Using your values calculate the average amount of time each student spends talking.

Do you feel that any changes are needed in the discourse pattern of your classes?

Encouraging student participation

Practice is one of the best methods of increasing a person's language store, and of developing skills in the use of words. Teachers should encourage their students to talk and write as much as possible in order to get the best out of a learning experience. This can be achieved by creating a rewarding atmosphere in which students can attempt to put into their own words the concept being taught and be given an opportunity to discuss related precepts. The teacher can help by carefully choosing the words used to introduce the concept, by putting questions, by seeking opinions and by making the most of resulting exchanges.

The type of question which elicits a greater amount of student response is of the open-ended type where a number of different answers are often quite acceptable. Reasoning-type questions also call for students to think aloud and to construct or synthesise from memory a logically organised sequence of ideas. Observation-type questions relate to demonstrations and phenomena which students may observe and which require them to perceive certain things. These questions provide good sources of student activity and are therefore to be preferred to closed questions which have only one acceptable answer, or naming questions which invite a response without requiring the student to demonstrate insight.

Assignment 6.4 – **Communicating in teaching and learning situations**

Identify the different ways in which communication may occur in your own classes and consider whether your teaching style is really appropriate to the style of communication demanded by the needs of your students.

To what extent would it be necessary, possible or desirable to change your method of delivery to meet their needs?

6.003 The importance of communication style

The four basic language skills

There are four basic language skills that a teacher needs to own: reading, writing, speaking and understanding. Proficiency in these skills can only be acquired by practice and not simply by reading. Competence in each must be demonstrated when teaching.

Teachers need to be able to 'correctly' pronounce words that they are using in class and must also be able to explain their meanings using several examples as and when required. The problem is in deciding what is meant by the 'correct' pronunciation.

Custom and practice changes from county to county, and regional or class dialects govern communication forms, particularly as different pronunciations are used by people from different parts of the country. However, the effects of unemployment, job searches, mobility and migration across the country is now reducing the once considerable differences between the 'standard English' of the BBC and the spoken word heard in closed, long-established communities. Under these circumstances, established usage by the teaching profession or by the majority of educated communicators has been suggested as a possible standard that could be used when comparing 'correctness' of pronunciation.

Differences also exist between the spoken and written word. When conversing in informal situations, the language style will often be more familiar and less precise in its form and will include slang, local expressions and examples of terminology picked up from the media.

The written word is governed by sets of grammatical rules that have been derived over the years by experts who have studied language and the works of notable writers and speakers. In the written form, words, phrases and sentences need to conform more closely to the rules of grammar, while maintaining an acceptable level of readability, and greater care needs to be exercised when composing the work. Short, uncomplicated sentences comprising standard words in everyday use are preferable to longer sentences containing many difficult words arranged in a complex form. These longer sentences are a 'turn-off' to learners and hinder their perceptions. However, for teachers to prepare written work in a form that would be used when talking to students about the same concept would probably be unacceptable.

When new words, definitions and concepts are being introduced it has been proposed that students should first listen to the words, then read what has been spoken, and then write down what they have read. This sequence is thought to enhance learning that is associated with language usage. Students can be encouraged to verbalise their thoughts and ideas as an aid to learning, by being taught to ask themselves questions, prepare in their minds possible answers and hold a conversation with themselves. With practice, competence in oral presentation will be improved.

For students learning to use language, or to apply specific terminology to their subject, it is not enough to set about learning by rote a set of rules, or building up a bank of information by chanting or repetition. Teachers need to train students to use what they have learned to solve problems and to communicate their specialist knowledge and skills effectively and with insight.

Students' vocabularies will vary with age, cultural and socio-economic background and it will often be the case that the language of the classroom will be vastly different to that of the home. In practice, it will be found that each student has a 'language ceiling' beyond which level it is harder to make progress in learning. Teachers should aim to enable students to learn as much as possible within this limit.

Having an awareness of the limitations imposed by such constraints in vocabulary and usage will cause teachers to understand that they have a duty, when preparing and delivering material, to arrange things so that the learners are able to learn in the most pleasant, efficient and effective manner. To expect learners to be able to do something for which they are ill-equipped due to lack of language is unreasonable; to knowingly ask the student to do it is unforgivable. Regrettably, a lot of damage can be done by this. The student's motivation and self-esteem will take a hard knock and it may be difficult and time-consuming to put things right, even if it is still possible to do so.

Pedagogical concepts

Pedagogy is a word that is used to describe the art and science of teaching. Pedagogical roles are the many and varied roles that a teacher may perform while teaching, and include key roles, such as structuring, soliciting, responding and reacting. Other roles involve: assessing, criticising, discussing, encouraging, enquiring, evaluating, explaining, giving individualised instruction, lecturing, organising, presenting, questioning and answering, recapitulating, repeating and reviewing, step-by-step instruction, team teaching and tutoring.

It will be appreciated that each and every one of these roles involves aspects of language that are reflected by factors such as vocabulary, communication style, speech patterns, pronunciation and dialect, the construction and level of written English, the degree of abstractness or concreteness of the language used, and the clarity or vagueness of the delivery agent.

In order to measure up to the responsibility that rests on the shoulders of teachers in tems of likely pedagogical roles that they will adopt, it is necessary for them to appreciate the need for competence in the four basic language skills outlined at the start of this section.

The effect of excessive detail in the learning process

When an object stands out prominently from its background we perceive it instantly. Infantry training in fieldcraft recommends soldiers to peep around the side of walls rather than stick their heads up over the top. This is said to reduce the chances of getting a bullet through the head! Camouflage and concealment reduces the chances of troops being spotted, the object being to blend with the terrain so as to avoid detection.

In the same way, when a concept is embedded in a complex pattern it is difficult to comprehend. The greater the amount of detail presented at one time, the longer we take to perceive individual parts. Students can be easily confused when confronted with a mass of detail and unconnected facts, especially when irrelevant information is included. It is better to present important basic principles together with key facts and to understand these, rather than to waste time and effort on superfluous content and lose the students in the process. Nobody can give complete attention to more than one thing at a time. Excessive detail tends to weaken concentration, thereby reducing learning efficiency.

A possible approach to the problem of eradicating excessive detail is to determine first the performance differential expected from the group of students — that is, to fix the difference between what they are able to do before training and what they will be expected to be able to do on completion of the learning session. This should enable the teacher to avoid too much repetition of existing knowledge. It should also limit the content broadly to that which the students need to know in order to satisfy the learning objectives. The resulting lecture content should include core knowledge which the students must know, together with an element of that which they should or could know.

The presentation should include a brief introduction outlining the scope of the lecture and should be related, wherever possible, to the students' experiences. Core content should be highlighted and other information must not be allowed to cloud the key points. Once the key points have been mastered, other facts may be introduced in discrete stages at a rate to suit the group.

Communication skills are the essence of effective teaching and learning. Communication is an integral part of the whole process of expressing, presenting and exchanging ideas between teacher and learners. It cannot and should not be treated as an isolated competence that is acquired independently of other aspects of a teacher's role. The use of language in teaching and learning serves to convey information. It is important that teachers when writing lesson notes for themselves, expounding or encouraging student note-making, do so with learners' needs foremost in their thinking.

Assignment 6.5 – **Effective communication**

Write down what you consider to be the key steps in giving explanations.

Check your resources and consider their suitability for an identified group. Analyse content, search for and edit-out redundant, irrelevant or confusing detail. List possible communication problems that may arise when working with this particular student group.

Discuss your findings with a colleague or in a small group and record the outcomes which will be useful to you when planning your lessons.

Produce a sample resource for one of your classes and exchange it with that of a colleague for criticism.

By monitoring before a lesson what you intend to say when delivering a topic, you will have avoided some of the pitfalls that you will identify while working on this assignment.

The advantages of using block diagrams

Have you ever walked into a classroom, slapped a transparency onto the projector, switched on, and then tried to introduce the subject? If you have, you will probably have wasted your time! The students' attention is attracted by the projected visual image and they are busy scanning it. While you talk they are trying to make sense of it. As it is impossible to give full attention to more than one thing at a time, your words pass largely unheeded.

Have you ever tried asking a few questions or making reinforcing statements while students are copying notes from the board?[7] If so, you will have once again wasted everyone's time. Maybe you have tried to describe in words alone a flower arrangement, a dance sequence, or the basic construction of a machine? If so, how much were the students able to recall of what you said?

Problems of attention and overloading are easy to incur. The teacher should therefore try to make it easier for the students to absorb detail and should present information in a way that enables them to do so.

Block diagrams are an excellent aid to conveying information. Diagrams giving key facts are prepared before the lesson and the first diagram to be presented should give an overall picture of the system or process to be discussed. Printed words are kept to a minimum, and each word should count. After a brief introduction of the subject, the first block diagram is displayed. The students' attention will immediately be attracted to the diagram and the general pattern of the whole will be taken in. Their gaze will shift from one part of the diagram to another until they have a mental picture of the process. Only then will it be possible for the teacher to effectively present verbal information relating to the process. To do so before sufficient time has been allowed for students to satisfy their initial curiosity would be unproductive. They would not be listening to what is being said. Their attention would be focused on the diagram, rather than on the words being spoken.

If control is lost, it may be helpful to briefly remove the display by covering the diagram or switching off the overhead projector. Once attention is regained, it will be possible to return to the diagram so that relationships between the blocks can be discussed and individual blocks selected for in-depth study.

Block diagrams can take several forms. For example, movement of fuels from oilfields to filling stations is shown in Figure 6.2. This is an elementary example of a flow diagram tracing a concept from 'start-to-finish'.

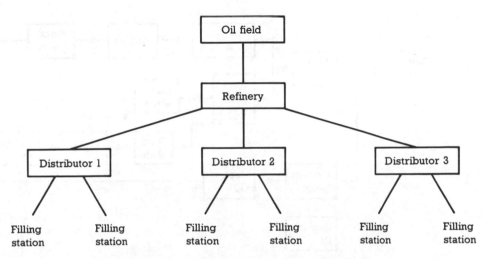

Figure 6.2 Block diagram of movement of fuel oils

178   Communication

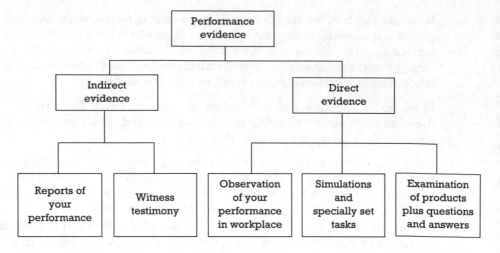

Figure 6.3 Performance evidence

Three main types of evidence are used in the S/NVQ assessment process: performance, supplementary and prior achievement. Key features of performance evidence are shown in the block diagram reproduced in Figure 6.3.

A systems approach showing the construction of a centre lathe with inputs and outputs relating to each main component part is given in Figure 6.4. Arrows indicate how individual blocks making up the system relate. Using the diagram as an aid helps the teacher convey an overall picture of the lathe to the students' minds. Each block may then be examined in detail, using actual machine components wherever possible.

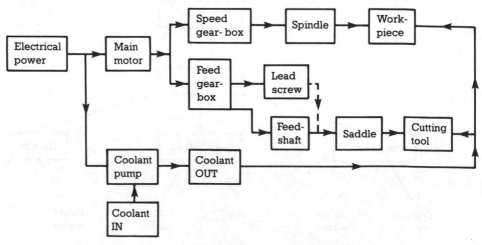

Figure 6.4 Block diagram of a centre lathe

Assignment 6.6 – **The importance in communication of speech and written language**

In its in-service handbook, the National Association for Staff Development pinpoints the importance of teacher competence in communication skills: 'Activities in which the tutor's own example ought to be impeccable include

– speech before and with the group
– the production of notes and 'handouts'
– writing on the chalkboard/whiteboard or in the production of visual aids.'[8]

Evaluate the quality of your work by checking preparation, handouts, visual aids, boardwork and delivery in terms of the correctness of spelling, punctuation and usage of language. If you consider that there are deficiencies in your ability to use oral or written language, have a word with your tutor or colleagues and agree an action plan designed to find effective ways of improving the presentation and delivery of your lessons.

6.004 Selecting the communication mode

The mode of teaching and conditions for learning should be considered when designing a lesson plan. According to R.M. Gagné[9] there are eight classes of learning, ranging from **signal learning** to **problem solving**, each class involving a different level of complexity and calling for different teaching and learning modes (see Chapter One). The lesson plan should therefore provide for the appropriate activities and conditions needed to achieve the desired outcome.

Transfer of training should also be allowed for when planning the lesson sequence. When building on previous knowledge, the teacher should be aware of the difficulties encountered by learners where tasks appear to be similar to those previously learned, but which in fact differ importantly. Advantage should also be taken of the positive effects of existing knowledge or skills which may be drawn upon to speed up the learning of similar tasks. The importance of the learning of core skills and the need to instil in students the concept of searching for ways in which new knowledge and skills can be incorporated into other aspects of their work should be at the forefront of every teacher's thinking. The relevant unit of the DfEE that has replaced the Employment Department Group – Training, Enterprise and Education Directorate (TEED) (previously the Training Agency and before that the Manpower Services Commission) places great value on the philosophy of teaching for transfer and there is a need to integrate college-based learning with work-placement and other off-college activities.

Reviews and recapitulations play an important role in reinforcing knowledge recently acquired and where learning appears to grind to a halt; recognition and understanding of the phenomena known as **learning plateaux** may help to explain the temporary lack of progress.

Alternative strategies to be employed if things go wrong due to inadequate preparation or inactivity should be included in the lesson plan. Students should be kept busy doing things whenever possible. The quality of presentation and learning outcomes depend to a considerable extent on a well-thought-out lesson plan which promotes effective communication and reveals competence by selection of the most suitable mode of delivery.

Identifying appropriate modes

1 Teachers communicating by writing

Some students are highly literate and scholarly and have little difficulty with written communications. There are others who really want to learn but have difficulties with language, handwriting or spelling that cause them unwanted problems in the classroom. Against this backcloth, teachers need to be aware of the wide range of student attitudes and abilities and be able to perform at the appropriate level to encourage interest and progress. It may be that with Class A, the teacher will frequently need to use short simple statements when writing on the board or when giving notes. With Class B, some students may demand very full notes or handouts that they can take away, study and précis as part of their preferred learning style. With Class C, some students' experience of writing may be confined to little more than filling in spaces on official forms, so that 'gapped handouts' may be a valuable classroom resource for them. In any of these situations the teacher needs to bear in mind that not all students will have identical requirements; mixed ability within the class also has to be taken into account. For some, linking the ways of saying things with ways of writing what is said is probably a good way to encourage and develop writing skills. For complete understanding, others may need to relate what is said or written to the rules of grammar. Teachers need to be able to select and apply different modes of speed and writing appropriate to their students and to the different educational situations that may confront them.

2 Teachers communicating by exposition

Many students do not like taking notes. It can be a timewasting, passive and boring activity, where little more is achieved than a neat (or not so neat) set of notes that may possibly be used later for revision or reference. However, older students often feel reassured by a good set of notes and do not feel satisfied unless they have a full and ample set to take home.

Some teachers prefer to write on the board rather than on an OHP transparency while giving key facts. They either keep their back to the class or adopt an agonising stance while trying to keep their eyes on the board and on the class at the same time. Everyone is working hard writing, but one wonders just how much learning is going on during the process.

Where very limited dictation is deemed to be absolutely necessary, the speed and clarity of the spoken word must be adjusted to the norm for the class. Some teachers appear to be oblivious to the fact that the activity can be more like a speed test, during which the sheer number of words recorded in a given time is the critical factor.

When practising the writing of modern languages, the right speed will be determined by practice and observation, since no two classes perform at the same level of skill. It is most important to perceive signs of confusion, and to note whether anyone has difficulty in keeping up with the others. Frustration results if teachers lose their place and fumble with papers trying to locate the last word, or miss a line or two and then realise what has happened and ask the class to cross things out or squeeze words in. It is easy to 'lose' or alienate the class during such sessions. Encouraging learners to make their own notes is a far more valuable method of transferring information, though of course dictation has its place in the teaching of certain subjects such as speedwriting, shorthand and languages.

Pace and **punctuation** are important both during periods of exposition and when giving notes. When teaching, it is good practice to punctuate the delivery with pauses at selected points during the input. When planning the lesson there will be clearly identifiable 'break points', similar to those used in the process of method study. Starting with an introduction, a pause will allow students to absorb the scope of the lesson that will follow. Then, at intervals, brief silences will signal the information that the listeners should be doing something. That is, they should be organising the material in their minds before progressing to the next stage. It is therefore recommended that lessons and other verbal exposition such as lectures should be punctuated in much the same way as written work. In a lecture, for example, the lecturer will vary the pace of delivery, slowing down to stress important points and speeding up for less important material. Tone and loudness of voice, coupled with gestures also help to identify and stress important points. If one spends too long explaining a point, uses every example that can be thought of to reinforce the concept, or rambles on with lengthy answers to a question, the class will lose interest and will probably end up more confused than they were to start with.

When giving instructions it is important to first ensure that all are attentive and ready to receive the information. No one should be writing, shuffling papers or otherwise distracted. Silence can be a very powerful weapon in a teacher's armoury. If a break in attention occurs due to a distraction, stop speaking, show firmness and control and wait for silence and attention to be restored. Then resume.

Subject-specific language is important and often its usage is unavoidable, since such vocabulary is used to give precise meaning to concepts that cannot otherwise be adequately described. In this and other contexts, it is important for teachers to be able to spell general and subject-specific vocabulary correctly. They are expected to check and rehearse their preparation before delivery, and consequently any words that are new to them should be checked too.

During the preparation stage it is always a good idea to think of possible questions or extensions of ideas that could crop up during the lesson. Time spent searching for relevant terminology is time well spent. Teachers of English as a second language will appreciate how stressful it would be for the unprepared teacher to teach technical English, to keen non-native-speakers with relatively small vocabularies.

Perhaps one of the more important features of a lesson is the **question-and-answer method** of developing a subject. The method is useful when introducing a whole range of subjects. It provides a good background for the later development of ideas, and encourages students to contribute by relating their work experience to the discussion. The technique can be applied effectively to any subject, hobby or topic and is used very effectively when teaching languages and many of the adult education subjects offered.

The use of a short question-and-answer session at the beginning of each lesson can help in several ways. Questions can be used to arouse interest and curiosity, while at the same time allowing the teacher to determine the existing level of knowledge of the subject. No matter how complex the topic for discussion may be, a good number of responses will relate to it in some way.

The development of autonomy in students should be encouraged, but there will be times when the teacher needs to help. Students' replies may need to be amplified in some respects and this can be done either by asking them for further clarification; or by asking others to enlarge on the statement. Students will clam up completely if they are ridiculed on account of an incorrect answer. They will remember that there is safety in silence and the teacher will have lost them.

If questions and comments are encouraged to flow naturally as the lesson develops, the result is greater participation by group members. The thing to bear in mind at all times is that, in general, students learn most when they are actively contributing to the lesson.

Many student-generated questions are directly related to statements made by the teacher or other students, or to theory and calculations written on the board. Wherever possible, the question should be broken down into a series of mini-questions and thrown back to the group, so that students formulate their own answers to the problem. If, after cueing, this ploy fails, the question has to be answered directly by the teacher. Questions may be asked by students simply because they are confused. The expression on an individual's face will signal bewilderment and an able teacher will take steps to restore the balance. This can be done by repeating the subject-matter more slowly or by putting it another way with a series of check questions interposed at suitable break points.

With a more formal teaching style, **key check questions** should be thought out and recorded in the lesson plan well before the event. Planned questioning serves to stimulate, encourage and consolidate learning as the lesson proceeds and creates self-confidence in the students, especially if they are rewarded for correct responses.

A prepared list of questions relating to the subject-matter may be put to the learners towards the end of the lesson. This enables the group to evaluate teaching and learning. It also serves to reinforce key points. Any difficulties apparent may be rectified there and then, and the lesson plan modified, ready for next time.

Questioning techniques: a checklist
To provide a greater level of usefulness to the student, the teacher should remember to:

– use unambigious language which is easily understood
– use questions which cover the subject step by step
– use also questions calling for considerable thought and longer responses
– put questions to the whole group, then pause for up to five seconds, then name the person to respond. (Some are opposed to the use of this technique on the

ground that learners may feel threatened and clam up, so it should be used with discretion)
- be reasonably sure, when choosing a respondent, that the person chosen is likely to be capable of correctly answering the particular question
- repeat answers slowly (only if reinforcement is necessary, as this can disrupt concentration)
- give praise for correct response and redirect question to others for confirmation of their agreement and understanding
- involve all class members at some stage of lesson; do not rely on students who volunteer answers all of the time
- encourage slow learners by cueing until correct response is elicited
- avoid irrelevant or trick questions
- avoid questions with yes/no answers as they have a 50/50 chance of being answered correctly by guessing
- avoid answering your own questions unless you really have to.

The use of incomplete statements by a teacher as a form of questioning requires little effort on the part of the learner. Be on your guard against this practice. As a teacher you will be tempted to put words into the mouth of a learner who is unable to answer. When the question has been answered you are 'off the hook' and many teachers will go to great lengths to achieve this happy state.

Assignment 6.7 – Self-diagnosis in questioning skills

Increasingly over the past twenty years teachers have been encouraged to improve their classroom skills by recording and analysing micro-teaching sessions. By carrying out these and other self-evaluations and reviews of frequently used components of teaching practice, deficiencies in current performance may be identified and updating training effected.

Research effective questioning skills and produce a profile checklist of at least 10 questioning skills that a competent teacher needs to own in order to perform at an acceptable level in classroom or workshop. Discuss and compare your profile checklist with colleagues and with the course leader. Modify or add to the list if necessary.

Videotape a 10 minute mini-lesson using questioning techniques as the main element of delivery. Replay the tape and review your performance using the profile checklist as a basis for diagnosing the degree of competence demonstrated during the mini-lesson.

Assignment 6.8 – Matching mode to method

Identify possible modes of delivery when teaching, and consider the speed of exposition or writing that would be most appropriate to each mode that you have listed.

6.005 Communicating effectively with students

Establishing credibility

In the teaching situation, the purpose of communication is to promote a change in the behaviour of students. The aim is to cause a change to occur either in the amount of knowledge held by students in a given topic area, or in their ability to perform certain tasks.

Effectiveness of the teaching will depend not only on adequate preparation of subject-matter but also on the way students evaluate the communicator. If the teacher is seen to be credible, that is, to be reliable and qualified by experience and ability in the task area, then there should be a significant change in behaviour. On the other hand, if the teacher professes to be an expert and is seen by the students to lack this expertise, the discrepancy will be noted and little, if any, positive behaviour change will occur. Disruptive activities will probably replace supportive and helpful interaction.

A communicator is more likely to induce attitudinal change if credibilty is high, so it is essential for a teacher to win the group's confidence and approval very early in the source or lecture.

Student responses

A **response** is the behavioural result of stimulation brought about by exposure to verbal or non-verbal signals from the environment which impinge on the recipient. A stimulus produces a response in a living organism. It may also rouse a person to action or increased action. Stimuli are important in gaining attention. The most significant properties are intensity, size, contrast, colour and movement.

When a stimulus attracts our attention we respond by performing certain body movements that improve our reception of the stimulation. Orienting reflexes result. If we hear our name, we look toward the speaker. If an intense light flashes, we look in its direction. In the classroom situation we pay attention when the teacher speaks. If he or she writes on the chalkboard or switches on the overhead projector, we read what is written or take in information given in the projected image.

The main problem in gaining attention is that people are usually preoccupied with messages circulating in their inner systems. These messages may result from having received stimuli from the surroundings or from thought processes. While these take precedence, little or no effective communication can take place. To gain full attention, irrelevant sensory inputs must be filtered out so that the students concentrate only on those directed to them by the teacher.

Attention involves motivation, while personality factors and nature of the task are strong influences on students' behaviour in class. The main aims of the teacher are to transmit and share with the student words, ideas and concepts. Therefore, for successful communication the student must be interested in what is being transmitted, and having received the message must decode it in terms of previously known information. What is perceived and the meaning attached to it is determined to some extent by the student's needs and values, and this perception must coincide with the teacher's intended communication in order to be effective.

Teaching for desired responses

No learning can take place without active responses from the student. A teaching situation can be said to have been successful if the teacher's actions result in a sought-after change in student behaviour. Throughout the lesson the teacher's role is that of enabler, providing a framework within which desired responses may occur.

Attention peaks at the beginning of a lesson. This is the time to outline the ground to be covered and to fuel the students' imagination and interest. Learning objectives should be spelled out and overall direction indicated. The expected terminal behaviour resulting from the lesson should be made known to the students, and if evaluative tests are to be included, this fact should be indicated before instruction commences.

The teacher should analyse the material to be taught in terms of 'previously learned material' and 'material to be learned'. The means of obtaining the necessary responses from the students follows the usual form — introduce stimuli, elicit response and obtain feedback. Verbal material used should be meaningful to the student and should progress from the known to the unknown, from the familiar to the unfamiliar and from simple to complex. Ample opportunities should be provided for the students to make the necessary responses, and practice on a massed or distributed basis should be scheduled.

Correct responses should be rewarded and knowledge of test results or performance on a task should be fed back to the students as quickly as possible. Increased motivation can often be obtained by relating material to the work situation or real world, and by indicating the benefit to the students of successfully mastering the work.

Keeping lines of communication open

Words or phrases may be perceived differently depending upon circumstances in which they are spoken, so that a communication may be interpreted both in terms of the message and the context in which it occurs.

A communication comprises three elements: a measure of the communicator's feelings, the form and style of the message, and an indication of the desired behaviour or response. The feelings expressed may include those of sincerity, hostility, irony, humour or sadness. The style may be technical or non-technical, and the message may be formed in such a way as to produce a specific response.

The communication channel is opened by attracting the receiver's attention and is maintained by words backed up with non-verbal signals. Verbal and non-verbal signals combine to convey the three elements of communication and the way in which the total communication is perceived governs its effectiveness.

Information is not merely transmitted and received; it is also interpreted. The message is frequently distorted as it passes through barriers to communication and interpretation of content will be affected by previous experience or personal values. The message taken in and meaning ascribed to it will govern the receiver's behaviour.

Effective communication results when a student's response corresponds with the teacher's intentions and vice versa. Communication failure results when a teacher's intention and a student's response are incompatible. In order to avoid misunderstandings due to ambiguity, complexity or sheer volume of message content, feedback should be provided between the student and teacher to ensure that correct interpretation has been made. A second feedback link enables the student's response in terms of what is done to be compared with the teacher's intentions. This is particularly necessary in the workshop, laboratory or work placement as a means of checking that orders or instructions have been carried out effectively.

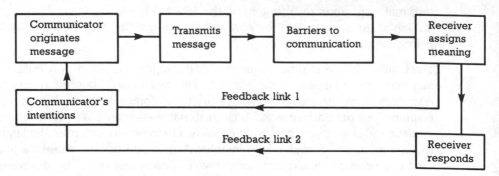

Figure 6.5 Communication system

Barriers to communication

Barriers to communication take two forms — **extrinsic** and **intrinsic**. Extrinsic barriers relate to external influences bearing on the communication and they include noise, language code used and the environment in general. Intrinsic barriers are set up within the receiver and include attitudes based upon past experience, feeling, emotions and internal thought processes relating to both the communicator and message content. All of these factors affect the receiver's perception of the communication.

Psychological imbalance between teacher and student

There is frequently a psychological imbalance between teacher and student, especially in the more formal classroom situation. This is particularly so in the case of mature students who have not been exposed to formal education for many years or adults who are undergoing various forms of government-sponsored training and re-training. For them, the classroom itself is likely to bring back memories of schooldays and of cold, unsympathetic, detached figures commanding obedience from the podium by virtue of the authority vested in them as teachers.

In further and adult education or in industrial situations, a different type of imbalance is to be found. The student or trainee perceives that the teacher or instructor possesses superior skills, knowledge and ability. As the master of a craft or subject and as the source of information, the teacher directs the activities of the student. The student engages in tasks set, supervised, monitored and evaluated by the teacher. The teacher is a source of social reinforcement who holds the power to reward or punish according to assessment of the outcomes.

Punishment may take many forms. The application of sanctions is not the only way to punish. Ill-conceived statements of rebuke uncaringly uttered are far more hurtful to a relationship than a democratically conducted objective review of 'what was good and what was bad' about the performance. If the student does well, praise and reward may be forthcoming. A poor performance may result in criticism of an unhelpful kind, in which case a loss of esteem inevitably results and it will take a long time to repair the damage.

Power is vested in the teacher's expertise and position in the institutional hierarchy. The teacher should be aware of this, and needs to take steps to reduce the accompanying emotional tension by providing a secure, sympathetic atmosphere within which learning will be encouraged. It is just not possible to simply 'pour in knowledge'. Learning is dependent on a healthy rapport between teacher and student, and a commitment of both to achieving the desired outcomes of instruction.

It is not always easy to breeze into a classroom brimming with energy and enthusiasm. Some classes are more difficult to teach than others. Sometimes the teacher has domestic worries, sickness at home, pressures and stresses brought about by the ever-increasing demands being made of teachers outside the classroom. But the teacher needs to overcome any such negative attitudes; unhelpful students who lack motivation will quickly observe how one feels and will seize the opportunity to behave disruptively given half a chance, while committed students will feel unable to apply themselves to work in which the teacher seems to be uninterested.

Under normal circumstances, students should be encouraged to speak freely and if similarities between teacher and student are perceived, these similarities tend to increase, resulting in better rapport and enhanced self-esteem for the student. The degree of familiarity should however be controlled relative to the pertaining circumstances.

The teacher should avoid sarcasm and should at all times be respectful to the students. A teacher's behaviour should be irreproachable and a model for the students to follow. Teacher talk should be uncontaminated with bad language, even when interacting with students who appear to adopt non-standard English as their norm. Where the opportunity exists, the teacher needs to correct communication styles as and when examples crop up in class. Possibly the best way of introducing a positive attitude towards improving language and communications skills is to provide examples of good practice when using the chalkboard, transparencies or handout materials.

Integrity and high personal standards will go a long way towards overcoming obstacles to effective communication with students and colleagues.

Assignment 6.9 – **Effective two-way communication**

Identify and analyse some significant problems of communication encountered in the context of teaching your group.

Consider how you might improve your person-to-person and person-to-group communication and in particular ask yourself whether you are:

- asking the right questions in the most effective way
- recognising and correctly interpreting the signals emanating from the group
- listening and using silence effectively
- talking the students' language.

6.006 Enhancing student communications

The teacher needs to be able to identify ways in which students may be assisted during a course of study to communicate effectively, but more importantly, to be able to arrange learning opportunities for students to demonstrate their communicating skills.

The role of perception in communicating and learning

Before considering ways that students may learn to communicate more effectively, it is necessary to examine the important role of perception in communication when teaching and learning. The intended meaning should be communicated with the help of words and images that carry the messages to and fro between teacher and students. However, what is perceived will depend to some degree upon past experiences, immediate needs and what we expect or wish to perceive.

Perception involves two important processes: the gathering of signals carrying information, and its subsequent decoding in the brain, where previous knowledge of such information is stored.

Information is received in the form of stimuli picked up by the five senses: smell, touch, taste, hearing and vision. These senses link the central nervous system with the environment and allow us to react to given stimuli.

The **behaviourist** school of psychology proposes that animal and human behaviour results mainly from the more or less automatic responses of a body to stimuli, playing down the role of the brain as a processor of information. The **Gestalt** school proposes the 'laws of perceptual organisation' including theories of continuity, closure and similarity. Gestaltists suggest that in perception, 'the whole is greater than the sum of its parts' and that **insight** plays an important part in problem solving. The brain in some ways organises individual stimuli into patterns so that dots, lines or musical notes are combined to form a meaningful whole rather than a set of random entities. They consider that this ability to structure and organise is innate.

At birth, babies are unable to perceive the environment as adults do, although after a while they do learn to perceive and build up a meaningful picture of the world around them. As time passes, the process of information gathering and decoding becomes almost automatic, and so a knowledge of the environment and learning is formed. The effect of personal experience on the learning process must also be taken into account.

Animals have been used in experiments designed to investigate brain activity. In one experiment a very fine electrode was inserted adjacent to a neural cell in the cortex. The pattern of electrical activity was monitored, amplified and recorded. The record showed bursts of spontaneous activity occurring every few seconds. Such activity continues throughout life, even during sleep, until brain death occurs, when no electrical activity can be detected.

When a sense organ detects a stimulus, the rate of brain activity increases and cells in different areas respond, depending upon the nature of the stimulus. The brain also serves as a storage device. Information is picked up by receptors located in the sense organs and is interpreted by the perceptual apparatus. It is then fed into a storage/retrieval system within the brain, where it is stored, possibly as a result of neurological, biochemical or electrical changes in the neural circuitry. The way in which an event is perceived, therefore, affects the way it is stored as knowledge.

We are constantly being bombarded with stimuli which reach us from the environment. We become aware of anything directly apprehended by the senses. We perceive it, although not necessarily as it really is. What can you detect from your surroundings? Perhaps you can hear a clock ticking or smell the coffee brewing, or see a car passing, or feel a warm cup in your hand or taste a mint sweet. These stimuli are obvious, but there are many other, less obvious items of information reaching you every second, each giving intelligence relating to the nature of the environment.

Much of the information received is either apparently ignored, as no action from the receiver is required, or else is responded to in a seemingly unconscious, automatic manner. However, particular sensations may be singled out for attention and interpretation. These stimuli reach the sense organs and are relayed to the brain, where they are interpreted on the basis of past experience and the requisite responses made. We perceive by comparing the particular sensation with previous learning and knowledge of identical or similar situations which have been coded and stored in the mind.

Different people perceive a given phenomenon in different ways and what is perceived depends to some extent upon past experiences, present needs and also upon what we expect and wish to perceive. In an instructional situation the aim of the teacher is to direct the learner's attention to specific communicable items of information. As communication is a two-way process, the learner is required to attend to what the teacher is imparting, to perceive, and hence to learn.

In order for active participation to take place, the learner must find the lesson content interesting and rewarding enough to displace other stimuli competing for attention. Creating this atmosphere is the main task confronting the teacher.

What is attention?

Attention is the selective focusing of the mind upon a given phenomenon. A sudden flash of light, a loud bang or an appearance of the unexpected will all attract our attention. We turn towards the phenomenon and try to make sense of it. If it has disappeared, we maintain our gaze in the direction of its original appearance, or strain our ears trying to detect the origin of the sound. Attention is maintained for a while, and if there is no recurrence of the phenomenon, we soon return to our own private thoughts or to whatever held our attention before the incident occurred.

Attention is a function of our senses, perception and instincts. Our senses detect a change in the environment. We try to relate the change to something we have experienced before and to categorise it in some way according to our previous knowledge of apparently similar events. If we perceive the change to be potentially dangerous, our attention is riveted to the phenomenon and survival behaviour is adopted. Attention can only be maintained if our interest in the event is maintained.

In the instructional situation, audio-visual aids and models initially attract attention. It is the task of the teacher to maintain attention by causing the learner to concentrate on what is being said, by attempting to shut out competing stimuli which interfere with the learning process. If interest is allowed to flag, attention will be lost to more rewarding student activities.

Attention is also related to both motivation and complexity of task. If a person is highly motivated by financial reward or other extrinsic factors, attention is likely to be maintained. Similarly, if the task is relatively complex and within the capability of the learner, this, together with other intrinsic factors such as challenge and mastery, will also maintain attention.

On the other hand, loss of attention often occurs in the performance of simple, repetitive factory work, tasks calling for little mental effort and work where there is a fear of failure. Probably the overriding factor relating to a person's ability to pay attention is the state of alertness. This, in turn, is a function of physical and mental states at a given time, so that fatigue or mental tiredness govern the degree of attention which may be maintained.

Role of attention in the process of perception
Attention leads to a keen awareness of an event which is taking place in a person's immediate environment. The person focuses attention on the occurrence and through the process of perception becomes aware of the object or behaviour which constitutes the event. The environment in which the event takes place is important in determining the responses resulting and while the event may be unambiguous, a number of observers will probably perceive it in different ways. The significance attached to the event will guide subsequent behaviour according to how the individual perceives it. Perception is not simply the passive reception and interpretation of stimuli according to some invariable register of meanings located in the brain. What is perceived is affected by **set** and **experience.** 'Set' describes a tendency to react in a certain way when a particular stimulus is presented, and may stem from previous experience or from instructions given in advance by a teacher.

An example of set is the readiness of a learner driver to perform an emergency stop when the driving test examiner bangs a clipboard on the dashboard or taps the windscreen with a pencil. A bus driver displays a similar readiness when reacting to stimulation resulting from the sound of a buzzer. At the bus stop, two buzzes are heard and the driver moves off. If the road becomes congested the driver slows down; if clear the driver speeds up. A single buzz is interpreted as a normal stop signal while a rapid series of buzzes causes the driver to make an emergency stop. Experience has dictated reactions to visual stimulation due to traffic conditions, while set accounts for a readiness to respond to the buzzer.

In the classroom, students perceive very little in the way of lesson content unless something attracts their attention and compels them to concentrate on it. An overhead projector projects a picture of an object, attracts attention and stimulates the student. The student tries to perceive the meaning of the event. However, perception is never instantaneous. At first, there is an awareness of a change in the environment; then follows a sequence of perceiving: background or field, shape, outline, colours, brightness, general classification and finally, naming the object. If two almost similar objects are displayed simultaneously, it may take some time to identify their dissimilarities, and more attention will be required in order to perceive these differences.

Excessive stimulation of a single sense, or inputs to several senses at one time, often produces sensory overload and leads to disruption of attention, hence breaking down the process of perception. On the other hand, sensory deprivation where a person is starved of sensory inputs leads to boredom and inability to concentrate, and once again attention is lost. In order to hold attention, the requisite input of sensory information must be provided and active participation encouraged so that perception may be maintained.

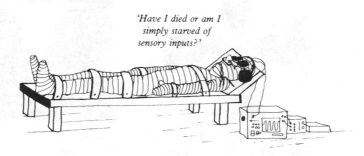

'Have I died or am I simply starved of sensory inputs?'

Figure 6.6 Sensory deprivation

Perceptual experience defined

Perceptual experience is obtained from exposure to objects or situations. Such experience enables the individual to construct a store of knowledge based upon identifiable objects and to draw upon this store when confronted with the same object or situation at a later date. The process is continuous, and the store is being added to daily as learning experiences are encountered. For example, we learn by experience the form, function and attributes of a motor car and also how to react to one when crossing the road. If, while standing in the road, we hear the sound of an engine running or its exhaust noise, we immediately identify the source as a motor vehicle. If we narrowly avoid being run down, we are wary and behave in an appropriate manner when crossing the road on future occasions. If we hear a louder, deeper exhaust noise, we classify the source as a heavy vehicle and, when it appears, find it fairly easy to identify the vehicle as a coach or truck. If, however, the distant noise of an engine running can be heard but the source cannot be seen, perception is ambiguous. Further information is required before the source can be classified as a motor car, van, truck, coach, bulldozer or stationary engine.

Perceptual experience, then, involves the interpretation of the main features of an object or action based upon information which has previously been categorised and stored in our memory bank.

The importance of perceptual experience in the learning process

Discrimination

The ability to differentiate and to discriminate greatly affects perception. Discrimination relates to the ability to detect differences between two stimuli. Drawings have been produced by experimenters in order to show that it is possible for a person to perceive a shape either as figure or as a ground. Figure and ground reversal always occur in such drawings. Figures 6.7 and 6.8 illustrate the effect. If the drawings are studied for a short time, at first, perhaps black stands out as the figure against a white background, and then the next instant, reversal takes place. In no case does the figure merge into the background. Who can say which colour is intended to form the figure?

Figure 6.7
Figure and ground reversal (i)

Figure 6.8
Figure and ground reversal (ii)

Adapted from N.L. Munn, *Psychology. The Fundamentals of Human Adjustment*, 3rd edition, George C. Harrap and Co. Ltd

False perception and optical illusions

Both optical illusions and problems of false perception highlight difficulties encountered in the process of perception. Examples of figures illustrating well-known illusions are given in Figures 6.10 and 6.11. Study them before reading on. It would appear that our eyes are not to be trusted!

In his study of the development of sensory organisation, Leeper[10] used three figures, those of a young attractive women, an old hag and one which could be perceived either as the young woman or as the old hag. Leeper's subjects were shown a figure of the young woman followed by the ambiguous figure and a high proportion identified the ambiguous figure as that of a young woman. Others were shown a figure of the old hag followed by the ambiguous figure and identified the latter as an old hag. These results suggest that 'recency effects' brought about by prior presentation of one or other of the unambiguous figures, or 'expectation', that is, a readiness to perceive certain aspects of the ambiguous figure (resulting from presentation of the first picture) determines to some extent how things are actually perceived.

A picture similar to the one used by Leeper is shown in Figure 6.9. The picture illustrates problems of false perception. At first glance the picture may appear to be that of an old hag but if gaze is maintained the old hag disappears and is replaced by an attractive young woman. In this case, neither recency effects nor expectation aspects apply, no other pictures having been presented.

Figure 6.9 Ambiguous figure-ground effects

Adapted from *Introduction to Psychology*, Ernest R. Hilgard, Richard C. Atkinson and Rita L. Atkinson, 5th edition, Harcourt Brace Jovanovich, Inc.

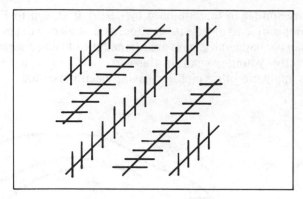

Figure 6.10 Zöllner illusion

In the Zöllner illusion (Figure 6.10), the longer lines appear to be converging whereas they are parallel.

In the Hering illusion (Figure 6.11), parallel lines superimposed on a system of lines radiating from a central point appear curved.

Perceptual illusions have been the subject of extensive research, but to date no universally accepted theory explaining the phenomenon has been expounded.

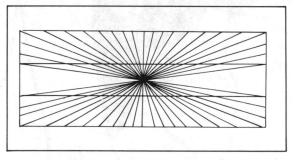

Figure 6.11 Hering illusion

Adapted from N.L. Munn, *Psychology. The Fundamentals of Human Adjustment*, 4th edition, George C. Harrap and Co. Ltd

Past experiences

Behavioural aspects of perception greatly affect the interpretation of events. Knowledge of results of exposure to a given occurrence is stored in the mind, and when a similar occurrence is experienced, the response made is often biased by what happened during the original event. If, however, there is some small difference which passes unnoticed, the response made may be totally inadequate or incorrect. Attitudes are formed as a result of subjection to an influence, and they lead to a readiness to respond in a predetermined manner. As a result, behaviour can be a function of either prejudice or opinion.

Language

The quality of perception is greatly affected by the language available to an observer. Appropriate language must be accessible in order for an event to be fully appreciated. If the meaning of an occurrence cannot be explained in words, then the mind cannot efficiently interpret the concept elicited by a given stimulus, given that thought processes involve a kind of inner conversation carried on in the brain. The role of language in human perception, thinking and teaching is more fully discussed in Section 6.002.

From what has been described in this section, it would appear that if drawings can be perceived in more than one way, and events falsely interpreted in the light of past experience, then it is not unreasonable to suggest that perceptual experience in the learning situation can be plagued by similar processes.

Using checklists of core skills in effective communication

A list of core skills used in the Youth Training Scheme provides a useful checklist around which to design with students a range of assignments that can be completed, preferably by small groups. A teamwork approach is likely to greatly enhance the communication abilities of each student, particularly if roles such as secretary, reporter, resource manager and the like are allocated to team members and a student-centred reporting session or review is conducted regularly.

The list, incorporating six important groupings covering the kind of communicating channels used in day-to-day problem solving is reproduced below:[11]

1 Planning, determining and revising courses of action

- plan the order of activities
- plan who does what and when
- plan all resources needed for a task
- plan the arrangement of items in a job, project or sequence
- plan how to communicate for a given purpose
- plan how to find and present information
- diagnose a fault or problem
- plan for contingencies, hazards and difficulties that may arise
- plan how to deal with things that have gone wrong

2 Decision making: choosing between alternatives

- decide when action is required
- decide which category something belongs to
- decide between alternative courses of action
- decide how to make the best of an awkward situation
- decide on the best response when accidents or emergencies occur

3 Monitoring: keeping track of progress and checking

- check that a person is performing a task to standard
- monitor a process or activity
- monitor the availability of resources
- check the quality and condition of resources
- check written information
- monitor the safety of the environment
- notice that things have gone wrong and that action is required

4 Finding out information and interpreting instructions

- find out information by speaking to other people
- find out information from written sources

- find out information by observing
- interpret spoken instructions
- interpret written instructions
- find out the needs of other people in the workplace or project group
- find out the facts about things that have gone wrong
- find out the needs of customers, clients or colleagues

5 Providing information

- by speaking to customers, clients or colleagues
- in writing and by means of tables and diagrams
- by demonstrating to other people
- by answering questions in the course of the job or project
- by explaining to others about problems that have occurred

6 Working with people

- notice when to ask other people in the workplace for help
- ask others for help
- notice the needs of others and offer help
- react appropriately to requests from others
- discuss with others how things are to be done
- react appropriately to complaints from others
- converge with others in order to establish or maintain an appropriate relationship
- notice where people behave exceptionally and whether action is required

The checklist given above provides a basis on which to negotiate and write a set of **competence objectives** that may be used to assess the effectiveness of student's communications and hence to yield information for profiling purposes.

The main advantages of using competence objectives are that:

- tasks that students will be able to do are listed and known to all concerned
- the objectives are unambiguous and understandable to teachers, students, employers and others
- teachers and students using the objectives can assess whether or not the outcomes have been demonstrated
- the objectives are usually written in occupational terms or at least as clearly recognisable activities
- checklisted competence validated by assessments of 'can do' outcomes are readily marketable to employers.

Developing effective communication by problem solving

The main advantages of group problem-solving exercises are that they involve mutual participation, criticism and correction behaviour by group members. Students tend to express themselves more freely and take advantage of the fact that the group is often leaderless and free of direct control by the teacher.

It is useful to set up a problem-solving exercise in order to study the behaviour pattern of a team when presented with a problem. A non-participating student acting as observer records impressions of the process on a report form and when the problem has been solved, feeds back observations to the team. Observers may be changed after each exercise, and it has been found that the observer often learns more about group behaviour and problem solving by looking at the process than by actual participation in the action.

Several types of report form are available depending upon the particular aspect of the behaviour being studied. One relates to the number of times each team member speaks; another records the type of statement being made by each person. These statements are usually classified as being related to the task itself or to group cohesion. They are sometimes called **product skills** and **process skills** (see Chapter One). Other factors which may be recorded include interpersonal communication skills, communication patterns, major roles and leadership styles.

Assignment 6.10 – **Improving the effectiveness of student communications**

List the ways in which students may be assisted during a course to communicate effectively.

Assess the quality of your own students' communication skills and decide whether any of the ways of increasing effectiveness that you have listed can be introduced in your classes.

Discuss your list and proposals with colleagues and evaluate the feasibility of actually introducing the new methods and the likely outcomes of the innovation.

Notes and references
1   B. Bernstein, 'Social Class Language and Socialisation' in S.A. Abramson (ed.), *Current Trends in Linguistics*, Mouton Press, The Hague 1971.
2   The title of the package is, 'RP390 Materials Pack — Staff Development for a Multicultural Society' and further information is available from FEU, Elizabeth House, London SE1 7PH.
3   *FE can really change your life*, FEU/NUS, 1987.
4   See R. Bandler and J. Grinder, *Frogs into Princes: neuro-linguistic programming*, Real People Press, Moab, Utah 1979. R. Bandler and J. Grinder, *ReFraming: neuro-linguistic programming and the transformation of meaning*, Real People Press, Moab, Utah 1982.
5   R.E. Young, R. Arnold and K. Watson, 'Linguistic Models' in *The International Encyclopedia of Teaching and Teacher Education*, (ed.) M.J. Dunkin, Pergamon Press, Oxford 1987, pp 49–58.
6   J.McH. Sinclair and R.M. Coulthard, *Towards an Analysis of Discourse: the English used by teachers and pupils*, Oxford University Press, 1975.
7   Getting students to copy notes from the board is considered by many to be of little or no value. 'Taking' (as opposed to 'making') a 'good set of notes' provides no evidence that learning results from the practice.
8   A. Castling (ed.), D. Scott *et al.*, *The New 730 – A Handbook for Use in the Part-time and In-service Training of Teachers in Further and Adult Education*, National Association for Staff Development, Colchester 1987, p 60.
9   R.M. Gagné, *The Conditions of Learning*, Holt, Rinehart and Winston, New York 1965, p 58.
10 R. Leeper, 'A study of a neglected portion of the field of learning — the development of sensory organization, in *Journal of Genetic Psychology*, 46, pp 41–75.
11 Source: *Core Skills in YTS (Part 1)*, Manpower Services Commission, September 1984.

CHAPTER SEVEN

Role

Aim: To enable teachers to make effective appraisals of their own professional responsibilities and teaching styles

7.001 Describing further and adult education

Adult education

In a contribution to Blond's *Encyclopaedia of Education*[1] Brian Groombridge writes:

> Adult education is inevitably the most compendious, heterogeneous and imprecise of all categories of educational provision. Unlike the others (primary schooling or higher education, for example), adult education does not cater for any particular academic level, it is provided by a large number of dissimilar agencies, and the age span it covers is exceptionally wide.

Groombridge describes the wide range of studies and activities embraced by adult education providers and gives examples of the type of classes covered, with the Adult Literacy Programme at one end of a continuum, and maintaining the knowledge of graduates at the peak of contemporary scholarship and research at the other. He goes on to suggest that between the two extremes it is possible to find students studying at all levels in order to satisfy educational needs derived from say, imperfections in schooling, leisure occupation or advances in knowledge itself. Adult education enables people to

> . . . undertake studies or pursue activities which while they may be attempted in schools or colleges, make better sense to people with some experience of life — aspects of literature, political studies and history, parentcraft, for instance — or for which the need may not have made itself felt until adult life.

At one time 'adult education' was thought of as being education for adults that was non-vocational and did not lead to qualifications. Clearly, that concept is no longer valid, since the modern adult education service is very much a route for continuing education, progression, and nationally recognised qualifications and training. In addition, it is an important provider of education in leisure-time occupation, specialised interests, skills associated with organised cultural training and recreational activities.

Adult education programmes for the public and their own members are provided by organisations such as the trades unions, The Industrial Society, The Workers' Educational Association, National Federation of Women's Institutes, National Farmers' Union; and the many social and cultural associations, trade federations, sports clubs and youth organisations.

The demand for adult education is increasing as a result of current trends in work and leisure patterns; it has also been promoted by the examples set by the Open University and Open College and by relatively greater governmental enthusiasm, and not least by the long-established and excellent provisions of adult education across the UK.

A teacher's professional relationships with colleagues, customers and other further and adult education establishments is discussed in Appendix F.

Further education institutions

Further education (FE) is an educational facility for those who have left school and wish to participate in part-time or full-time vocational or non-vocational studies. Pupils of schools also use further education facilities in connection with link courses and work experience. Work-related courses, vocational training inputs and assessment and relevant underpinning knowledge training is also provided. Government-sponsored initiatives also make extensive use of further education college facilities backed by the commercial and industrial expertise of lecturers.

The term 'further education' incorporates education provided by the University of Industry, national colleges and institutions of higher education, evening institutes, colleges of further education, organisations that specifically cater for the 16–19 age group and sometimes overlap sixth-form school provision; and monotechnics specialising in one particular subject or discipline such as agriculture or art.

Governance

The Government White Paper, *Higher Education: A New Framework*, and the two volumes of *Education and Training for the 21st Century* are documents that had profound implications for the future of providers. As a result, LEA-maintained colleges were taken out of the local government sector and established as corporate bodies, with a distinct legal identity and with charitable status. As such, they were given powers to provide services, employ their own staff, enter into contracts, and manage assets and resources. This innovation was later implemented and operating but in the process created considerable flux with LEAs and FE and adult education agencies.

From April 1993, the further education sector comprising colleges of further education, tertiary colleges and sixth-form colleges which previously received grants direct from the Government were duly given the autonomy to manage their own affairs. This meant that under the watchful eye of the relevant governing body, finance and management issues could be resolved in-house and all organisational matters including pay and conditions of service contracts could be determined.

Provision of learning opportunities

The DfEE considers that typically, a large FE college offers a highly flexible and comprehensive platform for lifelong learning, catering for both young people or adults by offering full-time, part-time or distance learning in most academic, vocational and professional qualifications subjects ranging from foundation to degree level.

Local authorities are responsible for making adequate provision for educational opportunities available to individuals seeking courses that do not lead to formal qualifications.

Tuition fee structure

Colleges are free to formulate their own strategy for setting the level of tuition fees for students over the age of 18 years. Tuition fees are not normally levied for 16–18-year-old local and EU students in full-time education. Students of any age, whether full time or part time, may be charged other fees such as registration, examination and certification fees.

Students of any age attending part-time courses may be charged tuition fees, and colleges must set out clearly their approach to charging such fees, including any arrangements for reducing charges in specific instances. Further education colleges may charge students for registration fees, examination entries and certification fees, books, equipment or other study material.

Further Education Charter

The Further Education Charter sets out national targets which all colleges are expected to meet. It tells local employers and members of the local community what service they have a right to expect from a college. It also gives advice on what to do if things go wrong.

Responsiveness

In order to maximise responsiveness, funding mechanisms for colleges and universities are designed to encourage them to react to student demand and to build partnerships with business. The rapid growth in student numbers and the growing diversity of programmes provided reflects the responsiveness of institutions to changing demand.

The Learning and Skills Council (LSC)

The national Learning and Skills Council (LSC) was set up to oversee and implement strategies focused on the needs of individuals, businesses and communities in partnership with other key bodies backed by a rigorous independent inspection regime to underpin the LSC's focus on improving the quality of learning.

The local LSCs, now responsible for planning and funding all post-16 education and training up to HE (in England), will ensure that community needs are met and FE will be well placed to meet requirements, the training and education responsibilities of the FEFC[2] and the TECs having been transferred to the LSCs.

Developing post-16 teachers and trainers

The following quotation, taken from the DfEE's publication *The Learning and Skills Council Prospectus – Learning to Succeed* (1999) describes how the LSC proposes to ensure the quality and effectiveness of practitioners' teaching, training and learning skills and the involvement of the standards-setting agencies in preparing compulsory teaching qualifications for teachers in further education and trainers in work-based learning.

High quality provision relies on people with the necessary skills. All providers will need to demonstrate to the local LSC that their staff have appropriate, nationally recognised qualifications or have personal development plans leading to appropriate, nationally recognised qualifications or units. In addition, all staff will be encouraged to undertake continuous professional development or education. The LSC will base its requirements on the work being carried out by DfEE in consultation with the Employment National Training Organisation (ENTO) which sets standards for trainers in work based learning, and the Further Education NTO, which sets standards for further education teachers.

Assessment

The Learning and Skills Bill set the legislative framework for proposals embodied in the White Paper *Learning to Succeed – A New Framework for Post-16 Learning* (1999) and provides for a common inspection framework between the Office for Standards in Education (OFSTED) and the Adult Learning Inspectorate (ALI). The ALI remit includes the inspection of further education training funded by the LSC in whole or part; LEA-funded further education; training provided by the Secretary of State; and other education and training as may be prescribed.

The remit of HM Chief Inspector of Schools (HMCI) (OFSTED) will be extended to include education of the under-16s in colleges, further education within the FE sector or provided by LEAs for those aged 16–19.

In practice, ALI and HMCI is required to advise the Secretary of State on the quality of education and training, the standards achieved, financial efficiency and value for money. This will be achieved by carrying out inspections and providing reports. Providers will be required to provide action plans on any inspection report.

Higher education

A large proportion of young people (about one-third in England and Wales and almost half in Scotland) continues in education at a more advanced level beyond the age of 18. This higher education (HE) sector provides a variety of courses up to degree and postgraduate degree level and carries out research. Increasingly the sector is also catering for older students. Over 50 per cent of students are now aged over 25 and many study part time.

Governance

Higher education institutions are legally independent corporate institutions, accountable through individual governing bodies which carry ultimate responsibility for all aspects of the institution.

Universities have substantial freedom from central control and are able to appoint their own staff, decide which students to admit, what and how to teach, what research to undertake, and which degrees to award. Each institution can decide on the qualification level at which they are prepared to accept student applicants. Special admission arrangements can apply for older students whom the higher education institution believes could benefit from a course of study.

The Higher Education Charter sets out the standards of service that should be available from higher education institutions in England. In Scotland the equivalent charter is the Further and Higher Education Charter. (Source: DfEE)

Assignment 7.1 – Relationships between establishments

Broadly identify and describe the nature and function of, and the relationships between, institutions and agencies of further, higher and adult education.

Assignment 7.2 – Purpose of the continuing education

Find out all you can about underlying concepts relating to the terms: 'community education', 'education permanente', 'lifelong education' and 'recurrent education'.

Use the information gathered to make a case for the education of adults and for the maintenance or expansion of lifelong learning opportunities as an essential part of national policy.

Consider the function of continuing education as a 'remedial' or 'second chance' activity and discuss the value of education and training as a means of meeting individual and community needs.

Assignment 7.3 – Describing the nature and function of continuing education services

Two definitions of 'adult education' are given below. Consider whether in your opinion either one adequately defines the function, purpose and role of the institution where you teach. Justify your conclusions.

A 'Adult education is the organised provision of learning situations to enable mature men and women to enlarge and interpret their own living experiences.'

B 'Adult education is education provided for adults for general educational rather than vocational reasons. It has much in common with 'education permanente', 'lifelong learning' and 'recurrent education'.[3]

7.002 Identifying institutions and agencies associated with further and adult education

Looking now at the concept of external agencies, suppliers and customers it is clear that teachers will need to be able to identify and describe those institutions and agencies with which post-16 education and training is concerned. They then need to establish links with those people responsible for features of the service that they, as teachers or referral agents, may need to access.

1 The DfEE (now DfES)

While knowledge of the aims, goals and objectives of the Department for Education and Employment (DfEE) may seem somewhat remote from the day-to-day work of the practitioner, they should be aware of its function, its overall strategy and its relationship with the institution in which they work. Additionally, knowledge of the DfEE's goal to combat discrimination based on gender, race and age in employment and education is fundamental to the teacher's role. Its strong commitment to information technology and its intent to establish a network of learning centres linked to the National Grid for Learning and the University for Industry is also worth noting.

An account of the DfEE **workplan** formulated for the early 2000s might be a suitable way of outlining the nature of the government department responsible for education. The plan specified the Department's aim and a number of objectives and targets for 2002. The aim was: *To give everyone a chance, through education, training and work, to realise their full potential, and thus build an inclusive and fair society and a competitive economy*. In order to achieve the desired outcome three key objectives were specified.

The **first objective** was to *ensure that all young people reached 16 with the skills, attitudes and personal qualities that would give them a secure foundation for lifelong learning, work and citizenship in a rapidly changing world*. In order to meet this objective, schoolteachers and support staff would be the key players in providing a firm foundation for children's education, and where necessary steps would need to be taken to improve school standards. This was backed up by increasing nursery places, reducing the number of pupils in infant classes of over 30, reinforcing numeracy and literacy support programmes, reducing school truancies and exclusions, and seeking to increase the success rate and improve grades in GCSEs.

The **Qualifications and Curriculum Authority** (QCA) was called upon to review the National Curriculum so that a revised curriculum could be implemented in schools, with further revisions being planned for the future. Effective implementation of the improvement of school standards would be enhanced by facilitating an action plan that was drawn up to create a better led, better rewarded and better trained teaching profession.

Leaving school with good grades and the requisite level of foundation and key skills would obviously open up more routes for progression to H/FE learning opportunities and/or vocational qualification programmes, training and work.

The **second objective** was to *develop in everybody a commitment to lifelong learning, so as to enhance their lives, improve their employability in a changing labour market and create the skills that our economy and employers need.* The achievement of this objective would therefore be a key factor in the attainment of **objective three**, which was *to help people without a job into work.*

Significant improvements were made to the quality of vocational qualifications, making ownership of related qualifications more attractive to employers. Accordingly, in order to improve employability the DfEE set targets for increases in the proportion of those aged 19 achieving Level 2 NVQ and 21 year olds with a Level 3 qualification. The target for Level 4 qualifications was also raised. The importance of the **Investors in People** programme in supporting would-be NVQ candidates and other learners was recognised because without the support and commitment of employers to the **lifelong learning** strategy little of real value would be achieved.

National Traineeships focusing on NVQs at Level 2 were greatly expanded, pre-vocational provision for those who most needed help and support was developed, and the Right to Time Off for study or training for 16- and 17-year-old employees was implemented. Other Government-supported training included **Modern Apprenticeships** and Work-Based Training for Adults.

Modern Apprenticeships are open to young people between the ages of 16 and 19 to enable them to train for jobs at craft, technician and trainee management level. They provide training within industry-designed frameworks under an agreement between apprentices and their employers. The apprenticeship leads to a Level 3 NVQ or SVQ and includes core skills.

Today, young people beyond compulsory school age who do not continue in school or further education have access to work-based training aimed at providing skills and underpinning knowledge applicable to their chosen job or occupation. Employers pay for the majority of all work-related training.

Individual Learning Accounts (ILAs)

The Inland Revenue Tax Relief for Vocational Training (VTR) entitlement was scrapped in 2000 to be replaced by a national framework for the provision of **Individual Learning Accounts** (ILAs). The ILA was designed to encourage people who were not currently investing in their own learning to make a start in gaining new skills or updating existing knowledge or skills needed to survive in today's volatile workplace. When first introduced, applicants would register on the scheme and show commitment to the programme by making savings (or an investment) of £25 towards the ILA. Once the applicant was registered, an amount of £150 was added by the funding agency towards the cost of learning.

The Government's Welfare to Work programme, the implementation of the New Deals for Young and Adult Unemployed, and Lone Parents into Work were designed to meet the **third objective**, which was to help people without a job into work.

New Deal

The Government also provides financial support for training young people, unemployed people and other priority groups, and was concerned to ensure that all unemployed people received every opportunity to improve their employability and contribution to society. Accordingly, young people between the ages of 18 and 24 who had been unemployed for more than six months were offered several options, each of which included a training element. Some over 25s were offered a chance to study full time for up to a year while remaining on benefit. (Source: DfEE)

All of these initiatives and others led directly or indirectly to more work for FE colleges.

2 Adult guidance services

A key function of a **careers service company** is to contribute to the learning and prosperity of individuals. It does this by providing impartial information, guidance and help to enable people to enter appropriate education, training or employment. In doing so it must promote equality of opportunity and raise aspirations.

Local careers service companies are required to be actively involved with careers teachers/advisers in schools and colleges in planning and delivering high-quality careers information and programmes of careers education and guidance.

Careers services therefore offer help in achieving career potential through a range of consultation services designed to assist clients to plan their future. The aim is to help people reach confident and informed career decisions which lead to success in learning and work, or to provide guidance and support for people facing redundancy or redeployment.

A careers service aims to help individuals move from full-time education into suitable work or further training. It provides a guidance, information and employment service to young people, their parents and employers. There are also professionally qualified advisers who specialise in working with handicapped young people, pupils of high academic potential, students in further and higher education, the unwaged and young people undergoing vocational training.

The basis of any good career decision is up-to-date careers information, and careers advisers spend much of their time interviewing and supporting people at appropriate stages in their personal development. They also help in job searches and improving application techniques.

In order to provide reliable vocational guidance, careers advisers need to be well versed in the use of modern methods such as vocational assessment tests, aptitudes assessment, personality profiling, CV design, personal interview coaching and use of careers information databases and libraries. Then by discussing with clients the various options that are available, the careers adviser can help clarify the client's thoughts, making sure that they are aware of the full range of opportunities available to them.

Careers company offices normally have access to a careers library with a wide range of books and pamphlets, and advisers can contact sources holding other information relating to careers, employment, further, higher and adult education, sponsorships and sources of funding, and training courses. Prospectuses of many universities, colleges and other training providers are normally held.

3 Referral agencies

Particular learning difficulties or problems that cannot be readily resolved with the teacher, and those needing help with organising themselves may be referred to qualified people in the special needs unit, educational guidance and counselling unit, student support services or specialist training providers as appropriate.

Referral is the act of directing a student or colleague to a practitioner who is specially trained or equipped to meet that person's special needs. Alternatively a special programme of support could be made available, using a mentor. People seeking advice will expect teachers to respond quickly to requests for information about where to seek help and who to contact at referral agencies. Knowing whom to contact and establishing linkages with the referral agency or support person is therefore a must for teachers.

4 The Youth Service

The Youth Service, which in Scotland is part of the Community Education Service, is a small, complex and diverse service, essentially local in nature, managed by local authorities and voluntary bodies. Its primary purpose is to promote the personal and social education of young people aged 11–25, with a special focus on the 13–19 age group. It offers challenging experiences and opportunities designed to help young people develop their potential as individuals and members of groups in the transition from childhood to adult life. It is largely funded through local authorities with some direct contributions from the Government. (Source: DfEE)

5 Education services in prisons and youth custody centres

The Prison Service is legally obliged to offer educational opportunities to all prisoners including those who are unsentenced, sentenced and young offenders (under 21). The aim of the education provision is to ensure that inmates are given the appropriate skills and experience to enable them to take up further training or employment on release in order to live a 'good and useful life'.

The Prison Service has contracted out, through a national competitive tendering process, the delivery of education services in each of its establishments. The contracts were awarded in January 1999, mainly to colleges of further education. A few private training organisations were also awarded contracts. The contractors are required to deliver a specified core curriculum including literacy, numeracy, social and life skills and information technology. Other courses are provided based on an initial needs assessment conducted during the induction period. Contractors are required to ensure that high-quality externally accredited courses are delivered by qualified, experienced and well-trained teachers.

It is estimated that at least 50 per cent of prisoners are excluded from 95 per cent of jobs in the community because they have low ability in areas of literacy, numeracy and work-related skills. Much of the prison governor's budget for education is therefore devoted to redressing these deficiencies.

A typical prison education programme will attempt to meet the assessed needs of its population and usually includes some or all of the following elements:

- induction testing, assessment, reviewing
- basic and post-basic literacy and numeracy
- examination courses leading to external accreditations including the Open University
- vocational education and training courses that integrate practical and theoretical skills and knowledge (most of these are provided directly by the Prison Service)
- application of information technology
- open learning opportunities for inmates who wish to pursue minority subjects
- social education and pre-release courses which provide careers advice and job-seeking skills
- evening courses which encourage the development of recreational skills or hobbies
- full-time education for all inmates of school age.

The cost of providing education services in prisons is met by the Prison Service through individual prison governors. (Source: Peter Blunt, Strode College)

6 NACRO

The National Association for the Care and Resettlement of Offenders (NACRO) is an independent voluntary organisation dealing constructively with offenders. It manages a wide range of projects across the UK and its work in prisons includes training workshops. Other projects concern working with education authorities to help young people return to mainstream education or other training.

NACRO also provides people to help the community by offering services for the elderly, disabled and single-parent families such as draught-proofing, loft insulation, painting and decorating, or gardening. Some educational establishments are actively involved with NACRO, and skills relating to instructional techniques in these topics may have valuable transferable elements.

7 Training centres

There are many different types of commercially operated training centres providing training on a long-term or drop-in basis. Their function is to serve the training and development needs of local companies, many of whom would be unable to support a major in-house training provision; and also Government-sponsored learning opportunities.

In the case of an industrial training centre, skills training might be provided in electronics, electrical engineering and electrical installations, production and mechanical engineering, auto engineering, plant maintenance and industrial automation and control.

8 Qualifications and Curriculum Authority

The Qualifications and Curriculum Authority (QCA) came into being on 1 October 1997. This new organisation brings together the work of the National Council for Vocational Qualifications (NCVQ) and the School Curriculum and Assessment Authority (SCAA), with additional powers and duties.

At the heart of QCA's work is the establishment of a coherent national framework of academic and vocational qualifications. Teachers will therefore be concerned with the lifelong learning aspects of QCA.

9 Workers' Educational Association

The Workers' Educational Association (WEA), founded in 1903, is a nationwide democratic voluntary organisation composed of student members, individual sub-scribers and affiliated organisations. Registered as a charity, it has no party political or sectarian ties. Through its network of branches WEA involves students in choosing and planning their own courses.

Day, evening and part-time courses are available in a wide range of non-vocational and liberal studies. Study tours are also organised by the WEA to various locations at home and overseas, and a number of short courses are also mounted.

The WEA operates in cities, towns and rural villages. It is always ready to expand its activities to new locations and would welcome help from people willing to undertake social, administrative or lecturing duties in their locality.

10 Adult numeracy and literacy

Adult basic education seeks to help people to acquire fundamental skills and knowledge that include:

> ... literacy and other verbal skills, including English as a second language; basic skills in number; and a body of general knowledge relevant to the day-to-day lives of adults in society; together with those other elements of education, both formal and informal, without which an adult might find himself cut off from continuing education, vocational preparation, or cultural and recreational activity.[4]

The setting up of future learning opportunities will involve a great deal of planning by people who are experienced in the field of basic education, if they are to provide the right level of flexibility, response to student needs and easy access to education for all. In the publication: 'A workshop approach to basic skills',[5] Chris Maples highlights lessons learned from the experience of running a workshop for four years and gives a diagrammatical representation of the workshop (see Figure 7.1). The aim of the

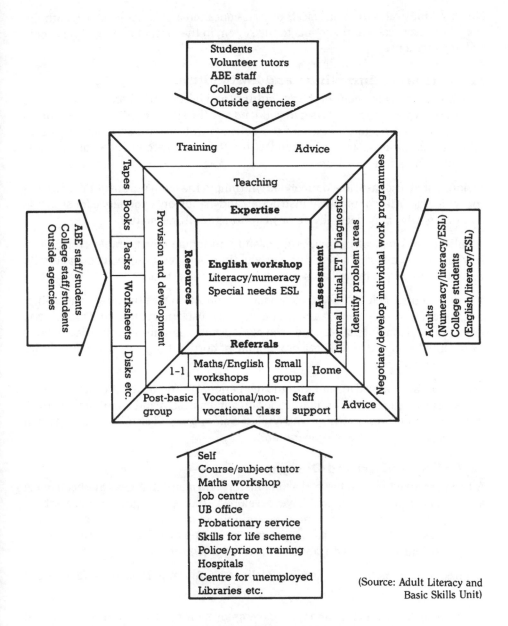

Figure 7.1 The workshop as a central focus for adult basic education (ABE) provision throughout an area

workshop is, 'to offer help and support to any individuals from the community or students on college courses whose lack of literacy skills prevents them from achieving their goals.'

Figure 7.1 illustrates the many facets of basic education provision and shows both the workshop resources and the inputs to the system in the form of participating people and organisations.

11 Colleges of Agriculture and Horticulture

Education for employment in the agricultural and horticultural sectors takes place in these colleges. They may be set in parkland and the size of estates may amount to several hundred hectares. Many of the colleges will operate sizeable farms that reflect the farming systems to be found within their wide catchment areas as well as national trends in agriculture.

Various enterprises are run commercially, although the main purpose of the farms is to provide facilities for practical instruction and 'hands-on' experience for students and others who may need advice or help on agricultural matter.

A college farm typically provides grassland and forage crops, arable crops, dairy sections, calf-rearing and beef cattle production facilities, poultry, game and milk products, flocks of sheep, herds of pigs and other livestock.

A general course includes: livestock production; nutrition, health and stockmanship; crop production – cereals, grassland and arable crops; farm vehicles and machinery; farm and estate maintenance; and farm management. A range of countryside skills would also be offered as well as a programme of horticultural courses, plant clinics and demonstrations.

Courses are also offered in: amenity and recreational horticulture; groundsmanship and sports turf management; landscape and garden design and maintenance; fruit, vegetable and flower growing; botany; flower arranging; glasshouse work; garden machinery maintenance and operation.

12 Colleges of Art and Design

Art and design education has had a long history and many changes have been made as the subject and profession have developed. Today, colleges are successfully meeting the demands of both industry and individual students, having organised themselves to meet modern day commitments relating to vocational design courses as well as long-established traditional art and design work.

A **mission statement**[6] of a leading College of Art and Design is reproduced below:

> To satisfy local, regional and national employment needs for staff educated and trained to various levels of creative sensibility and technical competence to carry out design-related activities in a variety of occupations dependant upon the particular area of specialisation.

> To provide each student with an accurate and realistic insight into design-related employment opportunities, requirements and prospects; to structure their courses to provide every student with the educational and professional

experiences necessary to enhance their employment prospects and to develop their creative, intellectual and craft skills to a high level; to encourage the students' personal development and their ability to adapt to changing circumstances; to provide encouragement, advice and assessment to fully realise their individual potential.

A management tree showing how a large art and design college may be structured is given in Figure 7.2. The example shows the very diverse work of an enterprising college.

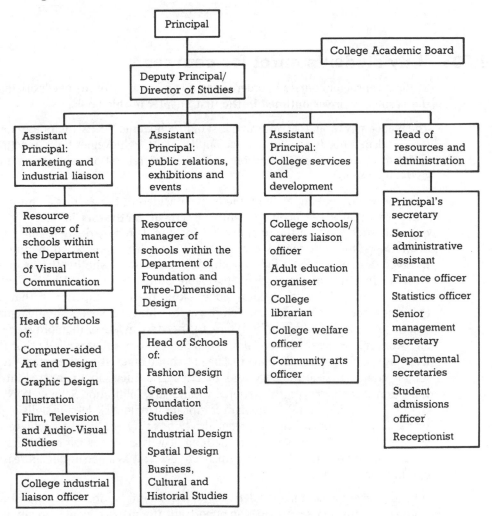

Figure 7.2 Structure of a College of Art and Design

Assignment 7.4 – Identifying interacting institutions and agencies

It is important for teachers to have a basic knowledge of the national structure of the education system and an up-to-date knowledge of those institutions and agencies with which you and your employer interact. You can test and develop your knowledge and understanding of the system by carrying out the following:

- broadly identify and describe those institutions and agencies with which further and adult education are involved
- produce a diagram showing the linkages between your own college or centre with other colleges and referral agencies in your catchment area. Add a brief description of each.

7.003 Why students enrol for courses

Students enrol for courses in order to satisfy one or more of the needs arising from the secondary drives outlined in the first chapter of this book.

The reader may recall that 'Murray's List of Psychogenic Needs' includes references to a student's needs concerning accomplishment, achievement and recognition; self-respect and esteem; ambition and prestige; relaxation, entertainment and social interaction.

Another way of looking at the topic is by considering the extrinsic and intrinsic motivators that cause people to enrol. **Extrinsic motivators** include vocational concepts such as when the unemployed enrol to gain a marketable skill that will open doors to work where the new skill can be applied and remuneration received — in other words, for some kind of actual reward whether this be in money terms or in terms of some other observable outcome. Included in the extrinsic category would be gaining knowledge, skills or work experience that would enhance career prospects, promotion or employability prospects should a planned change of occupation be sought. Where the need to update or to improve academic and work related qualifications prompts a person to enrol, it is likely that further learning opportunities will relate to a need to build on existing strengths. Students join a course to learn theory and practice and then obtain accreditation or validation of competences (the National Vocational Qualification Scheme [S/NVQs] is an example of this) or otherwise obtain certification for knowledge and skills acquired. **Intrinsic motivators** provide a potent drive to satisfy the need to achieve or for challenge, or the desire to master something new. This need is felt by the individual concerned, and others may be quite unable to detect it as a person's main reason for enrolling on a course.

Interest and enjoyment may be derived from social interaction with other students. Going to evening classes provides an opportunity for married women to mix socially with others and to enjoy a refreshing break from the disciplined constraints of caring for others in the home. A desire to become healthier may motivate someone to join a yoga, macrobiotics or keep-fit class. Likewise a desire to become more attractive and have greater choice in fashion wear may lead a person to the local weightwatchers group.

The pleasure derived from study itself may become habit-forming, so that one becomes a 'permanent student'. Adult education classes may be a very useful way of occupying spare time, especially when making the transition to retirement, or when being threatened with idleness due to unemployment.

Obviously, mainline further and adult education offers just about every type of subject and course that could be conceived and accommodates a very large clientele drawn from all industries, commercial enterprises and institutions. Local and national government, the health service, public utilities and the many large and small businesses will each supply many thousands of students, enrolling for different reasons. The teacher needs to be prepared for anything when it comes to the personal needs and reasons behind the enrolment of his or her student group.

Unfortunately many will have aspirations and needs that neither they nor you can hope to fulfil, and that is why careful selection may in some cases be necessary in order to avoid later disillusionment and feelings of failure. It will not always be possible to negotiate individual learning programmes, especially where budgets and staffing are limited. Alternative methods of study such as open-learning, distance learning, learning shops, learn direct, the BBC learning zone at www.bbc.co.uk/ learning zone or other Internet locations may need to be recommended to meet the student's needs.

Some subjects are followed particularly as a means of improving employability and career prospects. They include: construction trades such as brickwork, painting and decorating, plumbing, carpentry and DIY; car maintenance; business studies, particularly bookkeeping, accounting, office practice and skills such as shorthand and typing; computer studies; small business topics; cookery and catering; horticulture, gardening and flower arranging; and beauty therapy.

Other subjects that are very popular include: foreign languages; English literature and language; social work and social services; art, including painting, pottery, handicrafts and jewellery making; leisure, sport and gymnastics.

Assignment 7.5 – Factors causing students to attend further and adult education courses

'Adult education refers to any learning activity or programme deliberately designed for adults. Its ambit is taken as spanning non-vocational, vocational, general, formal, non-formal and community education and it is not restricted to any particular level.'[7]

Part A
Write down a statement that in your opinion describes the word 'adult'. Your statement may well embrace those attributes or parameters that relate to an adolescent; someone who is termed 'adult' because they have attained the age of 18 years; someone who has completed 'normal' full-time education; a 'mature' person or any other concept you may have.

Part B
With reference to the client groups attending your own classes list the factors that you have found to be prime factors causing and motivating them to enrol for courses.

Part C

Use your findings relating to A and B as the basis for a group discussion.

Consider how the outcomes of the discussions might influence your teaching style or learning methodology.

7.004 Appraising social and educational backgrounds of student groups

The main relationships between social class and educational opportunity and attainment

> The backbone of class structure, and indeed of the entire reward system of modern western society, is the occupational order. Other sources of economic and symbolic advantage do co-exist alongside the occupational order, but for the vast majority of the population, these tend at best, to be secondary to those deriving from the division of labour.[8]

Primary inequalities in Britain are made up of differences between individuals and groups in the form of income, wealth, class and power from which stem secondary inequalities, including inequality in the areas of health, housing and education. In order to consider inequalities within the educational system, it is first necessary to look at the primary sources of inequality.

The most commonly used indicator of social class in Britain and the USA is occupation. Blau and Duncan[9] suggest that the occupational structure in modern industrial society not only constitutes an important foundation for social stratification, but also serves as the connecting link between institutions and spheres of social life, and hierarchies of prestige, economic class, political power and authority. They go on to say that the occupational structure is the link between the economy and the family through which the economy affects the family's status, and by which the family supplies manpower to the economy.

Income is, in general, directly linked to occupation, with managers, scientists and professionals receiving higher remuneration than labourers for example. This difference in income and social class deriving from occupation, forms the basis of one of the primary dimensions of inequality and directly affects an individual's education. Educational inequality is therefore essentially a social problem.

Recent psychological knowledge indicates that ability is largely acquired, and that children can become more or less 'intelligent' according to the kind of family they have, together with the social and educational experiences they receive. Family background and lifestyle play an important part in the development of a child's academic performance, and where home values and norms correspond to those of the school, the child has a greater opportunity to succeed in school-valued tasks. Professor Bernstein's theory of linguistic codes (see Chapter Six) stresses the importance of language and learning, and points to disadvantages in coming from a home where public language or restricted code is spoken, in view of the fact that schools are essentially middle-class institutions.

If children are labelled 'culturally deprived', teachers will have lower expectations of them — expectations which the children will undoubtedly fulfil. The children will be expected to drop their social identity, way of life and values at the school gate and switch on to a completely different culture more representative of a middle-class lifestyle — supervised by teachers, the majority of whom either originated from middle-class families or adopted middle-class values during the course of their education or teacher training.

In an attempt to reduce educational inequalities in the United States and Britain after the Second World War, priority was given to egalitarian reforms. In Britain, this was evident in policies to abolish selection to introduce comprehensive education and to promote positive discrimination in favour of the most disadvantaged groups. The Plowden Report findings indicated that socially disadvantaged children need a greater slice of the education cake in the form of positive discrimination. This was to be in the form of better schools and better teachers, trained to teach a curriculum to suit the children's needs and aspirations. Comprehensives were introduced to reduce some of the inequalities of opportunity existing in society and to eliminate inequalities that go with low income, broken homes or living in difficult conditions in inner city areas.

Political processes for school provision in the form of the variety of schools provided by the state, school-leaving age, buildings, staff/student ratios and political processes at local level, greatly influence the education opportunities available to children within a given area. The area of residence directly affects educational opportunities, depending on range and number of places available. In 'The State in Capitalist Society'[10], Ralph Miliband says that educational institutions at all levels generally fulfil an important conservative role and act, with greater or lesser effectiveness, as legitimising agencies in and for their societies. He goes on to say that today, as in the past, elite schools consciously seek to instil into their charges a conservative philosophy based on tradition, religion, nationalism, authority, and hierarchy, together with an exceedingly narrow view of the meaning of democracy, and hostility towards socialist ideas and purposes. While entry to an elite school is theoretically open to all members of society, a tight selection process operates, which works in favour of children from higher social class background and incomes.

Non-school factors at the level of the home, local authority and central government affect the life chances of children; while factors such as streaming, selection and type of school attended can contribute to educational inequality. In some cases, schools do no more than train children for future role performance, often as low-paid, low-skilled workers, thereby confirming their class destiny and station in life. For some, the school provides the means of upward mobility, and a few may be creamed off into a class higher than the social class of their parents. For the majority it will be the means of providing advanced capitalist society with a pool of trained personnel to keep the system going.

This state of affairs is likely to persist unless primary dimensions of inequality in society are eliminated by radical government policy, after which, secondary inequalities such as educational inequality will be alleviated. In the meantime, differences in learning abilities of young adults and their attitudes toward learning will create problems for the teacher in further and adult education — problems that demand a sympathetic approach and much resolve on the part of the teacher to help students overcome the adverse effects of an unfortunate start to their lifetime of learning. However, an equal commitment is needed from the learner if progress is to be made.

The social development of adolescents

The modern adolescent is growing up in a turbulent world. The rapid social change which followed the Second World War still continues today. Urban growth, together with its attendant infrastructure, has produced a revolution in the fields of communications and technology. Knowledge and the development of high technology required to cope with the demands of a relatively affluent society have caused greater pressures on young people than those experienced in the past. Human aspirations have reached new high levels, fired by the effect of mass media, and modern youth has been caught up in the spiral of increasing industrialistion and consumerism.

Automation eliminates the need for skilled operators, although the need for highly skilled technicians remains. Fewer jobs for unskilled and semi-skilled workers are now available as the silicon chip and computer-controlled robots take over. Competition for jobs is now becoming fierce and many school leavers are finding it difficult to obtain employment. To stand any chance of obtaining meaningful employment with prospects, job applicants must obtain good grades at school, and leave with adequate qualifications.

Numeracy and literacy standards become critical. To lack them as a result of underachievement is economic suicide, and for low achievers it means a permanent low level life standard. The need to find a job becomes of paramount importance to a young person, for without a job he or she lacks status and position in the social world. Pressures bearing on young people are further increased by instabilities in international politics. Teenagers are aware of the threat of nuclear holocaust, germ warfare and death. Radio and television broadcasts publicise the social and economic imbalance between the developed countries and the Third World. Eminent scientists disagree over the environmental future of the planet. In addition to these broader concerns, there are numerous day-to-day pressures — for example where poor communications exist between the police and adolescents, especially in the areas of motorcycle spot checks. Is it any wonder, then, that many young people challenge societal standards, attack conventions and live for the present?

Early socialisation takes place within the family unit. At first, language, culture and moral values are acquired through a process of interaction between the child and members of the immediate family, and later, with a wider circle of friends and acquaintances. Social learning theory suggests that learning takes place as a result of the child imitating those who are close, and receiving reinforcement and approval for desired behaviour. Within a nuclear family the parents are directly responsible for discipline and determine, to some extent, the child's formation of attitudes.

Adolescence is a time when the young person becomes involved in greater activity and social interaction outside the home. Greater freedom from direct parental control and increased mobility bring emancipation and greater personal responsibility. In their search for independence and a new identity, young adults are drawn into a world in which family links are weakened. The media bombards them with advertisements designed to stimulate demand for certain types of entertainment and products in the huge teenage markets. Money, required to satisfy needs arising from such sources, becomes important, and while wishing to become free agents, they are not in a position to give up the security and lack of responsibility which goes with continued economic dependence on parents. They live at home, subsidised by parents, either unable or unwilling to accept full responsibility for their own support. While living in the family home they come under pressure from parents to conform to their ideas of social norms. Friction arises as a result of conflicts of opinion. Aggressive outbursts are commonplace and defiance of parental authority results. The generation gap becomes apparent. Many people forget the problems of their own transition to adult status, and the adolescent often refuses to accept values of the older generation. Parental attitudes towards sex before marriage and adult expectations relating to commitment to work and studies conflict with the way adolescents see things, adding to the difficulties normally experienced in growing up.

Some are unable to make the adjustment to work and cannot find a niche to fill. They become alienated, drop out and seek status in other fields. They dress outrageously (in conventional terms) in an attempt to beat the establishment. However, thankfully, the vast majority of adolescents make the transition to adulthood without serious difficulties.

Assignment 7.6 – Students' social backgrounds

Some teachers suggest that there is a relationship between the student's social background (in terms of family lifestyle and environment, socio-economic status, and life outside the classroom) and classroom behaviour (in terms of general academic and task related activities, work placement outcomes, levels of achievement, degree of disruptive social behaviour, attitudes to learning, co-operating when learning and attendance patterns).

Some determinants of social backgrounds that have been used as bases for discussion include

- income, occupation and profession of parents
- education of parents and others in family
- family (cultural background, race, nationality)
- family (size and composition)
- material resources (property, district, and wealth)
- home environment and facilities
- availability of space, learning resources and media
- leisure activities, pastimes and pursuits.

Discuss with others your experiences and opinions, and relate the findings to your plans and intentions for the groups that you are teaching.

7.005 Relating group appraisals to planning

Teachers who adopt a caring approach to their work tend to get to know a fair bit about each and every one of their students. Adult students are quick to spot teacher interest, and once this is perceived, responsiveness and enthusiasm pervade the group. This helps teacher and students to give of their best. Even those teachers who may not wish to get so closely involved need to show that they do understand that students have different interests, needs and abilities. Some students will need specific guidance and advice, but all will seek either the physical or the mental well-being associated with participating in the learning opportunities provided. They will also seek the enjoyment and companionship to be shared in attending classes.

Formal or informal appraisal of group and individual needs is an essential prerequisite of successful planning for effective teaching and learning in adult education. The ability to determine with learners their educational needs, hopes and aspirations is a key teacher competence.

Learner needs

Learners come to the classroom or training centre with certain needs and expectations which they hope to fulfil. These expectations include social needs, such as taking an active part in group activities and competing with others. They also come with intrinsic needs such as the need to make progress, to satisfy curiosity and to perform a task well.

The arena is set when the group assembles. It is at this point that the teacher must be fully aware of their expectations and be prepared to help them fulfil their needs during the teaching and learning session planned for the next few hours.

Learner capabilities

More often than not, groups are formed randomly rather than by IQ, ability or expertise in certain topics. This is particularly true with mature students, open-learning students, the adult unemployed, and those receiving industrial and commercial updating and training.

All too often teachers pitch instruction at a predetermined level that they have set without reference to anyone else. They then proceed to work through the subject-matter assuming that everyone understands, unless students ask questions or otherwise seek clarification. There is often little likelihood of anyone interrupting the flow, since many learners are reluctant to tell the teacher that they do not understand. However, they should not need to. Well-prepared and considerate teachers will have anticipated areas of difficulty and will be asking check questions of an appropriate type to clarify what has been said or done.

Few questions are asked during badly prepared or hurriedly delivered lectures as it is often the case that to do so could be embarrassing for the students concerned. They fear the prospect of losing face and do not wish to expose themselves to the possibility of ridicule. Sometimes, each student assumes that the others clearly understand and that to ask a question is frankly a confession of ignorance. There is safety in silence, so, 'let it all go over my head' is an attitude that often prevails. To reduce the probability of this kind of situation developing, the teacher should at a very early stage, and preferably before classes commence, establish the level of existing knowledge and individual abilities.

If the first lesson is chosen for the diagnosis then the teacher could usefully spend time establishing a level by carefully framing questions, putting them to the group and obtaining responses from each individual during the session. Having established a suitable level, instruction should be pitched accordingly.

A 'planning-led' approach

A description of the characteristics of a 'typical' learner group may be drawn up either by researchers or by other means such as standard setting bodies, college 'gatekeepers', subject specialists, the learners themselves or analyses of statistical data relating to others who have followed similar courses. From any such reliable base, an attempt at planning can be made.

It is of course necessary to co-ordinate the needs of the individual with those of the institution and of other interested external agencies, and the teacher's plans and intentions for the group must ultimately result in the satisfaction of these needs.

Tyler[11] proposes four fundamental questions that must be answered in developing any curriculum and plan of instruction. The questions are:
– What educational purposes should the school seek to attain?
– What educational experiences can be provided that are likely to attain these purposes?
– How can these educational experiences be effectively organised?
– How can we determine whether these purposes are being attained?

Tyler suggests methods for studying these questions, but makes no attempt to answer them since as he says, '. . . the answers will vary to some extent from one level of education to another and from one school to another.'[12] It would however be helpful to list some of the sources from which to obtain information relating to the four questions.

In connection with the objectives of the provider institution, Tyler suggests a number of sources including:
– the learners themselves as a source of objectives
– studies of contemporary life outside the institution
– suggestions about objectives from subject specialists
– use of a psychology of learning and philosophy in selecting objectives.

Because the institution's objectives may have been derived from a number of the sources listed above, '. . . it is desirable to state these objectives in a form which makes them most helpful in selecting learning experiences and in guiding teaching.'[13]

Having dealt with the educational purposes of the institution, the next question posed relates to the identification of learning experiences that will lead to the attainment of the objectives written. In this respect, Tyler states: 'Learning takes place through the active behaviour of the student; it is what he does that he learns, not what the teacher does.'

This statement must be remembered by teachers. It is important to realise that it does not matter how expert we may be at lecturing, very little may be learned unless students are actively engaged themselves and have the opportunity to practise the behaviour implied by the objective. Tyler goes on to list four other general principles relating to learning experiences:

–Learning experiences must be such that the student obtains satisfaction from carrying on the kind of behaviour implied by the objectives.
–The reactions desired in the experience are within the range of possibility for the students involved.
– There are many particular experiences that can be used to attain the same educational objectives.
–The same learning experience will usually bring about several outcomes.[14]

When dealing with the question regarding the effective organisation of learning experiences, Tyler carefully considers the procedures for organising learning experiences into units and courses. Regarding organising principles, he writes:

> It is not only necessary to recognise that learning experiences need to be organised to achieve continuity, sequence, and integration, and that major elements must be identified to serve as organising threads for these learning experiences, it is also essential to identify the organising principles by which these threads shall be woven together.[15]

We must therefore be aware of the need to arrange for a meaningful and properly thought out course to be presented that has real utility for the students. They will value their learning experiences if they can organise them into a logical framework, internalise them and fit them into their life worlds; whether this be in the home, at leisure or in the workplace.

The final question, concerning evaluation, is a matter that now concerns all teachers. The monitoring and evaluation of educational processes, together with the need to maintain quality in an efficient and effective institutional environment is now a universal requirement.

Monitoring 'keeps the train on the rails'. In other words, by continuously observing and reporting on method, content and outcomes, control of the educational experiences can be maintained and if necessary, changes made in response to feedback coming from the monitoring process. Evaluation is a process of establishing precisely what has happened during the educational experience and measuring against some standard the efficiency and effectiveness of the learning process. Assessing the extent to which the institution's, teacher's and student's educational objectives have been met is an essential part of the evaluation process.

Feedback from the evaluation of learning is one of the keys to validating plans and intentions for the group and it is hoped that the information contained in this section can be 'fed back' into achieving the objective we started with, namely, relating group appraisals to the teacher's own plans and intentions for the group.

Assignment 7.7 – **Relating appraisals to planning**

Select one of your classes for this assignment and carry out an appraisal of their social and educational backgrounds.

Consider whether the course you have prepared for them adequately meets their needs and whether or not your own plans and intentions for the group were appropriate. Using the information given in the text evaluate the course in respect of its effectiveness in

– meeting institutional objectives for the course and client group
– providing learning experiences that usefully and efficiently enable students to attain their own and course objectives
– organising instruction and providing continuity, sequence and integration of learning experiences
– enabling a process of monitoring and evaluation to take place.

Assignment 7.8 – **The effects of group composition and group size on planning teaching strategies**

Teachers tend to react differently to individuals and small groups than to large groups. If this is so then there will be differences in relationships between teachers and their students. There will also be substantial differences in student involvement and in the feedback behaviour of teachers. Strategies for teaching effectively and efficiently so as to promote student achievement will need to be planned taking into account group composition and size.

Examine the instructional behavioural concepts given below:

– structuring
– soliciting
– responding
– reacting.

Give examples of each of these concepts as applied to teachers and students interacting in the teaching and learning situation.

Consider how group size and composition could affect classroom management and the degree of active student participation. Think about how the interaction between teacher and students could be affected, particularly when initiating activities, eliciting student response, giving feedback and conducting question and answer sessions.

Discuss your findings with colleagues and reflect on how theory and practice may be related to your own groups.

Assignment 7.9 – **Equal opportunities when selecting and recruiting students**

An important duty of teachers is to operate a policy within their employers' guidelines that provides for equal opportunities for both sexes. In the Coombe

Lodge Report[16] Steve Crabbe gives a 'Checklist for Equal Opportunities (Gender)' and explains that the draft checklist has been written 'in order to focus attention on the steps needed to be taken to ensure that educational establishments are providing equal opportunities with respect to issues of gender and sex discrimination.' The checklist contains a section relating to students in which the questions reproduced below are posed:

– Have steps been taken to ensure that both sexes are treated fairly in terms of selection and recruitment for courses and subject options? Have staff been alerted to possible unconscious prejudice and stereotyping in selection techniques, interviewing and publicity for courses?
– Are careers teachers and advisers aware of possible sex-stereotyping when giving guidance to students on employment and training?
– Are amenities and facilities for students in all buildings and departments equally available to students of both sexes?
– As far as you are concerned are you providing equal opportunities to those with whom you are involved?
– Are you free of bias when counselling, giving guidance or enrolling?
– Are you happy with the facilities provided for both sexes?

Survey the arrangements within your employing institution. List suggested improvements in provision of equal opportunities that you feel would be helpful.

7.006 Creating an environment conducive to learning

Establishing a rapport

Student-teacher relationships in the classroom are one of the more important factors in the learning process. Little or no learning can take place unless the students want to learn. The general assumption is that the majority of students enter a classroom with a desire to learn something, this being an intrinsic human characteristic. The outcome depends largely upon the teacher's apparent attitude towards them. How this is perceived can make or mar a lesson. Similarly, if the students themselves cannot identify with the teacher, the result can be disastrous. The ability to establish rapport rests upon the teacher's demonstration of a sympathetic attitude towards the group, and on the group's willingness to follow the teacher's lead. Mutual co-operation and support is the keystone of success.

Rapport is a difficult concept to describe and involves many facets, such as respect, regard, concern, harmony, solidarity and affiliation. If rapport can be established, the group will probably see eye-to-eye and a bond of union will be forged. This will result in the group acquiring a sense of belonging, a team spirit and good relations. A smooth pattern of interaction should then follow.

To some extent personality traits govern a teacher's ability to encourage rapport; but a trait is yet another elusive concept. One school of thought holds that a personality trait is a mental structure based upon consistent behaviour in a large number of situations. This would suggest that a teacher is always easy-going or aggressive, or persevering with every group during every lesson. Another theory suggests that there is no constant trait, but that behaviour depends upon past experiences with different groups.

It may be that teacher plus Group A are very compatible with a rapport well established, whereas the same teacher with Group B just cannot make headway due to an inability to establish rapport. The difference between the two groups will certainly show up when educational attainment is compared.

Possibly the best means of establishing rapport is to exhibit a firm, fair, warm and friendly attitude and to show empathy towards the group. Attention should be paid to making eye contact with each member of the group and speaking in a pleasant tone of voice. Group members should be treated as equals, within limits, and attempts made to break down social barriers. A keen interest should be taken in listening carefully to responses from the group when accepting answers, and if an incorrect response is offered, anxiety should be relieved by preserving the respondent's self-esteem.

Motivation and attention

G.K. Chesterton once wrote: 'There is no such thing on earth as an uninteresting subject; the only thing that can exist is an uninterested person.' If this assumption is correct then a way must be found of arousing interest and maintaining attention so that learning may proceed.

Knowledge of the learners' reasons for attending the learning session is of great help to the teacher. If the learners can see some personal gain at the end of the course and the content is relevant to their individual lives, the teacher starts with an advantage. If, however, the learners are present only because they have been told to attend or are under some form of duress, the teacher has problems.

An audience of 'pressed persons' is difficult to deal with. In such cases, the concepts to be discussed should, wherever possible, be based upon the learners' practical experiences or on things that are known generally; gradually developing the concept towards the more specific. At all times the teacher should be careful to use appropriate language and terminology.

Regardless of how complex the subject matter may be, answers to questions put to the group will reveal, more often than not, that several members know something about the subject or something closely allied to it. This information can be used to develop the theme and once the group starts to contribute, interest is aroused, even to the extent that some start competing to give information.

Manner

Teachers are not all cast from the same mould. Some blend easily with their new classes and quickly build up good face-to-face communication. Others find it difficult to achieve the right level of sensitivity and seem quite unable to see themselves as others do.

One's manner should reflect the importance attached to shared values, and the teacher's approach should be open enough to encourage the students to tap into these. This implies practising the skill of teamwork and negotiation, achieving co-operation through relationships.

If the teacher appears to be enthusiastic about the subject, the students will see the possibilities that lie ahead, and will be encouraged to work toward these goals.

Listening for the meaning behind the words used, and understanding what is intended when the students ask questions or seek guidance, is an important facet of a teacher's role. Whether or not the teacher takes the trouble to give the person asking for help a fair hearing will be registered and remembered by all present. This will affect attitudes formed by the group.

There is always a possibility that conflict within the group will manifest itself. It may be that tough decisions will need to be taken but it is how class members perceive the teacher's management of the problem that will make or break his or her reputation. The teacher will need to demonstrate how an institution builds and achieves a common approach to the maintenance of core values and how this applies equally to the class members.

When teaching mature adults, the range of experience possessed by the group can be considerable. It may be that teachers will need to learn how to feel comfortable saying that they are not able to answer a question at once. But it is knowing how to acknowledge and use the talents that others in the group have — and that you may not have — that will convince the students of your worth.

If you bear these things in mind when preparing and delivering lessons, you will find they go a long way towards creating an environment and pattern of relationships that is conducive to learning.

The manner in which the teacher sets about handling people is what classroom management is fundamentally about. It is this process of managing people which determines whether the lessons and learning outcomes are successful or not.

Assignment 7.10 – **Assessing ability to establish rapport**

The teacher is faced with problems of communication and control when commencing a lesson. This is particularly true when meeting a group for the first time. An important objective for teachers who are candidates for the CGLI Further and Adult Education Teacher's Certificate is that they should be able to create an environment and pattern of relationships conducive to learning.

Plan and deliver a micro-training session designed to demonstrate competence in some of the techniques that are used to establish rapport with a group. The aim of the session is to record a teacher's attempts to establish a friendly democratic relationship with the group, so that the intentions and expectations of the group coincide with those of the teacher. The videotaped recording may be played back after the micro-training session and discussed with colleagues or the tutor.

Make a note of techniques that others use, review the list and adopt those that you feel would suit your own style.

7.007 Health and safety in the learning environment

Health and Safety at Work etc. Act 1974

The Health and Safety at Work Act received the Royal Assent on 31 July, 1974 and it provides a comprehensive system of law covering the health and safety of people at work.

The Act comprises four main parts:
- Part 1 is concerned with health, safety and welfare in relation to work.
- Part 2 relates to the Employment Medical Advisory Service.
- Part 3 amends the law relating to building regulations.
- Part 4 deals with various and general provisions.

Since the Act was introduced, teaching and non-teaching staff in further, higher and adult education have been affected by its implications and the legislative framework provided by the Act has had considerable influence and effect on day-to-day operations within and outside academic establishments.

The Act covers all staff employed in an educational establishment, all students, visitors and contractors, and it gives statutory protection to anyone who is present on the college site. It is concerned with:
- securing the health, safety and welfare of persons at work as described in Part 1 of the Act
- protecting persons other than persons at work, against the risks to health or safety arising out of, or in connection with the activities of persons at work
- controlling the keeping and use of explosives or highly inflammable or dangerous substances. Preventing people acquiring, possessing or illegally using such substances
- controlling the emission of noxious or offensive substances from any area.

Basic obligations of employers
Employers (including LEAs and college managements) have a duty to ensure that their activities do not endanger anybody and are required to provide the following so far as is reasonably practicable for employees and other persons:
- healthy and safe systems of work with safe plant, machinery, equipment and appliances all of which are maintained in good working order
- safe methods for use, handling, storing and transporting materials, articles or substances
- healthy and safe working environments including premises with adequate amenities
- adequate instruction and training for employees including such information and supervision by competent personnel as is necessary to ensure the health and safety at work of employees.

Basic obligations of employees
Quite apart from any specific responsibilities that may be delegated to them, teachers have a legal obligation, as do all employees in industry, commerce or elsewhere (except domestic service) under Section 7 of the Health and Safety at

Work Act 1974; namely, to take care of their own health and safety as well as that of students and of any person who may be affected by their acts or omissions.

They have also a responsibility for

- co-operating with their employers so far as is necessary to perform any duty or comply with any requirements imposed as a result of any law that may be in force
- making themselves familiar with and conforming to any statement of Safety Policy or Safety Code of Practice issued by principals or governing bodies
- avoiding the possibility of committing criminal offences due to putting the health and safety of themselves or other persons at risk
- conforming to safety instructions issued by principals or governing bodies and sharing their responsibility for safety, health and welfare
- reporting any hazard, accident or dangerous occurrence to their immediate superior and to their Safety Representative, whether or not physical injury has occurred.
- using and ensuring that students use the appropriate protective clothing, equipment and safety devices at all times and ensuring that any such equipment or devices are maintained in a safe working condition
- complying with improvement notices or prohibition notices that may have been served on them as employees
- complying with the duty not to interfere with or misuse things provided pursuant to any of the relevant statutory provisions
- setting a good example to students, colleagues and the public in their approach to health and safety matters.

Duties and responsibilities of teachers in the classroom
A teacher must ensure that students are carefully briefed about safety arrangements when in unfamilar surroundings. Examples of such situations might be with newly enrolled students at the start of an academic year, or if transferred with a class to another annexe or site, or when practicals or laboratory work commences or in any other novel situation.

It is essential that the students know

- the fire exit route
- the location of the nearest first aid box
- the location, uses and methods of operation of fire extinguishers in the vicinity
- content and application of accident and fire regulations
- what to do in the event of an emergency.

When students are on the register, the teacher is in charge and must accept responsibility for all aspects of safety and control of the environment in which work is taking place. Any activities that the teacher is expected to supervise should be inherently safe. If a situation arises where any aspect of class work is judged to be hazardous to the health or welfare of students, such work should stop immediately and a report be made in writing to college management.

Since the teacher is ultimately in charge in a workshop or laboratory, support staff such as technicians and caretakers, whilst being helpful, can only offer advice to the teacher or to the students. The buck stops with the teacher in the classroom. It is the teacher who is responsible for ensuring that students are instructed properly and it is the teacher who is responsible for students operating machinery or processes safely, not the technician. It is the teacher who must ensure that no request is made of students or technicians to undertake operations that are or may be hazardous.

Burden of proof

In any proceedings for an offence under any of the relevant statutory provisions consisting of a failure to comply with a duty or requirement, Section 40 of the Act lays the burden of proof on the accused. It is usually the employer who will be required to prove that it was not reasonably practicable to do more than was done to safeguard employees or other persons injured or otherwise disadvantaged by a contravention of the Act.

Laboratory safety

Teachers responsible for chemistry laboratories and all that happens while they and students are working within them will need to be aware of the potentially hazardous conditions and dangers that exist. Some of these are given below:

– Over a period of time, materials will have been accumulating that may not be in regular use; large stocks of little-used resources may be held; quantities of flammable chemicals may exceed the permitted allocation or be incorrectly stored; and incompatible materials, poisons, gases or other dangerous chemicals may be stored unsafely. All of these promote a potentially dangerous environment.
– Disposal of chemical waste will present problems concerning washing down sinks, disposal by burial, burning or other methods.
– Practical work in laboratories will always be subject to physical hazards, and to hazards associated with chemical, electrical and mechanical processes and the use of power tools and appliances.

In discussing laboratories, Kenneth Ireland[17] writes:

> ... It would be pointless to detail all laboratory risks, to list forbidden substances in school and college laboratories – including biology laboratories – and forbidden experiments. Any teacher who knows the job and keeps up-to-date with information issued by the Department of Education and Science [now DfEE] is already aware of these.

> On the other hand the Health and Safety Executive Inspectorate have horrifying tales of the bad state and organisation of some laboratories. Some have been so bad, and have contravened so many regulations, that the Inspectors have photographed them as almost unbelievable examples. In every one of these cases, a qualified science teacher was in charge.

Assignment 7.11 – Conducting a laboratory/workshop safety check

How are things in your area of responsibility? As the teacher in charge you will have tacitly accepted responsibility for all aspects of safety relating to your class for its duration. Carry out a comprehensive check of your own laboratory and working environment, bearing in mind some of the points given in the text above, and confirm whether or not it is free of hazards.

Write a report of your findings and use this to feed back outcomes to your teaching establishment supervisor.

Discuss general concerns highlighted by your research with other members of the course.

Assignment 7.12 – Fire hazards

Fire prevention must be a high priority for all teachers, particularly when flammable liquids, gases, wood, paper, electrical power and other combustible materials are handled in class. Even when care is taken, volatile materials, heat sources, powders and appliances can start fires; negligence, discarded cigarette ends and thoughtless behaviour can add unnecessary risk. No extinguisher should be kept in anything less than a full state of readiness at any time, and everyone should be ready to react to fires.

Given that all reasonable precautions have been taken and yet a fire breaks out; what action should a teacher take when

– the establishment's fire alarm is sounded?
– a fire occurs in his or her classroom or laboratory?
– called by students to the scene of a fire?
– asked to classify and report a fire?
– asked to supervise evacuation of a complete area?

State what a teacher should know about fire fighting equipment and other things relating to fires including

– alarms	– escape notices
– blankets	– escapes
– buckets	– exits
– classification	– extinguishers
– doors	– hazards
– drill	– prevention

Make a plan of your classroom and/or laboratory, and note on the plan all references to fire precautions and fire-fighting equipment and escape routes. Check that all the equipment is serviceable and that you are competent to use it. Make sure your students know the drill before a fire occurs.

Assignment 7.13 – **Promoting a positive attitude towards health and safety at work**

Basic obligations of employees under Section 7 of the Health and Safety at Work Act 1974 are:

– They should act in the course of their employment with due care for the health and safety of themselves, other workers and the general public.
– They should also observe the provisions of the Act wherever applicable to them or to matters within their control, co-operating with employers so far as is necessary to perform any duty or comply with any requirements imposed as a result of any law that may be in force.
– They should not put the health and safety of themselves or others at risk.

An important duty of a teacher is to encourage maximum student participation in the creation, implementation and monitoring of health and safety policies, practices and activities both within the educational establishment and at the workplace.

– Consider how you will best be able to promote in your students a positive and enduring attitude towards the duties of an employee in terms of Section 7 of the Health and Safety at Work Act 1974.
– Share your ideas and discuss your suggestions with course or team members.

Assignment 7.14 – **Health and safety in physical education and games**

Reducing the probability of injury or accident during physical education, swimming and games activities must be an important item on the minds of many adult education teachers. Every kind of sporting activity has inherent risks and it is impossible to remove every aspect of danger from the material and physical requirements of sport. Teachers may also have to cope with students' self-imposed dangers such as exhaustion, strained muscles and raised blood pressure due to violent or inappropriate exercise patterns.

Consider the gymnasium, swimming bath, playing field, court, playground, or changing rooms; the range of physical education equipment that you use including the floor, trampoline, beams, vaulting equipment, ropes, weight-lifting apparatus or that equipment specific to your specialism; and the chemicals, lotions or preparations associated with the sport.

– Survey the risks and dangers associated with your resources and class members.
– Review your methods and facilities with a view to either confirming that you are not exposing your students to unnecessary risk; or producing an action plan for reducing dangers and improving safety aspects of your operation

Assignment 7.15 – Accident procedures

If there were an accident in your location would you know what to do?

- How would you set about calling an ambulance?
- How would you get hold of a qualified First-Aider?
- Do you know the locations of First Aid boxes and the nearest sick room?
- Should you leave the patient alone? Manipulate patient into the recovery position? Cover the patient?
- What if the patient has received an electric shock and is still in contact with the power source?
- Do you know where a phone connected to an outside line can be found in the evening?
- If you intended to report the accident by phone or runner, what information would you give?
- How would you manage to contact a parent, guardian, relative or friend?

Answer these questions and produce a schedule of actions you would need to take to meet the needs of such an emergency in your own establishment.

7.008 Counselling, guidance and classroom management

The counselling role

Counselling is a process whereby clients may be provided with help with personal problems that affect their educational progress. The source of the problem that results in a need for counselling may be connected with life outside college or with college activities.

Non-directive counselling provides a setting, a relationship, the conditions and opportunity for a client to discuss with a counsellor the situation that has led to the meeting. Attitudes, thoughts and feelings can be aired in a non-threatening atmosphere; alternative courses of action can be explored, and the consequences of each option can be assessed. In the end, it is the client, not the counsellor, who will discover answers and solutions and make decisions as to the course of action to be taken. The counselling role is therefore largely one of facilitating, by providing an arena and conditions that allow clients to recognise and resolve their problems.

Guidance is a term used to describe advising on vocational choice or other directive forms of help, as opposed to the non-directive help represented by counselling.

With guidance, the teacher will probably

- give information without any attempt at evaluating or pronouncing value judgements on the content
- offer advice based on knowledge and experience
- structure the client's learning experiences by taking positive action in the form of direct intervention.

Dealing with the stressful personal problems is a more serious aspect of counselling work that may best be referred to a **counsellor** who has been specially trained and is particularly skilled in counselling. A professional counsellor is normally very experienced and will be able to refer the client quickly to an appropriate referral agency if necessary.

Teacher counsellors may feel that they can adequately meet students' needs by offering information and advice on matters relating to their own specialism and shorter-term aspects such as enrolment advice and subject information. They may not have the time or the confidence and skill to deal with longer-term goals or serious problems, although a good deal of informal advice and support is regularly given by most teachers employed in adult education.

Implementation

Integrating counselling, guidance and support strategies within the course is an extremely important element of programme design, as is the facility for liaising with professional student counsellors and referral agencies.[18]

When considering the staffing of counselling and guidance sessions it is important to ensure that the teacher concerned is competent in these counselling skills:

– icebreaking	– questioning
– drawing out	– summarising
– listening	– advising
– managing silence	– target setting
– clarifying	– prescribing
– reflecting back	

Assignment 7.16 – **The pastoral and academic guidance role of a teacher**

The Team Leader has recognised the shortcomings of your institution with regard to its system for academic and pastoral student guidance and counselling and has discussed with staff the possibility of planning a departmental approach to improving matters. As a result, it has been agreed that elements of the problem will be delegated to teachers in the departmental team for research and action planning.

Your task is to prepare an action plan for

- the identification and referral of students with exceptionally high or low ability
- the identification, remediation and referral of students with behaviour problems.

Record your action plan and present it to the team for comment.

Assignment 7.17 – Evaluating the role of a teacher as student counsellor

'Lies' by Yevgeny Alexandrovitch Yevtushenko (b. 1933) is reproduced below.

– Analyse the work in terms of its value to you in your role as student counsellor in relation to careers, educational guidance and personal problems.

– Discuss your views with other course members and decide whether or not the underlying philosophy of Yevtushenko's piece has any relevance today as far as counselling is concerned.

Lies

Telling lies to the young is wrong
Proving to them that lies are true is wrong
Telling them that God's in his heaven
and all's well with the world is wrong.
The young know what you mean.
The young are people.
Tell them that difficulties can't be counted,
And let them see not only what will be
But see with clarity these present times.
Say obstacles exist they must encounter
Sorrow happens, hardship happens.
The hell with it. He who never knew
the price of happiness will not be happy.
Forgive no error you recognise,
It will repeat itself, increase,
And afterwards our pupils
Will not forgive in us what we forgave.

Assignment 7.18 – Handling a grievance

Students may become frustrated and angry about something that perhaps they in the end realise was not worth getting upset about. Alternatively they may indeed have a serious problem that they need help to overcome. Examine the following situation:

You are working alone in an office when the door bursts open and in rushes one of your female students. She is obviously very distressed, has lost control and is looking for a confrontation with you.

Although you do yet not know the reason for her unhappy state, it is due to the fact that she has compared her latest assessment result with those of friends and feels that you have been grossly unfair, have shown favouritism to others and are getting at her for earlier misbehaviour in class.

Given a scenario similar to that described above, explain how such situations should be handled in terms of

- how to remain calm and avoid an argument with the student
- how to relieve tension
- how to acknowledge the fact that the student has a grievance, either real or imagined
- how to frame and ask probing questions to define the grievance
- how to get the facts and how to decide what to do
- how to apply the skill needed to reach an outcome that satisfies both parties.

Classroom management

When we hear the word 'discipline' we tend to think of domination, severity, obedience, restraint and punishment. As teachers we should perhaps avoid being labelled as strict, if it is at all possible. It might be better to be thought of as being helpful, patient, unbiased, impartial or firm but fair. Many teachers could, if they wished, maintain tight control. The whole lesson could pass without a murmur from the group, but it is doubtful whether much learning would take place.

Self-discipline in the classroom is a two-way process; it depends on mutual recognition of relative responsibilities. A knowledge of relative responsibilities is therefore necessary to enable discipline to be maintained and for useful learning to take place.

A teacher's responsibilities are

- to plan the period of activity
- to provide adequate resources
- to prepare for teaching and learning
- to negotiate with student goals and standards
- to fit material to each individual's level of experience
- to promote ease of learning and to present information in a manner easily assimilated.

Learner's responsibilities are

- to behave at all times with due regard to others' needs and feelings
- to respond to reasonable requests made by the teacher or peers
- to give others a fair hearing
- to participate in the learning process
- to exercise self-control.

Why things go wrong

Unfortunately, not all students are highly motivated all of the time, and there is a tendency for disruptive behaviour to occur when there is a conflict between group tasks and individual desires. It is the manner in which the teacher deals with the situation that reveals his or her attitude to the group and ability as peacemaker and negotiator.

There are no hard and fast rules for deaing with communication breakdowns in the classroom. Perhaps a good starting point would be to consider the following quotations and evaluate your own performance with these in mind:
'Personally I'm always ready to learn, although I do not always like being taught.' (Winston S Churchill)
'This person was a deluge of words and a drizzle of thought.' (Peter DeVries.)

People are inquisitive by nature. Learning is taking place from the cradle to the grave, but each person prefers a different method of learning. So the learning method in use may not suit every individual. A perceptive teacher will identify those students who appear to be flagging and will notice the glazed eyes, the fidgeting, the chin-on-chest attitude, the doodling, the murmur of conversation and the laughter when one's back is turned. These are danger signals indicating that the time has arrived for contingency plans to be put into action.

If we accept that there is no such thing as an uninteresting subject, then we must assume that our presentation is lacking in some respect. By trying a different approach, introducing another activity or using an aid to give impact, we may revive interest. Learning is an active process. We learn by doing. So keep the lesson going and avoid gaps of inactivity.

Dealing with trouble
If one or more of the class get bored and decide to opt out, it is up to the teacher to try to regain attention and involvement. If students create a disruption and choose not to respond even when a new approach is adopted, or if they refuse to join in group activity, then action must be taken. The majority of the group will expect this.

Sometimes group reaction to the disturbance will be sufficient to curb troublemakers' efforts to draw attention to themselves. Lack of reinforcement and rejection by peer groups are powerful demotivators for actions which do not conform to accepted group goals. However, care must be taken that the teacher does not unwittingly reinforce the unwanted behaviour by outright public admonishment; this might be just what they are hoping for. If they find that they are irritating you, they will try it again or else one of their friends will.

Each incident is an individual affair and the teacher should avoid penalising the whole group for the actions of a single person. Avoid the temptation to base the method of control on the behaviour of minorities. Do not make threats. You may be challenged and may not have the authority to carry out your threat. It is better to provide reasonable opportunities for the infringer to save face. In any case if you win by force, you lose. If you embarrass students you will most probably have lost them for the duration of the course, and as the aim is to increase their stores of knowledge you need them on your side. So, avoid confrontation in public unless you wish to make use of group pressure.

Alienation from the group and the attending isolation is the last thing most individuals want, and rejection is, for most, unbearable. Praise and reward are better than blame and punishment; even a small amount of success can give a sense of achievement, so use a positive rather than a negative approach. Aim for an increase in activity, cooperation, creativity and interest rather than authoritarianism, compulsion and passivity, and never make sarcastic remarks. Try reason first. Try to be just and try to be unbiased. If the troublemakers fail to respond, then you will have no alternative but to apply appropriate sanctions.

Assignment 7.19 – Case studies in classroom management

Imagine that you are the course tutor and that you are responsible for counselling members of your course team and for dealing with disciplinary matters involving students that are referred to you by them.

For each case your aim is to agree some line of action, or otherwise to obtain a positive outcome, so that both teacher and student profit from the interaction. Punishment will probably be ruled out, although you may consider that some kind of sanction is necessary.

Read through the cases, draw upon your own experiences of similar problems, and write down brief notes on how you would handle things. Try to anticipate the ways in which both teacher and student will react to you and the line each might take.

Prepare a few questions that you could ask or be asked concerning the matter, and a list of possible actions that either or both could take to improve relationships and performance.

When you have finished, discuss your work with colleagues or with one of the tutorial team.

Case study A   Troublemaker, or victim of circumstances?

Ian Griffiths is a big fellow aged seventeen and although towering above his classmates, he is good-natured and certainly not a bully when out of college.

He left school at the age of sixteen and obtained employment as a trainee with a large company. Wherever possible, the company encourages its trainees to follow further education courses and Ian is now enrolled in the second year of a course at college. Having managed to scrape through the first year, Ian now finds the second year very heavy going. This is not surprising, since he is no great academic.

From his very first day at college, Ian had found himself in trouble. During an initial safety lecture for the entire first year intake, his chair collapsed with an almighty crash, drawing unwanted attention to himself. The teacher in charge reported him for horseplay. Week after week something just had to happen which landed him in trouble. It was largely his own fault for he had set himself up as the class clown.

Now, whether he likes it or not, his mates look to him for leadership in disruptive tactics in the classroom. Any attempt to co-operate with the teacher is seen as an act of weakness by Ian and his cronies, so that anyone wishing to learn is ridiculed; they soon discover that it is better to keep their mouth firmly shut.

At the company Ian is well liked by the men in his section and he throws himself into his work with great gusto. He tends to rush things so that although his output is high, the quality is low and accuracy doubtful. He lacks finish and dislikes detail.

Long-suffering teachers have tried to make allowances for his unhelpful behaviour in class. The company has been advised five times of his misdemeanours and he has had several warnings from the training officer.

The crunch comes when Ian returns late to class after lunch, reeking of beer. The teacher remarks on Ian's lateness and points out the fact that college rules state that no student will be admitted to class after consuming alcoholic beverages. Ian responds by telling the teacher to 'get stuffed'.

The teacher cannot cope with this kind of behaviour. He is not sure what to do and doesn't know whether he can send Ian back to work, suspend him or what the limit of his authority is. All he is sure of is that things cannot go on as they are. He decides to leave the classroom and refer the matter to you for immediate action.

Case study B   Disruption in the Spanish beginners' class

Lessons during the first week of the 'Beginners' Spanish Conversation' course have always been a bit of a trial for you — people strolling in, every few minutes, some clutching textbooks, dictionaries and notepads, others with nothing at all. Some have enrolled, others expect you to enrol them instantly.

Eventually you get going and after a while, one or two students get up and rush out mumbling something like, 'Sorry, I thought this was the Italian Beginners.'

You are pleased to see friends that sat in the same desks last year and the year before. You admire their tenacity and wonder why they turn up year after year. Their Spanish doesn't seem to improve, even though their tans show that they spend a lot of time abroad. But they don't give you any aggravation and they are helpful as a lifeline, you do at least know their names and can call on them to help get things going.

As you look down your register you are pleased to see that 'El Pain', alias Graham Pike has not enrolled this year, but as you are congratulating yourself on your good fortune, he bursts in. 'Buenos tardes senora! Como esta?', he blurts out, showing off with a few words from his very limited Spanish vocabulary, while eyeing up the women.

He continues his noisy entrance by shuffling chairs around, chattering all the time and squeezing past some elderly women, scattering their things on the floor in the process. His objective is a very attractive and affluent-looking woman in the second row. He plonks himself down behind her — he can't get any nearer this week.

As the lesson proceeds, Graham leans across his desk until his face is in contact with the woman's hair and starts sniffing. He turns on his best, but very amateurish 'sycophantic' behaviour, hoping to impress the wealthy one. He is, as usual, seeking attention and some kind of gratification. The woman flinches, but says nothing. She is obviously ill at ease. The trouble is that Graham behaves like a clown, playing to the captive audience trapped in the classroom. He thinks the group enjoys his fun and he really means no harm, although he does have a bit of a reputation as far as his romantic inclinations are concerned.

You had enough of Graham's disruptive behaviour last year. What are you going to do about him this year? Should you nip it in the bud? How should you deal with someone that you quite like even though he is a bit of a rogue? How are you going to maintain control of the group and get them speaking Spanish with someone like Graham present?

7.009 Involving students in curriculum matters

One of the principal objectives of any successful teacher or trainer is to help learners to understand their own learning, and to plan and approach it in the most effective way. While this is and always has been, central to the teacher's role, it is also a guidance role. Guidance is that essential component of education and training which focuses on the individual's personal relationship with what is to be learned.[19]

The aim of this section is to identify ways in which students supported by teachers can actively consider matters such as course design, content, method and assessment procedures, and to recognise the value and constraints of such involvement. Students who willingly involve themselves in planning an activity are more likely to be better motivated and committed to it than would be the case if they had no say in the matter.

Needs identification is a term that is relatively new to teaching, although teachers have been involved in this or similar activities for decades.

Practising teachers will be familiar with the terms: 'staff appraisal' and 'identification of training needs' since under recently introduced conditions of service, they are required to identify their own training needs annually, or preferably on a continuous basis.

Where a negotiated and non-threatening atmosphere exists, appraisal is well received. Enlightened teachers can see what benefit may accrue personally and for the institution from a co-operative approach to updating and improving knowledge and skills. This philosophy is transferable to a unified approach by teacher and student to curriculum development.

There are five important areas of curriculum development where students can be actively involved. They are given below.

1 Making a start: a needs analysis

Students should be invited to talk about their needs; perhaps during an initial 'brainstorming' session' held before entry to the course or during induction or when the class first assembles. Some students may be shocked, having never before been asked for their opinion about what is to happen during any course. Others may be confused because they may feel that they are not yet in a position to tell you what it is that they need to know.

A suitable starting point could be to ask the students to discuss among themselves or with the teacher, their aptitudes, abilities and extent of their experience; their background knowledge and standard of basic education; special learning difficulties; and what they hope to get out of the course. Whatever else happens during this session, the students will feel that their opinions, feelings, hopes and expectations are at least being taken into account and that the teacher cares about trying to meet their needs. It may be possible at this stage to agree realistic expectations and outcomes that will go some way towards fulfilling personal agendas.

2 Course planning and design

Using information derived from the analysis of need carried out earlier, aims that reflect clearly the learners' needs can be written, and programmes designed that are responsive to the needs of individuals.

Theory should always be related to practice and be introduced only where necessary, rather than as a general rule. The main purpose of theory is to throw light on a subject, leading to greater understanding and improved performance. While no one would dispute that it is better to 'really understand' what it is that one is doing, it may not always be a priority. The level of cognitive learning that is targeted will be the deciding factor as to whether recall will suffice or whether analysis, synthesis or evaluation should be the aim.

Negotiating with students will enable the teacher to set the right level and identify potential barriers to learning, thereby helping to avoid periods where no progress can be made. Relevant and appropriate learning experiences, validated by the learners in advance, will ensure progression through the course, attainment of individual learning agendas, and eventually course objectives.

3 Delivery

The teacher is responsible for providing adequate learning resources and for agreeing with the students a logical development and sequence of learning experiences. Right from the start, a process of mutual support should be aimed at. Confidence-building is extremely important where students are actively involved in course planning and delivery; this is particularly true with mixed ability groups. Ongoing support in the form of negotiation, counselling and guidance will link the teacher to students in a continuous dialogue which will nurture and maintain enthusiasm.

Experience/reflection learning conducted in small groups, or individualised learning specified by the learners themselves will allow them to build on strengths.

4 Assessment

Assessment procedures are a key factor in the learning process. It is during assessment that learners are able to review their learning experiences and realise what it is that they are now able to do that they were not able to do before.

Self-assessment of work; formative and summative assessments made with the help of the teacher or some other person; coursework subject to continuous assessment; competence testing; certification of skills or external examinations – all these serve to confirm in the learner's mind what they have learned and what skills they now own.

Now, more than ever, students are being invited and required to play a key role in assessing their own achievements.

5 Reviewing the programme with learners

Programme planning may be seen as the province of the teacher, with learner involvement restricted to merely soaking up and regurgitating what is prescribed for them. Alternatively, an assessment of learner requirements and diagnosis of what members of the group think most beneficial to them could lead to a mutually negotiated and highly prized developmental learning programme that best matches individual needs, awarding body standards and organisational requirements.

For off-the-shelf courses an overall impression of the curriculum and course design may be obtained by assessing learner progress and their perceived quality of the learning opportunities provided. Opinion could be based on accurate formative assessments supported by learners' views about their progress and the teacher's management of the learning programme. Reviewing progress and conducting formative assessments is now becoming a day-to-day occurrence, and the reviews are of paramount importance to learners whether acting alone or interacting with their teachers or peers.

In order to accurately evaluate outcomes, information gathered during reviews must be correctly matched with syllabus content and relevant learning objectives, thereby ensuring that valid and reliable judgements may be made about the degree to which standards have or have not been met. Continuous feedback from learners and other stakeholders is very important, but its true worth can only be realised if it is acted upon. Learners will expect their teacher to act on the feedback they provide if motivation and co-operation is to be maintained. Analysing feedback may be the best way of discovering any learning problems and deficiencies in the delivery system.

Adaptations to the learning programme will be expected if the system is thought by learners to be letting them down. If this is the case, necessary changes in the teacher's and learner's contributions must be planned and executed by taking account of feedback resulting from learning experiences and assessments.

6 Monitoring and evaluation of outcomes

Throughout a programme, the value of student involvement in course operation can be recognised, particularly if they are invited to participate in continuous monitoring of activity and outcomes. Feedback provided by **student monitors** can help maintain course quality and validity of learning experiences provided.

It may be possible in some cases to set up **quality circles** consisting of three or four students from the same course, who meet regularly in class time in order to talk over problems experienced while learning. The leaders subsequently report back to the group, outlining problems highlighted with suggested solutions.

The quality circle concept is identified with Japanese industry and over ten million Japanese workers are involved in circles. In industry, support from management is essential for the successful operation of circles. In the classroom, teacher support and encouragement will be necessary to ensure fruitful outcomes from the quality circle problem solvers.

During the evaluation stage, when jointly analysing the 'fit' between student achievement and course aims, the worth of student participation in course design, method of delivery, assessment and monitoring may be realised. Their contribution to the evaluation and subsequent revision of the curriculum in response to recommendations for improvements and changes, will be of great value to those who will undertake the revised course when it is re-offered.

Assignment 7.20 – Involving students in curriculum matters

Identify ways in which your students may be actively involved in matters such as the following: course design and content; teaching and learning methods; the monitoring, assessing and evaluating of the process and outcomes.

Consider also how the value and constraints of student involvement in curriculum matters may be recognised and assessed.

7.010 Promoting students' participation in their professional and personal development

When children are very young they know of only a few occupations, which usually include spaceman, train driver, policeman, nurse and suchlike. Between the ages of seven and nine they become aware of a wider range of jobs occupied by neighbours, relatives and friends' parents. By the age of twelve, fantasies are discarded and replaced with a first career choice, although these choices do not necessarily accord with academic ability.

Today, more than ever before, pupils have a chance to take a hand in their own personal and career development before leaving school. They are given an opportunity to share with teachers the responsibility for learning outcomes and are encouraged to make the most of learner-centred methods and practices designed to develop confidence and enquiring minds. In order to meet these opportunities, teachers involved need to be able to promote in their pupils a desire to further their career prospects and a commitment to participate fully in the process of learning.

Perhaps a brief discussion of some earlier characteristics of the transition from school to work may help to focus on present-day needs in terms of promoting student participation in their personal development.

Up to and throughout the 1970s, the type of school attended, together with the range and level of subjects studied, related directly to the choice of career available to an individual. Unfortunately, a large majority of pupils had no plan worked out well in advance and little or no idea of their eventual career. Labour turnover in industry was affected by the school-leaver's choice of employment. Many were attracted to an occupation purely by chance. An advertisement caught their eye, a company had a recruiting stand in a shopping precinct, a friend told them of a vacancy or the careers master directed them to a few companies. It was often the case that school-leavers had acquired ideas about what work would be like, and were shocked when they discovered that the world of work was completely different to their expectations. The absence of industrial or commercial experience before leaving school was a contributory factor to a high labour turnover and poor adjustment to work.

At the age of fifteen years the prospect of leaving school and the need to find a job made the task of career choice more worrying, especially when linked with the transition from adolescence to adult status. Many apprenticeships were geared to a sixteen-year-old entrant, and the decision to remain at school until eighteen added further anxiety. If pupils stayed on until the age of eighteen and did not do well in 'A' levels, they were likely to experience some difficulty in finding a job due to the inflexibility of many training schemes and the difference in wage rates payable which were governed by age. Teenagers who had failed to make any career decisions found themselves pigeonholed into jobs, either by their parents or schools careers teachers whose main interest appeared to be in getting them into some kind of job, the actual job being immaterial.

Insufficient guidance was given to pupils. They were often expected to make up their own minds first, and then careers teachers provided information as to how the chosen ambition might be realised. Once in a job, teenagers often complained that the careers staff in schools were unqualified to meet the demands made of them. The staff were considered to be orientated towards the world of the school and out of touch with the real world of work outside the school gates.

Fortunately, over the last ten years, work-experience involvement has become more widespread and pupils are now sent from schools to work in factories and offices. There, they gain first-hand knowledge of the type of work involved. Now NVQs and GNVQs are paving the way for better links with the world of work. Work-experience components forming integral parts of the schemes now bridge the gap between school and industry, enabling students to sample a variety of careers before leaving school.

Assignment 7.21 - **Comparing then and now**

Read through the passage above and consider whether the content is representative of the situation during the 1970s and before. Consider the present-day philosophy as it relates to vocational preparation and particularly preparing pupils and school leavers for the world of work. Highlight the differences and list competences that today's teachers will need to satisfy student expectations as far as teacher support in career and personal development is concerned.

Evaluate your own staff development needs in this area of a teacher's work.

The need for guidance

Three main areas within which students may seek help or guidance are the educational, personal and vocational aspects of their professional and personal development.

Each of the three areas, although separate in some respects, are to some extent interrelated and together form a key component of professional and personal development. Failure to progress in any one of the three areas will probably affect the others, whereas progress in each area will maximise the person's potential to succeed in their chosen career. A balance needs to be maintained by placing necessary emphasis on each area so that the linkages remain firm. By concentrating too much effort in one area it is possible to neglect the other two and reduce the effectiveness and impact of employability and self-actualisation.

The need for **educational guidance** and support may arise when a client is unsure whether joining a course or training programme, or progressing within an existing course, will fulfill their own perceived needs. In such cases it may be necessary to examine with the client the importance of the educational input and related learning outcomes to professional and personal development. Obviously, if the client is unable to see clearly how the education and training will help to meet needs identified as being relevant to life chances, then motivation will either be poor or non-existent.

In the case of **personal guidance**, support may be needed when a young person is making the transition from school to work or from puberty to adulthood. In Britain today, young persons attain adult status at the age of eighteen, become independent and assume full responsibility for their actions. The several years preceding this momentous occasion are busy times for the teenagers who have to cope with the process of sexual maturation along with social and physical growth. Greater freedom from parental control and wider involvement in social pursuits outside the home adds to their responsibilities, while media advertisements arouse needs thereby creating a demand for more money. Lack of sufficient cash to fund the changes in lifestyle adds yet more pressure. During late adolescence an urgent need to acquire the academic qualifications to gain a place in higher education or for a decent job, together with the transition from school to work, bears heavily on the adolescent.

With older people the transition to retirement may become problematic for those concerned, and this is where guidance may be needed to smooth the path to a world of leisure, maybe in a hardship context, too. This is where the adult education service has a great deal to offer, and where staff need to demonstrate high levels of commitment and skill in human relations.

Vocational guidance is concerned in particular with employment and other matters concerning occupation and entry into employment. In the case of younger people, needs will probably focus on obtaining initial employment or obtaining and matching skills to the type of work that may be found in the district.

Unemployment or early retirement may give rise to the need to provide guidance on career opportunities and support that will help those displaced from work. The clients will need to be helped to see for themselves the value of trying to update their skills or the benefits of carrying out effective job-search activities.

The purpose of guidance is to provide support and to promote self-development in co-operation with other agencies, not to provide an opportunity for a 'hard sell', or for the imposition of personal decisions. The client should be recognised as the prominent player and every effort should be made to encourage participation in what is really, for the client, a developmental decision-making process. An important role of a guidance person is that of a 'middleman' who either outlines 'off-the-shelf' opportunities available to a client, who then chooses the option that most nearly suits them; or works with a client who attempts to make or to persuade others to provide an opportunity for satisfying individual needs.

In general, for young people leaving school and starting a new life the options comprise

- employment with or without access to formal education
- education and training provided by further and higher education establishments or universities
- education and training sponsored by the Government
- unemployment.

Teachers need to be able to offer guidance and counselling appropriate to each of these categories, and to provide the means by which clients can be helped to make good decisions about their personal development.

Assignment 7.22 – Researching personal development guidance facilities

The promotion of students' participation in their professional and personal development calls for a teamwork approach, since in general more than one teacher is responsible for this aspect of staff–student interaction.

Investigate the organisation of personal guidance provision in your institution and produce a chart showing the individual role holders and referral agents that you will need to work with to ensure that you are able to carry out your role in this important work.

- Compare the network operating in your own institution with that of members of your group and of the course provider.
- Do you have a professional and personal development promotional team to turn to for help?
- If not, what can you do about forming a team?

7.011 Identifying the roles of a teacher

The aim of this section of work is to identify some of the various roles that teachers may be called upon to adopt in the course of their duties, and to discuss how teachers may make effective appraisals of their own professional responsibilities.

The task of identifying possible roles that a teacher in further or adult education may need to exercise requires considerable research. Since no two educational establishments operate in precisely the same way, and post holder's contracts vary considerably, readers will perceive roles differently. Perhaps a start could be made by considering teachers' roles that relate either to their work 'in-college' or to activities 'off-college'. In-college roles have been the subject of many dissertations over the years and there are good accounts of what a teacher is expected to do while on site, but relatively little has been written about off-college roles. Before discussing self-appraisal of performance, these two aspects of a teacher's role will be considered.

Off-college roles

The teacher as consultant

A **consultant** may be defined as a qualified person who provides a service to industry, commerce or the public by identifying and investigating problems, recommending appropriate action and helping to implement the recommendations. A consultant may be required to probe a problem, gather and diagnose data, identify options, propose criteria, make recommendations and prescribe action for implementation designed to solve the problem.

Servicing clients' needs is being introduced into more and more aspects of the teacher's role; a range of skills for college consultancy and counselling activities is now necessary in order to function in the modern educational environment.

Today, teachers need to interact much more with clients from off-college locations than has been the case in the past; especially when seeking to attract fully-costed work as is the case when marketing and negotiating Services to Business type contracts. Maintaining good relations with employers' representatives when arranging work placements and visiting outstations is yet another example of the liaison role expected of enlightened teachers. In order to be really successful in handling contract type work, the teacher consultant needs to be able to demonstrate competence in skills such as
- proposal writing
- marketing programmes and ideas
- gaining entry to establishments and access to the right people and information
- establishing rapport
- adapting to change
- responding to needs
- contracting, that is, protecting the client from loss of operational control
- making a diagnosis
- synthesising data
- report writing

– problem solving
– team building
– conflict resolution
– process consultation
– training and development.

In general, consultation is a voluntary relationship between a consultant and client, where the consultant tries to help the client solve some kind of problem. Within college a teacher adapts the accepted role of consultant when tutoring or counselling students; but when interacting with external agencies, the teacher is not part of the hierarchical system operating and hence needs to establish credibility.

In an article concerning consultants published in *The Times*, Edward Fennell made reference to Employment Relations' suggestion that 14 different roles may need to be adopted by a consultant. The roles which are transferable to the work of a teacher and still valid in the 2000s are outlined below:

– **catalyst and adviser**   identifies issues and potential pitfalls in client situation and prompts/advises on appropriate action to reach long-term goals
– **fact finder**   gathers data and identifies key implications
– **auditor**   reviews client situation and problem areas; analyses and presents the results
– **technical expert**   provides technical information and suggestions for policy and practice decisions
– **system specialist**   applies specific methodology involving client participation
– **collaborator in problem solving**   operates as team member offering alternatives and advising in options
– **advocate**   proposes guidelines, makes recommendations
– **reflector**   raises questions for reflection
– **trainer and educator**   designs learning experiences and trains the client
– **solution provider**   provides discrete service or product specific to client's stated needs
– **enabler**   identifies alternatives and resources for clients and helps assess consequences
– **facilitator**   directs clients in the analytical processes, challenges thinking and conclusions, promotes broader capability
– **influencer**   seeks and gains broad commitment for specific action
– **implementer**   assists or leads implementation of recommendations.

At this point it might be useful to reflect on how the roles described relate to your perception of the role of a teacher, and specifically to your existing post.

In-college roles

If we can agree that the fundamental teaching role is one of facilitating learning by providing expertise, managing resources and encouraging learners to help themselves to attain their goals, perhaps other important roles that need to be considered include those of

– administrator and record keeper
– assessor

- change agent and innovator
- communicator
- counsellor and coach
- helper and supporter
- implementer
- market researcher
- monitor and evaluator
- motivator and team leader
- needs identifier and advisor
- organiser and planner
- publicity and promotional materials officer
- special needs or multicultural liaison person
- staff developer
- teaching and learning media expert
- tutor.[20]

When discussing the impact of additional non class-contact roles and 'subsidiary or departmental duties' on the effectiveness of their classroom teaching, teachers often complain that their workload increases almost daily. Some admit to being very worried about the possibility of their classes suffering due to teacher overload brought about by maintaining high self-imposed standards and attempting to meet increasing demands made by superiors. Trying to fit everything in can result in pressure and accompanying stress.

More than 10 years ago the implementation of procedures relating to the document *Managing Colleges Efficiently*[21] inevitably meant that staff at all levels needed to take on new roles and become more effective managers of resources; they also needed to become better administrators of correspondence, budgets, funding and other systems – and better communicators.

Innovation and the rapid rate of change in educational provision calls for relatively new roles for some as innovators or **agents of change**. They need to be conversant with staff development policy and provision designed to satisfy training needs thrown up by new types of teaching and learning methodology, together with advances in experiential and student-centred learning such as open-learning, computer-assisted learning and supported self-study. They need to examine strengths and weaknesses of existing provision and be able to perceive the need for change — for example, to introduce modular curricula where necessary and to experiment with cross-college integration of programmes. So as to remain active in some of the now fiercely competitive areas of what was, at one time, unquestionably further and adult education territory, innovators need to promote an entrepreneurial thrust and take other staff along with them.

Implementers need to be curriculum development experts who are also good communicators. They need to set up a teamwork approach to the course development task and be knowledgeable in relevant areas such as validity and reliability of aims, objectives, content, resources and methodology. **Communicators** with team building skills also play an important part in maintaining direction and harmony by encouraging a consultative atmosphere within the course team.

Quality controllers can ensure that assurance procedures are in place so that the quality and appropriateness of course materials and methods may be validated before delivery and during the later monitoring and evaluation checks. In addition to this, **monitors** should create opportunities to frequently review the course during delivery and advise on the effectiveness of the teaching and learning that is taking place. Information and opinion can be gathered, sifted and evaluated to ensure that everything is going well — or if it is not, to introduce improvements.

In consultation with monitors and course team members, **evaluators** can take decisions on the basis of data gathered during the monitoring programme. A key question that will always be in the evaluator's mind is: 'Has the right quality of learning occurred and has the learning experience been effective and as pleasant and rewarding as the students could reasonably expect?' Other matters of concern for evaluators involve the question of cost effectiveness of the provision. This sort of question will often give rise to conflicts relating to management needs to perform within targets or efficiency ratios and the teachers concerned who may well be committed to educational excellence at any cost. The planning and delivery of future courses will be affected by the outcomes of the monitoring and evaluation process and hence it becomes a very important task for any teacher.

Meanwhile, some or all of the transferable consultants' roles referred to earlier will still need to be fulfilled by teachers.

Assignment 7.23 – **Role of the teacher in adult and further education**

Write an essay on the role of the teacher in adult and further education. You will need to research the topic and include in your essay:
– evidence of systematic analysis of the role, giving appropriate source references
– an assessment of the degree to which the texts that you have studied are capable of being applied in the 'real world' of teaching and learning
– a description of the roles that you personally adopt when operating in your own field.

Note: City and Guilds of London Institute specify the requirement that Course Work assignments should be: 'structured, properly headed, illustrated where necessary with relevant data, well composed and carry appropriate source references.'

Professional and personal development

A **core objective** for teachers is that they will be able to *identify ways in which they may participate in, and contribute towards, their own professional and personal development, in order to respond flexibly as their own conditions and responsibilities change*. This objective complements the **training cycle key skill**: *evaluating training and improving own learning and performance*. What is important is that all concerned should recognise that quite apart from undergoing formal appraisals it is every teacher's duty to continuously evaluate their own performance day by day.

Specifying self-development needs in relevant key result areas is an essential feature of the **personal development process**. The object is to identify, set and prioritise clear and realistic goals and targets for one's own development based upon an accurate assessment of all relevant information. Clearly, there will be a need to keep abreast of current trends in teaching, training and human resource development practice.

Self-appraisal

In the current climate of change teachers should regularly measure their performance against relevant indicators and innovations in training and development and related matters. Methods of assessing your own work and achievement of current targets should be identified. Once these methods have been determined and implemented, your current competency as measured against essential teaching functions and job requirements could be **profiled**. Any self-development needs identified would be recorded in a **personal action plan**.

The **self-profile** shown in Figure 7.3 could be used as an aid to appraising your performance as a teacher and later when defining personal development targets. The profile is intended to help teachers keep under review their performance in seven broad areas of competency and to identify and articulate any personal development needs related to current job competency, foreseeable responsibilities, and institutional and career development. The diagram gives an indication of the linkages and interaction of each, and how each profile area may affect and influence the others.[22]

Personal action planning

Having identified areas for improvement, rationalised your goals and set targets, you will need to prioritise self-development needs and find learning opportunities that will enable you to satisfy your needs. A **personal action plan** is then written specifying the means by which your targets will be achieved, completion dates and typical activity. The plan can be used to keep track of your progress and updated to take account of changing circumstances.

Implementation

Your own facilitation skills should be developed in ways that will limit inconvenience to others. Teaching centres are ideal places in which to try out new methods as they offer facilities for any initial training, updating and ongoing personal development. Staff tutors will be there to help and there may be other experienced teachers present who would be able to lend a hand or give sound advice. Other possibilities include in-college staff development activities, teamworking and self-help groups. New teaching techniques can be developed by first watching films or videos illustrating examples of good practice and then trying them out during microteaching sessions.

Micro-training

The aim of micro-training is to help inexperienced teachers acquire and develop basic practical teaching skills and to help established teachers improve their lecturing skills. Micro-training incorporates such elements as lesson-planning, verbal exposition (lecturing and addressing the students), questioning and discussing. It encourages the participants to be self-critical. The technique promotes the learning of social skills involved in motivating and controlling groups, and heightens perception of quality of classroom management and interaction. It also serves to validate new approaches to the teaching of a subject.

Figure 7.3 Activities forming basis of a self-profile

The teacher concerned prepares a short lesson or the opening of a lesson and delivers it to a small group. The lesson, usually devoted to a particular skill, may last up to about 15 minutes. After delivery, the teacher reviews the strengths and weaknesses of the presentation and then with the group discusses how improvements could be effected. The teacher then repeats the lesson with another group, incorporating the improvements suggested, and re-evaluates the outcomes.

The value of micro-training is that the teacher can plan and deliver a short piece of instruction before launching into longer sessions, and receive early feedback on performance, together with valuable guidance from peers and experienced tutors.

It has been found helpful for initial sessions of micro-training to deal with only one aspect of teaching, such as introducing a topic, explaining a single aspect, organising a short question-and-answer session, giving directions, using aids or gaining the attention of students.

Videorecorded feedback sessions
By participating in videotaped practice lectures, teachers may obtain the benefit of feedback using a resource which may be played back and analysed immediately, or retained to compare improvements in their lecturing ability over a period of time.

In an article reporting on a study of lecturers' reactions to the method of staff development which involves giving practice lectures that are videorecorded for playback and analysis, Patricia Cryer[23] gives details of advice offered by the participants of video feedback sessions during the study:

'Try to forget that the camera is there — you will anyway once you get started.'

'Make sure you are well prepared with a topic that interests you and should interest your audience.'

'Look forward to constructive criticism. See what you can find out about yourself.'

'Avoid the temptation to regard unpalatable comments as biased.'

'Don't be downcast by your faults. Now you know them you'll be able to put them right.'

'Don't be over self-critical. Many normal, useful and expressive gestures look silly on screen.'

'Choose a simple topic so that you can concentrate on outward factors such as voice level, stance and eye contact.'

'Think of it as fun being able to see yourself on the screen afterwards.'

'Study the video very carefully by yourself afterwards.'

'Try to learn from seeing other people's lecturing as well as your own'.

Two of the useful pieces of advice to tutors running video feedback sessions reported by Cryer are: 'Give the person doing the lecture the chance to criticise it before throwing the discussion open to the group' and 'Try to get participants to be less polite to each other because over-politeness results in helpful advice not being given.'

A schedule that may be helpful when carrying out a self-appraisal of a videorecorded micro-training session is given in Figure 7.4. Although grading or marking appraisals is not now encouraged, some people like to grade themselves using a marking scheme, so that they have a 'mark base' for establishing in their own minds where they stand against some standard that they set themselves. For this reason a rating scale has been provided on Self-Assessment Sheet A in Figure 7.4.

Teaching performance

While undergoing training, teachers need to conduct lessons and use self-assessment checklists or rating sheets to analyse their effectiveness.

During discussions with the course tutor or others delegated to help and advise during counselling and review meetings following an observation, comments on strengths and weaknesses of the presentation, preparation, and style of delivery should be exchanged. The object of the review is to share experiences and to negotiate areas where improvement could reasonably be attempted. These reviews and discussions should be seen as part of an ongoing formative assessment and self-improvement process carried out in a non-threatening manner.

The final report or profiling in the form of a summative assessment record should include details of coursework, teaching practice outcomes and interaction with the course team and others involved in the teacher training process.

The CGLI 7307 Scheme Pamphlet lists the following guidelines for the assessment of teaching.

Candidates will demonstrate that they can:

— show evidence of planning
— communicate objectives to their students
— relate sessions to a learning programme

Practical Teaching Performance

	Self Rating %

Name _____

Poor	Fair	Good	Very Good	Excellent
1	2	3	4	5

1 Presentation

Was your introduction satisfactory?
Were the key points presented in logical sequence?
Were the explanation and development clear?
Conclusion: key points restated, content summarised, action recommended,
    (plug line?)

2 Information

Was the content related to subject of talk?
Was the terminology clearly understood?
Was the information easily assimilated?
Were the facts and figures supported by evidence?

3 Interest

Did you hold your students' attention?
Did you relate facts to their experience?
Were the appropriate visual aids used?
Was there an opportunity to ask questions?

4 Delivery

Were you relaxed?
Was your manner warm and friendly?
Did your eyes roam over the whole group?
Did you have any irritating mannerisms?

5 Speech and language

Was your speech clear?
Was the appropriate language code used?
Were the important points stressed or emphasised?
Were the concepts you introduced explained in simple language?

Rating % = Total Mark $\times$ 4

Figure 7.4 Self-assessment sheet A

– relate their chosen material to students' learning needs
– create a safe and effective learning environment
– design and use a suitable range of learning materials
– establish and maintain good rapport
– behave appropriately and in a professional manner at all times
– demonstrate appropriate equal opportunities behaviour and anti-discriminatory practice
– show adequate command of the subject
– relate the material to varied student abilities
– use strategies appropriate to the size and needs of the group
– manage teaching and learning resources and activities effectively
– use appropriate written and spoken communication
– monitor student progress
– assess student achievement, using appropriate methods
– give feedback to students in a positive manner
– evaluate their own teaching and learning
– complete necessary administrative tasks.

A checklist that could be of use for assessment or evaluation of performance is given in Figure 7.5. The lesson plan and appraisal given in Figures 7.6 and 7.7 may also be helpful to both teacher and tutor when appraising teaching.

Name _____

Factor	Poor ←					→ Excellent	
	1	2	3	4	5	6	7
Clarity of objectives	....	....	....	....	....	....	....
Appropriateness of objectives	....	....	....	....	....	....	....
Organisation of lesson	....	....	....	....	....	....	....
Selection of content	....	....	....	....	....	....	....
Selection of materials	....	....	....	....	....	....	....
Beginning of lesson	....	....	....	....	....	....	....
Clarity of presentation	....	....	....	....	....	....	....
Pacing of lesson	....	....	....	....	....	....	....
Group participation and attention	....	....	....	....	....	....	....
Ending of lesson	....	....	....	....	....	....	....

Comments

....
....

Figure 7.5 Self-assessment sheet B

<u>Lesson Plan</u>.   <u>Location</u>   B'mth + Poole College of Further Education
                                  Constitution Hill , Poole.

<u>Course</u> : A level Art	<u>Subject</u> : Illustration	<u>Students</u> : 8F 6M 14 students - mainly 16yrs, (couple of them slightly older)
<u>Room</u> : 1123	<u>Time</u> : 11.15 - 1.00	<u>Date</u> : 16.1.9-.

<u>Aim</u> :   To develop layout and illustration abilities.
                   To demonstrate how to use gouache + paint to get a flat colour.

<u>Objectives</u> :   ✶ Students shall be able to produce an illustration
                     relevant to their rough layout designs.
                   ✶ Students will be able to use gouache paint to produce
                     a flat colour illustration.

<u>Equipment</u> :   For demonstration,
                   Frisk film
                   gouache paint
                   CS10 board with pencil drawing on
                   Scalpel + scalpel blades
                   metal shield
                   palette / plate
                   brushes
                   pencils
                   rubber
                   masking tape
                   red film

<u>Other</u>   Chalk + chalkboard (BB)
<u>Equipment</u> :   Rough layout (RL)
                   Graphic Source Book
                   Examples of Posters.   CONTINUED OVERLEAF ▶

Figure 7.6 Sample lesson plan (continued overleaf)

Time	Stage	Method	Activity	Aids
11.15	**Introduction:** Why do graphic designers do rough layouts for projects? Show example - explain I'll look at theirs later.	VE Q & A		RL felt tip pens & paper
11.25	Students copy project brief from blackboard. Any questions.	Q & A	Writing from board. (I prepare demonstration)	BB
11.30	**Development:** Form class into groups and demonstrate gouache paint technique - for flat colour illustrations.	VE Demo.	Paint a small section of a drawing.	Paints. Frisk film. Scalpel. cs 10 board. Metal shield. Pencil. Rubber. Plak. Brushes. Masking tape.
11.45	Rearrange classroom and students start practical illustration.	Individual attention discussing homework & the illust. to be produced.	Painting / drawing	Pad & felt tip - for rough sketches.
12.30	Students continue practical - I write graphic supply shops addresses on board.			BB
12.45	Conclusion: Recap on project. Homework: Continue illustration. Next week: How to present work for Jan.30? Bring mounting card. Any questions. Write down addresses of graphic suppliers - and then they can go.	V.E. Q & A	Copy notes from board	BB

CITY AND GUILDS OF LONDON INSTITUTE - 7307 FURTHER AND ADULT TEACHER'S CERTIFICATE	*The* BOURNEMOUTH AND POOLE
TEACHING PRACTICE APPRAISAL	*College* OF FURTHER EDUCATION

Name: JANET YOUNG   **Date:** 16.1.0-   **Time:** 1115 - 1300

Course: 'A' Level Art   **Students:** 15 - 8 female / 7 male   **Venue:** U23 - Upper Const. Hill Site

Subject: 'ILLUSTRATION'

Teaching characteristics	Comments
Preparation: Aims and objectives	Given perfectly on lesson plan but not presented well at start of lesson.
Plan	Comprehensive and clearly laid out. A good deal of thought had been applied to the plan.
Environment	Rather cluttered but the lecturer made the best possible use of available space. A nice informal atmosphere prevailed.
Presentation: Beginning the lesson	Could have been more positive. Focus attention using a practitioner's layout or finished project. Establish credibility and urgency.
Development	Good logical development. Progressive with no padding.
Ending the lesson	Need to review positively and effectively - the key points - using newsprint sheets as discussed.
Delivery - voice, gesture, use of language etc.	Fast, fluent and interesting. Consider possibility of slowing down in places. Stress important points.
Techniques and aids: A/V aids	Flip chart type presentation using two flip charts could be effective - as discussed. Consider use of CCTV.
Question and answer technique	Good. You made a lot of use of this - but allow adequate time for responses. Develop each answer and share around the group.
Other evaluative procedures	Guided discussion and review
Class control	Students riveted to lecturer's delivery.
Demonstration	Effective, but always use the instruments you specify for the task (i.e. round edged scalpel). Avoid saying one thing and doing another.
	Productive individual work on projects. Could have got them going a little earlier.

Figure 7.7 Sample appraisal (continued overleaf)

Student response:	
Participation	Keen, well motivated group. Nice, friendly and helpful students.
Attention and interest	Interest maintained totally throughout whole lesson.
Rapport	Excellent, especially as lecturer had taught class only once before.

General comments: (Teaching practice Assessor)

Although some of the comments overleaf may at first sight appear highly critical this is not the intention.
You prepared very, very well indeed.   You delivered with great gusto and keeness.   You worked very hard and all enjoyed the learning experience AND learned a lot from your input and their own participation.
You have high credibility and the group appear to trust and value your judgement.   You are a competent illustrator and own many important teaching skills.   All you now need is more classroom practice.   You may need to slow down a bit in places and use the question and answer procedure to reinforce learning.   Remember always to actively encourage the learners to seek clarification and to fully express their views.
Negotiate content as the lesson develops and target your input on learner requirements that come to light when they are sharing their experiences with you.   Their needs and preferences will probably match your own intentions but they will feel even happier about joining in.
During Q & A sessions and reviews wait patiently for answers or observations and get other students to comment on their peers' offerings.
I enjoyed the session immensely, Janet.   Thank you for making the effort to plan and deliver an interesting lesson and for preparing content that the learners will I am sure remember. I look forward to seeing you again soon.

Signed: *Les Walklin*   Date: 16 January 200–
     Les Walklin/Staff Tutor

Self-evaluation: (FAETC Student)

In which part of the lesson did you experience the most difficulty?
Briefly speculate on the reasons.

The beginning - I didn't state clearly my aims + objectives - + spoke too quickly. I think this was because I was not relaxed enough.

In which part of the lesson did you experience the most confidence?
Briefly speculate on the reasons.

Examining student's work - and demonstration. I enjoyed seeing how each student had interpreted the project.

Briefly describe any aspects you would consider doing differently next time you taught the topic.

I would give a clearer start to the lesson. I would make better use of the flipchart - possibly using two. I would slow down in places.

Additional comments:

I think with more teaching practice I would slow down + not rush so much. The teaching practice assessment helped me by highlighting aspects of the lesson that succeeded and those that were not so successfully handled.

Assignment 7.24 – **Writing a self-evaluation analysis prompt list**

The purpose of writing a prompt list is to give yourself something to use when reviewing your strengths and weaknesses during the process of self-evaluation. It is easy to give oneself a false sense of security by making subjective self-assessments in which everything appears to be fine. Nobody has complained or voted with their feet. Results seem to be no better nor worse than any other teacher's. Students appear to like what is going on in the classroom, teacher is working hard. There are no problems — or are there?

Consider two important aspects of teaching performance — classroom management and relationships.

- In what ways to your personal standards affect your students?
- Do you have a positive or an adverse effect on their attitudes and behaviour?
- Apart from academic learning, what else to they take away from your lessons?

A prompt list for use when reviewing performance in these areas might include questions such as:

- Am I always in the classroom well before the lesson is due to start?
- Am I clean and tidy and dressed appropriately?
- Do I bring my personal problems into the classroom?
- Do I set a good example?
- Do I maintain fair and honest relations with all students?
- Do I show respect to other members of staff when being observed by students?
- Do I work hard in the classroom and give a fair account of myself?
- Do I when on duty present a highly ethical and moral model?
- Is my diction, language and manner appropriate to my role?
- Do I always present a responsible image?

Using the seven main areas of activity shown in Figure 7.3, produce a set of prompt questions that you could use during self-assessment, or when interviewing other members of your group.

Assignment 7.25 – **Analysing your own and other teacher's presentations with reference to stated objectives**

Each member of the group should be invited to

- choose a topic for a short piece of instruction
- write down the elements forming the instruction
- write a set of learning objectives for the topic
- prepare an assessment designed to evaluate the effectiveness of the delivery

- deliver the instruction
- apply the assessment
- evaluate the responses.

After presenting an instruction and evaluating the assessment responses, each teacher should be asked to outline what they consider to be the strengths and weaknesses of their presentation.

The group should then be asked to discuss how well the stated objectives were met, and to comment on the effectiveness of the teaching and learning experience.

7.012 Identifying and evaluating characteristics of personal teaching styles

Self-evaluation by reflection

Competence-based and performance-assessed teaching skills may be evaluated by reflecting upon experiences gained in the classroom, laboratory or other teaching arenas. Such reflection and evaluation forms the basis for continuing professional development; and probably the most important aspect of self-evaluation is that the evaluator (oneself) will be credible and knowing. Nobody can better know the reality of any strength or weakness than the practitioner, so the process of review and development should be valued by the individuals who have taken responsibility for the assessment of their own teaching competence.

Whenever possible, performance should be assessed against measurable standards, but when these are not to hand teachers can usefully assess their performance against national standards, self-imposed goals or organisational performance targets. Appraisals are used to assess performance and to talk about a teacher's recent accomplishments. Feedback from learners and teaching practice observers can be of great value to any teacher. For example, evidence collected could indicate that your teaching methods may be too pedantic, thereby encouraging learner dependency when a rather more learner-controlled self-directing approach might be more suitable to your group. If this is the case then a more democratic, collaborative and informal structure based upon negotiated and agreed objectives and a high degree of learner involvement could replace a formal, competitive and autocratic regime where the teacher is the predominant figure.

When evaluating personal teaching styles it might be helpful to reflect on your attitudes, team skills, interpersonal skills and approach and style of facilitating learning when using methods such as:

- experiential learning, work experience, laboratory work, discovery learning and trial and error
- demonstration–explanation–imitation–practice and coaching
- discussions, simulations, games, interactive exercises, role play and tutorials
- researching, resource-based learning and problem solving
- lectures and exposition-style sessions.

It has been found to be helpful when planning self-evaluation to write a list of competencies to be attained, together with associated statements of how the skills may be demonstrated. Alternatively, the standards and checklists of performance criteria for current City and Guilds of London Institute Training and Development NVQs and series of trainer, APL adviser, assessor, verifier, coaching and other trainer competencies may provide ideas for developing your own procedures for self-evaluation. Alternatively, one or more of the assessment procedures listed above may suffice.

Teaching styles

Instructors and teachers are not all cast from the same mould. Personalities vary from person to person and the list of desirable traits required of a 'perfect' teacher is long. No one person can hope to possess all of the qualities required. Perhaps some of the best results are obtained by teachers who may be described as sociable, approachable and friendly extroverts; though of course these characteristics are not necessarily a single or accurate measure of quality in a teacher.

There are fortunately some aspects of a teacher's performance that have been suggested as indicators of a 'good teacher':
– enthusiasm and interest in the subject being taught
– ability to organise and deliver content
– ability to motivate, stimulate and maintain interest
– good classroom management skills
– honesty, reliability and conscientiousness
– absolute fairness in awarding marks and grades
– resourcefulness and persistence
– sense of humour.

Obviously, it is important to be seen to be enthusiastic about the subject being taught, since enthusiasm is infectious. Students are quick to spot a flagging teacher and quickly adopt a similar attitude or worse still, divert their energies to unscheduled activities.

It may be helpful on occasion to be something of a showperson, to brighten things up when the going is hard and to establish a warm and friendly atmosphere. But here the mode of instruction governs to a degree how teachers behave and how their students perceive them.

Above all, a teacher should behave naturally. If a person is normally quiet and reserved, or stern, it would be a mistake to try to adopt a false identity in front of a group. We are transparent when exposed to the gaze of our students and they would be unlikely to appreciate any form of attempted deception. Sometimes a joke does not go amiss, but this practice is dangerous. If you are not a natural comedian, forget it. Alternatively, if you are a comedian, keep it for the club. Some jokers spend more time telling jokes in and out of class than they do working productively. Staff and students alike can be seen to be carrying out avoidance tactics whenever the joker appears and in the end really do not value the time-wasting involved.

Early efforts should be made to establish rapport. Let the learners see that you are on their side and trying to help them. Never talk down to them. Avoid being too familiar but at the same time avoid being a martinet. Try to strike a happy medium. Ill-judged familiarity breeds contempt and disrespect, while an authoritarian attitude quickly alienates a group. A friendly, democratic style usually produces more work and better attitudes towards the subject and teacher. Approval for good work and prompting or coaxing for the strugglers is better than punishing or showing disapproval.

Learners often have several teachers during the same day and they compare notes about methods, attitudes and manner. Teachers tend to forget this and then wonder why they have a hard time while other teachers have little or no trouble with the same group of students.

Teaching styles in military and civilian contexts

It is interesting to contemplate whether or not there are differences between teaching styles in the armed forces and other 'service-type' institutions and those commonly found in other further and adult education establishments. Figure 7.8 indicates some of the perceivable differences.

Aspect	Military school	College of F.E.
Course structure	Intensive block full-time	Block/day/evening Full-time/part-time
Course character	Continuous	Continuous/periodic
Validation	Normally objective testing	Continuous
Departmental organisation	Hierarchical Instructor specialisation Central direction and control Centralised training support, resources and function Some integral administrative support	Open/fluid Broad-based lecturing duties Peripheral (individual) effort Largely integral responsibility Variety of college/departmental administrative support organisations
Student characteristics	Similar range of age/experience within group Similar personal and work circumstances Similar range of attitudes and motives within group	Unlimited range of age/experience Widely disparate personal circumstances Wide variety of attitudes and motivation levels
Approach to students	Structured relationships with overt status differentials Wide instructor responsibility for dress/behaviour/welfare Student attendance mandatory Range of sanctions available	Negotiated relationships with little emphasis on status Formal responsibility for teaching only Attendance optional within limits Few sanctions available
Instructor	Functional specialist from non-educational career (exempt RAEC)	Professional career lecturer or consultant

Figure 7.8 Perceived differences between teaching experience in military training establishments and civilian colleges of further education

As there is a growing number of public service officers and warrant and non-commissioned officers from the armed forces enrolling for the FAETC and other teaching qualifications, it is likely that many readers will be working or studying alongside someone who is used to a different style of teaching and a different type of client group.

Assignment 7.26 – **Assessing differences between civilian and military teaching styles**

Study the list given in Figure 7.8 and discuss with colleagues the validity of the comparisons made.

Adjusting to teaching in civilian life: a case study

The modern British army, navy air force and other services are vastly different to their predecessors, as a result of progress in the technology, communications and training of today's services. In order to maintain efficient forces, a very high level of technical and instructional skill is demanded of the trainers. But, inevitably, these highly skilled servicemen return to civilian life and many take employment as technicians or teachers in adult and further education.

Service personnel undertaking teacher training have frequently requested the opportunity to participate in discussions based on a case study that addresses the problem that some feel they may have in making the adjustment to teaching in civilian life. Accordingly, the case study[24] that follows has been prepared in the hope that it may be helpful to such people. Although it is couched in military terms, many of the concepts included relate to teachers generally.

Subject: John Carpenter aged 40 years
Service career: Army apprentice promoted to Warrant Officer
Class 2 REME (AQMS)
Artificer – Vehicle mechanic 'B'
WO2 Instructor, SEME Borden – specialist in wheeled
vehicle applications
Civilian job: Currently a lecturer in Motor Vehicle Engineering at Charlton Marshall College
Background: John Carpenter joined the Royal Electrical and Mechanical Engineers as an army apprentice at the age of 16. His interest in, and aptitude for mechanical engineering meant that he was recommended to attend an artificer's course after some years working as a vehicle mechanic. He passed the course without difficulty and was promoted to sergeant relatively early. There was no doubting his technical merit, and he had the ability to devise elegant and cost-effective solutions to engineering problems which was both respected and recognised by his colleagues and superiors.

As a senior NCO his ability to deal with, and get the best out of his soldiers in a working environment, was not so good. While his engineering excellence was admired, his subordinates viewed him as somewhat aloof and not very approachable.

His man-management suffered in consequence, and after a number of welfare and disciplinary cases had been poorly handled, his further promotion was delayed. A posting to a vehicle trials team where his technical expertise could come to the fore helped to restore some balance to his career prospects, and John Carpenter eventually achieved Warrant rank in his last three years of service. These were spent at the School of Electrical and Mechanical Engineering in the instructional field.

He worked in a training wing which was well organised and equipped to appropriate scales. He enjoyed this experience and, having completed his 22 year engagement, he undertook a resettlement course in instruction and training techniques. After unsuccessfully following a number of training job leads with major vehicle manufacturers, he obtained a probationary post as a lecturer with his local college, teaching motor vehicle engineering.

Current employment: John Carpenter took up a vacant post at Charlton Marshall College within the Engineering Department. The vehicle engineering course he teaches had been discontinued as an economy measure for two and a half years prior to his arrival, and although there is a departmental technical library he feels that the availability of reference and study material does not meet more than half of the needs that are implied by the course syllabus. Most of that which is available is out-of-date to some extent, and he is attempting to amend it as and when time allows. Similarly, while classrooms are adequately equipped with basic training aids, there is a dearth of technical display material and his instructional workshop is shared with a DIY class who are accustomed to treat the workshop as 'their own'.

The workshop technician — Tom Payne — is nearing retirement. Safety checks are not properly or clearly recorded, and many of those tools which are available — hand and machine — are unserviceable. The elderly technician grumbles about 'neglect' of the workshop, and confines his efforts to complaining about the mess that students leave, pushing a broom in desultory fashion and making sure that 'No Smoking' signs are prominently displayed about every bench.

John Carpenter recognises that the workshop technician is a key figure in the success of the re-instituted motor vehicle engineering course. He made an early attempt to encourage Tom Payne to sort out the workshop area and re-introduce proper standards but met with resentment. There has been little noticeable improvement. John has therefore shelved this problem for the time being until he has the time to devote to resolving it.

The Head of the Engineering Department is Pat Morgan. He was involved in John Carpenter's job interview and following John's appointment, Pat Morgan made a point of welcoming him to the Department. During the preliminary discussion, the course syllabus was clarified and Pat Morgan produced some previous programmes upon which John could base his own programming until experience dictated otherwise. He then gave John a brief tour of college facilities, introduced him to Tom Payne in the workshop and left him alone to get on with it.

The students on the motor vehicle engineering course vary in age and circumstances from 17-year-old school-leavers to a couple of mature students well over 30. The majority are under 25 and several are unemployed, although John suspects that at least some of these may be unofficially working for cash on the black economy, since their reasons for non-attendance at some sessions do not ring wholly true. Most are sponsored by their employers or by a government training programme. One or two are paying for the course out of their own pockets.

John does not admire some of the standards of dress and behaviour that are evident, but has been unsure of how to deal with this. He is also somewhat puzzled by the informality of approach and by what he regards as the 'free-wheeling' attitudes that he has encountered at unexpected times. He feels more attuned to his mature students but has had one or two surprises even within the older age bracket. The students' responses to the early stages of the course have been somewhat mixed, and John Carpenter is aware that both he and the course are being judged.

He has improvised where possible to overcome the lack of study material. While this has been feasible for the early basic lessons, he is uneasily aware that he cannot go on producing hastily amended but otherwise out-of-date material, to support the more advanced and complex areas of study which will be upon him shortly. He is well aware that effective teaching depends upon proper planning and preparation.

Current developments: At the end of an all-day session that John feels has gone rather well, one of the younger students asks to see him privately. After some hesitation, it comes out that this individual — having missed one of the evening sessions the previous week — has been unable to grasp today's course work, despite having previously had the reading materials covering the missed instruction.

After some probing, it also transpires that, having sought help from two of the class during the lunch break, neither had been able to satisfactorily resolve the bewilderment of this particular student. John's immediate reaction is one of irritation. He conceals this, while reflecting that it would be more productive if students who did not understand a topic clearly would say so at the time.

He arranges a time for a tutorial session the following day, reassures the individual he has been talking to and sends him away. He then sits down to reflect upon his current position, and to decide what must be done . . .

Assignment 7.27 – Adjusting to teaching in civilian life — John Carpenter

Read the case study given above and either individually or as a group member assess John Carpenter's position and produce an action plan that would lead to an improvement in his situation. During the course of your deliberations it may be necessary for you to

– analyse John Carpenter's situation as objectively as possible
– identify the problems taking care to look below the surface in order to define the root problems

- identify and write down John's overall aim and any supporting or subsidiary objectives that he will need to achieve
- set time priorities and time scales for achievement
- make outline plans to achieve objectives and ultimately to fulfil overall aim.

Discuss and record how the other additionally relevant questions listed below may be satisfied:

- How can John ensure the support and active co-operation of an already well-disposed head of department without losing face?
- The motivation of the workshop technician will need careful handling and a strategy for this must be agreed with the head of department. How should this problem be overcome?
- In order to derive short-term and then long-term solutions to his resourcing problems, how would John set about investigating the sources of capital and revenue funding and writing up a proposal in the form of a bid?
- John needs to seek advice about his puzzlement in the field of his relationships with students and needs to obtain help in clearly defining his responsibilities. Where would he find this support and how might his problems be resolved?
- Design a format that could be used to enable teachers in similar situations to carry out a self-analysis that would at least be helpful in identifying and prioritising their problems.

Assignment 7.28 – Strategic planning — using a SWOT analysis

A **SWOT** analysis is carried out to determine a company's strategic position in terms of its **strengths, weaknesses, opportunities** and **threats** to itself (SWOT). Strategic planning is concerned with the longer-term future of a company and it involves identifying any changes required in order to ensure a successful future. Clearly, the process involves thinking ahead, building on what is good and overcoming weaknesses. This idea of strategic planning can also be used to help teachers make choices about their future activities.

Produce a SWOT analysis by writing down on a flipchart a summary of your perceived strengths, weaknesses and resourcefulness; and the opportunities and threats present in the environment in which you are teaching.

Review your analysis with the group, a colleague, mentor or course team member and write a strategy describing how you intend to exploit your strengths and opportunities and overcome weaknesses and threats.

The outcome of this assignment will be that you and others will be able to improve and develop yourselves as effective practitioners by the processes of self-analysis and self-criticism. The SWOT analysis should provide an opportunity to explore personal qualities and lead to an awareness of the knowledge, skills and techniques needed to improve future performance.

Assignment 7.29 – Evaluating the performance of an experienced teacher

Observe and evaluate the performance of an experienced teacher teaching your group or some comparable group. You will need to negotiate the arrangements for this activity with the help of the course tutor if necessary.

– Note the strengths and weaknesses of the teacher's performance and judge the suitability of the delivery method, style, checks of learning and use of aids. Consider also how the teacher handled classroom management and relationships with the students.
– Contrast the teacher's level of competence with your own and identify areas that you may need to review and improve upon.

Assignment 7.30 – Compiling a list of classroom management strategies

This assignment calls for group activity and may involve the design of a survey or questionnaire to enable a wider sample of teachers to be reached.

Part A
Every experienced teacher has ideas about the ways and means of establishing effective classroom management while maintaining good relationships with students. Unfortunately, new teachers do not often have the opportunity to see this experience in action and so these strategies are not shared.

– Talk to some of the more experienced teachers that you know and find out some of their 'trade secrets'.
– Ask each member of your teacher training group to tell you about strategies that they have found helpful in managing their classes and compile a list of useful ideas.
– Ask your student group to tell you about the characteristics of teachers whose strategies have resulted in what have been, for them, enjoyable and productive learning experiences.
– Compile a list of useful ideas, share them with your class colleagues and decide how the strategies listed could be used during the teaching of your own classes.

Part B
Kurt Lewin was the psychologist who contributed to work in the field of group dynamics. He was particularly interested in the concept of a social climate and his work was applied to the educational field in terms of classroom climates resulting from formal control or the absence of it by teachers who could be described as being either 'authoritarian', or 'democratic' or 'non-interventionalist'.

Find out more about Lewin's work and write descriptions of the classroom climates and traits of the teachers who introduce the climates. For example one of the climates may involve a very formal teacher-directed learning situation in which everything is planned, timed to the minute and very highly organised.

266 Role

There may be high output while the teacher is around but very little when his back is turned. Students may respect the teacher but not enjoy the learning experience. The teacher may be a strict disciplinarian who is very decisive and uncompromising, while at the same time being a keen subject expert committed to giving of his very best.

Having finished your analysis of the three styles, plus any others you may identify, decide which one or combination would apply to your style of classroom management and whether a change in style could be advantageous.

Assignment 7.31 – Roles and responsibilities in quality assurance

When operating a Total Quality Management (TQM) policy the roles and activities of key people should be defined and those accepting roles should be fully briefed as to how they will be involved in planning and implementing policies.[25]

Describe how your employer's quality policy affects your day-to-day work and how you are involved in planning and implementing TQM.

Notes and references

1 B. Groombridge, 'Adult Education' in Blond's Encyclopaedia of Education, (ed.) Edward Blishen, Blond Educational Ltd, London 1969, pp 8–12. Brian Groombridge was formerly Education Officer, Independent Television Authority and Deputy Secretary, National Institute of Adult Education.
2 Many FE teachers knew the Further Education Funding Council (England) as the FEFC. It made funding for education and training available to further education and sixth-form colleges (and certain other institutions). Its principal legal duty was to ensure that there were sufficient further education opportunities for young people and adults throughout England. It allocated finance to colleges through its funding system and provided incentives to colleges to recruit and retain students as well as rewarding the college for high levels of student attainment.
3 G. Terry Page, J.B. Thomas and A.R. Marshall, *International Dictionary of Education*, Kogan Page, London 1977 p. 13.
4 Advisory Council for Adult and Continuing Education (ACACE), 'A Strategy for the Basic Education of Adults', 1979.
5 C. Maples, 'A workshop approach to basic skills', Adult Literacy and Basic Skills Unit (ALBSU) insert in Newsletter No 30, London, Summer 1988. ALBSU publishes a free newsletter that includes articles of interest to those who teach adult literacy, second language and basic skills.
6 A 'mission statement' defines the philosophy that underpins the operations of a college or organisation. The statement expresses in the broadest way its organisational objectives, its direction and underlying purposes.
'Organisational objectives' tend to be rather more specific and are statements of intent concerning goals for the whole college or organisation, but each department will have its own 'unit objectives' and probably different sets of 'course objectives'.
7 OECD Paper of 28 April, 1975, referred to in: D. Legge, *The Education of Adults in Britain*, The Open University Press, Milton Keynes 1982, p 3.
8 F. Parkin, *Class Inequality and Political Order*, Paladin, St Albans 1975, p 18.
9 P.M. Blau, and O.D. Duncan, *The American Occupational Structure*, Free Press, New York 1978.
10 R. Miliband, *The State in Capitalist Society*, Quartet Books, London 1976, p. 214.
11 R.W. Tyler, *Basic Principles of Curriculum and Instruction*, The University of Chicago Press, Chicago 1969, p 1.
12 *Ibid*, p 1.
13 *Ibid*, p 44.
14 *Ibid*, pp 63–7.
15 *Ibid*, p 95.

16   A. Spencer, N. Finlayson and S. Crabbe, *Coombe Lodge Report, Volume 20 Number 3*, 'Women in Further and Higher Education Management', The Further Education Staff College, Coombe Lodge, Blagdon, Bristol 1987, p 172. (Checklist reproduced with permission of Avon County Council.)

17   K. Ireland, *Teacher's Guide to the Health and Safety Act*, The Schoolmaster Publishing Co. Ltd. Kettering 1979.

18   For information on the guidance and counselling role of the tutor see J. Miller, *Tutoring*, FEU/NICEC 1982.

19   See *The Challenge of Change*, Unit for the Development of Adult Continuing Education (UDACE) 1986. See also Bulletin Number 2 in a series on 'The Role of Guidance in Education and Training', FEU, October 1988.

20   For information on the guidance and counselling role of the tutor, see: FEU publications *Tutoring*, June 1982 and *Teaching Skills*, June 1982.

21   *Managing Colleges Efficiently* (report of a study of efficiency in non-advanced further education, for the government and the local authority associations), Department of Education and Science and the Welsh Office, 1987.

22   *A Self Profile for Continuing Professional Development*, FEU, London 1987.

23   P. Cryer, 'Video Feedback Sessions for Improving Lecturing: Participants' Reactions to this Method of Academic Staff Development' in *Programmed Learning and Educational Technology* (Journal of AETT) Kogan Page Ltd, London, Volume 25, Number 2, May 1988, p 116. Patricia Cryer is a lecturer in the centre for the Advancement of Teaching in Higher Education in the Department of Educational Studies at the University of Surrey.

24   This case study was prepared by a lieutenant-colonel of the Royal Transport Corps and a major of the Brigade of Ghurkas, aided by senior training officer, George King.

25   For information about implementing quality assurance in education, training and service businesses see: L. Walklin *Putting Quality into Practice*, Stanley Thornes (Publishers) Ltd, Cheltenham 1992.

CHAPTER EIGHT

Features of the FAETC NVQ3

Aims: To examine the 7306 award structure and features of the qualification standards, and to consider ways of gathering and presenting evidence relating to key roles and competences

8.001 Introduction

The 'new' C&G 7306 Further and Adult Education Teacher's Certificate (NVQ Levels 3 and 4 qualification framework) was introduced in September 1994 and programmes are currently being offered by a number of colleges and other providers throughout England, Wales and Northern Ireland. At the time of writing the proven and well supported C&G 7307 version is still operating and will continue to do so while demand exists. However, the current revised 7306 programme is designed somewhat differently and is undoubtedly now more user-friendly and much improved on the earlier version available in 1993.

An important feature of the new 7306 Level 3 version of the FAETC is the designation of 17 TDLB defined units – seven core units and ten optional units covering five key purposes – plus two optional MCI units. The full C&G 7306 Level 3 qualification now comprises seven core units plus any three optional units and providers will negotiate attendant assessments of competence and the recording of achievement with individual candidates. A Foundation Certificate based on Level 3 NVQ Units and unit certification will also be available. However, teaching competence and the ability to facilitate learning effectively remains the essential focus for experience and certification.

Candidates following the 7306 NVQ format will need to demonstrate competences that will be assessed and judged against award performance criteria. Being able to meet unit requirements entails not only the ability to provide performance evidence at the right level but also the ownership of sufficient underpinning knowledge that supports such behaviour. A portfolio of supplementary and other supporting evidence associated with the elements assessed can be built up and used to support performance and knowledge evidence demonstrated during assessments. But care should be taken to ensure that the teacher-candidate is neither encouraged nor required to join in a 'paper chase' nor to 'jump through hoops'. In general, alternative sources of evidence are only required when performance evidence does not cover all the specified criteria and contexts defined by range statements.

This additional chapter has been added in order to provide useful information and insight about interpretation and possible approaches to development activities concerning some of the new FAETC Units. Unfortunately, due to constraints in space available, only a few key topics about which teacher-candidates and facilitators of the earlier 7306 have sought information will be discussed. However, Appendix E provides details of where other relevant underpinning knowledge relating to other C&G 7306 Units may be found in this book.

8.002 Award structure

The key roles and competences shown in Figure 8.1 form a logical approach to the work of people engaged in teaching and training occupations. The well established cycle commences with a training **needs analysis,** leading to the identification of training requirements of an organisation, department, group or individual. This is followed by a strategy for identifying **learning objectives** and planning, developing, organising and resourcing **learning opportunities**; implementing training by selecting methods and facilitating and **enabling learning** to take place; monitoring and **assessing achievement** and reviewing and **evaluating outcomes**.

The earlier prescriptive competence-based 7306 made it near impossible for many practitioners working in non-NVQ areas to qualify satisfactorily for the award. Thankfully, the number of optional units now available affords teacher-candidates considerable choice and will promote valid, reliable and relevant assessments. The clusters of units offered fit neatly into the training cycle framework and it is pleasing to note that five optional units are now available under the heading *Assessing achievement*. This will make the new award possible to achieve and far more relevant to the many practitioners who work in leisure, non-vocational and non-NVQ/SVQ areas of education and training who would otherwise experience considerable difficulty in meeting the requirements of D32/D33, the ownership of which carries with it responsibility for maintaining fair and valid assessment of candidates for NVQ/SVQ units.

8.003 Portfolio building

Evidence requirements

Many teacher-candidates starting work on NVQs such as the 7306 pose the question, 'What evidence can I collect to meet the assessment criteria for this particular competence?' The FAETC facilitators respond by suggesting certain performance evidence and supplementary evidence but notice that the candidates' eyes are glazing over and frowns are appearing. So they patiently try again and again, slowly digging their own grave. Explaining evidence requirements and range statements can be a very slow process for programme facilitators. Also when the NVQ/SVQ assessment model is new to them and the wording of standards difficult to cope with, trying to grasp what is involved becomes a painful process for candidates. With this in mind, diagrams giving an overview of the assessment model and showing the types of evidence that may be gathered are given below, together with brief explanations.

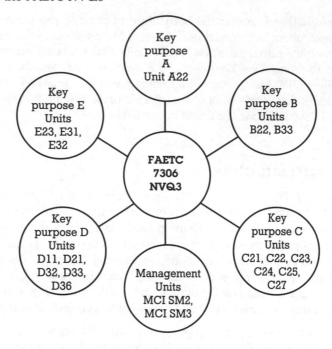

Key roles and competences

Establishing learner needs
A22*   Identify individual learning needs

Organising and resourcing learning opportunities
B22*   Design training and development sessions
B33*   Prepare and develop resources to support learning

Facilitating and enabling learning
C21*   Create a climate conducive to learning
C22   Agree learning programmes with learners
C23*   Facilitate learning in groups through presentations and activities
C24   Facilitate learning through demonstrations and instruction
C25   Facilitate individual learning through coaching
C27   Facilitate group learning

Assessing achievement
D11   Monitor and review progress with learners
D21   Conduct non-competence based assessments
D32   Assess candidate performance
D33   Assess candidate using differing sources of evidence
D36   Advise and support candidates to identify prior achievement

Evaluating developmental outcomes
E23*   Evaluate training and development sessions
E31*   Evaluate and develop own practice
E32   Manage relationships with colleagues and customers

Management
MCI SM2   Contribute to the planning, monitoring and control of resources
MCI SM3   Contribute to the provision of personnel

Note: The full C&G7306 Level 3 qualification now comprises seven mandatory core units* plus any three units from the options.

Figure 8.1 C&G 7306 Level 3 (Training and Development) FAETC Award structure

Gathering evidence against standards

Coverage

When candidates are preparing for assessment they must assemble the necessary evidence to cover all unit criteria and range statements. The evidence needed will fall into two main categories: performance evidence and product evidence. Performance evidence will be provided by demonstrating activity defined in the performance criteria while being observed by an assessor or perhaps while being videoed at work. Product evidence is gathered for examination and supplementary evidence may also be required. If performance evidence and examination of products and questioning do not alone cover performance criteria the assessor will call for further evidence of process skills or underpinning knowledge. Evidence presented must confirm competent performance.

Criteria for evidence presented

All evidence presented for assessment must satisfy four criteria: validity, currency, sufficiency and authenticity. This is essential, whether the evidence derives from prior achievement, experiential and informal learning, life skills, work experience, simulations or written sources.

```
Criteria for
evidence
presented

Validity
Currency
Sufficiency
Authenticity
```

Figure 8.2 Criteria for evidence presented

Historical evidence

Historical evidence relates to events of the past. The adviser or assessor concerned will need to check whether or not evidence which the client intends to present is up to date, meets current standards and is relevant to the performance criteria being considered. If this can be confirmed then the evidence will meet the requirements of **currency** and **validity**. **Sufficient** evidence must be provided to meet all unit performance criteria and must cover all range statements in terms of context and sources of evidence specified in the standards. Evidence presented must be **authentic**, that is, it must be of undisputed origin. Clients must 'own' the evidence. It must be genuine and reliable – a valid and accurate representation of facts and clearly the work of the person claiming ownership.

8.004 Assessment model

Gathering evidence for assessment

Features of the evidence gathering process are given in Figure 8.3. Assessment decisions are made by judging evidence presented against national standards. Plans agreed between candidate and assessor will describe the conditions and circumstances relating to the assessment, and detail evidence to be gathered which could comprise a mix of performance, supplementary and prior achievement. A suitable portfolio is then built up which contains supporting evidence.

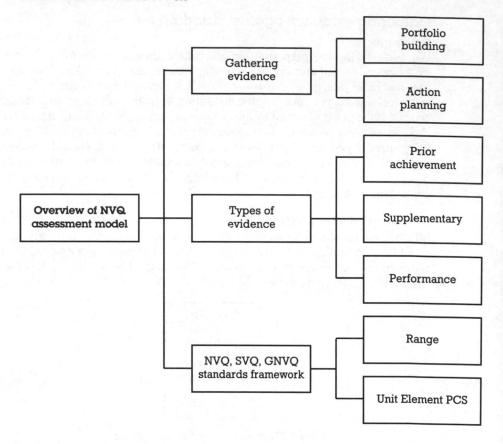

Figure 8.3 Gathering evidence for assessment

Types of evidence

Three main types of evidence are used in the NVQ/SVQ assessment process: performance, supplementary and prior achievement. Key features are shown in Figure 8.4.

Performance evidence

Performance evidence is current evidence – **direct evidence** of present competence. It is tangible, observable and naturally occurring. Performance demonstrated unaided while providing a service or creating a product are prime examples of direct evidence, but other sources include employers' letters of confirmation of current competence at work backed by written, material or computer generated products and assessor questioning. **Indirect evidence** includes archive materials produced by the candidate, testimonials, certificates of achievement, licences, log books, media articles, references and letters from present and past employers, accounts of unwaged work carried out, videoed activity and computer programming, or in fact any relatively recent and current supplementary evidence that satisfies unit criteria.

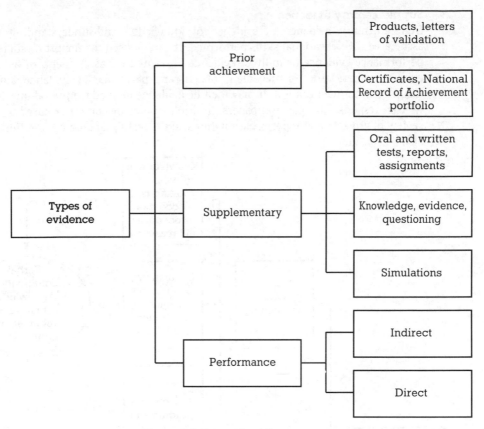

Figure 8.4 Types of evidence

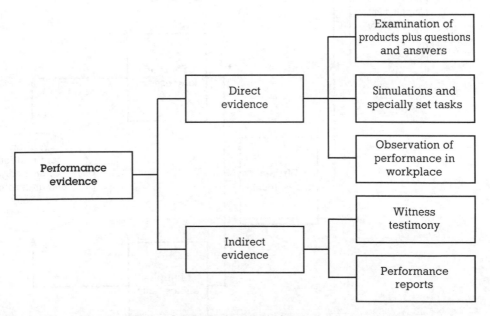

Figure 8.5 Performance evidence

Supplementary evidence

Supplementary evidence is evidence of knowledge and understanding that is associated with vocational skills performed. It can be used to support or supplement performance evidence or indirect evidence presented for assessment, or as 'top up' evidence where prior achievement or current performance evidence alone are insufficient to meet criteria. It may include evidence derived from: oral questioning, written responses to question papers, multiple-choice or computer-based testing or review of projects and reports. Simulations, skills testing and demonstrations could also be considered.

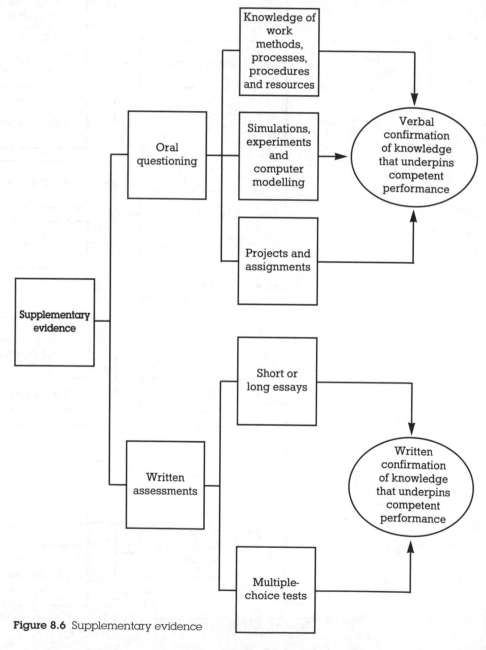

Figure 8.6 Supplementary evidence

Prior achievement

Prior achievement derives from relevant past experiences that have resulted in learning and the ability to perform tasks to the required standard. Acceptable evidence might include: contents of the candidate's National Record of Achievement file, certificates, awards and qualifications, authenticated letters of validation confirming achievement matched with relevant elements of competence during recent employment or while undertaking unpaid work. The assessment of prior learning and achievement is further discussed in Appendix D.

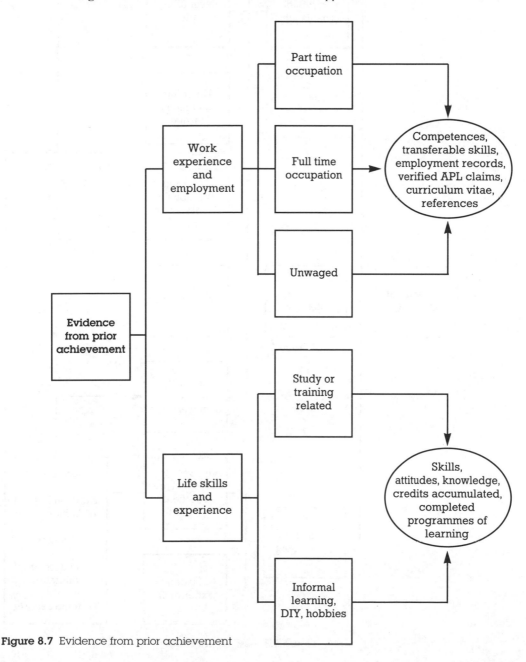

Figure 8.7 Evidence from prior achievement

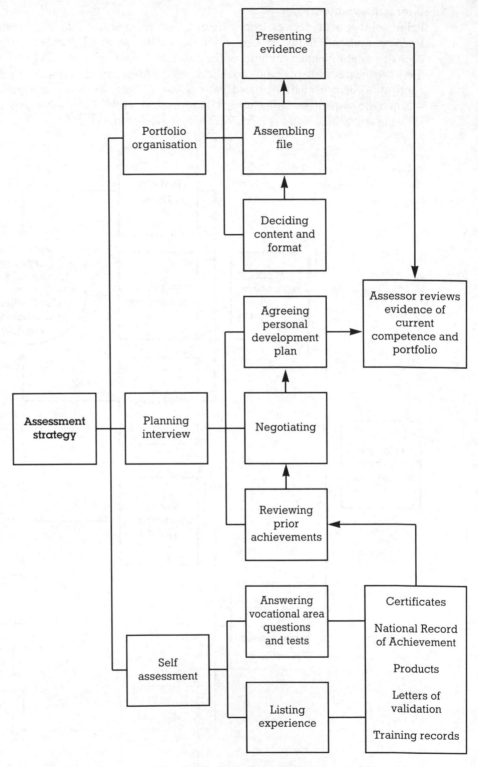

Figure 8.8 Assessment strategy

8.005 Assessment strategy

Stages

Overview

An overview of a strategy adopted when preparing for assessment is shown in Figure 8.8. As can be seen, candidates are encouraged to self-assess initially or otherwise establish where they are against unit criteria and range statements and then create a list of evidence to be gathered before joining an APL adviser, identification of training needs (ITN) analyst, learning needs identifier or teacher-assessor at a planning interview. A review of prior achievements and any evidence put forward is followed by negotiation and agreement of either a **personal development plan** and **top-up training** or an **assessment plan** (see the example given on page 321).

A contents list is drawn up and portfolio content is gathered ready for presentation to the assessor concerned. For ease of identification care must be taken to cross-reference evidence produced against unit criteria.

Assessing achievement

Assessing candidate performance

The five optional 7306 units available, D11, D21, D32, D33 and D36, cover important functions concerned with monitoring and reviewing progress and achievement, conducting non-competence-based assessments and assessing candidates using the many different sources of evidence that could be presented. Teachers will need to be able to negotiate assessment plans effectively; collect information on learners' progress, judge performance and knowledge evidence presented by candidates against criteria; make and communicate judgements, give constructive feedback and record achievement.

It is well known that account must always be taken of unit standards, range statements, the assessment specification and evidence requirements when considering a valid starting point for any assessment strategy. Numerous references to these important concepts are made earlier in the book; however, additional comment on approaches to gaining Units D32 and D33 will be given after discussing the key role of adviser and ITN analyst.

8.006 Identifying individual learning needs

Importance of establishing needs

A suitable starting point for any educational or training proposition is the establishment of learners' requirements. In the past, provision was often heavily supply-led. A menu of 'courses' was offered on a take-it-or-leave-it basis, rather than demand-led learning opportunities resulting from market research, data gathered from existing students or inquiries made by prospective customers. Some people have registered for training and development opportunities only to find later that the provision did not really meet their individual requirements. Others realised that they were going over old ground and quickly lost interest, while others found things too difficult or irrelevant to their needs and made their feelings known by voting with their feet or disrupting other learners.

The importance of the learner's role is recognised by the 7306 award design team, and the designation of units A22, *Identify individual learning needs* and C21, *Create a climate conducive to learning* as an essential core unit backed by optional unit C22, *Agree learning programmes with learners* reflects this view. This cluster of related units provides an opportunity for teacher-candidates to adopt an integrative approach to gathering evidence that will support claims for recognition of their competency in a number of units, rather than a hotchpotch of bits and pieces that they hope will fit in somewhere. With this in mind a *Client's Charter* has been devised which teacher-candidates find useful when matching evidence of their competency in particular skills with the complex role of facilitating learner achievement.

General principles and other matters relating to establishing learning needs are described in Appendix C.

Client's charter

Suggested fundamental roles for a teacher-adviser who is operating a guidance and support service for candidates are given in Figure 8.9. Action verbs describe each part of the role, which if carried out will result in unit-specified performance that can be observed or otherwise assessed and achievement recorded. Considerable benefit can derive from forming teams of teacher-advisers, each charged with the task of identifying members' prior achievements, identifying current training needs, agreeing realistic goals and establishing priorities for action and recording action plans with those concerned. This enables the complete ITN process to be demonstrated by role play, while other criteria such as facilitating collaborative learning and managing group dynamics may also be observed and assessed.

8.007 ITN interviewing and planning

Establishing current achievement

Initial self-assessment
Clients seeking NVQ and other qualifications will need help in identifying the gap between what they can already do and what they need to be able to do in order to meet award criteria. They will expect to be provided with **unbiased** and sufficient **relevant** information about the APL or ITN process, and **guidance** when completing *listings of experience, self-assessment instruments* and *assessment tests* and *identifying previously acquired competence*. Teams of teacher-candidates and others working towards the C&G 7306 and D36 APL Adviser's Award have found documents similar to the ones reproduced below helpful when gathering portfolio evidence. Role plays enable group members take it in turn to adopt the role of adviser, client and observer and hence gain valuable experience in identifying needs in a collaborative learning situation.

Listing experience
Having set the client at ease, explained the ITN process and provided award criteria,

the adviser sets about gathering information about potential areas of relevant current experience. The client is asked to complete forms similar to those given in Figures 8.10 and 8.11. Some people find it difficult to recall relevant past experiences and prior achievement and write no more than a few lines. This is when the adviser may need to provide considerable support.

Client's Charter

Adviser's Mission
My key purpose is to provide an excellent advisory, guidance and support service for clients, covering a range of vocational schemes and educational programmes.

Role of Adviser
My role as adviser is to:

ESTABLISH a sympathetic relationship and create an atmosphere conducive to establishing rapport with clients.
EXPLAIN the 'Assessment of Prior Learning and Achievement' (APLA) and 'Identification of Learning Needs' (ITN) processes to clients.
SUPPORT the principles of equal opportunities and best non-discriminatory practice; make arrangements to meet clients' special needs and requirements; and strive to break down personal and structural barriers obstructing access to learning opportunities.
ESTABLISH with clients the target qualification with reference to the NCVQ database of NVQs, GNVQs, SVQs, College prospectus, Careers Service, Training Access Points (TAPS) and other sources of information.
ARRANGE an initial diagnostic and assessment session within a comfortable and friendly environment while maintaining clients' confidence and self-esteem. Provide prompt constructive and objective feedback on outcomes.
INTERVIEW clients. Put them at ease and encourage them to self-assess prior accomplishments, review sources of achievement and complete a listing of experience.
ASSESS whether the individual client is likely to benefit from APLA, and whether their previous learning experiences would be likely to generate evidence of achievements.
IDENTIFY, PRIORITISE AND AGREE learning needs with clients.
ADVISE clients on the conditions and characteristics of assessment, training and personal development opportunities available and provide guidance on progression.
REGISTER clients for an award (where appropriate).
NEGOTIATE AND CREATE with clients learning programmes, action plans and assessment plans.
ARRANGE top-up training and where necessary facilitate individual or collaborative learning opportunities within a healthy and safe working environment.
PROVIDE guidance on identifying, selecting and gathering evidence.
PROPOSE a suitably structured folder or similar means of containing and presenting evidence, and guide portfolio composition and preparation.
MAKE AN APPOINTMENT – on the client's behalf – with a vocational or accredited assessor for the target qualification sought.
SUPPORT clients at all stages of the process, from initial assessment to final accreditation.
MAINTAIN the security, accuracy and confidentiality of clients' records.

Adviser _____   Client _____

Figure 8.9 Client's charter

Listing of Experience

Please list here potential areas of relevant current competence

Examine all criteria for the NVQ or other qualification that you are seeking and write down any prior learning, experience or achievements that you consider to be relevant.

Describe things that you have done in full-time employment or unpaid work, at college or while undertaking other education and training, during leisure activities, hobbies and DIY projects. Include also details of relevant written assignments, reports, investigations and any other documentary evidence.

Date of planning interview _____

Adviser _____   **Candidate** _____

Figure 8.10 Listing of experience

Initial Self-assessment

Please carry out a self-assessment

Identify areas where you think you can gain exemption from some units of the award chosen and others where you will need to do some extra work, attend skills-building sessions, obtain coaching in the workplace or find training opportunities elsewhere before seeking assessment.

Complete this self-assessment and also the listing of experience form. Then make an appointment with your adviser who will help you to identify existing competence and either arrange suitable learning opportunities for you or for assessment of your evidence.

Date of proposed planning interview _____

Adviser _____   **Candidate** _____

Date seen _____   **Date written** _____

Figure 8.11 Initial self-assessment form

Occupational area question checklists
Sometimes it will be necessary to apply written tests or questionnaires to establish currency and sufficiency of the client's knowledge and understanding. In such instances it would be helpful if the adviser had lists of preset questions available to supplement other self-assessment information gleaned.

Occupational Area Question Checklist

TOPICS AND QUESTIONS

Target qualification sought _____

Title _____

Occupational area questions
Please note: The primary role of your adviser is to *advise* and not to *assess*. The purpose of the questions listed below is to help you, the candidate, estimate the current level of your occupational area skills and underpinning knowledge concerning those units you intend to claim on the basis of existing competence. Please attempt all the questions. There is no time limit. When you have finished, review your responses with the adviser.

Unit title _____

Element title _____

Q1

Q2

Q3

Q15

Element title _____

Q1

Q2

PREPARE WRITTEN QUESTIONS FOR ALL UNITS AND ELEMENTS BEING REVIEWED

Questions prepared by _____

Figure 8.12 Occupational area question checklist

Interview checklist
In order to carry out a comprehensive and logically ordered review of current competency and to identify learning needs the adviser should prepare a list of topics to be raised and questions to be asked. The **checklist** given in Figure 8.13 could be complemented with **interview notes** recorded on a form such as the one in Figure 8.14.

Interview Checklist

TOPICS AND QUESTIONS

Target qualification sought

What is your present occupation?

Have you any changes in mind?

Which qualification are you seeking?

Is your work creating a need for you to go for the award?

Will you get any support from your employer?

Generally speaking, do you know what is involved in working for the award?

Are you familiar with the units and performance criteria involved?

Key prior achievements

Have you done anything like this before?

Do you have any formal qualifications that might be relevant to the award you are going for?

Have you done anything before that could be used to gain exemptions or credits for any part?

Have you done any part-time work that might be compatible with the award you are seeking?

Voluntary or other unpaid work?

Simulations?

Leisure activities?

Previous education and training?

TV, radio or reading-assignments, projects or similar?

DIY?

Units to be claimed

Have you identified any units you feel you can claim credit for right away?

Shall we now go through your listing of previous experience and sort out any potential areas of current   competence that would apply to the new award?

Now that we have done this we shall need to make a note of what you think you can claim and create an assessment plan.

Portfolio of evidence

Identifying evidence

Do you feel confident that the evidence you intend to present for assessment will cover all the unit requirements?

What do you understand by the term *direct evidence*?

Do you intend to provide any direct evidence for assessment?

What do you understand by the term *indirect evidence*?

Do you intend to provide any indirect evidence for assessment?

What do you understand by the term *performance evidence*?

Do you intend to provide any performance evidence for assessment?

What do you understand by the term *knowledge evidence*?

Do you intend to provide any knowledge evidence for assessment?

Let us make a note of the evidence you have identified for collection and presentation for assessment.

Gathering evidence

Do you foresee any difficulties in collecting the evidence?

You will need to match your evidence against the elements and performance criteria.

Will you need any help with this matching?

If you experience difficulties with interpreting performance criteria where could you get help?

I suggest that you file and index your evidence in a ring binder as soon as it becomes available. This will prevent a confusing build up of paperwork that takes some sorting out if it gets out of hand. Remember that you need to produce only sufficient recent evidence related to the units being claimed. In some cases you may need to demonstrate competence where evidence from prior achievement is not available.

Notes

Adviser _____

Figure 8.13 Interviewer's checklist

Interview Notes

TARGET QUALIFICATIONS AND PREVIOUS ACHIEVEMENT

Target qualification identified

Key prior achievements

Units to be claimed

Evidence to be gathered

Top-up training needed

Referral agency to be consulted

Assessment plan created and agreed   YES ☐   NO ☐

Notes

Adviser _____   **Candidate** _____

Interview date _____   **Date of next meeting** _____

Figure 8.14 Interviewer's notes

Action planning

Before concluding the session an action plan is agreed and recorded. The form and scope of the plan is a matter for negotiation, and content and context will vary according to individual needs identified. The action planning process is summarised in Figures 8.15 and 8.16.

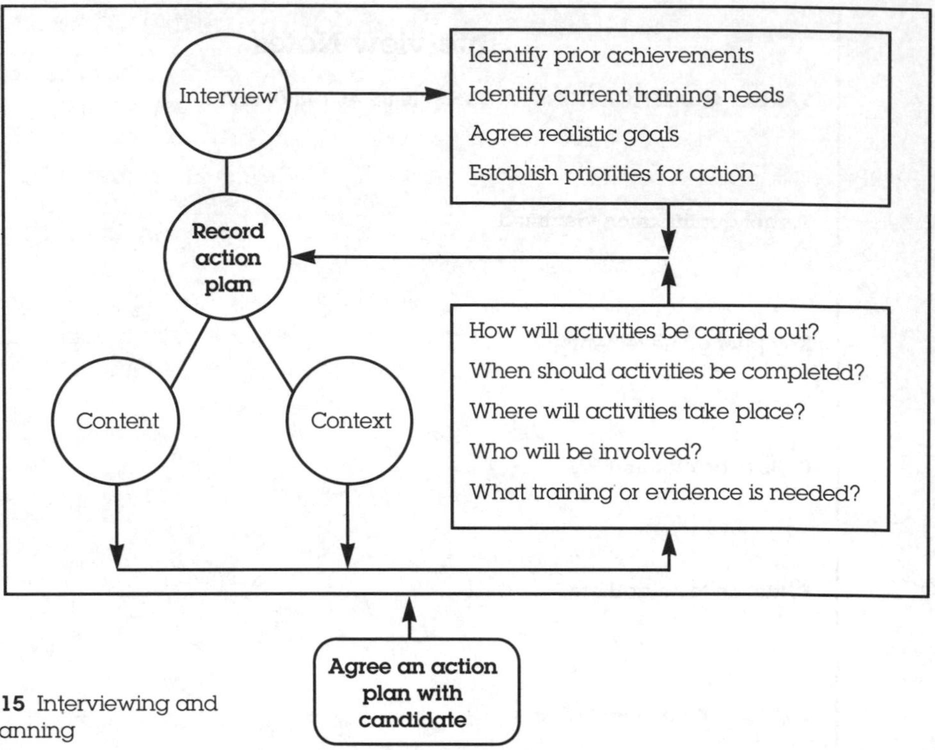
Interview
Identify prior achievements
Identify current training needs
Agree realistic goals
Establish priorities for action
Record action plan
How will activities be carried out?
When should activities be completed?
Where will activities take place?
Who will be involved?
What training or evidence is needed?
Content
Context
Agree an action plan with candidate

Figure 8.15 Interviewing and action planning

Action plan

Candidate name: ____________________

This assessment plan created during the planning interview held today has been agreed by the undersigned

Career goals:

Qualifications sought:

Target date:

Review dates:

Context for activity:

Location:

Performance criteria:

Resources:

Assessment arrangements:

Support required:

Other comments:

Adviser ____________________ **Candidate** ____________________

Date of planning interview ________

Figure 8.16 Action plan format

Assignment 8.1 – Discussion brief: Identifying training needs

A training needs analysis is carried out in order to obtain up-to-date information about a client's current competency and to establish personal needs. Once the data has been collected the training gap can be identified and suitable personal development opportunities provided, backed by effective training. Define and discuss each of the steps that should be taken in order to identify the training needs of individuals. Suggested steps are listed below, but you may add any others you consider necessary.

Prepare a group report covering each step. Add any points raised and comments made during the discussion. Include in your report conclusions and recommendations about how carrying out training needs analyses could be integrated with other teacher roles.

Suggested steps

Identify the individual or client group concerned.

- Explain the ITN procedure to clients.
- Clarify expectations and aspirations.
- Carry out the ITN using established procedures (or write your own).
- Collect data.
- Analyse findings.
- Identify the training gap.
- Write a report or prepare individual action plans.

Note: An effective training strategy would then be created that would enable initial training, top-up training or updating to be provided taking account of the individual's personal development objectives or group needs and priorities. Progress would be monitored and outcomes evaluated.

Assignment 8.2 – Writing an ITN information sheet

Design and produce an information sheet covering the range outlined in Figure 8.17 below. Consult with others about their perceived needs for sources of easily understandable information that will help overcome obstacles and break down barriers blocking access to learning opportunities. Ensure that your information sheet covers any particular requirements of clients from your own catchment area, the needs of the unwaged and people of differing cultural and racial background.

Information sheet

PRINCIPLES AND IMPLEMENTATION OF THE ACCREDITATION OF PRIOR LEARNING AND IDENTIFICATION OF LEARNING NEEDS PROCEDURES

Write up a draft form ready for use with your clients
Teacher candidates should add information here that they consider necessary for their candidates (clients, customers, students or trainees) to know about APL and ITN processes. Copies of the briefing document produced would be discussed, handed to or posted to clients seeking learning opportunities when or soon after the first contact is made. Being observed while administering the information sheet could serve as evidence towards units A22 *Identify individual learning needs* and C21 *Create a climate conducive to learning*.

Content could include:
– Statement of principles, philosophy and operation of APLA and ITN
– Methods of identifying learning needs
– Commitment to equal opportunities and non-discriminatory practice
– Types of information that could be supplied by candidates for reviews
– Types of candidate support that you/the employee/the training provider can offer
– Potential sources of experience that could be discussed during the ITN review or considered for APL assessment
– How the review and identification of candidate current status will be conducted
– Where detailed information about learning programmes may be obtained
– Notes on resources available and organisational requirements

Date information provided _____

Adviser _____ **Candidate** _____

Figure 8.17 Information sheet

Self-assessment questions 1

Helping candidates to identify areas of current competence

1 Explain how candidates can be provided with clear and accurate information on the principles and implementation of accreditation of prior learning and achievement and ITN.

2 Describe how you would encourage candidates to carry out a broad review of all their relevant experience.

3 Explain how the following five sources of experience could provide material that might be included in a Listing of Experience:
– full time employment
– part time employment
– unpaid work
– leisure activities
– education and training.
Can you suggest any other potential sources of experience?

4 Describe how a Listing of Experience could be used to help you and the client accurately identify and analyse potential areas of their current competence.

5 Explain how your style of support encourages self-confidence and promotes self-esteem in your candidates.

6 Describe other relevant means of support that you know of which could be helpful to your clients.

7 Describe how your approach changes (if at all) when helping people who are:
  – young adults as opposed to mature adults
  – employed/unemployed
  – confident/non confident
  – those with special needs, including physical or intellectual impairment.

Agreeing action plans with candidates

8 How can realistic client expectations and attainable career aspirations be encouraged?

9 Explain what is meant by NVQ/SVQ levels 1–5.

10 Describe where information about a wide range of occupational areas can be obtained.

11 Why it is necessary when advising clients to identify accurately units which they might claim?

12 Describe how appropriate target vocational qualifications can be identified and matched to a candidate's current competence and future aspirations.

13 With reference to action plans which you have prepared, explain how you have provided realistic learning opportunities for your clients. Describe how your approach changes (if at all) when helping people who are:
  – young adults as opposed to mature adults
  – employed/unemployed
  – confident/non confident
  – those with special needs, including physical or intellectual impairment.

14 Explain how you maintain records of interactions with your clients.

Helping candidates to prepare and present evidence for assessment

15 Describe how you can help your clients prepare and present their portfolio of evidence for assessment.

16 Describe and give examples of portfolio content that you may be called upon to handle.
  What is:
  – direct evidence?
  – indirect evidence?
  – performance evidence?
  – knowledge evidence?

17 Explain the means by which you liaise with your client's assessors and describe some purposes and outcomes of liaison activities.

18 Explain how you help your clients maintain confidence and motivation to succeed.

19 In what ways would you adjust your approach when giving support in the case of:
– one-to-one?
– group?
– self-study?
20 How can you ensure that awarding body documentation, recording and procedural requirements are met?

8.008 Assessing achievement

Assessing candidate performance

Process
When assessing candidate performance teacher-candidates will need to follow the now well established assessment process: negotiating, agreeing and if necessary reviewing action plans and assessment plans; collecting and judging performance and knowledge evidence against criteria, making assessment decisions and providing feedback. This process is reflected in performance criteria specified for D32 and D33, but is also very relevant to D11, D21 and D36.

Assessment model
A model showing how the assessment of achievement against criteria could be carried out is given in Figure 8.18. While there is no one system that will meet every assessment requirement, many key features are included in the diagram. However, effective communication and cooperation are absolutely essential features of amicable and constructive assessment. This holds true whether the teacher is conducting formative assessment with learners, reviewing progress, assessing candidate performance or otherwise making judgements about another person's achievements.

Pressures
When conducting assessments it is not difficult to upset a candidate whose perception of what constitutes competent performance may vary considerably from that of the assessor! For many candidates gaining the tick is what it is all about, rather than reward for credible achievement. With this in mind, the assessor foolish enough to adopt an authoritarian 'inspector' stance can expect trouble. Arguments can easily start which create poor relations and all kinds of tactics will be employed to get the all important tick.

In an effort to get a quick decision from a pressurised teacher-assessor who happens to have 25 or so to 'assess' before the end of a session, some candidates will adopt a quick-talking market trader approach. They reel off facts and launch into lengthy justifications while turning over pages of their file so quickly that vision is blurred, hoping to push their work through before the assessor has chance to think. Others may attempt to play off one member of the course team against another by saying something like, 'Chris (another teacher) said if I did this it would be OK.', or 'Briggs signed off Mark's. Mine's better than his. Why won't you sign this off?' Aggressive or over assertive attitudes will be adopted by a few who realise that some teachers who perform poacher–gamekeeper roles will be anxious to please and maintain motivation, and could even have the 'payment for successful outturn' concept pressing on their minds. Faded manuscripts curling at the edges and containing snippets of far from recent evidence dotted about here and there will be presented. No attempt will have been made either to highlight or justify relevance to the element now being claimed, or match it to performance criteria. But try explaining why such evidence is invalid to the person concerned and note well their attitude and responses. Assessors prefer to say 'Yes' and dislike saying 'No', and few candidates find it easy to walk away without their tick, regardless of the quality of feedback shared.

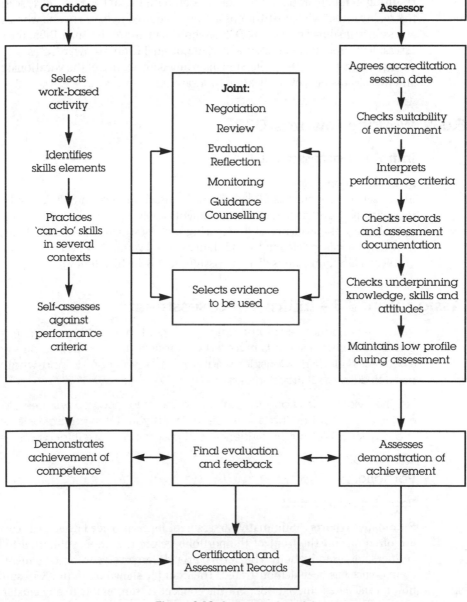

Figure 8.18 Assessment model

The examples given above illustrate the downside of 'assessment in action'. Fortunately for the growing army of vocational assessors, the number of candidates who neither appreciate nor value the requirement to present authentic, sufficient, current and valid evidence seems to be outweighed by those presenting high quality evidence to support claims of achievement.

Concerns

Professor Alan Smithers of the University of Manchester School of Education has expressed concern about deficiencies of the assessment system[1]. Considerable support for Professor Smithers' views has been forthcoming from practising teachers, resulting in much argument and discussion both for and against his assertions. But the reality is that while institutions are now required to have anyone who carries out assessment qualified by owning D32 or equivalent awards by April 1995, the quality of assessment processes operated and value of qualifications awarded as a result will depend ultimately on the professionalism and competence of the vocational assessors and the effectiveness of verification by awarding bodies.

8.009 Working towards D32

Initial self-assessment

Personal action plans

Initial self-assessment has already been discussed in Section 8.007. The benefits of reviewing past experiences and achievements apply equally when devising a strategy for collecting the evidence and preparing for assessment. A suggested approach to identifying needs in relation to D32 standards and gaining an overview of the content of a personal action plan is given in Assignment 8.3 which follows.

Assignment 8.3 – Initial self-assessment

Read the performance criteria, range statements and evidence requirements for Unit D32. Consider what is involved and reflect upon what you already know about each element. Consider what you think you can do and what you will need to do to meet requirements.

List the evidence you already have and the evidence you will need to gather, and specify your training needs. Discuss with your tutor, adviser or supervisor a strategy for collecting the evidence and preparing yourself for assessment.

Portfolio

Record of achievement

Summative reports   Summative assessment forms provided by accredited assessors are often filed at the front of the portfolio before the file is submitted to external verifiers for examination. The forms provide an overview or statement of how competence has been demonstrated. The example shown in Figure 8.19 summarises how a candidate achieved D32, but the concept is transferable to any cluster of units or complete award.

Assessment Record

Unit D32
Assess candidate performance

Candidate _____

Summary of assessment

The City and Guilds Vocational Assessor Candidate demonstrated competence in all elements of D32. Performance and supplementary evidence presented including the following:

D321   Identifying opportunities for the collection of evidence of competent performance.
Creating and agreeing with a client an individual assessment plan which covered three elements

D322   Carrying out an assessment by observing a candidate and collecting and judging performance and supplementary evidence against criteria.

D323   Devising sets of checklisted occupational area questions.
Using the questions while collecting and judging knowledge evidence to support the inference of competent candidate performance.

D324   Making assessment decisions and providing constructive feedback and advice to candidates.
Completing individual records of assessment, updating group records and reporting outcomes to the Training Standards Group.

                                        Signed: **Candidate** _____

Date _____   **Assessor** _____

Figure 8.19 Assessment record

Portfolio evidence list

When assembling the portfolio a sheet listing the contents should be filed near the front. Figure 8.20 gives an example. Evidence which is cross-referenced to criteria can then be inserted in numbered plastic pockets. The same piece of evidence can sometimes relate to several elements and this must be clearly specified to avoid confusion. Candidates are generally very familiar with the amount of evidence filed and its location and know just where to find documents; assessors may not be, especially when files containing a mass of irrelevant material are thrown together. The inclusion of summary evidence sheets helps to overcome this problem.

Summary evidence sheets

Header sheets listing documents relating to particular elements are prepared using a format similar to that shown in Figure 8.21. Evidence is cross-referenced to the element numbers concerned and added to the file in correct sequence. Separate header sheets are used for the performance, prior achievement and supplementary evidence contained in the portfolio.

Element	Ref	Title	PE	PA	SE
D321	01	Assessment plan agreed with candidate The plan to cover a minimum of three elements Plan must cover all performance criteria	*		
	02	Other assessor qualifications		*	
D322	01	Assessment plan (See D321)			*
	02	Other assessor qualifications (See D321)		*	
	03	Unit, elements and pcs (for 3+ elements to be assessed)	*		
	04	Assessment Task Sheet	*		
	05	Assessment Checklists	*		
	06	Oral/written (product) evidence from simulations			*
D323	01	Assessment plan (See D321)	*		
	03	Unit, elements and pcs for elements to be assessed (See D322)	*		
	07	Assessor-devised occupational area questions (1 set x 15+ Qs covering at least 3 elements) relevant to Assessment plan and actual D322 assessment undertaken (with sample answers)	*		
	08	Other sets of written questions used during vocational assessments	*		
D324	01	Assessment plan (See D321)	*		
	02	Other assessor qualifications (See D321)		*	
	03	Unit, elements and pcs (for elements to be assessed) (See D322)	*		
	04	Assessment Task Sheet (See D322)	*		
	05	Assessment Checklists (See D322)	*		
	09	Individual Achievement Record for one candidate covering at least 3 elements	*		
	10	Group Achievement Record *(Note: Ref. 09/10. Evidence that records are passed to next stage of the recording and/or certification process.)*	*		
	11	C&G *Access to Assessment – Special Needs* Policy Statement			*

Note: PE = performance evidence
         PA = prior achievement evidence
         SE = Supplementary evidence

Figure 8.20 Contents list of an evidence file for D32

Evidence presented

Candidate assessment plans   A personal assessment plan agreed with candidates is an essential prerequisite when preparing for assessment. It provides an overview of the forthcoming assessment and specifies what the candidate will be doing and methods to be employed, together with a description of how evidence will be collected against award criteria. There is no set format for plans as candidate circumstances and award standards will vary considerably within and across occupational areas. The importance of agreeing a plan lies in the fact that the candidate will have considered arrangements and actions carefully with the assessor or advisor and agreed them in advance. This collaborative approach will ensure a clear sense of direction, respect for the candidate's rights, maintenance of self-esteem, a fair degree of autonomy and acceptance of responsibility for outcomes.

A sample assessment plan is given in Appendix C on page 321.

Summary of performance evidence

TDLB Unit 10 (D32)   Element D322

Ref	Evidence presented
03	Units, elements and performance criteria for elements assessed
04	Candidate's Assessment Task Instruction Sheet
05	Assessor's Assessment Checklist

Candidate's signature _____   Date _____

Name: _____

Accredited assessor's signature _____   Date _____

Name: _____

Figure 8.21 Summary of performance evidence presented

Standards
Performance must be judged objectively against standards. Assessors will compare performance and knowledge evidence collected using the performance criteria and associated range statements which together form an element. For the assessor to perform effectively, knowledge and understanding of the standards is an essential prerequisite. A copy of the standards must be available to teacher-assessors when planning and conducting assessments.

Access to assessment
Teacher-assessors will need to ensure that all candidates presenting themselves for assessment are treated fairly in terms of equal opportunity regardless of gender, age, racial origin, sexual orientation, religious persuasion or disability. Discrimination and inequality must be eliminated from assessment techniques, practices, resources and their application, and all reasonable steps must be taken to meet candidates' special assessment requirements.

Access to assessment must be appropriate to candidates' needs. Assessment arrangements should therefore be adjusted to take account of the needs of candidates with hearing, visual or physical impairment or those with specific learning difficulties of a dyslexic nature. The services of a signer, specialist communicator, interpreter, reader or someone to take dictation may be required.

Knowledge and application of the policies presented in the documents *Access to assessment–candidates with special needs* and *Equal opportunities*[2] adequately covers D32 evidence requirements. These statements are available from City and Guilds. Equal opportunities and special needs are further discussed in Appendix C.

Assignment 8.4 – Creating an assessment plan

Obtain a set of standards set out in an awarding body's candidate pack, together with the log book, and the assessment specification or the NVQ/SVQ units, elements and performance criteria to be assessed. Using the standards as a basis for discussion, identify and agree with the candidate the unit to be assessed and opportunities for evidence collection. Consider all possibilities, including products, activities both work-based and outside work, simulations, questioning and any other feasible sources of evidence.

Determine the context in which the assessment will take place. Include details of what is to be assessed, how it will be assessed, where and when the assessment will take place and who is involved.

Review the outline content and write an assessment plan using your own format or one similar to that shown in the example on page 321.

Assessment task instructions
In general, unless tasks are clearly specified in relevant log books, candidate packs or similar award body documentation, candidates for assessment should be provided with written assessment task instructions. Tasks must clearly relate to valid standards. Oral briefings should be unambiguously presented using plain language. Candidates who do not understand what they are required to do must be given an opportunity to have the instructions clarified. Instructions should contain sufficient information to elicit required behaviour and no more. Far from helping to make the task appear crystal clear, irrelevant detail tends to confuse and bewilder.

Assessment task checklist
Preparing **assessor's checklists** and marking up the lists during assessment sessions are two of the core skills essential to effective judging of performance. A recommended sequence of operations is written, deriving from a method study of experienced workers performing the task or from careful examination of the standards. The list is then checked for validity and completeness, ready for use as a checklist during the observation session on assessment day.

Some people will argue that using a checklist and recording observations relating to candidate activity while the candidate is working, and a written question checklist later is a waste of time. Comments like, 'I don't need paperwork. It's all in my head. I've been doing this job for years.' will be heard. But can consistent, valid and reliable judgements be made without checklists?

Candidates may find the assessment checklist given in Figure 8.22 helpful when preparing for assessment against D322 standards.

Assessment Checklist

Element D322
Collect and judge performance evidence against criteria

Candidate _____

Performance criteria	Was this met? Yes	No	Assessment method Observation	Product	Comments
a) advice and encouragement to collect evidence efficiently is appropriate to the candidate's needs	☐	☐			
b) access to assessment is appropriate to candidate's needs	☐	☐			
c) only the pcs specified for the element of competence are used to judge the evidence	☐	☐			
d) evidence is judged accurately against all the relevant pcs	☐	☐			
e) the evidence is valid and can be attributed to the candidate	☐	☐			
f) any preset simulations and tests are administered correctly	☐	☐			
g) the assessor is as unobtrusive as is practicable whilst observing the candidate	☐	☐			
h) evidence is judged fairly and reliably	☐	☐			
i) difficulties in judging evidence are referred promptly to an appropriate authority	☐	☐			
j) the candidate is given clear and constructive feedback and advice following the judgement	☐	☐			

Range statement

Source of evidence:

Observation of process ☐
Simulations ☐
Examination of products ☐

Candidates:

Experienced in presenting evidence ☐
Inexperienced in presenting evidence ☐
With special assessment requirements ☐

Evidence seen

One individual assessment plan ☐
Standards – elements and pcs ☐
Written assessment task instructions ☐
Assessment task checklists ☐
Simulator briefings and reports ☐

Other evidence

C&G 730 Certificate ☐
Other assessor qualifications ☐

Notes from guided discussion (including guidance on further evidence or action if required)

Candidate's signature _____   **Assessor's signature** _____

Figure 8.22 Assessment checklist

Assessor's checklisted questions

Teachers will probably have already demonstrated competence in using questioning techniques during teacher training programmes and teaching practice assessments. They will have frequently used written and oral forms of questioning and associated techniques in their normal course of duties as facilitator, trainer and assessor. All truly effective teacher-assessors will own the skills listed below, backed by adequate underpinning knowledge of how to frame, adapt and ask questions:

– planning and managing assessment sessions
– questioning techniques
– devising questions
– oral, written and live observation techniques of testing and assessing
– gathering evidence
– sharing feedback
– reliability and validity
– purposes and applications of various types of tests
– self-appraisals and assessment methods.

Sets of assessor-devised questions covering the occupational area must be available for use when collecting and judging knowledge evidence.

Assignment 8.5 – Collecting evidence

Assume that an assessment plan has already been agreed with your candidate. You are aware of the assessment arrangements but need to consider how the assessment task will be introduced and how candidates will know what they are required to do. You are not happy about relying on an oral briefing and decide to prepare a written assessment task instruction sheet that will be given to the candidate before starting their demonstration.

Carry out an analysis of the assessment task concerned and produce a document similar to the example shown on page 54. Using the analysis as an aid, develop an assessor's checklist ready for use as a tick list during the observation session on assessment day. (Note: The task analysis process can also be useful when lesson planning.)

Write a suitable assessment task instruction sheet specifying the task to be performed by the candidate. Ensure that the information contained will neither help, hinder nor lead the candidate when performing the task. Alternatively, photocopy the relevant sheets from award body documentation and prepare to use the documents during an actual assessment.

Devise sets of occupational area assessor-devised assessment questions, based on performance criteria, that will be used during the assessment session when collecting and judging knowledge evidence to support the inference of competent performance.

Individual achievement records

Valid and reliable records of current achievement should be updated at the earliest opportunity.

Formative or summative achievement records should be signed up, entries made and outcomes logged on databases as appropriate. Information must be stored securely and confidentiality maintained when communicating assessment decisions to authorised persons.

Group records

When monitoring progress and planning assessment schedules, teacher-assessors working with large groups will find it helpful to maintain group records in the form of a matrix. Names are listed vertically against NVQ/SVQ elements listed horizontally. Boxes can be dated and initialed as and when candidates gain unit credits.

Assignment 8.6 – Judging, decision making and recording

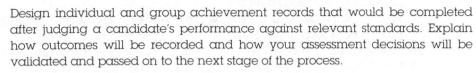

Design individual and group achievement records that would be completed after judging a candidate's performance against relevant standards. Explain how outcomes will be recorded and how your assessment decisions will be validated and passed on to the next stage of the process.

Self-assessment questions 2

Agreeing and reviewing a plan for assessing performance

1 What types of evidence could be used for assessment purposes?
2 What is meant by a realistic work environment?
3 Explain how naturally occurring evidence could be collected.
4 Why is it both preferable and important to assess candidates while they are performing their normal work role?
5 What steps should be taken to minimise disruption to normal work routine when planning assessments?
6 What other settings or contexts are acceptable and under what circumstances would they be adopted?
7 How would you set about collecting collect performance evidence?
8 Give examples of supplementary evidence that you might also need to collect.
9 Why is it important to collect evidence of underpinning knowledge?
10 Why is it important to negotiate and agree assessment plans with candidates?
11 What other people might be involved at the assessment planning stage?
12 Specify the minimum number of elements to be assessed at one time.
13 What is meant by performing across the range?
14 What would you do if the candidate presented evidence that was not on your list of acceptable evidence?
15 If you needed to assess a simulation, how would your plan differ from that of a 'natural performance' assessment plan?
16 How would you ensure access to fair and reasonable assessment?
17 In what circumstances and for whom might you need to make special assessment arrangements?

18 What important and relevant legislation protects people from unfair discrimination?

19 What options are available to candidates if there is disagreement when negotiating assessment plans?

20 When planning assessments, how could you minimise costs of the assessment process but still carry out a valid and reliable assessment?

Collecting and judging performance evidence against criteria

21 When collecting and judging performance evidence against NVQ/SVQ or other criteria, why is it important to consult the assessment plan?

22 What is the point of using an assessment checklist when collecting evidence?

23 How can you be sure that the candidate's performance activity meets all the performance criteria being assessed?

24 Why is it important that the candidate takes responsibility for identifying and presenting relevant evidence?

25 How could you encourage candidates to collect their own evidence?

26 How would you gather performance and product evidence during a simulation?

27 Why is it important to remain unobtrusive when observing a candidate in action?

28 Explain how you would maintain adequate observation at all times while still keeping a low profile.

29 What type of evidence would you expect to collect while the candidate is performing in the workplace?

30 Under what circumstances would you use preset tests or simulations when collecting evidence?

31 What important conditions must prevail when administering tests and simulations?

32 Why must standards be referred to when assessing a candidate's performance?

33 If there were difficulties in interpreting the performance criteria or standards to whom would you turn for advice?

34 If you were assessing product evidence only, how could you ensure that it was the candidate's own work?

35 Why should the candidate be allowed to complete the assessment task unaided?

Collecting and judging knowledge evidence to support inference of competent performance

36 Explain the importance of checking knowledge evidence during the assessment process. Why is it important to ask questions concerning underpinning knowledge?

37 What are the available sources of knowledge evidence?

38 Describe the range of questioning techniques that could properly be used when gathering evidence. Give an example of circumstances where each would be used. Why would you use the methods described?

39 Specify any other types of questions and tests that you would need to use as a qualified vocational assessor.
40 Describe the type of preset questions and tests you would use for assessment purposes.
41 Where could you obtain other sets of preset tests if needed when assessing candidates?
42 List the assessment instruments you have in your resource bank.
43 In what circumstances would you need to construct your own assessment questions?
44 What is meant by the term *validity*?
45 When constructing tests, how can you ensure that the questions are valid?
46 Why is it important to restrict the scope of questions asked to the unit that you are assessing?
47 What is meant by *leading* candidates when asking questions?
48 Why must the adequacy of candidate answers be judged? How is judging effectively carried out?
49 Why is it important to involve the candidates sufficiently in their own assessment?
50 What action would you take when certain performance criteria have not been met?
51 Why is it important to give feedback as soon as possible?
52 How is consistency and reliability maintained when assessing different candidates?
53 How, where and when must candidate achievement be recorded?
54 Describe how your assessment provision allows access that matches individual candidate's needs and requirements.

Making assessment decisions and providing feedback
55 Describe how the assessment specification ensures that the evidence selected will match the stated performance criteria.
56 What factors should be considered when choosing a location to share feedback with the candidate?
57 Why is it essential to reduce (or preferably eliminate) disruption in the workplace when you are carrying out an assessment and giving feedback?
58 What features of a normal work environment could adversely affect a candidate's performance?
59 How can you be sure that you use only the specified performance criteria when making your assessment?
60 What positive or negative biases to candidates might you experience?
61 How can you be sure that the candidate clearly understands which performance criteria have been met?
62 What action would you take when certain criteria have not been met?
63 Why is it important to give feedback as soon as possible after the assessment?
64 Why is it essential to give constructive feedback?
65 Why should you encourage candidates to ask questions about their assessment?

66 How might your approach change when dealing with candidates who were either very confident, lacking confidence or having special assessment requirements?

67 What are the benefits of keeping records of achievement/assessments?

68 Why is it important to complete records at the time of assessment?

69 How are your records transferred between different parts of the recording system?

70 How and where are the records stored?

71 Describe what is meant by the term *verification*.

72 What is the procedure for obtaining countersignatures?

73 What can be done to ensure that candidates understand what they need to do in order to meet the required standard of any performance criteria that have not been met?

74 How can anxiety be reduced when candidates present themselves for assessment?

75 What is meant by the concept *quality assurance in assessment*?

Notes and references

1   See A. Smithers, 'All our futures – Britain's education revolution. A Dispatches report on education' published by Channel 4 Television, London, 1993.

2   Available from Sales Section, City and Guilds of London Institute, 1 Giltspur Street, London, EC1A 9DD.

APPENDIX A

Making OHP transparencies

Prepared by staff of the Department of Educational Resources, Head: C.H. Teall, BA, Dip Ed Tech, and reproduced by kind permission of K.G. Lavender, BSc (Eng) (Hons) C Eng, MIEE, M Inst W, Principal, South Thames College.

First attempts

```
MATERIALS YOU WILL NEED

Squared drafting paper
1 set thin felt tip OHP pens
1 set thick felt tip OHP pens
Box of acetate sheets
Masking tape
OHP Transparency frames
Sheets of transparent self-adhesive
  colour film
Bottle of cleaning fluid
Sharp-pointed knife
```

1 To plan the transparency you need the squared drafting paper. Lay the transparency frame on a piece of squared paper and draw round the outline of the aperture. Plan the layout of your visual within this boundary.

2 Fix a piece of acetate over your draft with small pieces of masking tape. This keeps acetate and paper in register.

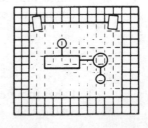

3 Using the pens of your choice draw the outlines of your visual. Add colour and lettering as planned.

4 Select a frame of the correct size. This will be A4, 10″ × 8″ or 10″ × 10″ aperture. Some 10″ × 8″ (rectangular) frames have push out sections to make them 10″ × 10″.

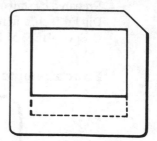

5 Position the Vufoil on the table and place a frame over it so that the cut off corner is to top right.

6 Turn frame and Vufoil over and secure all edges with masking tape.

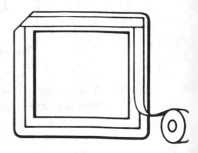

7 If overlays or masks are required they should be positioned correctly and fixed to the top of the frame with self-adhesive aluminium foil hinges (Techinges) or masking tape.

8 Label frame clearly for filing, write notes on frame edge.

This of course is the simplest way of making your visual. Higher quality lettering can be obtained by using dry transfer lettering (Letraset or Letterpress) and large blocks of colour can be added with the self adhesive transparent colour film or transparent coloured tapes (these are very useful for graphs or bar charts).

Applying Transpaseal

1 Select the colour and place the sheet of the Transpaseal over the area to be covered.

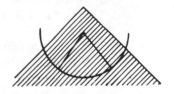

2 Using scissors cut out a piece slightly larger than that required.

3 Peel off the backing and carefully apply to the Vufoil surface rubbing with a circular motion from one end so as to exclude all the air bubbles.

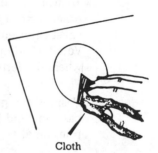

Cloth

4 Using a sharp knife, cut round the true edge lines using the lines of the diagram as guides. Only press hard enough to penetrate the Transpaseal. Do not cut through the Vufoil. Avoid cutting beyond the lines on the diagram as this will leave a scratch line on the acetate which will project as a black line.

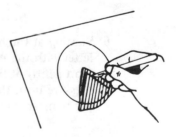

5 Carefully peel off the surplus Transpaseal and discard.

Dry transfer lettering

1 Place a sheet of ruled paper under the Vufoil and clearly indicate the base line to be followed. This is to be aligned with the guide lines below the letter.

Position of letters

Guide line

2 Where positioning of words is left to right start from the first letter.

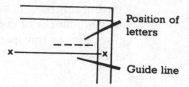
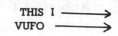

3 When positioning of words is central, work out the middle letter and start from there. Remember however that not all letters take up the same space, (If 'A' is standard, 'I' takes up 0.5 the space and 'W' 1.5 times.)

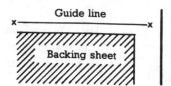

4 To avoid accidental transfer of letters on to other parts of the Vufoil, keep the backing sheet between the Projecta-type and the Vufoil, positioning it to expose the area where the letters are to be transferred.

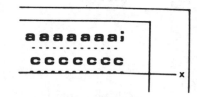

Guide line

Backing sheet

5 Position the guide below the letters on the base line and locate the letter to be transferred.

6 Starting at the top, rub down the whole letter with the rounded end of a pen. Start gently at first and increase pressure until the letter separates from the transfer sheet.

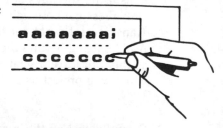

7 Slowly pull the sheet of letters from the Vufoil, leaving the letter adhering to the Vufoil. Hold the sheet in position until you are sure the whole letter has been transferred.

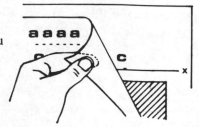

8   Proceed exactly as before to complete the lettering using the spacing marks on the sheet.

9   When all the letters have been transferred, place the backing sheet over the letters and rub down with a thumbnail or rounded pencil end to ensure transfer.

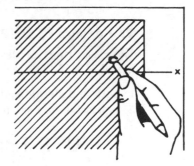

10 Replace the backing sheet on the sheet of lettering and place in the storage wallet.

Making transparencies using photocopiers

Most offices, educational and training establishments have some type of photocopying equipment. In the majority of cases transparency material is available for these copiers although the range will vary considerably.

Some photocopiers will only take a single sheet — while others will accept a book or other bound material. The most useful copier (and often the cheapest) for making OHP transparencies is the heat copier since a wide range of specially treated acetate is available. By buying different acetates you have a choice of black or coloured lines on a clear background, black lines on a coloured background or white lines on a black background. You can, of course, make your base visual this way and add colour with pens or the transparent self adhesive film.

Heat copiers will only accept single sheets and the original must be drawn in a carbon or metallic based ink or in pencil since they are 'blind' to colour inks.

True photocopiers will produce half tones but usually the quality of a transparency made on these machines is poorer.

Using computers and printers

Some of the methods suggested above may seem somewhat dated compared to today's methods of resource production, but they still have considerable utility in terms of cost effectiveness (materials/machine costs).

Larger organisations will probably be equipped with computers and laser printers, which can be used to produce high-quality colour transparencies. The process can be completed in very little time providing the teacher has mastered the computer program and has the necessary resources. But for some the capital expenditure and high costs of consumables may not be justified, so that it is likely that the well-established 'hand' methods will be used for some time yet.

Nowadays pictures and data can be downloaded from the web (subject to any copyright restrictions) or desktop publishers may be used to generate high-quality handouts and transparencies, but the fact remains that teachers need to be able to operate anywhere in the world — even in places where computing facilities may not be available.

The design of OHP transparencies

The basic rules of design apply but in addition you will find the following useful.

1 Lettering should be large enough to read from the back of the room. Ordinary typeface is too small.

USE THIS SIZE AS THE MINIMUM.

2 Do not try to squeeze too much information onto one transparency.

3

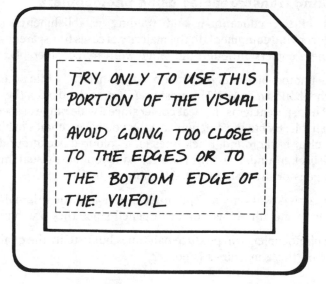

TRY ONLY TO USE THIS
PORTION OF THE VISUAL

AVOID GOING TOO CLOSE
TO THE EDGES OR TO
THE BOTTOM EDGE OF
THE VUFOIL

- Do not over-crowd your transparency with too much material or print.
- Get the spacing right.
- Make sure the material is clear and easy to read.
- Try to achieve some visual interest and appeal. Use visual symbols not words.
- Keep it bold and simple.

APPENDIX B

Stages in producing an objective test

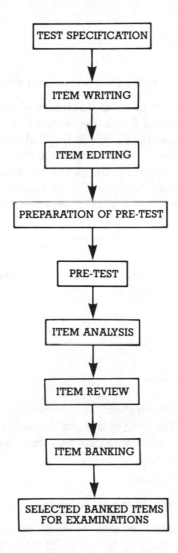

```
┌─────────────────────────┐
│   TEST SPECIFICATION    │
└─────────────────────────┘
            │
            ▼
┌─────────────────────────┐
│      ITEM WRITING       │
└─────────────────────────┘
            │
            ▼
┌─────────────────────────┐
│      ITEM EDITING       │
└─────────────────────────┘
            │
            ▼
┌─────────────────────────┐
│  PREPARATION OF PRE-TEST │
└─────────────────────────┘
            │
            ▼
┌─────────────────────────┐
│        PRE-TEST         │
└─────────────────────────┘
            │
            ▼
┌─────────────────────────┐
│      ITEM ANALYSIS      │
└─────────────────────────┘
            │
            ▼
┌─────────────────────────┐
│       ITEM REVIEW       │
└─────────────────────────┘
            │
            ▼
┌─────────────────────────┐
│      ITEM BANKING       │
└─────────────────────────┘
            │
            ▼
┌─────────────────────────┐
│  SELECTED BANKED ITEMS  │
│    FOR EXAMINATIONS     │
└─────────────────────────┘
```

The following extract is from the City and Guilds of London Institute *Manual on Objective Testing*.

An assessment guide, *Setting Multiple Choice Tests*, Ref. No. TS-00-5001 is currently on sale and may be purchased from the Sales Section, City and Guilds, 1 Giltspur Street, London EC1A 9DD.

Definition and types of objective items

An objective test may be defined as a series of items, each of which has a predetermined correct answer so that subjective judgement in the marking of each item is eliminated.

1 There are a number of types of objective item:
– multiple-choice
– multiple-response
– matching block
– assertion/reason
– true/false.

The Institute has concentrated on the **four-option multiple-choice item.**

A **multiple-choice** item consists of a **stem** in which a question is either asked directly or implied, followed by four answers called **options**. Three of these are incorrect, called **distractors**, and one is correct, called the **key**. The candidate is required to select the option he or she believes to be the correct answer. The correct answer must be clearly acceptable to the more able candidates but each distractor must be sufficiently plausible to appeal to a reasonable proportion of the less able candidates. An item of this type is shown in Example 1.

Example 1

The maximum voltage at which one-piece construction on pin-type insulators can be used is

a   11 kV
b   33 kV
c   66 kV
d   132 kV   (Type of Knowledge – I)

This particular item tests the recall of an important piece of **factual knowledge** (Type of Knowledge 1). The same format can also be used, however, to test higher types of knowledge, and the Institute currently deals with two of these, that is

type II – comprehension
type III – application

which require a more thorough understanding on the part of the student.

Test constructors often find that the allocation of a type of knowledge to a particular item is a difficult stage. It may be helpful to remember that
(i)   one should concentrate on deciding what needs to be tested, i.e. forget about the learning steps that lead to it.
(ii)   the knowledge categories are hierarchical, i.e. if an item is testing in the application category, it will at the same time be testing in the two lower categories, comprehension and factual knowledge.

Examples of items: testing types of knowledge II and III follow.

Example 2

The main purpose of the vehicle in a printing ink is to

a   produce properties relating to colour
b   transfer the pigment to the paper
c   control the rate of drying
d   prevent set-off set on the paper.   (Type of Knowledge – II)

Example 3

An exterior architectural subject is to be photographed in colour. The lighting is brilliant sunlight and it is necessary to reduce the image illuminance without affecting colour reproduction or depth of field. Which one of the following filters would do this?

a   Colour correction filter
b   Polarizing filter
c   Suitable contrast filter
d   Graduated sky filter.   (Type of Knowledge – III)

2 Multiple-response. A type of multiple-choice item in which one or more than one of the possibilities given below is correct, as in Example 4.

Example 4

Which of the following features should be found in concrete when used for the construction of a small estate road?

1   Air entrainment
2   Sulphate resisting cement
3   Low to medium workability
4   High cement content (not less than 400 kg/m^3).

a   1 and 2
b   1 and 3
c   2 and 4
d   3 and 4.

3 Matching block. This consists of two lists of statements, terms or symbols and the candidate has to match an item in one list, as in Examples 5 and 6. (In these examples the method of answering has been laid out in four-option form for ease of marking, but this format is not the only acceptable method of presentation.)

Example 5

	List 1			List 2
A	Permanent wave solution		1	Lawsonia alba
B	Permanent hair dye		2	Magnesium carbonate
C	Red henna		3	Para-phenylene diamine
D	White		4	Ammonium thioglycollate
			5	Azo-dyes

Which one of the following shows the correct order for matching the items in List 1 with those in List 2?

a	List	1	A	B	C	D
	List	2	4	3	1	2

b	List	1	A	B	C	D
	List	2	3	4	2	1

c	List	1	A	B	C	D
	List	2	4	3	5	1

d	List	1	A	B	C	D
	List	2	3	5	2	4

Example 6

	List 1		List 2
A		1	Fuse
		2	Battery
		3	Transformer
B		4	Variable resistor
		5	Capacitor
		6	Inductor with core
		7	Filament lamp
C			
D			
E			

Which one of the following shows the correct order for matching the items in List 1 with those in List 2?

a List	1	A	B	C	D	E
List	2	5	3	1	6	4

b List	1	A	B	C	D	E
List	2	2	1	3	6	5

c List	1	A	B	C	D	E
List	2	5	3	4	6	7

d List	1	A	B	C	D	E
List	2	2	5	7	6	1

In Examples 5 and 6, the possibility of a candidate getting the last answer correct by a process of elimination has been avoided by making List 2 contain more topics than List 1.

4 Assertion/reason. This type of question consists of an **assertion** followed by a **reason** and the candidate has to decide whether assertion and reason are individually correct or not, and, if they are correct, whether the 'reason' is a valid explanation of the 'assertion'. The items are usually laid out as in Example 7.

Example 7

Assertion
Metallic or inorganic dyes are often used in a hairdressing salon.

Reason
Metallic or inorganic dyes are progressive dyes and develop slowly by oxidation.

a   Both assertion and reason are true statements and the reason is a correct explanation of the assertion.

b   Both assertion and reason are true statements, but the reason is NOT a correct explanation of the assertion.

c   The assertion is true, but the reason is a false statement.

d   The assertion is false, but the reason is a true statement.

---

5 True/false. An item consisting of a statement which has to be judged true or false, as Example 8.

Example 8

Delete either the word 'true' of the word 'false' after each of the following sentences to indicate whether or not they are correct.
(i)   The coal and shale constituents of true middlings can be liberated by crushing.   TRUE/FALSE
(ii)   The calorific value of a middlings is higher than that of its shale constituent.   TRUE/FALSE
(iii)   The ash content of a middlings is less than that of its coal constituent.   TRUE/FALSE
(iv)   The constituents of true middlings are more intimately mixed together than are those of false middlings.   TRUE/FALSE

This type of question is open to the criticism that, as it requires the candidate to choose only one of two possible answers, it may reward guessing because a candidate has a '50/50' chance of arriving at the correct answer.

Conclusion

Although other types of item (multiple-response, matching block, assertion-reason) have advantages for at least some types of subject matter it has generally been found that the four-option multiple-choice is the most useful and flexible of item types. Institute policy is therefore to concentrate mainly on the four-option multiple-choice type of item, including item groups.

Computer assisted assessment (CAA)

Computers are now being used to deliver, mark and analyse objective tests. They can also be used for diagnosing and assessing prior knowledge as well as newly acquired knowledge. Results of these tests and other examinations can subsequently be accessed when making formative and summative assessments.

City and Guilds has been at the forefront of objective testing for many years, and the growing use of CAA to deliver a range of objective tests nationally (including the Theory Test for Car Drivers) enables a wide syllabus to be examined quickly and reliably.

Factors that might be considered when contemplating the use of CAA include the:

– advantages and disadvantages of CAA
– maintenance of security and authenticity
– feasibility of on-line testing.

Item groups

An 'item group' is a series of items which all relate to a given situation presented at the beginning, either in the form of a sketch or as a description. The item group is a useful method of testing knowledge of laboratory or practical situations as several aspects relating to one job can be tested, and candidates are then asked to apply their knowledge in a realistic manner.

Example of an item group based on a description (Hairdressing)

The following four items refer to the situation described below.

A client has tinted hair and requires a permanent wave which can be dressed into soft wave movements and loose curls. The hair is thick, abundant and inclined to be porous. In order to obtain the best results, procedure would be as follows:

1   The hair should be prepared for permanent waving by cleansing with

    a   clear soapless shampoo

    b   egg shampoo

    c   beer shampoo

    d   lanolin shampoo.

2   The hair should be cut by

    a   thinning and tapering thoroughly

    b   clubbing all over

    c   layer cutting thoroughly

    d   lightly thinning and tapering.

3   A special reagent should be chosen because tinted hair is likely to

    a   process more quickly

    b   process more slowly

    c   take a loose curl

    d   develop a darker colour.

4   The first test for movement should be made

    a   after winding a few curlers and when half the head is wound

    b   five minutes after winding is completed

    c   when winding is completed

    d   ten minutes after winding is completed.

Further items may follow on similar lines.

Examples of an item group based on a diagram (Welding Engineering)

Questions 1–4 refer to Fig. 12.

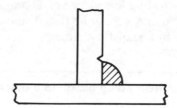

FIG.12

1   The type of joint in Fig. 12 is a
    a   corner
    b   butt
    c   tee
    d   lap.

2   The defect shown on the weld in Fig. 12 is
    a   undercut
    b   porosity
    c   overlap
    d   cold lap.

3   In Fig. 12, the weld has a face which is
    a   convex
    b   concave
    c   mitred
    d   flat.

4   In Fig. 12, the fusion zone of the weld would lose most of its heat by
    a   convection
    b   conduction
    c   radiation
    d   penetration.

Item writing principles

Choose an item of knowledge on the syllabus.

Ensure that the item tests knowledge important for the candidate to know and understand.

Ensure that the item is technically accurate.

Ensure that the aim of the item is clearly presented in the stem.

Ensure that the wording of the item is as brief and clear as possible.

Use diagrams where appropriate.

Ensure that the item has **one** correct answer which appears as one of the options.

The key should usually be of about the same length as the distractors, not consistently longer or shorter.

All distractors must be plausible to the level of candidate being examined.

Avoid giving clues in the stem of the distractors.

Avoid overlapping options. (Options showing numerical values are particularly prone to this.)

Avoid negatively phrased stems. If this is unavoidable emphasise the negative.

Avoid the use of 'none of these' as a distractor.

Avoid the use of the word 'you', i.e. what would you do ...?

Item editing schedule

Relevance
Is the item on the syllabus?
Is it worth asking?
Is it appropriate for the level of candidate?
Is the type of knowledge tested correctly indicated?

Technical content
Is the stem technically correct?
Is the key technically correct?
Are the distractors technically plausible?

Stem
Does the stem present a single question?
Note: The stem may be either a direct question or an incomplete statement; in either case it should usually be possible to supply the correct answer without reading the options.
Is the stem clearly and simply worded?

Key
Is the key the only correct answer to the question presented?

Key and distractions
Does each option follow grammatically from the stem?

Are there any words or phrases in the options which are also used in the stem and which may serve as clues towards eliminating the distractors or selecting the key?

Is each distractor likely to be plausible to students who have insufficient knowledge of the subject-matter?

Establishing Learning Needs

Role of training needs assessor

Role

Teachers will need to understand the purposes and techniques of assessing learner needs, and adopt the supporting role most appropriate to the learner's experience and requirements.

Occupational activities

Teachers co-ordinate and facilitate learning opportunities that are available to learners. But before teachers are ready to accept this role they must be competent to carry out each of the key tasks listed below. It will be readily appreciated that none of the tasks stand alone since effective teaching is a technique that integrates multiple skills, knowledge, experience and attitudes. This calls for 'helicopter vision' when meeting with clients for the first time and seeking to help them identify and clarify their training needs. The teacher must demonstrate ownership of an adequate level of related knowledge and skills backed by a wealth of experience when establishing learner needs.

Tasks

- Check provision and resources, verify accuracy and reliability of learner performance standards and discuss associated teaching programmes with other staff.
- Advise learners of the range of opportunities available and explain relevant context, content, procedures and standards.
- Familiarise learners with the concept of giving credit for relevant knowledge, skills, experience and ability and explain the practice of APL in terms of recognising the value of awards already held and prior experience gained.
- Provide information and resources to enable individuals to identify their current competences.
- Explain techniques of initial self-assessment, assist individuals who wish to access information banks and support learners who may be experiencing difficulties.
- Define and agree current competence of individuals.
- Negotiate developmental action plans and learning programmes in accordance with the needs and abilities of individual learners.
- Provide the best match reasonably and economically possible either by devising new schemes or by adapting available programmes to meet learner needs and where necessary group or sponsor's requirements.

Identification of needs

Object

Matching individual needs and expectations with a personalised training programme is an essential ingredient in any successful learning proposition. The object of **initial assessment** is to help teachers and prospective learners sort out what it is they wish to achieve. Action plans can be produced and relevant individualised training programmes based upon an analysis of training need can be arranged.

Quite apart from socially derived needs relating to leisure-based activities and work-related demands, there will be clients who are directed to the college or other training provider by businesses seeking to invest in training for their people.

Ageing population

Teachers will need to take account of strategic priorities for action to meet the challenges of the 2000s that have been identified by the Government.[1] These include the need for businesses to invest in training and to take account of the fact that 1 million fewer under 25s will be available by 2001 whereas the 25–54 age group will increase by 1.6 million. This could mean that a greater proportion of older people will present themselves for training or upgrading and their needs will probably differ from those of young people.

Motivating and guiding

People will need help and advice in planning and developing skills to meet the needs of the economy as well as to achieve their own full potential. In this case the teacher will need to be able to motivate those without any formal qualifications to take up the challenge of learning so as to help them make their way in life or find a job. There will also be a requirement to give guidance to others with qualifications who are seeking to become more competitive in the labour market by gaining related awards.

Developing potential

Clients will appreciate advice on how to set about making the most of the chance to use their unfulfilled potential and so move their career along. The initial assessment session provides a setting in which to introduce the concept of being responsible for one's own learning outcomes and career development, and to assist clients by offering a flexible programme that maximises learning opportunities.

Difficulties

Clients with particular learning difficulties or problems that cannot readily be resolved with the teacher during the initial assessment, and those needing help with organising themselves, may be referred to qualified people in the special needs unit, educational guidance and counselling unit, student support services or specialist training providers as appropriate.

Identifying the current competence of individuals

Initial meeting

First impressions
First impressions are important. How clients feel about someone when calling at the assessment centre, reception or departmental office, or when telephoning or meeting them for the first time, will influence their attitude towards them on subsequent meetings. This is very true when a person is contemplating spending a considerable sum of money on professional tuition and also making a big investment in terms of their time. Besides seeking good value for money, clients will be entitled to expect a friendly and enthusiastic reception. A better attitude will result when a little time is spent welcoming people and giving them a chance to settle down.

Initial assessment

Structure of assessment
Having acquired experience elsewhere some clients seek the services of a qualified professional teacher when they feel they are almost ready for the assessment. A different approach would be

required here to that used for a complete beginner, but in both cases, sooner or later, clients would need to be completely familiar with assessment structure and content.

Teachers will probably need to describe assessment requirements and give details of how the assessments will be organised. They must be prepared to discuss with clients any aspect of an assessment structure and procedures.

In order to do this the assessor will lead the candidate through a number of stages:

- assessment administration
- practical or performance assessment
- oral assessment used when seeking supplementary evidence.

Initial learning status

Many new learners will have acquired knowledge and skills either by private practice or experientially through day-to-day living or from work experience. For example, transferable skills will have derived, say, from riding a bike or as a road user on foot and these experiences could be formalised and authenticated when assessing a person's claims of previous experience in roadcraft.

Prior learning can be quickly accredited by arranging an assessment so that the learner is able to validate any claims made. This enables a better estimate to be obtained of the time needed to reach assessment standard. Oral assessment will reliably confirm the candidate's status of knowledge of unit or award content.

APL advice – accreditation of prior learning

Information relating to the accreditation of prior learning (APL) is given in Appendix D. However, the City and Guilds definition of APL and guidance for tutors and candidates that now follows gives a clear picture of what is involved:

> 'The accreditation of a candidate's current competence, based upon evidence of past achievement or past demonstrations of competence. APL allows assessment and certification of competence without the need for candidates to undertake a formal period of study. This open access to assessment simply requires candidates to demonstrate their current competence. APL also allows candidates to put forward evidence of past achievements. This will mean that they will need to keep records of achievements. Current trends are moving towards achievements being kept in a personal portfolio with examples of reports, teaching notes, examples of materials, endorsements from employers and such like.'[2]

Analysis of skills

A review of skills already owned and an estimate of learning needs may be carried out together with the teacher or by **self-analysis**. The analysis should preferably be carried out during the first meeting. Some people will be surprised to be asked for their personal views, and for many, this will be the first time in their life that they have been actively involved in making an assessment. They will expect to be told what they need to do and ready to take the medicine. Others may be confused because all they will know is that they want to go for a certain qualification and will feel unable to tell the teacher what they need to do about it. But by building upon what they can already do, feelings of inadequacy will be swept away and a positive **self-image** formed.

It may be possible at this stage to agree realistic expectations and make an estimate of programme duration, although as already suggested, an assessment will be necessary to confirm previous achievement claimed. A valid and objective assessment can only be made against a prepared **checklist of competences**. The result obtained can then be compared with assessment criteria. The difference between what new learners claim they can do and what they need to learn to do is known as the **training gap**. Once the gap has been agreed, the next stage will be to establish a learning programme and create an **individual development plan**. Teachers should operate a system for recording, categorising and prioritising learners' needs.

Equal opportunities

Teachers may need to consider developing provision for clients with special needs, and providing equal opportunities with respect to social and religious background, ethnic or national origin, marital status, intellectual or physical capacity, age and gender. Care must be taken to avoid harassment, sex discrimination and sexist stereotyping. In some cases there has been a lack of adequate provision for learners with disabilities and insufficient thought is given to compensating for serious and minor handicaps and temporary indisposition.

Handicaps

Where a client has a handicap that hampers or hinders learning, or a physical disability or disadvantage resulting from either physical or intellectual impairment, it may be possible to adapt the learning opportunity so as to overcome the difficulty or provide help to assist cognitive or motor learning. Teachers will certainly be expected to take account of learners' needs and where possible to modify their plans and give advice and relevant guidance.

Illiteracy and dyslexia

An **illiterate** person is either unable to read or write *or* incapable of attaining the standard of reading and writing required for a given purpose. Illiteracy does not mean that a person is 'uneducated' in worldly matters or that they are ignorant or uncultured, but they will need the teacher's help. In the case of new learners the teacher may be required to give help directly or arrange language support for those needing it. This is because new learners will need to adequately meet language requirements pertaining to their chosen learning programme.

Dyslexia is also known as 'word blindness'. It is the name given to an impaired ability to read. Dyslexia is neither caused by nor associated with low intelligence or stupidity and does not reflect a person's IQ. In formal academic situations and when sitting written examinations candidates may be allocated a 'reader' who reads the questions aloud to them. In such cases the examining board concerned must be contacted well in advance so that necessary arrangements may be made to accommodate the candidate.

Teachers should be prepared to suggest ways and means by which illiterate and dyslexic clients may familiarise themselves with curriculum content and be able to cope with essential written, verbal and oral communications.

Creating personal action plans

Short and long term aims

During the initial assessment session a **developmental action plan** may be negotiated that is designed to meet the client's present aspirations. The plan gives details of previous experience and achievement and describes how the learner will attain long term aims and shorter term objectives. Being individually negotiated, the plan lists groupings of compatible learning objectives for each phase of the proposed training programme, and a progressive route towards meeting assessment requirements. Obviously, the key long term aim will be to meet all award performance criteria and accomplish any complementary self-set goals, while shorter term objectives may concern achieving particular elements or units of an NVQ. But teachers will probably agree that learning and achievement does not always go according to plan and it will therefore be necessary to continuously review progress and update the developmental action plan.

Performance criteria

An explanation of what is needed to meet assessment performance standards could be given together with an outline of what the client needs to do to meet the requirements. Spelling out specific performance criteria in great detail would probably overload and unnerve the client and this is best left to later sessions.

Individual programme

The plan will detail the negotiated programme of activity. If an action plan is produced the teacher will need to check that the content and sequence of learning agreed will in fact give the best match between the learner's needs and their current learner status.

Teachers need to put a good deal of thought into preparing and planning the learning programme and providing opportunities for the new learner to learn effectively, confidently and enjoyably. The way people prefer to learn and the pace of learning varies from one person to another and there is no set pattern of learning that suits everyone. For these reasons it is essential that the method and content is negotiated and agreed as far as is possible during the initial stages of course or learning programme.

Clients will be drawn from at least three categories of learner: the **complete beginner**, those with **some experience**, and people approaching **assessment standard**. Each group will have different needs and the teacher's approach used will vary accordingly.

Beginners may be new to and completely inexperienced in the award content. They will need to be tactfully introduced to the learning programme and may require a good deal of encouragement and counselling. Initially, progress may be somewhat slow and uncertain and it may take some time before such learners can gain sufficient confidence and ability to accept responsibility for outcomes themselves. The teacher will therefore need to exercise a considerable degree of control over the learners' behaviour and relieve their anxiety if they become stressed.

The **partially trained** learner will already own certain learning skills and have acquired a body of related knowledge. The teacher will need to assess the current level of skill and the relevance of existing know-how and experience. Rudimentary knowledge can be reinforced and basic and fundamental skills can be perfected, practised and built upon before progressing to higher skill levels.

Learning with parents and friends may not be the most effective way to learn although it is the way that many new learners start. Resulting lack of patience and poor teaching skills can really upset such learners and seriously affect their confidence level. They are left feeling mixed-up and frustrated, leaving the unlucky new learner totally lacking in confidence. Here, the teacher would need to correct poor techniques and rebuild shattered confidence.

When the learner is **approaching assessment standard** the role of the teacher becomes that of a facilitator and assessor. If necessary, learners may wish to practise unobserved typical assessment tasks or perform a number of dummy runs made under assessment conditions while the teachers or peers record and judge their performance against criteria.

After each demonstration the teacher gives feedback and reviews outcomes with the learner, who is encouraged to self-assess his or her own performance. Advice may be offered that will help the learner reach levels of competence demanded by the assessment. The run-up to the unit assessment provides an opportunity for learners to become more self-assured and better able to take full responsibility for their actions. It reinforces the need for them to work independently and confidently, and to allow for varying conditions and local circumstances.

For some reason it may be necessary for new learners to take later assessments at a centre located elsewhere. In this case teachers will need to help learners adjust to behaviour patterns that may vary considerably from that of their familiar surroundings. Even though centres are carefully chosen to ensure reasonable compatibility wherever the assessment is held, there will always be an element of uncertainty about specific equipment, unfamiliar staff and the like.

Confidence can be gained and uncertainty overcome by practising 'out of class', 'off college' or under simulated assessment conditions. This is one of the needs that may be identified during initial assessment sessions for learners who feel that they are approaching assessment standard.

Assessment plan

A personalised assessment plan format developed by the author for use when negotiating with candidates for the City and Guilds Vocational Assessor Award is reproduced on the following page. The plan can also be related to Units D32 and D33 which are included in the C&G7306 FAETC structure.

Notes

1   *Labour Market & Skills Trends* (SEN 32), Employment Department Group, Moorfoot 1991. pp. 3–6.
2   C&G7306 FAETC (NVQ) Candidate Packs can be obtained from the City and Guilds of London Institute, 1 Giltspur Street, London EC1A 9DD.

Assessor-candidate Assessment Plan

Assessor-candidate name: Kelvin Arthur Hellings

Unit D33   Assess candidate using differing sources of evidence

Element D331

Objective: To assess the Assessor-candidate's ability to identify opportunities for collecting evidence and to agree and review candidate assessment plans

Target date for assessment: 23 June 200–

Context for assessment
Kelvin will be in his normal work role, that of Group Training Manager, senior instructor, assessor and examiner operating a training and assessment system in a working environment within the Auto Engineering School.

Assessment methods
I will examine the assessment plans that Kelvin presents and compare them with the candidate's assessment specifications. Kelvin will describe how the assessment plans meet all the D331 Performance Criteria. I will seek supplementary evidence of Kelvin's competence by asking him oral questions using my own checklisted written questions and judging his responses.

Evidence
Performance
Kelvin will present **three** different candidate assessment plans each of which should cover at least **two elements** and **three sources of evidence** chosen from: natural performance, examination of products, simulations, projects and assignments, questioning, candidate and peer reports, or the candidate's prior achievement and learning. Each plan could if necessary cover the same elements.

Plan One will include **natural performance**, followed by a **question and answer** session and **examination of products. Plan Two** will include the examination of **projects** and **assignments**, **questioning** and review of **candidate and peer reports. Plan Three** will include **natural performance**, evaluation of **candidate reports** and **judgements of other assessors**. The plans will take the varying needs of candidates into consideration and will be agreed and signed by those involved.

Supplementary
Kelvin will be prepared to answer questions on the underpinning knowledge relevant to D331 performance criteria and range statements (as listed in the assessment specification for D331). He will also answer questions, explain and demonstrate that he is able to prepare assessment plans that include **simulations** and **candidate prior experience**.

Other relevant information and action agreed
Kelvin is self-studying up-to-date literature relating to the assessment of performance and competence in real work environments. He is relating what he learned recently while working towards his C&G7307 FAETC Award, and integrating new knowledge and skills gained while preparing for the Vocational Assessor Award with his day-to-day managerial work and training and assessment duties within the Auto Engineering School.
Kelvin will join the current Vocational Assessor's training programme and will meet me and other candidates as and when required prior to assessment of Unit D33 to review matters of mutual interest and to clarify any queries. I will be available at any time for telephone tutorials/discussion and for face-to-face meetings as required by Kelvin and other candidates. He will assemble current evidence relating to this element in his Evidence File ready for presentation.

Chris Greenaway and Ben McKaigg, the Auto Engineering School APL Advisers, will support Kelvin throughout the process.

Candidate signature _____   **Assessor signature** _____

Assessment plan

Assessment Plan

Candidate name: _____

Unit No. and title _____

Assessment location _____

Evidence to be presented	**Details**
☐ Natural performance in the workplace	
☐ Simulated work activities	
☐ Carrying out pre-planned tasks	
☐ Written projects and assignments	
☐ Review of written records	
☐ Completed assessment question papers	
☐ Records of prior achievement	
☐ Reports from colleagues	
☐ Reports from supervisors in workplaces	
☐ Q&A/products/any other evidence	

People involved in my assessment

☐ Assessor

☐ Supervisor

☐ Clients

☐ Others

Special assessment requirements and what I need to agree with the people concerned

Continued overleaf...

Schedule for assessment and review	Date: Purpose:	Date: Purpose:	Date: Purpose:

Candidate	Date plan agreed	Vocational Assessor

© LW

APPENDIX D

Assessing prior learning and achievement

The accreditation of prior learning and achievement is fast becoming a key function of teachers and trainers who are involved in the education and training of adults. Its importance lies in the need to recognise and give credit for the knowledge, skills and attitudes that together make up the many competences already owned by people who are seeking acknowledgement in the form of NVQs and other qualifications.

Basic techniques used involve tutors or helpers working with candidates to assemble a portfolio of evidence of previous learning and achievement which can then be presented to a qualified APL assessor for evaluation and accreditation either manually or with the help of computer-based 'expert' systems.[1]

The text that follows is intended only to provide an insight into the concept of APLA and perhaps to promote an interest in current developments in this important topic. How the process of assessment is planned and conducted and how it links to the wider learning programme is described clearly in *The Assessment of Performance and Competence.*[2]

The impact of change

There is now a powerful force challenging the status quo and compelling almost all educators and trainers to address anew their way of assessing. As traditional barriers between education and training break down, more and more teachers, trainers and workplace supervisors will find themselves in new-style assessor roles. Experienced practitioners are being asked to learn new tricks and consequently the need to breathe fresh life into teaching styles is fast becoming an essential requirement rather than an optional extra. The need to keep up with developments in learner assessment, and assessment in a **real work environment** must now be nagging away in the back of teachers' minds. If it isn't, it should be.

Full implementation of **National Vocational Qualifications (NVQs)** and **Scottish Vocational Qualifications (SVQs)** will call for considerable change in training philosophy and the assessment of work-related competences in every occupational area as well as in GNVQs and other recent innovations. The arrival of competence-based qualifications impacts on the standards required to achieve vocational qualifications. It also affects the way students and trainees are assessed, the way assessment relates to learning and also, therefore, the learning process itself. The impact of the change described will stretch right back to the moment learners begin their courses or negotiate their assessment plans.

The use and understanding of a wide range of assessment techniques is now an essential ingredient in the teacher's pack of skills. Acquiring these and becoming certificated for doing so is essential not just for full-time teachers in the education and training system but is also vital for the growing army of assessors in industry who may be in supervisory or other positions which bring them into contact with the NVQ process.

Initial assessment

It is important to assess all people seeking access to education and training opportunities, the purpose being to help them to plan their future education and training programme. Initial assessment helps the provider and the learner sort out what it is they wish to achieve. Credit for prior achievement can be given and action plans can be agreed and relevant training arranged to meet identified needs and the ability of individuals to attain their goals. Matching needs and expectations with education and training provision is the key to success in the attainment of competence or achievement in academic subjects.

Access

Access to suitable learning opportunities has not always been easy and, at best, it has been a compromise between what the client was seeking and whatever course or training was ready-made and on the shelf. Today, the demand for a wider range of training provision is clear. This extended range is needed to fulfil the expectations of employers seeking to provide quality products and services backed by a well-educated and competent workforce. A responsive education and training service is called for.

Motivational aspects

Showing approval and giving credit for good work can motivate people to strive even harder to meet self-imposed goals. Formally acknowledging skilled status and recognising a candidate's claim of being competent to carry out certain tasks at work or in a simulated work environment can also serve as effective motivators. This is why it is so important to give recognition for prior achievements when a client is seeking access to a new learning opportunity. Knowing that they will not have to 'jump through the hoops' again before moving on to fresh ground acts as a spur and motivator and gets learners off to a good start. Time is precious and adult learners will not relish the idea of wasting several attendances going over old ground just because it happens to suit the teacher's scheme of work.

Accreditation of prior learning and achievement

Prior learning and achievement

Prior learning is learning that has occurred in the past. Prior learning leads to **prior achievement** and it is the achievement aspect that is particularly relevant when a client is seeking admittance to a particular course or formal learning opportunity, and not the formal or informal learning process that led to the achievement. Evidence of prior achievement is used by assessors to give credits toward NVQ units.

Unintentional learning deriving from every-day life experiences, independent self-study out of college, such as by correspondence courses and watching TV programmes, and experiential learning in the workplace, at home or on DIY projects are prime examples of the means by which prior learning and achievement may occur.

The client is now seen by many providers as the central figure in the educational process. This was not always the case and even today there is still much evidence of teachers adopting the role of authoritative central figures who direct and control every aspect of what is offered to learners. These 'pillars' or 'guardians of institutional standards' often held the key to the door of learning and could easily exclude anxious learners on the grounds that they 'did not meet the formal entry qualifications for the learning opportunity sought'.

Nowadays the introduction and growth of formal **accreditation of prior learning and achievement (APLA)** is changing matters for the better. Candidates are now better able to claim their entitlement to a place on a given course and exemptions, or credits, toward a particular qualification.

Route to progression

Initial assessments and APLA sessions provide opportunities to collect and judge oral and written evidence brought forward from existing experience. Present levels of achievement can be established by asking a series of carefully framed assessor-devised questions or administering preset tests covering the performance criteria of the unit or element being assessed.

Being able to objectively specify just where the candidate stands enables the APLA assessor to outline what is on offer and to negotiate the learner's way forward up a 'ladder of opportunity'.

Claiming credit for competence

Assessment in NVQs

NCVQ says of the use of evidence from prior achievement:

> Evidence of past achievements, if properly authenticated, may be equally or more valid than evidence from a test or examination. . . . Prior achievements are simply those which have occurred in the past. . . . If a candidate has practised the required competencies, in work or outside, and can produce evidence of his or her competence from past performance, this could provide an alternative source of evidence that could be taken into account for the award of a qualification.[3]

Experiential learning

The term **experiential** may be applied to learning deriving from experience. In vocational training the term **prior experiential learning** describes learning and associated achievement demonstrated as a result of learning by 'doing' things in everyday life rather than from contrived learning situations in classrooms, workshops or simulations. Informal learning evidenced by correctly performing tasks in **real work environments** (natural performance) therefore provides a valuable source of evidence of prior achievement.

Experiential learning is defined as:

> The knowledge and skills acquired through life and work experience and study which are not formally attested through any educational or professional certification.

> It can include instruction-based learning provided by any institution, which has not been examined in any of the public examination systems.

> It can include those undervalued elements of formally provided education which are not encompassed by current examinations.[4]

Assessment centre staff

Trained assessors

Trained and qualified assessors must be aware of the regulations, assessment processes and requirements of the awarding bodies and they must be able to meet quality assurance procedures administered by internal and external verifiers consistently.

Assessors will be required to make decisions about the **amount** of evidence needed to support candidates' claims for the accreditation of competence. They will need to be able to judge the **validity** of evidence presented and ensure that the content adequately underpins the competence claimed. They must ensure that **sufficient** evidence is presented so that all performance criteria comprising the element being assessed are covered. Evidence gathered from more than one source must be **consistent** and must support the notion that the competence has been correctly demonstrated on a number of previous occasions in different contexts and can still be demonstrated at the required standard – it must be **current**. They must be satisfied that the evidence presented is **authentic** – it must be genuine and must relate only to the candidate.

APL advisers

An **APL adviser** is someone who is qualified to give guidance, on-going support and direct help to candidates who are seeking recognition of previously acquired learning and achievement. Advisers will suggest how to gather and put forward evidence drawn from past achievements and past demonstrations of competence when seeking accreditation of current competency.

APL advisers will indicate how information stored in **National Records of Achievement** and evidence such as certificates, training records, employers' letters, skills tests, projects, assignments and reports stored in personal portfolios can be used to validate claims of prior achievments. Products may also be presented to assessors but supplementary evidence in the form of oral questioning, multiple-choice tests or short written answers to pre-set tests may be needed to allow valid assessments to be made.

Advisers may offer suggestions regarding how to set about making initial self-assessments and writing lists of evidence to be gathered before an assessment plan is devised. They will arrange access to trainers and tutors who are able to help the candidate top-up their achievement so as to match outstanding elements or performance criteria. Or they will refer the candidate to assessors with whom they can negotiate formal assessment against award criteria.

Vocational assessors

Assessors will be responsible for judging evidence of prior learning presented and for negotiating and agreeing with the candidate a suitable assessment plan covering remaining elements. Candidates will be briefed on the assessment process and how a valid assessment specification will be used when making assessment decisions.

Occupational area assessors must be familiar with all types of evidence that may be provided and must adopt the agreed assessment process. Immediately after the assessment task has been completed the assessor must give the candidate accurate, objective and constructive feedback.

Where all performance criteria are met the assessor will make his or her decision known and complete all relevant assessment records and other documentation needed. Where criteria are not met, the assessor and candidate will discuss and agree the way forward and update the candidate's assessment plan accordingly.

Internal verifiers

The **internal verifier** is a quality assurance agent. The verifier must be able to confirm whether or not standards are being maintained within the assessment centre and among assessors so that a reliable assessment service may be provided. They will need to check the process and determine the correctness of the vocational assessors' use of valid assessment specifications and interpretation of qualification standards or performance criteria, consistency and accuracy of judgements made, usefulness and completeness of feedback shared with candidates, completeness and correctness of records kept.

External verifiers

The **external verifier** is the guardian of **awarding body standards**. His or her role is to ensure that the internal verifiers are carrying out their responsibilities properly. External verifiers will check that the assessment centre systems and documentation, candidate achievement records and internal verifiers' and vocational assessors' performance consistently meets the specification and requirements of the award body concerned. In this way national standards can be assured.

Evidence from prior achievements

Gathering evidence

Candidates will be responsible for gathering and assembling evidence that they intend to present during an APL session. In principle this is fine, but in practice it is time-consuming and is often the cause of people withdrawing from the process or simply failing to turn up on the day. The burden of responsibility for organising themselves and their material proves too much for some candidates and they walk away from the task. Others after initial discussion will declare their intention to start from scratch and will subsequently confirm that they find it easier to provide new evidence than face the ordeal of trying to meet all elemental requirements with what they originally had in mind to offer.

The prospect of going over what they have already achieved once again as a 'revision' or 'confirmation' appeals to some candidates and they seem happy to do so provided that they are not made to 'jump through hoops' just to please assessors. But there will always be occasions when there will be a need for candidates to convince assessors that evidence presented is: accurate and soundly based, covers all specified performance criteria, is representative of competence demonstrated over an acceptable period, is genuine and confirms that knowledge and skills claimed are still current.

For those wishing to go ahead with APLA sessions, methods of assessment will include:
– asking the candidate questions relating to essential underpinning knowledge (This will entail assessor competence in asking open-ended, closed and confirmation type questions.)
– reviewing portfolios
– examining reports, documents and products, design work, computer programs, projects and assignments, peer group reports, testimonials and letters of validation from employers. (This will entail assessor competence in establishing and matching evidence with relevant performance criteria, and checking authenticity, validity, currency and sufficiency of evidence presented.)

Supplementary evidence

Supplementary evidence may be called for where assessors are not satisfied that evidence of prior achievement alone is entirely satisfactory, or when they are unable to assess, by observation of performance, a candidate's competence over the full **range** outlined in the assessment specification for the element concerned. Assessors must be convinced that the candidate can or will be able to perform competently in the full range of contexts in which they reasonably can be expected to work. Various methods of assessing the knowledge and understanding that underpins competent performance can be employed. Typical sources of evidence that could provide the confirmation sought include:
– oral questioning
– guided discussion
– open-ended written answers given in short or long essay form

- multiple-choice tests
- skills tests
- demonstrations
- interview notes
- computer interrogation and print-outs
- live or video taped demonstrations
- simulations
- role plays
- projects and assignments
- products.

Credit transfer

Credits for prior achievement can be awarded against one or more element of a qualification offered by a school, college or training provider. For example, a candidate holding a C&G9292 Staff Assessor Award would be entitled to credit for six of the seven elements comprising the updated C&G7281/91 Vocational Assessor Award, provided that satisfactory evidence of prior achievement was presented to the APL assessor. Recent C&G7306/7 FAETC Awards would probably be acceptable as credits for Parts I and II of the Certificate in Education (H/FE) leaving only Part III to be obtained. Credits for prior achievement are usually offered before a learning programme is negotiated.

Credit accumulation and transfer schemes operate for NVQs and a wide range of other qualifications offered in further and higher education.

Client portfolios

As suggested above, gathering and collating evidence is not an easy task for some candidates. They really struggle to sort out valid and acceptable supporting evidence from archives, ring binders and material from sources that may well be widely dispersed. The task can be so off-putting that it deters candidates from going any further. They tend to give up unless there is someone on hand that they can turn to who is experienced in advising them what is required. Help will be needed when cross-referencing evidence selected from award performance criteria, indexing portfolio content, writing up self-analyses and specifying what further evidence needs to be gathered before going to the APLA session.

Recording achievement

Statement of achievement

A **statement of achievement** is recorded during, or immediately after, the assessment of evidence gathered and presented by candidates who are seeking accreditation of prior learning achievements. Its content confirms competence deriving from earlier experiential learning or contrived learning situations. Evidence of current competence is inferred from an assessment of the candidates' claim of prior experience when judged against relevant assessment specifications.

It is the actual **achievement** that is recognised and not simply participation in learning experiences that led to attainment of the competence achieved. A learner can take part in a learning opportunity but may not meet all specified performance criteria that include competent performance and hence achievement of a particular NVQ element.

Statement of competence

A **statement competence** lists the performance criteria, range statements and sources from which evidence has been collected and evaluated during the assessment of a candidate against, for example, an NVQ unit or element. Achievement is judged against the criteria and records of assessment are completed and processed. Successful candidates will have their training log, diary, or Record of Achievement endorsed or a statement of achievement will be printed out.

Accreditation

Accreditation of an awarding body's NVQ qualification means that NCVQ has accepted and validated its submission. Candidates for an NVQ award may than be assessed and certificated. The candidate's performance will have been 'certificated', 'credited with NVQ units' or 'accredited', and they will then receive their individual NVQ award.

Notes and references
1   See 'The Assessment of Prior Learning and Achievement – The Role of Expert Systems', RP448, FEU, London 1990.
2   L. Walklin, *The Assessment of Performance and Competence*, Stanley Thornes (Publishers) Ltd, Cheltenham 1991.
3   'Assessment in National Vocational Qualifications – the use of evidence from prior achievement', NCVQ. See Foreword by Geoffrey Melling (Director, Further Education Staff College) in Richard Gorringe, 'Accreditation of Prior Learning Achievements: Developments in Britain and Lessons from the USA', Coombe Lodge Report, Volume 21, Number 5, Further Education Staff College 1989, p 320.
4   N. Evans, 'Curriculum Opportunity', FEU, London 1983, para 1.

APPENDIX E

Cross reference of chapter content with the author's interpretation of units, elements and performance criteria relating to the City and Guilds 7306 NVQ Level 3 Further and Adult Education Teacher's Certificate.

Please note: Relevant underpinning and supporting knowledge can be found within the chapters under reference numbers specified in the table. Additional information about topics marked with an asterisk may be found in L. Walklin, *The Assessment of Performance and Competence (APC)* and comprehensive coverage of all C&G7306 FAETC and NVQ3 Training and Development units is provided in L. Walklin, *Training and Development NVQs: A Handbook for FAETC Candidates and NVQ Trainers*.[1]

Units		Chapter references
A22	Identify individual learning needs	1.002, 1.003, 2.001, 2.004, 4.001–4.004, 5.004, 5.005, 7.003, 7.005, 7.009–7.011, 8.005–8007, Appendix C, Appendix D *See also APC chapter 2 'Initial assessment and induction' and chapter 7 'Assessing knowledge skills and evidence'.
B22	Design training and development sessions	2.001, 2.002, 2.006, 3.001–3.003, 3.006, 4.001–4005, 5.001–5.006, 7.008 *See also APC chapter 2 'Initial assessment and induction' and chapter 3 'Planning and preparing training'.
B33	Prepare and develop resources to support learning	2.002, 3.001–3.006, Appendix A, Appendix B
C21	Create a climate conducive to learning	1.001, 6.001–6005, 7.006, 8.006, Appendix C *See also APC chapter 2 'Initial assessment and induction'.
C22	Agree learning programmes with learners	1.002–1.005, 2.001, 2.002, 2.005, 2.006, 3.002, 3.006, 4.001–4.005, 5.005, 5.006, 7.005, 7.007–7.010, 8.005–8.007, Appendix C, Appendix D *See also APC chapter 1 'Developing standards' and chapter 3 'Planning and preparing training'.
C23	Facilitate learning in groups through presentations and activities	2.001–2.006 *See also APC chapter 4 'Planning and delivering training'.
C24	Facilitate learning through demonstration and instruction	1.001–1005, 2.001–2.006, 3.001–3.006, 4.004, 6.001–6.006 *See also APC chapter 4 'Planning and delivering training'.
C25	Facilitate individual learning through coaching	2.002, 2.003 *See also APC chapter 4 'Planning and delivering training'.
C27	Facilitate group learning	1.004, 1.005, 2.001–2.006, 7.005, 7.008 *See also APC chapter 3 'Planning and preparing training'.

D11	Monitor and review progress with learners	5.001–5.006, 7.005, 7.008, 7.009 *See also APC chapter 7 'Assessing knowledge skills and evidence', chapter 8 'Assessing competence' and chapter 9 'Feedback, records and certification'.
D21	Conduct non-competence based assessments	5.001–5.006 *See also APC chapter 7 'Assessing knowledge skills and evidence'.
D32	Assess candidate performance	2.001, 2.006, 4.002, 4.003, 4.005, 5.004–5.006, 7.008, 8.007–8.009 *See also APC chapter 7 'Assessing knowledge skills and evidence', chapter 8 'Assessing competence' and chapter 9 'Feedback, records and certification'.
D33	Assess candidate using differing evidence	5.004–5.006, 7.008, 8.007–8009 *See also APC chapter 7 'Assessing knowledge, skills and evidence', chapter 8 'Assessing competence' and chapter 9 'Feedback, records and certification'.
D36	Advise and support candidates to identify prior achievement	8.003, 8.004, 8.007, Appendix C, Appendix D *See also APC chapter 2 'Initial assessment and induction' and chapter 7 'Assessing knowledge, skills and evidence'.
E23	Evaluate training and development sessions	2.002, 2.006, 4.002, 7.005, 7.011 ** See also *Putting Quality Into Practice* chapter 6 'Service design' and chapter 9 'Monitoring and evaluating the service provision'.
E31	Evaluate and develop own practice	7.005, 7.011, 7.012
E32	Manage relationships with colleagues and customers	6.001–6.006 *See also APC chapter 5 'Communication in training and assessment'. **See also *Putting Quality into Practice* chapter 4 'TQM – putting the customer first'.
MCI **SM2**	Contribute to the planning, monitoring and control of resources	3.003, 3.005, 4.002, 4.004, 4.005, 7.005, 7.007 **See also *Putting Quality into Practice* chapter 6 'Service design' and chapter 11 'The curriculum audit'.
MCI **SM3**	Contribute to the provision of personnel	7.011 **See also *Putting Quality into Practice* chapter 7 'Service delivery' and chapter 10 'Audits and probes'

1 L. Walklin, *Training and Development NVQs: A Handbook for FAETC Candidates and NVQ Trainers*, Stanley Thornes (Publishers) Ltd, Cheltenham 1996

*L. Walklin, *The Assessment of Performance and Competence*, Stanley Thornes (Publishers) Ltd, Cheltenham 1991

**L. Walklin, *Putting Quality Into Practice*, Stanley Thornes (Publishers) Ltd, Cheltenham 1992

Professional relationships with colleagues and customers

Professionalism and commitment

As professional teachers we should be committed to creating an enduring training provision and aim to be leaders in our subject area. Our teaching and training expertise are key to establishing a reputation as a caring and effective facilitator of learning. Learner achievement and satisfaction of learners' needs are measures of our success. It is this that provides a reward for our stakeholders and colleagues and secures a long-term future.

Having elected to become a teacher we must be seen by students to be always behaving properly and doing the right thing. It is our duty to treat learners decently, and to be accountable for our actions. We should never blame others for our own shortcomings. Our overriding aim should be to establish a rapport and bond with our learners, to put them at ease and to take responsibility for creating a safe environment where openness and co-operation is encouraged and where no stereotyping or bias is permitted.

Teachers should learn how to effectively manage classroom interactions. This would help them to address problems of difficult behaviour in the classroom and create conditions for good behaviour patterns to replace unhelpful ones. If instances of bullying crop up we must identify the causes and handle the case in such a way as to prevent its repetition, and in doing so discourage others from taking part in similar cruel practices.

When working with learners we as teachers and role models are obliged to demonstrate a high level of moral development, commitment and judgement when discharging our professional duties and in our dealings with them. We must not be found to be wanting when it comes to offering support, study guidance or advice on what might be done to overcome their difficulties. Self-imposed levels of student support could mean being available before or after a learning session to answer queries or help out with course administration. This would be particularly true if students have only limited access to classes as in the case of distance learning or tutor-supported resource-based learning. In such instances telephone or e-mail contact might be expected.

Taking pride in imaginatively anticipating and responding to national, regional and local training initiatives, matching these to our customers' needs and providing them with a wide choice of high-quality training and education opportunities in an attractive and welcoming learning environment should be our goal.

Creating an atmosphere in which our colleagues and students value one another and can develop their talents and contribute as part of an energetic and enthusiastic team should feature in our planning when devising learning opportunities. Getting involved in staff development training will be rewarded by enhanced performance when applying knowledge and skills.

Sharing a common interest with our referral agencies and other related organisations in meeting our customers' needs, and being fair in all our dealings and agreements with one another, will result in long-term relationships of mutual respect. As professionals in a very transparent occupation we should make a positive and responsible contribution to the lives of the community in which we live and work.

On the work-related training side we should provide each learner with an accurate and realistic insight into employment opportunities, requirements and prospects. Furthermore, we should structure learning opportunities so as to provide the educational and professional experiences necessary to enhance our students' employment prospects. A related role might be that of giving practical information about applying for jobs and hints on how to project a positive image of oneself when attending interviews.

We should strive to be recognised as unbiased supporters of equal opportunities and aim to help to bring educational opportunity to all. Our collective aim should be to develop the learners' creative, intellectual and craft skills to a high level, and to aid personal development and the ability to adapt to changing circumstances.

We should be proud to be employed in the teaching profession in which we are involved and work continuously to improve our standards of efficiency and effectiveness so as to manage our resources well and assure quality of provision.

Working with others

A favourable attitude to building relationships can be promoted by working professionally and co-operatively with other teachers, learners and support staff. When people work as a team, motivation increases and individual talents are utilised for the benefit of the group. Any tendency to unhelpful behaviour or lack of support is replaced by positive and helpful effort, leading to a responsible attitude and will to succeed. Results of teamwork can often be much better than the sum of individual efforts. Personal satisfaction is gained from helping one another to accomplish tasks confronting the whole group, and effective teachers have a high level of 'people skills' that contributes to lasting relationships with colleagues.

The ways in which teachers work with colleagues, customers, referral agencies and other institutions will determine the success of the teaching team and the effective ness and value of learning outcomes. Good communications and harmonious relationships can go a long way in promoting a tradition of service to others and bridge-building with other agencies.

The bulk of our customers will be learners, although in our teaching role we may serve several other stakeholders. Today the term **internal** customer refers to any person who is receiving a service from people like you who are providing the required service. But at the same time we could be customers of another supplier, such as the reprographics supervisor. It can be seen that all teachers and support workers are interdependent, and therefore to be successful we need to communicate well.

A starting point might well be to study the employer's mission statement, organisation chart and learners' charter, in order to get an overview of the key purposes of the organisation, its strategy and facilities for delivering the service offered. This would lead us on to gaining a clear picture of where we fit in and how we might be involved in establishing and managing relationships with our contacts, colleagues and customers. Our aim would be to share common goals and effectively carry out our roles and responsibilities.

Professional values

Colleagues and students alike can expect to receive our support when they need it, and we in turn can expect their support too. Ethical aspects of professional teaching practice are accounted for by establishing good working relationships, and are reflected by high standards of teacher conduct and by placing a great deal of importance in satisfying the interests of our learners. This entails demonstrating professional values and giving colleagues and learners a high level of support when and where they need it. This in turn requires that we have regard for the psychological and social effects that our behaviour may have on those with whom we interact on a daily basis.

When we notice signs of distress, overload or pressure on the people around us we need to offer our support and not stand back or look the other way. We need to offer advice and help where we can; to aim to work together in co-operative and collaborative ways; and to act in ways that safeguard the interest of our customers – our colleagues and students. But we can only do this by working hard at establishing and maintaining constructive relationships with the people we work with.

BIBLIOGRAPHY

P. Armitage and J. Fasemore, *Laboratory Safety – A Science Teachers' Source Book*, Heinemann Educational Books Ltd, London 1977.

R. Bandler and J. Grinder, *Frogs into Princes – Neuro Linguistic Programming*, Real People Press, Moab, Utah 1977.

R. Bandler and J. Grinder, *ReFraming – Neuro Linguistic Programming and the Transformation of Meaning*, Real People Press, Moab, Utah 1982.

D. Barnes, 'Language and Learning in the Classroom', in *Journal of Curriculum Studies*, 1971.

D. Barnes, *Practical Curriculum Study*, Routledge and Kegan Paul, London 1982.

B. Bernstein, 'Social Class, Language and Socialisation' in A.S. Abramson (ed.), *Current Trends in Linguistics*, Mouton Press, The Hague 1971.

E. Blishen (ed.), *Blond's Encyclopaedia of Education*, Blond Educational, London 1969.

P. Block, *Flawless Consulting*, Learning Concepts, Austin, Texas 1981.

B.S. Bloom (ed.), *Taxonomy of Educational Objectives: Handbook 1 Cognitive Domain*, David McKay, New York 1956.

B.P. Clarke, *Safety and Laboratory Practice Level 1*, Van Nostrand Reinhold Co Ltd, New York 1981.

L. Cohen and L. Manion, *A Guide to Teaching Practice* (Second Edition), Methuen, London 1983.

K.T. Collins, L.W. Downes, S.R. Griffiths and K.E. Shaw, *Key Words in Education*, Longman Group Ltd, London 1973.

J.M. Dunkin (ed.), *The International Encyclopaedia of Teaching and Teacher Education*, Pergamon Press, Headington 1987.

N. Flanders, *Analysing Teaching Behaviour*, Addison Wesley Publishing Company Inc, USA 1970.

D.S Frith and H.G. Macintosh, *A Teacher's Guide to Assessment*, Stanley Thornes (Publishers) Ltd, Cheltenham 1984.

R.M. Gagné, *The Conditions of Learning*, Holt, Rinehart and Winston, New York 1965.

D. Garforth and H. Macintosh, *Profiling – a user's manual*, Stanley Thornes (Publishers) Ltd, Cheltenham 1986.

A. Greer and G.W. Taylor, *Mathematics for Technicians – New Level 1*, Stanley Thornes (Publishers) Ltd, Cheltenham 1980.

S. Hawkins, I. Davies, K. Majer and J. Hartley, *Getting Started*, Basil Blackwell, Oxford 1975.

G. Highet, *The Art of Teaching*, Methuen and Co Ltd, London 1951.

B. Hodge (ed.) *Communication and the Teacher*, Longman Cheshire Pty Ltd. Melbourne 1981.

K. Ireland, *Teachers' Guide to the Health and Safety Act*, Schoolmaster Publishing Company Ltd, Kettering 1979.

D. Jarrett, *The Electronic Office – a management guide to the office of the future*, (Second edition), Gower Publishing Company Ltd, Aldershot and Vermont 1982.

R.L. Katz, *Management of the Total Enterprise*, Prentice-Hall, Englewood Cliffs, New Jersey 1970.

D.R. Krathwohl et al, *Taxonomy of Educational Objectives: Handbook 2 Affective Domain*, Longman, London 1964.

D Lawton, P. Gordon, M. Ing, B. Gibby, R. Pring and T. Moore, *Theory and Practice of Curriculum Studies*, Routledge and Kegan Paul, London 1978.

D. Legge, *The Education of Adults in Britain*, The Open University Press, Milton Keynes 1982.

R.F. Mager, *Preparing Educational Objectives*, Fearon Publishers, Belmont, California 1962.

Manchester Polytechnic Staff Development and Educational Methods Unit, *Safety at Work – Some Implications for Colleges* (Conference Paper No 8.), Manchester Polytechnic, Manchester 1977.

J. McCafferty, 'Innovation and Education', in *Education and Training, Vol 22, No 9*.

A. Morrison and D. McIntyre, *Teachers and Teaching*, Penguin Books Ltd, Harmondsworth 1969.

J. Murdoch and J.A. Barnes, *Statistical Tables*, Macmillan, London 1968.

H.A. Murray, *Explorations of Personality*, John Wiley and Sons, New York 1938.

NATFE, *Safety in Colleges*, National Association of Teachers in Further and Higher Education, London 1980.

J. O'Shea, *Learning and Teaching with Computers – Artificial Intelligence in Education*, The Harvester Press, Brighton 1983.

G. Terry Page, J.B. Thomas and A.R. Marshall, *International Dictionary of Education*, Kogan Page, London 1977.

E. Perrott, *Effective Teaching – a practical guide to improving your teaching*, Longman, London 1982.

E. Richardson, *Group Study for Teachers*, Routledge and Kegan Paul, London 1967.

A. Robinson, *Principles and Practice of Teaching*, George Allen and Unwin, London 1980.

J. Rogers, *Adults Learning*, (Second Edition), The Open University Press, Milton Keynes 1977.

G.J. Russell, *Teaching in Further Education*, (Second Edition), Costello, 1984.

J. Shelley, *Computers in the Office*, Pitman Books Limited, London 1983.

G.L. Simons, *Automating Your Office*, NCC Publications Limited, Manchester 1984.

L. Stenhouse, *An Introduction to Curriculum Research and Development*, Heinemann Educational Books Ltd, London 1975.

R.W. Tyler, *Basic Principles of Curriculum and Instruction*, The University of Chicago Press, Chicago and London 1949.

L.W. Walklin, *Instructional Techniques and Practice*, Stanley Thornes (Publishers) Ltd, Cheltenham 1982.

L. W. Walklin, *The Assessment of Performance and Competence,* Stanley Thornes (Publishers) Ltd, Cheltenham 1991.

L.W. Walklin, *Putting Quality into Practice*, Stanley Thornes (Publishers) Ltd, Cheltenham 1992.

C. Ward, *Designing a Scheme of Assessment*, Stanley Thornes (Publishers) Ltd, Cheltenham 1980.

D.K. Wheeler, *Curriculum Process*, University of London Press Ltd, London 1967.

R. Whitlow, *Notes for Guidance*, Bristol Polytechnic, Bristol 1982.

INDEX

accreditation of prior learning and achievement, 323–4, 329
action-centred leadership, 4
action planning, 248
activities, 46
adolescence, 217
adult education, 198
adult education learning opportunities providers, 198–9
adult guidance services, 205
adult learner characteristics, 6, 20–1, 39–40
adult numeracy and literacy centres, 208
affective domain, 58, 100, 103
objectives, 64, 66
agents of change, 246
aids, 78–98
advantages of, 83
audio, 80
audio-visual, 80, 83
CCTV, 81
CEEFAX, 85
chalkboards, 80
computers, 88
design of, 97
diagrams, 79
disadvantages of, 83
evaluating use of, 84, 97
films, 80
filmstrip projectors, 80
flipcharts, 80
interactive video, 81
loop projectors, 80
magnetic board, 80, 96
microfiche, 85
overhead projector, 80
paste-ups, 81
photographs, 79
pictorial, 79
slide projectors, 95
slide/tape programmes, 95
transparency making, 301–6
videos, 80, 81
white boards, 80
aim, 5, 100, 115
examples of, 116
fromulating, 99, 115
writing of, 99–101
algorithms, see teaching methods
analysis, 38
APL advisers, 318, 325
appraisals, 218, 221, 247, 248, 255, 257–8
aptitude testing, see testing

Argyle, M., 39
assessing
achievement, 277–8
candidate performance, 277–8
assessing prior learning and achievement (APLA), 322–9
assessing the lesson, 247–58
assessors, 325, 326
access to, 293
ALI, 201
checklist D322, 295
concerns, 290
model, 271, 288–9
plan, 160, 277, 292, 294, 321, 322
pressures, 288
procedures, 239
questions, 296
records, 291, 296
self, 239, 278, 290
Smithers, Professor Alan, 290
standards, 293
strategy, 276–7
task checklists, 294–5
task instructions, 294
assessment see also tests and testing, 134–63
classifying methods of, 151
of competence, 135, 151
formal, 145
formative, 145, 148, 239
group assessment profiles, 155, 158
informal, 145
initial, 148
methods compared, 147, 150
NCVQ, 151
objective testing, 142
objective test writing, 307–16
performance goals, 134
planning, 160
procedures, 239
profiling, 145–6, 151
specification, 134, 160, 162
standard tasks, 135
summative, 145, 148, 239, 250
attention, 189
gaining and retaining, 169
motivational aspects, 223

Barnes, D., 100, 115
behaviour reinforcement, 7, 234
behavioural objectives, 99–108
Bernstein, B., 166, 214
Bloom, B.S. see also Taxonomy, 19, 23, 57, 105, 160
boredom, 57, 191, 234

careers service, 205
cause and effect analysis, 38
chaining, 6, 9, 11
classroom
health and safety in the, 225–30
management, 49, 230, 233, 235, 265
teacher's responsibilities, 226
Client's charter, 278–9
cognition, 104
cognitive
domain, 58, 100, 104
domain objectives, 64
processes, 17
colleges see educational establishments
communication, 164–97
barriers, 175, 186
establishing credibility, 184
gaining attention, 169, 189
language codes, 165
lines of, 185
mannerisms, 170
modes of, 179
non-verbal signals, 169
one-way, 169
oral, 165
pace of, 181
and problem solving, 196
problems in, 165
pronunciation, 174
question and answer methods, 181
and socio-economic status, 164
and special needs, 165
spoken, 180
student responses, 184, 188
student sensitivity to, 168
subject-specific language, 181
strategies, 168
two-way, 169–187
vocabularies, 174
written, 165, 180
competence, 21, 106–8, 258
objectives, 125, 136
comprehension, 104
computer
assisted assessment, 312
assisted learning, 88–95
central processing unit, 90
health hazards, 92
input devices, 89
output devices, 89
programs, 93
teaching with, 88
concept learning, see learning

conditioning (instrumental), 67
confidence building, 18
continuing education, 212–14
core curriculum, 113
counselling, 44, 167, 230–2
credit
    for prior achievement, 328
    transfer, 328
criterion
    referencing, 138
    testing, 134, 149–50
course(s)
    content, 110, 113
    defined, 112
    delivery of, 238
    design, 238
    evaluation, 239
    integration components of, 126
    modular, 113
    monitoring, 239
    planning, 64, 238
curriculum, 99–133
    assessment, 111
    core, 113
    course design, 238
    delivery of, 238
    development, 99, 109
    evaluation, 111, 239
    equal opportunities in, 123
    modular design, 70
    monitoring of, 111, 239
    negotiated, 31
    objectives, 109, 125
    planning, 64, 238
    planning-led approach, 219, 238
    resource planning, 112
    special needs, 124
    strategies, 111
    structuring of, 111
    student involvement, 240
    team planning, 126
    work experience in, 124
    content, 110, 113
customers, 333–5

D32
    assessment records, 291, 293,
        295
    initial self-assessment, 278, 290
    personal action plans, 283, 292,
        321
    working towards, 290
Dalton Plan, 31
data processing (see aids), 88
demand-led training, 109
DfEE, 23, 178, 200, 201, 203–4
diagnostic testing, 144
discipline, 233–7

discrimination (bias), 123, 192
drive reduction, 3

education
    adult, 198, 208
    further, 199
    prison and youth custody, 206
educational establishments,
        199–212
employment testing, 143
enrolment, 212
equal opportunities, 123, 221, 318
ergonomics, 92
evaluation, 19, 104, 122
    of experienced teacher, 265
    of teaching methods, 52, 220,
        239, 240
    of test scores, 138–41
evidence
    criteria for, 271
    gathering, 270–72, 292, 296
    historical, 271
    of prior achievement, 327–8
    presented, 292
    requirements, 270
    types of
        performance, 272–3, 293
        prior achievements, 275, 327–8
        supplementary, 274
examinations, 136
experiential learning, 32, 38, 324
    assessment of, 163

facilitative teaching, 3, 19, 44, 67
FAETC NVQ3
    award structure, 269
    features of, 268
    key roles and competences, 270
feedback, 46, 157, 220, 249
FE
    charter, 200
    instiutions, 199
FEFC, 200, 266
Finney, P.J.M., 33–7
flexible learning, 62

Gagné, R.M., 6, 12–13
gatekeeping roles, 20, 221
Gestalt, 7, 8, 188
governance, 199
group
    appraisals, 218, 221
    assessment profiles, 155
    composition, 39, 221
    dynamics, 265
    pressure, 234
guidance, 20, 44, 230–1, 242–3
guides to training, 47

Health and Safety at Work etc. Act,
        225–30
human engineering, see ergonomics

identifying learning needs, 277, 285
illusions, 192
implementors, 246
Individual Learning Accounts, 204
industrial training centres, 207
information technology, 88–95
insight, 7, 8, 188
instrumental
    conditioning, 6, 7
    team learning, 33
intellectual development, 41
intelligence
    growth of, 42
    quotient, 41
internal customers, 335
internalisation, 103
invention, 105
IQ tests, 41
ITN
    action planning, 278, 283–4, 290,
        294
    establishing current
        achievement, 278
    information sheet, 285–6
    initial self assessment, 278, 280
    interview checklist, 281–2
    interviewing and planning, 278,
        283–4
    listing experience, 278, 280
    process, 277–88
    question checklists, 281

job
    competence, 107
    description, 107
    factors, 53
    instruction training, 52

kinaesthetic
    feedback, 15
    sensitivity, 15, 55
Kohler, W., 7–8
Kolb, D., 38
Krathwohl, D.R., 100, 103

language
    codes, 166
    grammar, 174
    learning and, 171
    perception and, 194
    pronunciation, 174
    register of, 171
    skills, 173
    subject specific, 181

teachers' uses of, 171
vocabularies, 174
law of effect, 7
leadership
    action-centred, 4
    capabilities, 4
    characteristics, 40
learner
    -centred approaches, 13, 31
    needs, 218, 316–20
    participation, 31
learning
    barriers to, 17, 175, 186
    chaining, 6
    communication in, 173
    computer assisted, 88
    concept, 6, 11
    conditioning, 6, 7
    contract, 31
    curve, 28
    difficulties, 43
    experience(s), 220, 238
    experiential, 32
    flexible, 62
    how people learn, 18
    Gestalt, 7, 8
    insight, 7, 8
    instrumental team, 33
    and language, 71
    MUD, 19
    methods of, 19
    multiple discrimination, 6
    objective see behavioural
        objectives, 99–108
    open, 62, 124
    participative, 33
    plateaux, 28, 179
    principle, 6, 11
    problem solving, 6, 8
    process, 5, 41
    reflection-type, 238
    resource-based, 125
    signal, 6, 179
    skills, 14
    stimulus-response, 6
    strategies, 127
    student problems in, 157
    styles, 42
    trial-and-error, 6, 7, 13
    validation, 136–7
    verbal association, 6
Learning and Skills Council, 200
learning resource centres (LRCs),
    84–5
lecture, see teaching
lesson(s), 114–121
    assessment of, 76
    conclusion of, 117–18

plan, 64, 71–5, 113, 219, 253
planning system, 64, 71, 219
preparation, 72

Mager, R.F., 100, 103
management, see also planning
    of change, 67
    classroom, 49, 233
    of learning, 69
marking scheme, 162
matching block items, 308
McCafferty, J., 59
methods see also teaching, learning
    didactic, 43–4
    heuristic, 31
micro-training, 224, 248
Miliband, R., 215
mission statements, 210
Modern Apprenticeships, 22, 165
modular course(s), 113
monitoring, 220, 239–40
Moseley, D., 172, 197
motivation, 1–2, 169, 223, 233, 323
    drive reduction, concept of, 3
motivators
    extrinsic, 212
    intrinsic, 212
motor skills, 19
MUD (memorising, understanding,
        doing), 19
multicultural education, 42, 166
multiple-choice items, 275
multiple discrimination, 10
multiple response items, 275
Murray, H.A., 3, 4, 212

NACRO, 207
naming, 9
National Traineeships, 204
needs
    adult, 16
    analysis, 237
    identification of, 237, 316–20
    learner's, 218
    psychogenic, 3, 212
neuro-linguistic programming, 171
New Deal, 22, 204
non-verbal signals, 170
norm referencing, 138
normal curve of distribution, 138–9
National Vocational Qualifications
        (NVQ), 151, 322, 324, 329

objective(s), 101–121
    and performance, 134
    behavioural, 63
    components of, 101
    competence of, 125, 136

criteria for success, 135
formulating and justifying, 114
recognising skills involved, 102
testing, 142
use of, 63
writing, 102
Open College, The, 11, 63
operant conditioning, 6, 7

pace, 181
participative learning, 32
pastoral role of teacher, 231–2
Pavlov, I., 6
pedagogy, 175
perception
    behavioural aspects of, 194
    definition of, 188
    false, 192
    self-, 39
perceptual
    discrimination, 192
    experience, 191
    illusions, 192
    judgements, 192
    organisation, 8
performance:
    judging design, 35–6
    objectives, 113, 136
    testing, 135
personal guidance, 242
personality traits, 222
Piaget, J., 31
planning, 45, 69–77, 115–119, 126,
        159–163, 195, 219, 238
portfolio
    building, 270
    client, 328
    D32 assessment record, 291
    evidence list, 291–2
    record of achievement, 290, 296
    summary evidence sheets, 291,
        293
    summative reports, 290
    candidate assessment plans,
        294
principle learning, 6, 11
prior experiential learning, 324–5
Prison Service, 206
problem solving, 6, 8, 13, 179
process skills, 23, 197
product skills, 23, 197
professional
    development, 247, 333–5
    values, 335
profiling, 145, 151, 155
programmed instruction, 55
programme review, 239
project work, 57–8

psychogenic needs, 3
psychomotor domain, 57, 100, 105
   objectives, 64
punctuation, 181
punishment, 235

QCA, 203, 207
question-and-answer techniques,
   173, 182
questions
   check, 182
   objective type, 307–16
   observation type, 173
   open-ended, 173
   reasoning type, 173
questioning skills (self-diagnosis),
   183
rapport, 222, 224
recall, 19, 104
recency effects, 192
records
   individual achievement, 290–1,
      296
   group, 297
referral agencies, 205–6
reliability, 136–7
resource-based learning, 125
resource planning, 92
resources see also aids
   compiling file of, 92–3
role (of teacher), 198, 231, 244–58,
   316
role play, 62

safety see Health and Safety Act
scheme of work, 113, 121, 130
self-appraisal, 248, 250–2, 257–8
sensorimotor skills, 14, 105
sensory
   deprivation, 191
   overload, 191
   perception, 19, 190
set, 190
signal learning, 6, 179
simulation exercises, 62
skill(s), 21–31, 53
   cross curricular, 26
   analysis, 53, 55
   clusters, 26
   development, 30
   generic, 26
   occupational area, 26
   ownership, 26
   process, 23, 197
   product, 23, 197
   transfer, 23
   transferable, 24
   vocational area, 26

special needs, 43, 124, 318, 319
standard deviation, 140–2
standard tasks, 135
statement
   of achievement, 328–9
   of competence, 329
stimuli, 10
stimulus-response learning, 6, 7
strategic planning, 264
student
   enrolment, 212–3
   monitors, 239
   participation, 173, 240
student-centred learning, 31
supervision, 46
supply-led training, 109
SWOT analysis, 264
syllabus, 112
synthesis, 38

Taxonomy (Bloom's) 23, 100
teacher
   appraisal, 247–8, 255
   as consultant, 244
   as facilitator, 3, 67
   as manager, 67
   -centred method, 2, 13, 67
   competence, 90
   expectations, 40
   roles, 108, 231, 244–58
   -talk, 171
teaching, 39–77
   computer assisted, 88
   facilitative, 3, 43, 44
   for transfer, 21–2, 28
   methods, 44, 45, 68
   in military/civilian contexts,
      260–4
   organisation of, 69–77
   performance, 250–52
   practice assessment, 247–59
   styles, 259, 265
   system, 69, 70
teaching methods
   algorithms, 58–61
   demonstration, 56
   discussion, 62
   flexible learning, 62
   job instruction training, 52
   lecture, 55
   open learning, 62
   project work, 57
   role play, 62
   simulations, 62
   strategies, 29, 127, 168
team
   effectiveness design, 33–4
   member teaching design, 33–4

teamwork, 3, 33, 35–6
teamwork critique, 33
test(s) see also assessment,
      134–63
   attainment, 144
   designing, 135
   diagnostic, 144
   evaluation, 138–41
   items, 143, 153–4
   objective, 142–3
   post-/pre-, 145
   purposes, 152, 159
   reliability, 136–7
   results, 138–9
   scores, 138, 141
   terminal, 159
   validity, 136–7
testing
   aptitude, 143
   criteria for success, 135
   criterion-referenced, 149–50
   diagnostic, 144
   educational, 143–4
   employment, 143
   group assessment profiles, 155
   interpreting graphs of results,
      139–40
   norm-referenced, 150
   objective, 307–16
   personality, 144
   phase, 144
   pre-requisite, 144, 159
   proficiency, 143
   selection, 144
   standard deviation, 140–2
   standard tasks, 135
   standardised norm, 144
   student attainment, 153
   trainability, 149
Thonrdike, E.L., 5, 7
training
   analysis, 134
   centres, 207
   evaluating transfer, 26–8
   needs analysis, 109
   plan, 129
   programme format, 128–30
   specification, 160–1
   transfer of, 179
trainability testing, see testing
transfer of training, see training
transferable skills, see skills
transparency making, see aids
trial-and-error learning, 7, 13
Tyler, R., 100, 109, 219–20

validation, see learning
verbal association, 9, 105

verifiers
   external, 326
   internal, 326
vocational guidance, 243
Vygotsky, L.S., 104

work experience, 124
Workers' Educational
      Association (WEA), 208
working with others, 334
workplan (DfEE), 203
Youth Service, 206